Tudor HISTORY of PAINTING
In 1000 Color Reproductions

Tudor HISTORY

Contributors Luc Benoist
Jean Cassou
André Chastel
Pierre du Colombier
Pierre Devambez
Jean A. Keim
Paul-Henri Michel
Michael Middleton
Joseph-Émile Muller
Claude Roger-Marx
Hertha Wegener
Jean Yoyotte

OF PAINTING
IN 1000 COLOR
REPRODUCTIONS

Under the general editorship of
Robert Maillard

TUDOR PUBLISHING COMPANY
New York

ND
1170
.H513

Translated, with the exception
of the English language contributions,
by Margaret Shenfield and Richard Waterhouse
from the French *Histoire Illustré de la Peinture*

This edition © 1961 Tudor Publishing Company

© 1961 Fernand Hazan Editeur, Paris

All rights reserved

Library of Congress Catalog Card Number: 61-17425

Manufactured in the United States of America

CONTENTS

JEAN YOYOTTE	Prehistoric Art	1
	Egyptian Painting	2
PIERRE DEVAMBEZ	Etruscan Painting	8
	Greek Painting	10
	Roman Painting	12
	Egypto-Roman Painting	15
JEAN KEIM	Byzantine Art	16
PAUL-HENRI MICHEL	Pre-Carolingian Miniatures	18
	Carolingian Miniatures	19
	Ottonian Miniatures	20
	Romanesque Painting	22
JEAN KEIM	Icon-Painting	26
ANDRÉ CHASTEL	The Duocento	28
	The Trecento in Florence	30
	The Trecento in Siena	32
	International Gothic	38
	The Quattrocento in Siena	42
	The Quattrocento in Florence	44
	The Quattrocento in Umbria	54
	The Quattrocento in Padua	58
	The Quattrocento in Ferrara	60
	The Quattrocento in Venice	61
	The Quattrocento in Florence	66
LUC BENOIST	Fifteenth-century France	72
	Franco-Flemish School of the Fifteenth Century	80
PIERRE DU COLOMBIER	Netherlandish School in the Fifteenth Century	81
JEAN CASSOU	Fifteenth-century Spain	96
	Fifteenth-century Portugal	97
PIERRE DU COLOMBIER	German School of the Fifteenth Century	98
ANDRÉ CHASTEL	The High Renaissance in Italy	104
LUC BENOIST	The Renaissance in France	126
PIERRE DU COLOMBIER	The Renaissance in Germany	132
	Netherlandish School of the Sixteenth Century	142

JEAN CASSOU	Sixteenth-century Spain	150
ANDRÉ CHASTEL	Caravaggio and Luminism	154
JEAN CASSOU	Seventeenth-century Spain	158
PIERRE DU COLOMBIER	Flemish School of the Seventeenth Century	164
CLAUDE ROGER-MARX	Dutch School of the Seventeenth Century	172
LUC BENOIST	Seventeenth-century France	184
	Eighteenth-century France	198
ANDRÉ CHASTEL	Eighteenth-century Venetian School	203
JEAN CASSOU	Eighteenth-century Spain	208
MICHAEL MIDDLETON	Eighteenth- and Nineteenth-century England	210
	The Pre-Raphaelites	222
PIERRE DU COLOMBIER	German Romanticism	223
CLAUDE ROGER-MARX	French Neo-classicism	224
	Nineteenth-century France	228
	Symbolism	242
MICHAEL MIDDLETON	Whistler	243
J.-E. MULLER	Impressionism	244
	Cézanne	256
	Neo-Impressionism	258
	The Reaction against Impressionism	260
	The Symbolists and the Nabis	266
	Fauvism	270
	The Reaction against Fauvism	278
	Cubism	280
	Futurism	294
	Metaphysical Painting	295
	Expressionism	296
	Rouault	298
	Die Brücke	300
	Nolde — Kokoschka	301
	Der Blaue Reiter	302
	Klee	304
	Flemish Expressionism	306
MICHAEL MIDDLETON	Twentieth-century England	307
J.-E. MULLER	Soutine	308
	Modigliani	309
	Chagall	310
	Naive Painting	311
	Utrillo	313
	Dadaism	314
	Surrealism	315
	Abstract Painting	318
HERTHA WEGENER	American Painting	321
	Index of artists	327

Tudor HISTORY of PAINTING
In 1000 Color Reproductions

PREHISTORIC ART

The earliest traces of pictorial activity are rock-paintings or engravings, which have survived owing to the difficulty of gaining access to their sites and to the fact that subsequent levels have obscured them. These remains of Palaeolithic culture, which are contemporary with the last Ice Age, date from 10,000 to 30,000 B.C. Their location depends on the nature of the ground, and the sites are obviously widely scattered. Nevertheless, the distribution of those that have so far been studied is virtually Euro-African, extending as it does from the Dordogne to Natal, through the Spanish Levant. The two most famous painted caves are Lascaux in France and Altamira in Spain.

As the men of that age were still hunters and shepherds, the subject represented may be animals, such as reindeer, mammoths, and bisons, that have since disappeared or migrated to other climatic regions, or else they may be cows and horses. These sometimes life-size animal figures are remarkable for the vigour of the handling, the perfection of the attitudes, and the sureness of the line, all of which bear witness to exceptional sensitivity and masterly skill. Executed with the finger, the graver, the bark-brush, or a straw, the paintings only entail the use of mineral colours: yellow-ochre, red-ochre, and black. They may represent hunting scenes or ritual dances, but most often they are of single animals. As for the explanations put forward to account for them, these range from the most elementary (magic to promote successful hunting) to the most lofty (a symbolic representation of the religious forces presiding over the course of the cosmos and the initiation ceremonies of the tribe). Since spiritual value is not measured by the same standards as economy, one may suppose that these painted caves, in which decorations are often hidden far away from the entrance, are the ancestors of the earliest rock sanctuaries of historic times.

THE LASCAUX CAVE.
BULL AND RED COW.
GREAT HALL,
RIGHT-HAND
GALLERY

THE LASCAUX CAVE.
BULL SUPERIMPOSED
ON RED COW.
GREAT HALL,
LEFT-HAND GALLERY

THE LASCAUX CAVE.
RED COW
AND HORSE.
PASSAGE OFF
RIGHT-HAND
GALLERY

ALTAMIRA CAVE.
BISON JUMPING
(TRACED BY THE
ABBÉ HENRI BREUIL)

I

EGYPTIAN PAINTING

WOMEN MAKING MUSIC.
THEBES,
TOMB OF NAKHT,
MIDDLE OF THE
18th DYNASTY

PORTRAIT OF A LADY.
THEBES,
TOMB OF MENNA,
MIDDLE OF THE
18th DYNASTY

SCENE SHOWING
FUNERAL BANQUET.
THEBES,
TOMB OF NAKHT.
MIDDLE OF THE
18th DYNASTY

From the time when they first developed their own style, in other words, at the beginning of the third millennium B.C., the ancient Egyptians made great use of polychromatic painting. Their art was a 'magic of forms', not in the metaphorical or metaphysical sense in which modern aesthetes use the term, but in a perfectly matter-of-fact sense. An image of a person or an object was a permanent reproduction of that person or object and reproduced its reality no less than its appearance: thus a portrait was as real and as much an entity in itself as the sitter, according to the principles on which sympathetic magic is based. In the same way the representation of a certain action was the same as the action itself, except that in the picture it went on repeating itself as long as the picture lasted. Thus in case of need, pictures were made in order to reduce the enemies of the gods, kings and men to impotence. In general, however, they served the purposes of white magic. Idols were modelled so that the bodies of the gods who protect this world could be cherished; statues were sculpted so that individual men might live on for ever. Pictures of various activities of the dead or the gods were painted on the walls of temples and mortuary chapels so that they should go on for ever.

Of necessity the graphic and plastic arts tend to create forms which express and preserve the true essence and attributes of living creatures. In addition life and super-life are determined to a large extent by the light of the sun. Colour is an essential identification-mark bound up with everything illuminated by light; therefore the Egyptians painted everything—buildings, statues and designs. The colours had to be 'real', which did not necessarily mean realistic, since it was their function to endow products of the imagination with an ideal life, as rich and beautiful as possibe. This is why, for some obscure reason, the standard type of handsome man, for example, was always painted a

2

EGYPTIAN PAINTING

virile brown, while the beautiful woman, her beauty shown as it was to last for eternity, was of a delicate pale yellow complexion. The drawing behind and round the colour had to be equally real: it emphasized the most important elements of a scene, the most characteristic and indispensable attributes of a person or object. Probably a spirit of 'abstract analysis' reigned over the elaboration of the conventions, or rather, the rules of expression, of ancient Eygptian art. The gods, kings and dead heroes were larger than the other figures to proclaim their superior powers. For greater completeness, portraits of human beings combined full-face and profile views; those of buildings were half-way between a plan and an elevation. Often pictures would give prominence to objects which, according to realistic perspective, should have been partially hidden from the spectator.

But it must be admitted that this selective process does not seem to have been taken to its ultimate conclusion by the first Egyptian artists — at least, looked at from the standpoint of our logic. Perhaps only an ancient Egyptian could explain why — with what mythological or magical reference — men drawn in profile have only one eye (as, indeed, the eye sees them) but an eye shown full face. In a completely abstract rendering two eyes would be shown. Perhaps the same Egyptian could explain why figures have two left feet or two right feet (which might be called restriction rather than selection). But would he know? After the beginnings of Egyptian art, the traditions and rules undoubtedly became standard because they were 'according to the will of our forefathers'. We know that in the Pharaohs' Egypt practices surviving from the past were held to be a legacy from the primordial golden ages and the ideal of truth and effectiveness in every sphere — political, moral or religious. Moderation, the gods' guarantee of happiness and success, was another central principle of Egyptian ethics:

WEEPING WOMEN. THEBES, TOMB OF THE ROYAL SCRIBE HOREMHEB, REIGN OF TUTHMOSIS IV

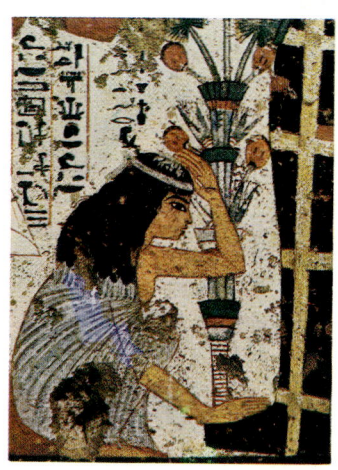

WIDOW'S FAREWELL TO HER DEAD HUSBAND. THEBES, TOMB OF NEBAMON AND IPU-KY, END OF THE 18th DYNASTY

FUNERAL BARGE SAILING TOWARDS ABYDOS. THEBES, TOMB OF MENNA. MIDDLE OF THE 18th DYNASTY

3

EGYPTIAN PAINTING

SURVEYING
THE CORN-FIELD.
THEBES,
TOMB OF MENNA.
MIDDLE OF THE
18th DYNASTY

HARVEST SCENE.
THEBES,
TOMB OF NAKHT.
MIDDLE OF THE
18th DYNASTY

TREADING
THE CORN.
THEBES,
TOMB OF MENNA.
MIDDLE OF THE
18th DYNASTY

WINE-HARVEST
SCENE: THE
WINE-PRESS.
THEBES,
TOMB OF IPU-Y.
19th DYNASTY

this may explain the typical restraint of Egyptian art. By means of carefully chosen groupings, symmetrical or otherwise, draughtsmen were easily able to suggest movement, speed, effort and so on, but even when showing the energetic actions of Egyptian peasants, fishermen or soldiers, they lent their gestures—of triumph or industry—a feeling of great serenity. Crowded, hurried, feverish and distorted effects were reserved for pictures of destruction (enemies or game).

To present-day spectators the most attractive ancient Egyptian pictures are not the ritual scenes in the temples—although these contain some vigorous set-pieces—but the pictures in the funeral chambers of the nobles. Sometimes they show the private activities of a dignitary, sometimes the public works of an official of the state, but in each case everyday life is preserved for immortality: farmers and workmen, the men who produce goods, and bureaucrats, the men who check and take a note of their efforts, are shown in their typical activities. Nor are the dead to forget the pleasures of life. The funeral banquet at which the living and the dead commune together is enlivened by attractions: bird-hunts and fishing are, in part, a magical way of laying low the enemies of the dead man, but also a genuine relaxation which he will enjoy in the refreshing marshes of the after-life. Every episode of life on this earth—down to the very last, the funeral ritual with its sadness and, at the same time, its resuscitating quality—is re-created.

Although these episodes are arranged in vertical ranks or horizontal panels, the visitor who enters an Egyptian funeral chamber does not feel at all as though he is surrounded by a gallery of pictures. The whole chamber is, so to speak, a single canvas on which art works its magic. (For critical purposes one has to divide the whole into 'pictures' and 'details' but this dissection contradicts the spirit of Egyptian art to a certain extent.) The lasting qualities of

EGYPTIAN PAINTING

that art are the marvellous skill in design (serving the purposes of the ritual rules which control the organization of the scenes), the love of real, everyday things, the discreet humour which appears in the 'anecdotes', the perfect rendering of atmosphere (pompous and bureaucratic, rural and jolly, etc.).

Essentially, of course, Egyptian art was the product of an industry which served a given purpose. But it would be a mistake to think that the Pharaonic painters were never moved by truly aesthetic motives. Working for a king or a temple, the artist was certainly a craftsman —sometimes considered on a par with the plasterer—but a craftsman of some distinction, with the status of a doctor or hairdresser. Painters were proud of their calling and nobles were glad to number them among their friends. As scribes, they were often learned about other things besides their own particular craft. In about 2400 a minister of state practised painting; in the fourteenth century the painters who were ornamenting the tombs of the Valley of Kings read the classical authors and some wrote psalms of a high poetical quality. Thus in her art as in her government, techniques and beliefs, Egypt combined two tendencies, one divine, superhuman, primitive and remote, the other human, everyday and modern. It is in the two-dimensional paintings in the Theban tombs of the eighteenth dynasty (1550-1340) that the modernism is most striking.

These tombs may well be called the flower of Egyptian painting, so long as one does not forget that they represent only a very small space of time and only one version of a graphic art that extended over three millennia. In them the artists were, it seems, aiming at 'mural appliqué work', but this conclusion must be put forward with some reservations. Normally the paintings on chamber walls were treated in low relief; the swellings and bumps, however broken up and subtle, represented the *volumes* of objects. In other

JOINERS.
THEBES,
TOMB OF NEBAMON
AND IPU-KY.
END OF
18TH DYNASTY

MASONS WORKING.
THEBES,
TOMB OF
REKH-MIR-E.
REIGN OF
TUTHMOSIS III

WEIGHING GOLD
FOR THE
GOLDSMITHS.
THEBES,
TOMB OF
REKH-MIR-E.
REIGN OF
TUTHMOSIS III

5

EGYPTIAN PAINTING

BIRDS
(DETAIL OF A
HUNTING AND
FISHING SCENE).
THEBES,
TOMB OF THE
ROYAL SCRIBE
HOREMHEB.
REIGN OF
TUTHMOSIS IV

BIRD-HUNT
IN THE MARSHES
(DETAIL OF A
HUNTING AND
FISHING SCENE).
THEBES,
TOMB OF NAKHT.
MIDDLE OF THE
18TH DYNASTY

words, the form of painting most in favour with the gods and the dead was not the 'fresco' but the painted bas-relief. However, if the rock out of which the tomb was cut was too crumbly—which was generally the case in the Theban mountains—it was covered with a layer of brick and with a layer of plaster, and the painting was applied without any relief. In the tombs of the nobles the best painters were able to develop a style more or less independent of relief and practise pure painting. Their basic canons, tools (large and small brushes), palette (charcoal, red and yellow ochres, blue and green frit) were the same as those of their predecessors. As early as the first two dynasties the mats painted in *trompe-l'œil* show great skill in completing the rhythm of geometrical motifs by means of colour-arrangements. From the

WILD DUCK
AND FISHES
(DETAIL OF A
HUNTING AND
FISHING SCENE).
THEBES,
TOMB OF MENNA.
MIDDLE OF THE
18TH DYNESTY

EGYPTIAN PAINTING

third dynasty artists knew pictorial methods of reproducing the grain in wood and the veining in granite. In Meidum under the fourth dynasty and Beni-Hassan under the twelfth, artists were already masters of most of the means at their disposal. But at the height of the New Kingdom Theban artists, discovering or rediscovering the joys of pure painting, reached a new peak of subtlety in colour and outline.

The first masters of the eighteenth dynasty, taking over from where the Middle Empire left off, juxtaposed images, often stiff, against bluish backgrounds; but by the reign of Tuthmosis III a sort of classicism had developed out of this archaism. In the work of the artists of the vizier Rekh-mir-e, whose iconographical repertoire is much more extensive, the graphic canons are strained a little, the forms are gently loosened, the groups denser and more animated, the colours more varied than in the past. Painting was asserting its autonomy. Under Amenophis II dignity gave way to spontaneity; the colours on the cream background were more melting. From the reign of his successor Tuthmosis IV (tombs of Nakht and Menna) one finds delicious female figures, transparent drapery, highly attractive 'still-lifes' and charming backgrounds of marshes. With Ramose, under the reign of Amenophis III, the style of the Theban painters entered a phase of high classicism, a mixture of almost excessive skill and affected attention to detail. At the beginning of the nineteenth dynasty the few walls showing everyday life (Ipuky) were still enlivened by a sort of good-humoured vulgarity, but while these scenes gave place to an exclusively religious repertoire, painters were reduced to 'enriching' the pictures of dead men in virtuoso fashion—with complicated jewellery, skilful folds and sacred trees treated like iridescent tapestries. With the decline of the New Kingdom, Theban painting became over-zealous craftsmanship, and eventually disappeared.

BIRDS ABOVE PAPYRUS THICKETS (DETAIL OF A HUNTING AND FISHING SCENE). THEBES, TOMB OF NAKHT. MIDDLE OF THE 18th DYNASTY

MENNA'S DAUGHTER HOLDING BIRDS AND LOTUS-BLOOMS. THEBES, TOMB OF MENNA. MIDDLE OF THE 18th DYNASTY

FISHES (DETAIL OF A HUNTING AND FISHING SCENE). THEBES, TOMB OF MENNA. MIDDLE OF THE 18th DYNASTY

GREEK PAINTING

HEAD OF A GIRL
('LA PARISIENNE').
CRETAN FRESCO,
c. 15th CENT. B.C.
ARCHAEOLOGICAL
MUSEUM,
HERACLION

CUP-BEARER,
CRETAN FRESCO
(MUCH RESTORED),
15th CENT. B.C.
PALACE OF MINOS,
KNOSSOS

HECTOR SAYING
FAREWELL,
c. 525 B.C.
WÜRZBURG
MUSEUM

The little face of a *midinette,* with a pug nose, lips that are too red, eyes that take up half the face, a kiss-curl on the forehead, and a great cascade of hair at the back of the neck—this is not the description of a Toulouse-Lautrec, but of a detail from a fresco that decorated the palace of Knossos, on Crete, some fifteen centuries B.C. Other paintings, contemporary with it or even older, give the same impression of freshness and spontaneity: flying-fish, their dance describing an arabesque against a marine landscape; a cat with watchful eyes and tensed paws, bracing itself behind a bush to leap on a pheasant; or else a crowd of ladies idly gossiping as they watch a bullfight. The artists of that age did not clutter themselves with rules. Instead, they looked at nature, enjoyed scenery, took pleasure in the liveliness of a movement; deliberately sacrificing all unnecessary detail, they aimed only to give the spectator a suggestion of their impressions.

Their pupils and successors in the Mycenaean age were actuated by the same desire; but these painters of a different race and a different spirit only succeeded now and then in rendering so intensely the most fleeting aspects of life. In their art, a kind of stiffness paralyzed the spontaneity that they vainly tried to acquire.

Entirely different tendencies appeared, when, towards the end of the second millennium B.C., invaders from the North conquered Greece, and a new civilization was established. For nearly two centuries a totally abstract form of art reigned supreme. Its decorative spirit appears in skilful compositions made up entirely of lines that bend sharply, intersect, or come together in chequers, triangles, meanders and swastikas. When, shortly after 800 B.C., the human form appeared again for the first time after this long interruption, it looked like a cardboard cut-out—all angles, and apparently conceived in purely geometrical terms. Since the painting of many following

10

GREEK PAINTING

centuries is hardly known to us except through designs in silhouette traced by craftsmen on the bellies of vases, can we really discuss it at all?

Mural decorations and easel pictures did indeed once exist, but, they have fallen victim to the ravages of time and been destroyed. We would have no conception of them, were it not for the very fact that the Greeks had a strong urge to make their terracotta vessels visually pleasing by means of decorations illustrating their heroic legends and the domestic detail composing their lives.

It is probably this fondness for images that prompted them to break away from geometric art. Throughout the seventh century B.C., they were learning, under the guidance of the Orient, how to draw living forms. These forms were not ones that they knew from direct experience, but monsters and ferocious beasts, which they copied, just as they were, from Asian models. They did, however, provide Greek artists with an opportunity of making their handling more supple and coming closer to life.

This experience enabled the painters to represent scenes of every variety, at first by causing their figures to appear as completely black silhouettes, and then by making the red colour of the terracotta stand out against a dark background. To begin with, they sought precision of line and purity of features; then, as their technique improved, they strove to render the expressions of their figures; and very soon, from the fifth century, they were tackling the complex problems of perspective and the third dimension. Very great artists, of whom only the names have come down to us (Polygnotos, Zeuxis, Apelles), mark the stages of this continuous progress. Starting from simple drawing uniformly coloured, without any shading or atmosphere, it gradually transformed Greek painting into an art remarkably close to that of modern times.

CUP OF HERA,
MIDDLE OF THE
5th CENT. B.C.
MUNICH MUSEUM

BOWL OF THE MUSES,
c. 440 B.C.
VATICAN MUSEUM

ACTORS IN
SATIRICAL DRAMA,
c. 400 B.C.
NAPLES MUSEUM

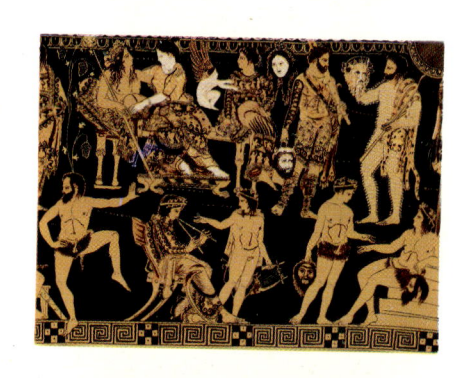

ULYSSES
AND THE SIRENS,
MIDDLE OF THE
4th CENT. B.C.
BERLIN MUSEUM

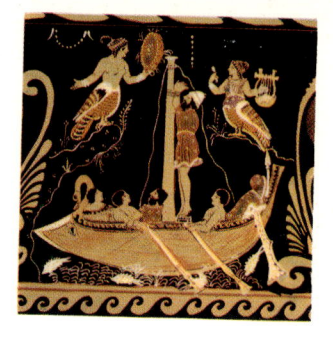

ROMAN PAINTING

It is natural for any one, who, in the Naples museum, looks at the frescoes detached from the ruined walls of Herculaneum and Pompeii, to wonder whether the works before him are Greek or Roman, and whether Rome ever created original art. Of course, the question is not limited to painting; but it is with these paintings that it comes most to the fore. Most of the subjects are Hellenic. The gods whose images we behold seem to have come directly from Greek models; and we are told of the exploits of Ulysses, and of Medea's misgivings when she is about to kill her children. Our mind turns to Homer or Theocritus, just as much as to Virgil or Catullus. There is not a single subject or type of work that had not already been used (often according to the same scheme) in Asia Minor, Alexandrian Egypt, or Greece proper. Is all this exceptional, peculiar to Pompeii? For Pompeii was a kind of seaside resort inhabited by rich, cultivated men who had been brought up on the Greek authors, and who were eager to introduce into their own homes copies of the masterpieces that they had learned to hold in their hearts. In reality, it seems as though it was a more general occurrence, and that, in painting as in sculpture, a taste for art only developed among the Romans when their generals brought back in their baggage thousands of pictures and statues looted during their conquests round the Mediterranean basin.

Nevertheless, such an interest could already have been aroused by other, more ancient models; for the Etruscans, the Romans' neighbours and once even their masters, could have prompted them to launch out in their turn into pictorial creation.

In fact, there had indeed been painters at Rome in relatively remote times, and we still retain a memory of Fabius Pictor, whose name and fame were perhaps only preserved because he belonged to one of the leading families of the city. Other artists, too, acquired

ALDOBRANDINI MARRIAGE (FRAGMENT). VATICAN LIBRARY

PORTRAIT OF LA DOMINA (DETAIL OF THE FRIEZE OF THE DIONYSIAN MYSTERIES), 1ST CENT. VILLA OF THE MYSTERIES, POMPEII

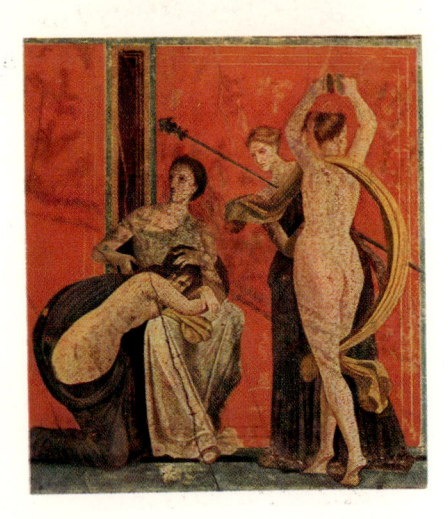

BACCHANTE DANCING (DETAIL OF THE FRIEZE OF THE DIONYSIAN MYSTERIES), 1ST CENT. VILLA OF THE MYSTERIES, POMPEII

ROMAN PAINTING

some glory through commemorating victories; but was it the talent displayed in these works that was valued—or was it not rather the memento of the Roman soldiers' heroism?

It really did require the stimulus from abroad, and the Greek craze disapproved of by Cato the Censor, to impel the Romans to introduce into their native land an art that had always been so foreign to them. Many of the executants had to come from Greece; those who were true Romans were trained by Greek immigrants.

For more than one reason, we can only rejoice at such a complete ascendancy; because it is certainly through these painters that we have our least imprecise and incomplete idea of what (particularly from the fourth century B.C.) was created by those Greek artists only known to us by name, but who aroused unqualified admiration among the ancients. Are we, however, to believe that the Romans, who considered themselves their pupils and reproduced their works, always behaved as conscientious copists deliberately suppressing their own personality purely in the interests of exactitude? This is unlikely, firstly because the ancients were never, in this respect, concerned about excessive strictness, and, like translations in seventeenth-century France, their copies could no doubt be called *belles infidèles*—'unfaithful beauties'; secondly, because the painters of Antiquity only very slowly gained full command of their means of expression, and, from the fifth and particularly the fourth century B.C., numerous technical advances were made. It is hard to believe that an artist of the time of Augustus or Nero would have forced himself to commit what he would have considered errors in drawing, purely out of fidelity to his model. The rendering of space, volume and perspective, all of which presented difficulties to Polygnotos and his immediate successors, were no longer very frightening problems. One could say the same

THE THREE GRACES (FRESCO FROM POMPEII). MUSEO NAZIONALE, NAPLES

PUNISHMENT OF CUPID (FRESCO FROM THE 'HOUSE OF THE PUNISHMENT OF CUPID' AT POMPEII), 1ST CENT. MUSEO NAZIONALE, NAPLES

MARS AND VENUS (FRESCO FROM THE 'HOUSE OF MARS AND VENUS' AT POMPEII). MUSEO NAZIONALE, NAPLES

ROMAN PAINTING

DOUBLE PORTRAIT KNOWN AS 'THE BAKER AND HIS WIFE' (PAINTING FROM POMPEII). MUSEO NAZIONALE, NAPLES

SPRING (PAINTING FROM STABIAE). MUSEO NAZIONALE, NAPLES

PORTRAIT OF A GIRL (PAINTING FROM POMPEII). MUSEO NAZIONALE, NAPLES

of the colours: how much richer the artists' palette had become since the beginning of the Hellenistic period!

But, the contribution of the Roman painters was probably not limited to this adaption to contemporary taste of purely technical processes. Though they borrowed several themes from Greek mythology, others appear to us more genuinely Roman. The Dionysiac initiation that provides the decorative theme for the Villa of the Mysteries at Pompeii is treated in a truly Classical spirit, directly inspired by that of Greece. Yet the god here being honoured is not altogether the same as the one revered by the Athenians.

Whether this applies to other works, of which the subject itself has been inspired by some Greek legend, is hard to tell. To all intents and purposes, a sort of common language and spirit had, since the Alexandrian conquest, become established throughout the eastern part of the Mediterranean basin. The Romans adopted both the language and the spirit with greater or lesser fluency, according to their own temperament. A girl taking a walk in a flowery meadow is well suited to the tastes of people familiar with Virgil's *Eclogues*; but had no similar subject already been created to bring pleasure to the artists of Asia Minor and the admirers of Theocritus?

Then we come to portraiture. That it was a branch of art that had greatly developed since Alexander, and of which the Romans were particularly fond, is borne out by numerous sculptured busts. As it was less expensive than a work in marble, a painting allowed a person of middling means to preserve a likeness of himself and pass it on to his heirs. With the submission to reality that was also shown by many other works, portraits like the one of the baker and his wife provide evidence that, at Rome, the art of painting had not just developed in the shadow of Greek culture.

14

EGYPTO-ROMAN PAINTING

Making allowances for certain universally accepted conventions, Egyptian painting had since remotest Antiquity been characterized by a desire for exactness sometimes carried to the point of caricature. Neither the passing of millennia nor the dominion of successive conquerors had changed the Egyptians' liking for strict realism. When Alexandria became one of the intellectual capitals of the Mediterranean, the art that developed in the Nile delta was no doubt imbued with a certain cosmopolitanism; but in the remote provinces the racial character remained quite unchanged. There is therefore no reason to be surprised at the very idiosyncratic features displayed by a type of portrait of which a series has been found in the oasis of the Fayum. These were funerary portraits placed on the mummy-case to provide an eternal duplicate of the dead person's countenance. Here, one recognizes the desire to perpetuate the appearance of the deceased so typical of the Egyptian mind; and this longing to last for ever was to continue right into Christian times in Coptic art.

Only the head and shoulders were represented of the man or woman whose mortal remains were contained, immediately underneath, in the mummy-case. The very humble craftsmen who executed these portraits deserve our admiration not just because of their fidelity in representing their subject's features, but for their attempt to render the inner life that had animated—and perhaps still animated—those withered bodies.

These works have considerable documentary value. Clothing, ornament and hair-dressing vary from one figure to the next, and, in particular, we see how, with a certain delay, the fashions of Rome and Alexandria found their way to the country districts. But what seems no less precious to us is the urge to express, in the deliberately enlarged eyes, the inquietude that from 100 A.D. heralded the fervour with which Christian mysticism was to be received.

FUNERARY PORTRAIT OF A WOMAN. ANTINOË, 2nd CENT. LOUVRE, PARIS

FUNERARY PORTRAIT OF A MAN. THEBES, 2nd CENT.

FUNERARY PORTRAIT OF A WOMAN. THEBES, 2nd CENT. LOUVRE, PARIS

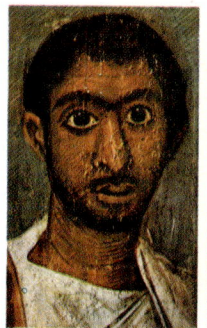

FUNERARY PORTRAIT OF A GIRL. FAYUM, 2nd CENT. LOUVRE, PARIS

BYZANTINE ART

THE GOOD SHEPHERD
(DETAIL OF THE
NORTH TYMPANUM),
c. 424-450.
MAUSOLEUM OF
GALLA PLACIDIA,
RAVENNA

THE TAKING
OF CHRIST (DETAIL),
c. 526.
SANT'APOLLINARE
NUOVA, RAVENNA

PROCESSION OF THE
VIRGIN MARTYRS
(DETAIL), *c.* 520.
SANT'APOLLINARE
NUOVA, RAVENNA

Under the heading 'Byzantine art' come all the works produced from 300 to 1453 within the orbit of the Christian state that succeeded Rome, and of which the influence extended to the Middle East, Italy, the Balkans, and Russia. Byzantine painting prolonged the tradition of the Greek and Roman painters; but though the authority of the capital was always apparent, regional character showed through.

The palaces and churches were decorated with wall paintings, most of which have disappeared. Only a few mosaics remain. A distinction is to be made between two great periods: one before the Iconoclastic Controversy, during which many works of art were destroyed; and the other after the victory of the pro-image party, when, in 842, the religious value of representations in human form of Christ, the Virgin, and the saints was recognized. By good luck, Ravenna, the capital of the Western Empire, has retained about a third of its treasures; less than a tenth remains in the rest of the Empire.

The Mausoleum of Galla Placidia (first half of the fifth century) is still completely permeated with the Romano-Hellenistic vision. Religious subjects—the Good Shepherd, the Apostles, and the Cross—continue to be symbolic, and the entire scheme is dominated by the floral and animal ornamentation. The mosaics are closely related to the walls, whereas those of the same period in Santa Maria Maggiore at Rome are simply enlarged illustrations from manuscripts. In the Baptistery of the Orthodox (second half of the fifth century), the same subjects reappear in a dazzling form, but one that has lost some of its simplicity. The early sixth-century figures in the Baptistery of the Arians have become independent, and the ornament is relegated to the background. At the same period, narrative cycles vividly treated made their appearance in Sant' Apollinare Nuova; they include the life of Christ, and processions of holy virgins and martyrs with representations of the

BYZANTINE ART

port and town. At San Vitale, after 547, the mosaics came to be completely incorporated in the structure of the building, and they display a wealth of colours: warm hues, deep greens, brilliant reds, and resplendent golds. Human forms have become symbols and the invisible has been made flesh in the Scripture scenes, while the emperor and empress, accompanied by their retinues, possess extraordinary presence and reality. In Sant' Apollinare in Classe, the temporal gives way to the eternal, with St Apollinarius and the Twelve Lambs beneath a huge cross in an immense symbol of the Transfiguration. Ravenna is not, however, unique. From the same period have survived the decorations at Parenzo in Istria; of St Demetrius at Salonica; the basilica on Mount Sinai; S. Maria Maggiore and S. Agnese in Rome.

After the victory over the Iconoclasts, representational art regained ascendancy. Buildings were covered with mosaics according to a programme in which figures had their appointed places: Christ in the dome and the Virgin in the apse. They were clearly arranged, with large empty spaces and a rhythmic balance of masses and colours. The Middle Ages have bequeathed us the splendid decorations of St Sophia, Constantinople, and the church of the Nea Moni on Chios and Daphni in Greece. From the twelfth century, the entire surface of the walls was covered with narrative cycles. A comparison of the Kahriyeh Djami at Constantinople with the Capella Palatina at Palermo in Sicily, the cathedrals of Monreale and Cefalù, San Zeno at Rome, Torcello, and St Mark's at Venice shows how Byzantine art was transformed through contact with old regional cultures. Byzantine influence continued to be felt in Greek, Yugoslavian, Bulgarian, Rumanian, Armenian, Georgian and Russian churches, where the icons shone with special brightness—and in the churches that would hold the works of the Italian primitives.

EMPRESS THEODORA (DETAIL OF 'EMPRESS THEODORA AND HER COURT'), *c.* 546-548, SAN VITALE, RAVENNA

EMPEROR JUSTINIAN (DETAIL OF 'EMPEROR JUSTINIAN AND HIS COURT'), *c.* 546-548. SAN VITALE, RAVENNA

EMPRESS THEODORA AND HER COURT, *c.* 546-548. SAN VITALE, RAVENNA

17

PRE-CAROLINGIAN MINIATURES

IMAGO LEONIS,
THE LION OF
ST MARK.
ECHTERNACH
GOSPELS,
NORTHUMBRIA,
MIDDLE OF THE
8th CENT.
BIBLIOTHÈQUE
NATIONALE, PARIS

LETTER I
IN THE FORM
OF A HUMAN FIGURE
WITH AN EAGLE'S
HEAD,
SO-CALLED
SACREMENTARY
OF GELLONE.
FLAVIGNY,
BETWEEN
755 AND 787.
BIBLIOTHÈQUE
NATIONALE, PARIS

ST MATTHEW.
SALZBURG,
c. 770.
STAATSBIBLIOTHEK,
VIENNA

As almost all the decorated manuscripts now in existence belong to the Middle Ages, we would be led to regard illumination as an exclusively mediaeval art, were it not for some rare but remarkable examples from Late Antiquity. The two Vatican Virgils (the *Vaticanus* and the *Romanus*), though very different in style, both belong to the fifth century, and both give proof of great mastery and a long tradition. A bible, contemporary with and treated in the same way as the *Vaticanus*, is known to have served as a model, during the ninth century, for miniaturists at Tours. Thus, behind late imitations, one sometimes glimpses a missing prototype.

In the sixth century (a period of transition from Late Antiquity to the Early Middle Ages) the monasteries were the only remaining centres of culture in Western Europe. From then onwards, the copying and decorating of manuscripts was for more than five hundred years a job reserved for the clergy, so that the development of illumination became tied to the expansion of the religious orders, especially the Benedictines.

In the seventh and eighth centuries, there were two main centres: the British Isles and Merovingian Gaul. Anglo-Irish ornamentation is characterized by a vigorous interpretation of the subject (men, animals, or plants) and an abundance of purely geometrical motifs. Here, the *Imago Leonis* from the so-called Echternach Gospels provides an example. The richness of the spiral or intertwining linear patterns is specially noteworthy in the large-scale initials and monograms.

In France, the abbeys of Luxeuil and Corbie were active centres from the seventh century. During the eighth, the scriptoria grew more numerous, and manuscripts were decorated in a less heirachic, livelier, more realistic style than in the British Isles. Large, whole-page letters gave way to ornamental capitals more in harmony with the calligraphy; and though geometrical

CAROLINGIAN MINIATURES

embellishment retained its importance, it was used more freely. The activity of Charlemagne and his successors on behalf of literature and the arts was also extended to the sphere of illumination. Continually growing in number, the scriptoria zealously vied with one another in complying with the orders of the rulers and dignitaries of the Empire, and in presenting them with sumptuously decorated books. Whereas the recipients of manuscripts from earlier periods are unknown, we are familiar with the Gospel-book of Charlemagne, that of Lothaire, the two Bibles of Charles the Bald, and so on. Several thriving schools divided up huge areas of France and Germany. The most renowned is the Palatine school, which, with Aachen at its centre, included the abbeys on the western bank of the Rhine. From the Palatine scriptoria emerged some of the most beautiful purple-and-gold manuscripts still in the great European libraries: the Gospel-book of St Maximinus, Trier; the St Médard (Soissons), Vienna, and Brussels Gospels; and (one of the earliest) the Gospel-book of Charlemagne (or Godescalc, after the name of the monk who received the commission). This beautiful work, produced to commemorate the baptism of Pepin at Rome in 781, was executed in the workshop (sometimes called after Charlemagne's legendary sister, Ada) of the Palatine Chapel. Preserved until the French Revolution in the church of St Sernin at Toulouse, it is now in the Bibliothèque Nationale. The highly monumental Christ in benediction, here reproduced, seems to have been inspired by an apse painting or mosaic. Amongst he other schools belonging to this period are that of the Loire (Tours, Fleury-sur-Loire); those of Rheims, Metz, and Corbie; and the so-called Franco-Saxon school, whose main centre has been placed by the experts at St Amand in northern France, and whose influence spread to the Germanic provinces of the Empire.

CHRIST. GOSPEL-BOOK OF CHARLEMAGNE, DIOCESE OF MAINZ, 781-783. BIBLIOTHÈQUE NATIONALE, PARIS

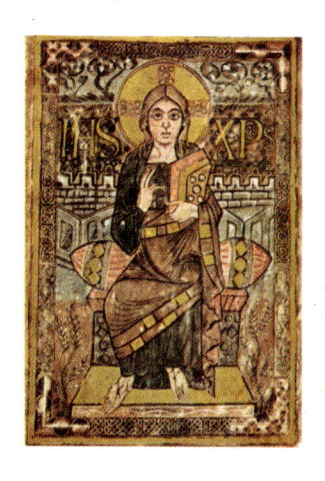

ST LUKE. GOSPEL-BOOK OF THE BENEDICTINE ABBEY OF ST MAXIMINUS AT TREVES, END OF 8th CENT. BIBLIOTHÈQUE MUNICIPALE, TREVES

ST LUKE. GOSPEL-BOOK, FULDA, SECOND QUARTER OF 9th CENT. UNIVERSITÄTS-BIBLIOTHEK, WÜRZBURG

OTTONIAN MINIATURES

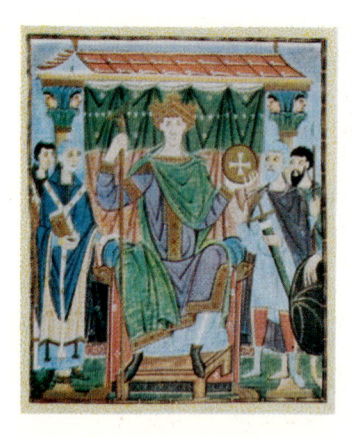

EMPEROR OTTO III. GOSPEL-BOOK OF OTTO III, REICHENAU, END OF 10th CENT. BAYERISCHE STAATSBIBLIOTHEK, MUNICH

CHRIST TALKING TO HIS DISCIPLES. PERICOPES OF HENRI II. REICHENAU, c. 1007-1014. BAYERISCHE STAATSBIBLIOTHEK, MUNICH

THE VESSELS OF WRATH. APOCALYPSE OF BAMBERG. REICHENAU, BEGINNING OF 11th CENT. STAATSBIBLIOTHEK, BAMBERG

After the Carolingian renaissance France had a century's inactivity; but for Western Europe as a whole the revival was assured by Germany under the Ottos and Henrys. The Ottonian golden century (960-1060) began shortly before the end of the reign (936-973) of Otto the Great, reached its height under Otto II and Otto III, and barely survived the death of Henry III (1056)—after which it was Germany's turn to remain in the shade. In each country, these ups and downs were linked up with the vicissitudes of political and religious life. An event like the marriage of Otto II to a Byzantine princess (972) is often given as an example of the direct action of political history on the history of art. It did, in fact, produce a flow of Oriental elements into Germany, and this influx had an influence on painting. All the same, with regard to illumination, it must be remembered that the Ottonian renaissance began at least a decade earlier. Its origins are obscure, but the movement seems to have started from the west (Metz, Trier, and neighbouring abbeys), and, as in England two centuries earlier, it appears to have coincided with a reform of religious life.

The chief centres of activity were Fulda, Hildesheim (Saxony), the island of Reichenau, Cologne (Rhenish schools), Echternach, Regensburg, Salzburg (Danubian schools). One of the originators of the Ottonian renaissance is known as the Master of the Registrum Gregorii. He worked at Trier for Archbishop Egbert (end of the tenth century), and was among those who helped to give manuscript painting the monumental character that became the rule in almost all the scriptoria, even those of Reichenau. There, however, the style was more linear, lively, and expressive, with a more frequent use of gold backgrounds replacing bands of plain colour. Both these forms of Ottonian art were to influence the taste of Romanesque painters.

ROMANESQUE MINIATURES

The further one advances in time, the more numerous and varied in style become the surviving examples. Carolingian and Ottonian art each had their own domain, the boundaries of which can be traced on a map, and it has been possible to locate their points of origin, too. Romanesque art, on the other hand, flowered throughout the whole of the West, while its chronology is no less imprecise. Secular themes enrich its iconography, and religious subjects are sometimes accompanied, in the borders, by freely handled incidental scenes. It even came to pass that a copist's portrait was represented in the middle of the page—a place once strictly reserved for religious imagery or the likeness of an emperor. These liberties were rare, though the harbingers of a new era.

A few examples will be enough to show how varied were the inspirational sources of pre-Romanesque and Romanesque illumination: the *Phaenomena* of Aratus draws on the most ancient traditions, and the constellation figure reproduced here is copied from a Carolingian model, which itself goes back to an Antique prototype; the intense contrasts of the Apocalypse of St Sever are due to the spirit of Spain; while, through its dramatic quality, the Sacrementary of Limoges, a masterpiece of Limoges illumination, evokes the Ottonian art of Reichenau.

Among the most notable types of decorated manuscript—whether innovations of the period or legacies from the past—are the Exultet rolls of southern Italy, with paintings that appeared to the congregation as the deacon unfurled the *volumen* and read the text; the Lives of the Saints, numerous in northern France, with full-page illuminations that developed the narrative cycle in a series of compartments; and, above all, the 'private psalters'—forebears of the books of hours—that began to increase in number from the twelfth century onwards, to satisfy the requirements of an enlarged clientèle.

CONSTELLATION FIGURE. ARATUS: 'PHAENOMENA'. NORTHERN FRENCH SCHOOL *c.* 1000. BIBLIOTHÈQUE MUNICIPALE, BOULOGNE

THE RAIN OF FIRE AND BLOOD. BEATUS DE LIEBANA: 'COMMENTARIES ON THE APOCALYPSE'. ABBEY OF ST SEVER, MIDDLE OF THE 11th CENT. BIBLIOTHÈQUE NATIONALE, PARIS

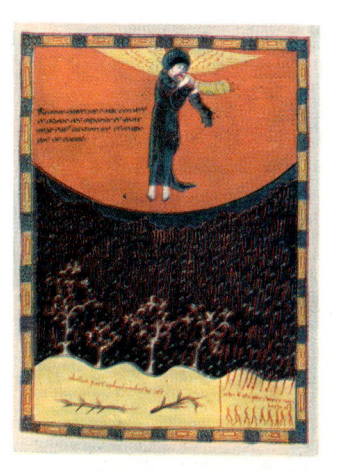

THE MARIES AT THE TOMB. SACREMENTARY OF THE CATHEDRAL OF ST ÉTIENNE, LIMOGES, *c.* 1100. BIBLIOTHÈQUE NATIONALE, PARIS

21

ROMANESQUE PAINTING

THE VIRGIN,
END OF 11th CENT.
CRYPT OF THE
CHURCH OF TAVANT

WOMAN PIERCED
WITH A LANCE,
KNOWN AS
LUXURY,
END OF 11th CENT.
CRYPT OF THE
CHURCH OF TAVANT

Inappropriate, though hallowed by use, the term 'Romanesque painting' serves to designate what, in Western Europe during the eleventh and twelfth centuries, followed Carolingian and Ottonian painting. It did more: it prolonged and gained inspiration from them, here retaining the liveliness and vehemence of the former, there the serene gravity of the latter. On these influences was superimposed—increasingly in the twelfth century—that of Byzantium. This variety of sources would alone explain the great diversity of Romanesque works; but one still has to take account of the local character that changed from one region to the next; of the movements of influential manuscripts; of the sometimes very long-range action of the great mother abbeys (e.g. Monte Cassino or Cluny); and the large number of itinerant workshops. Romanesque painting is ill-suited to geographical classification by regional schools, as affinities can be found between widely separated localities (Nohant-Vicq in Berry and Bohi in Catalonia), and profound differences between neighbouring sites (Tavant and Le Liget).

Yet, with these reservations, it *is* possible to distinguish a number of artistic regions. France was divided into two zones: a western one extending from the Loir valley

ENTRY INTO
JERUSALEM,
FIRST QUARTER
OF THE 12th CENT.
CHURCH OF
ST MARTIN DE VICQ,
NOHANT-VICQ

ROMANESQUE PAINTING

to Aquitaine through Touraine, Orléanais, Anjou, Poitou and Bourbonnais; and one more open to foreign and Oriental influences (it included Burgundy, Auvergne, and the Rhone and Alpine regions). In Spain, there was a single zone confined to the area in the north that had remained Christian. It comprised Catalonia, together with the French district of Roussillon, and a few scattered sites to the west (Leon) and south (Belanga and Maderuelo in Castile). Everywhere, however, the reflection of Mozarabic art was apparent. The majority of Spanish wall paintings have been detached, and transferred from the humble sanctuaries that originally contained them to the museums of Barcelona, Vich and Madrid. This is one of the reasons why they are better known to the public, and became the object of intensive study earlier than any others. The Italian focuses were Lombardy and Piedmont in the north; a truly Romanesque school that flourished in the central area; and, in the south, the school of Monte Cassino, the first to be affected by Byzantine art. Other regions included southern England, western Germany, Flanders, Switzerland, Austria, and a few small Scandinavian islands; each developed its own individual style.

Nevertheless, wall painting in the Romanesque period presents general features that necessitate a common name. As Prosper Mérimée rightly observed, when he discovered St Savin in 1845, it constituted the final phase of Antique art—the last stage of a slow evolution, during which certain technical, stylistic, and, in religious painting, iconographic traditions were maintained from the Early Christian period onwards. The sudden appearance of Gothic towards the end of the twelfth century set pictorial art on a new course. With regard to technique, Romanesque painting made no innovations, and remained faithful to age-old traditions. Each workshop had its own customs and methods, but all were dependant

THE DRUNKENNESS OF NOAH, FIRST QUARTER OF THE 12th CENT. NAVE OF THE CHURCH OF ST SAVIN

ST CLEMENT; MARTYRDOM OF ST PANCRAS, MIDDLE OF THE 12th CENT. CHURCH OF ST LÉGER, ÉBREUIL

TEMPTATION OF CHRIST. MIDDLE OF THE 12th CENT. CHURCH OF ST AIGNAN, BRINAY

23

ROMANESQUE PAINTING

APOSTLE (DETAIL OF MURAL PAINTINGS IN THE APSE). GINESTARRE DE CARDÓS, 12th CENT. MUSEO DE BELLAS ARTES DE CATALOÑA, BARCELONA

MARTYRDOM OF SANTA JULITA (DETAIL OF AN ALTAR DEDICATED TO SANTA JULITA AND SAN QUIRICO). DURRO, *c*. 1100. MUSEO DE BELLAS ARTES DE CATALOÑA, BARCELONA

VIRGIN (DETAIL OF THE 'WISE VIRGINS'). FRESCO FROM SAN QUIRCE DE PEDRET, 12th CENT. MUSEO DE BELLAS ARTES DE CATALOÑA, BARCELONA

on three main processes. Firstly, there was true or Italian fresco painting, in which the colours were applied *a fresco*—on a fresh, damp coat of plaster, that is to say. This plaster, composed of slaked lime and fine sand, absorbed the colours, and then dried hard, acquiring the strength of stone. Though very resistant and durable, the painting had to be executed swiftly, with no possibility of retouching. A few examples are to be found in France, at Auxerre (crypt of St Germain, ninth century) and at Berzé (crypt of the Château-des-Moines). Secondly, there was the 'Greek' method of painting on top of many layers of plaster. This support formed a crust almost a quarter of an inch thick, and on it, when dry, were superimposed two ground layers and two applications of colour (e.g., upper chapel at Berzé, France). Thirdly, there was distemper painting, in which the colours were applied to a layer of plaster that had been allowed to dry, but was dampened again when work began. As with true fresco, speed was essential and retouching difficult. This method was the one most prevalent in western France (St Savin, Tavant, etc.).

The styles are more varied than the techniques, and their diversity corresponds to that of the sources of Romanesque art, as well as to that of regional preferences and the temperament of individual artists. The examples reproduced here give an idea of these contrasts; but a more attentive study will reveal what they have in common: sobriety; the reduction of the subject to its essential features; an almost complete absence of accessories and marginal motifs, which is so striking when one compares it with their profusion during the succeeding periods. The Romanesque wall painters paid no attention to décor, and arranged their figures against a plain background, or one that was made up of parallel bands. Often, a single object was enough to set the scene: a seat if the action took place indoors, a tree or a stylized plant

ROMANESQUE MINIATURES

if it occurred in the open air. Such sobriety is suited to mural painting, and, in the same way, the general arrangement of a composition took into account the nature of the field to be covered, whether wall, vault, cupola, intrados, or apse. Anxious to adapt his work to the architecture, the painter made do with and emphasized surfaces, rejecting both the *trompe-l'œil* effect of modelling and the illusory depth of perspective. Finally, among the characteristics common to all Romanesque wall painting, is the use of an 'alphabet' of forms corresponding to the various objects to be represented—in particular, the parts of the human body, the folds of garments, and facial features. There were many of these alphabets, but the artist in charge of a project always kept strictly to the one that he had chosen. At St Savin, for example, the noses consist of two parallel lines ending in a sort of trefoil, which forms the nostrils.

A few examples from French and Spanish murals must suffice to sum up an extremely rich iconographical system common to the whole of Western Europe. Its principal themes came from the Orient, and they dated back to the first centuries A.D. The sources of inspiration were, above all, the Old Testament, with a marked preference for the Pentateuch; the life of Christ; the parables of the Gospels; and the basic concepts of Christian eschatology—namely, the Last Judgment, Heaven and Hell, and the visions of the Apocalypse. To these great subjects were added representations of the saints and episodes from their lives. Such themes were partly traditional (the Virgin, the Apostles, and the first martyrs), and partly more recent and more local in character, having been taken from history and the Golden Legend. There also appeared moral allegories (combats of the Virtues and Vices) unknown to the Early Christian and Oriental repertoire, and forming the West's most important contribution to religious iconography.

LAZARUS AT THE GATES OF DIVES. MURAL PAINTING FROM SAN CLEMENTE DE TAHULL, 1123. MUSEO DE BELLAS ARTES DE CATALOÑA, BARCELONA

THE FALL OF MAN (DETAIL OF A MURAL PAINTING FROM MADERUELO), *c.* 1125. PRADO, MADRID

ANNUNCIATION OF THE SHEPHERDS (DETAIL OF THE PAINTINGS OF SAN ISIDORO), SECOND HALF OF 12th CENT. SAN ISIDORO, LEON

ICON-PAINTING

ST BORIS AND
ST GLEB.
SUZDAL SCHOOL,
END OF 13th CENT.
RUSSIAN MUSEUM,
LENINGRAD

ARCHANGEL
MICHAËL.
NOVGOROD
SCHOOL,
BEGINNING OF
14th CENT.
TRETIAKOV GALLERY,
MOSCOW

THE PROPHET
ELIJAH.
NOVGOROD
SCHOOL,
END OF 14th CENT.
TRETIAKOV GALLERY,
MOSCOW

The icon is basically a sacred image, venerated 'with fear and trembling' by the pious. The icon-painter is not producing a work of art but making a gesture of piety by showing the heavenly kingdom in visual terms, in terms of the kingdom on earth. The themes were taken from the Holy Scriptures; the artist, often a priest, remained anonymous and merely gave an aesthetic form to the dogma and mysteries which are beyond man's understanding.

It was only at the beginning of this century that Russian icons were given a place in the history of art. After the Revolution of 1917 many of them were restored and classified so that it became easier to distinguish between different periods and schools. The fact that the most important works have remained in Russia explains why icon-painting is still a fairly unexplored territory and why it still has not attained the position it deserves. The icon, painted on wood, came to the fore in Byzantium after a ninth-century council had confirmed the defeat of the iconoclasts. It spread to Greece, Yugoslavia, Bulgaria, Rumania and even Ethiopia, but it was in Russia that, for eight centuries, it was at its richest.

When the founder of the Russian state was converted to the Orthodox Church in 989 he summoned Byzantine artists to his Court to decorate the first churches and train pupils. The buildings were mainly of wood so that they could not be decorated with frescoes or mosaics; hence the great use of the icon and, eventually, the iconostasis, a huge wall with a door in it which cut off the congregation from the sanctuary where the sacrament took place. Although the themes treated were traditional, the painters nevertheless exercised a certain freedom in the treatment itself. Works were not signed; artists collaborated in workshop-groups under the direction of one or more masters. Therefore we can only make out schools, apart from a few personal attributions.

Few works have come down to

ICON-PAINTING

us from Kiev, still thoroughly saturated with Byzantine influence. From the end of the eleventh to the sixteenth century Novgorod produced a number of extraordinary works — simple and powerful, brilliant in colour, supple in design, intellectual in conception. Monumentality vanished and rhythm took over, to produce a purely Russian style. The Suzdal school was more elegant and graceful; it unfortunately degenerated into affectation. But until the end of the fourteenth century Byzantine artists were still summoned to Russia and Russian artists modelled themselves on them. Theophanes the Greek, the last of a long line, worked in Moscow when that city was becoming an important — soon to be the most important — art-centre. Andrei Rublev (1360?-1430?) is the most famous of the Moscow artists; his works bear comparison with those of his contemporaries, Fra Angelico and Van Eyck. He managed to impart outstanding delicacy and charm to his painting; the soft forms of his figures, harmony of his colour, his sense of rhythm, majesty, spirituality and yet humanity make him one of the greatest painters in the world. Certainly his *Trinity* is the finest work in the whole of Russian art. The Moscow school followed the path marked out by Rublev; but towards the end of the sixteenth century the art of icon-painting gradually began to decline. The workshops of Stroganov produced pretty little icons in brilliant colours, tasteful miniatures in which decorative qualities have ousted life. In the seventeenth century Simon Ushakov introduced a note of realism. Only the subject remained religious; the spirit of painting became more and more secular under the influence of the West. Dutch engravings after Piscator's Bible came to be the favourite models. When, at the beginning of the eighteenth century, Peter I invited Italian, German and French artists to Moscow, he merely gave icon-painting the *coup de grâce*.

ST GEORGE,
END OF 14th CENT.
RUSSIAN MUSEUM,
LENINGRAD

ANDREI RUBLEV,
c. 1360-*c.* 1430.
THE TRINITY.
TRETIAKOV GALLERY,
MOSCOW

THE ENTOMBMENT,
END OF 15th CENT.
TRETIAKOV GALLERY,
MOSCOW

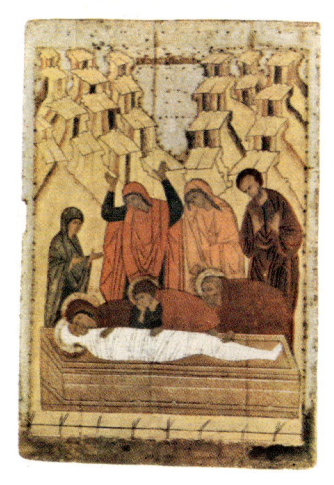

THE DUECENTO

GUIDO
DA SIENA,
MIDDLE OF
13th CENTURY.
MADONNA IN
MAJESTY,
c. 1260.
PALAZZO PUBBLICO,
SIENA

SCHOOL OF
GUIDO DA SIENA.
ANNUNCIATION
(PANEL OF ST PETER
ALTARPIECE).
PINACOTECA,
SIENA

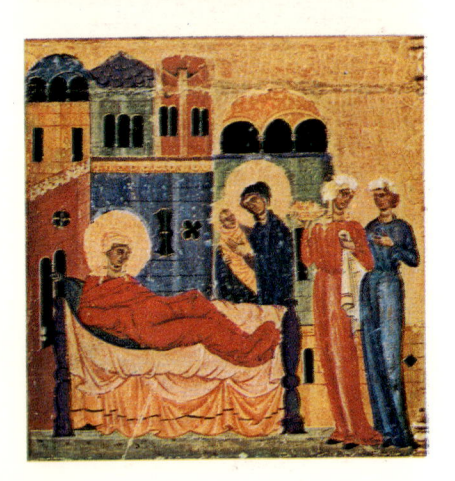

SIENESE SCHOOL.
BIRTH OF
ST JOHN
THE BAPTIST
(PANEL OF
ALTARPIECE OF THE
LIFE OF THE SAINT),
c. 1270-1280.
PINACOTECA,
SIENA

For centuries it was fondly imagined that Cimabue, the Florentine painter, was the first to react against the schematism of the 'Byzantine manner' and therefore the founder of 'modern' painting in Italy. Nineteenth-century critics tended to associate this shift in artistic outlook with the new religious sensitivity awakened by St Francis of Assisi (1182-1226), the new spiritual joy, humility towards nature, emotivity and feeling for the human pathos of the story of Christ. Today these ideas no longer seem valid.

The innovating movement sprang, not from the Franciscan spirit, but from a more general change in cultural and religious attitudes linked with the rise to power of the towns. It owed much to a certain renewed interest in 'imperial' greatness and the naturalism of Antiquity which characterized the art of the Ghibelline towns and of Rome under Boniface VIII at the same period, and which accounts, in large measure, for the power of, say, Cavallini's figures. Nor were the dramatic, expressionistic tendencies completely Franciscan; at this time they dominated all Greek monastic painting, and Italy cannot be viewed in complete isolation from the rest of the Mediterranean. Finally, it was natural enough that the existing mosaics, Roman and Florentine, should stimulate painters, who often worked in mosaic also, to revise the traditional schemes. When in 1280-1290 artists from all over Italy met at Assisi to decorate the church built over St Francis' tomb (in a splendid style quite opposed to the spirit of the saint—a fact which aroused not a little criticism), this manifesto of the new art already had the character of a vast synthesis.

Thus the movement did not stem only from Florence. Pisa and Lucca entered it somewhat earlier with their moving Crucifixions painted on leather or on carved wood; Guido of Siena probably anticipated Cimabue, although the date 1221 on his

28

THE DUECENTO

Madonna in Majesty in the Palazzo Pubblico probably refers to an earlier work for which Guido substituted this in about 1260. The Virgin was, significantly, the main theme of the earliest Sienese art. Later the school of Siena was distinguished by its elegance of line, the refined harmony of its colour, its poetic feeling and imaginative power. The tonal delicacy and grace of one of Guido's circle, the Master of the St Peter's altarpiece (Siena Gallery) already reveal a distinctive Sienese sensitivity.

The life of Cimabue, the Florentine innovator who early became a legend, remains, by and large, a mystery. He began his career as one of the team who decorated the Baptistery at Florence with mosaics; it was probably at Florence that he acquired his feeling for Byzantine splendour and gift for composition. At thirty he was in Rome with Torriti, the great mosaicist who restored to the Greek technique its Antique strength. Later, at Assisi, the central laboratory of Italian painting, he executed a *Virgin and St Francis* in the lower church and some amazingly assured frescoes, combining solemnity with animation, in the upper church (apse and transept). The penetrating portrait of St Francis in Santa Maria degli Angeli is also attributed to him. His famous *Madonna* in the Uffizi at Florence no doubt pleased the public, always impressed by three-dimensional effects, because of the skilful composition of volumes (note the heads of the figures at the bottom of the throne). He died at Pisa where he was making mosaics for the cathedral.

Like Cimabue, Pietro Cavallini (1250-1330) endowed Byzantine forms with new life and Classical nobility. He produced the mosaic *Story of the Virgin* in Santa Maria in Trastevere, a work more supple than the traditional renderings, and the *Last Judgment* in Santa Cecilia nearby. In its strict organisation, the latter is perhaps the most 'Classical' work produced in Rome in the Middle Ages.

CIMABUE,
c. 1240-1302.
VIRGIN AND CHILD.*
UFFIZI, FLORENCE

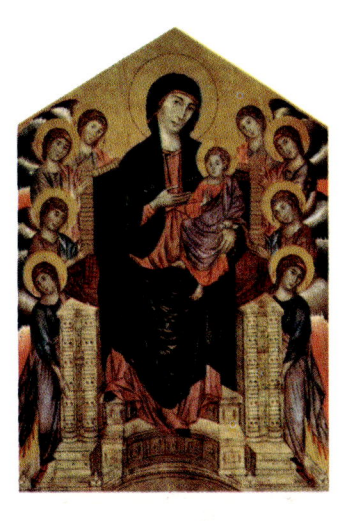

CIMABUE.
ANGEL
(FRESCO DETAILS).
UPPER CHURCH OF
S. FRANCESCO,
ASSISI

PIETRO CAVALLINI,
1250-1330.
APOSTLE
(DETAIL OF THE
LAST JUDGMENT
FRESCO). S. CECILIA
IN TRASTEVERE,
ROME

29

THE TRECENTO IN FLORENCE

GIOTTO DI BONDONE,
1266?-1337.
ST FRANCIS
PREACHING TO
THE BIRDS
(FRESCO),
c. 1300.
UPPER CHURCH OF
S. FRANCESCO,
ASSISI

GIOTTO.
ST FRANCIS
GIVING HIS CLOAK
TO THE POOR MAN
(FRESCO DETAIL),
c. 1300.
UPPER CHURCH OF
S. FRANCESCO,
ASSISI

GIOTTO.
THE DEATH OF THE
KNIGHT OF CELANO
(FRESCO DETAIL),
c. 1300.
UPPER CHURCH OF
S. FRANCESCO,
ASSISI

Giotto's art derives from Cimabue and the Roman mosaicists. According to tradition, he started life as a shepherd-boy in Mugello; as an apprentice in Florence in about 1280, he could have studied the mosaics in the Baptistery, including Cimabue's obviously 'pre-Giotto' *Story of Joseph*. At Rome, when the city was preparing for the great jubilee of 1300, he produced the famous mosaic of the *Navicella*, whose truth and dramatic intensity gripped contemporaries as they have posterity. In Giotto's work Cavallini's Byzantinism, with its Classical tendencies and imperial solemnity, loses what conventionality remained to it, while retaining its force and breadth. Already one finds the two elements with which Giotto came to be identified: 'Antique grandeur' and 'truth' (these may be roughly equated with the Roman tradition and Gothic contribution).

Like Cimabue, Giotto also learned from the heritage of Assisi. He was there in about 1300, but there is some doubt as to how much of the cycle of the *Life of St Francis* in the upper basilica is by him. This is the first cycle relating the life-story of the saint step by step according to the biographies which were declared official at that time. The style shows the influence of Rome; it has been suggested that the inequality of execution is due to Giotto's having started the system of 'teamwork' in such paintings. Those scenes which are certainly by him stand out on account of the monumental presentation of the isolated figures and, often, the use of an architectural setting to create space. The *Life* is in the grand style of history painting and has little to do with the Franciscan spirit, whatever older commentators said; the powerful, balanced forms echo the Patrician spirit of the towns. (Il Poverello's pictorial biographer, enriched by his art, composed a hymn to the glory of riches.)

The frescoes in the Capella degli Scrovegni in Padua (1303-1305) give the measure of his greatness.

THE TRECENTO IN FLORENCE

The chapel is a simple vaulted chamber whose walls are entirely covered with frescoes relating the Life of Christ and the Virgin in three rows of scenes; a *Last Judgment* on the west wall and an *Annunciation* on the triumphal arch, above two curious exercises in *trompe-l'œil*, complete the ensemble.

The iconography is traditional and the absolute simplicity of the arrangement suits the admirable conciseness of the composition in each of the panels: the figures or groups stand out powerfully against the sober background; the volumes, reduced to their bare essentials, are distributed with an acute feeling for balance. There is no room for empty formalism; all is subordinated to the story and the gripping power of the setting.

Spatially, Giotto's work does not emphasise either distance or the surface of the painting; each picture tends to be a narrow scene running parallel with the wall. The action also unfolds horizontally, thus avoiding any conflict between the massive volumes of the figures and their function as mural decoration. Though the facial expressions and gestures make the character and rôle of each figure abundantly clear, they do not isolate it from the action in general. But this dramatic quality makes a continuous frieze impossible; each scene forms a separate entity.

The intensity of every element and their perfect integration into a rational pattern are the distinctive qualities of Giotto's art and explain his great importance: in this he resembles Dante. His later Florentine works—the *Madonna in Majesty* in the Uffizi, the decorations in the Bardi and Peruzzi chapels in Santa Croce—take this Classical clarity and serene objectivity as far as they will go. After being invited to Naples and Milan and commissioned by Florence to supervise all the city's architectural projects, Giotto died, leaving behind him a school which rapidly degenerated into the picturesque prettiness which characterised minor Gothic art in the fourteenth century.

GIOTTO. FLIGHT INTO EGYPT (FRESCO DETAIL), 1303-1305. SCROVEGNI CHAPEL, PADUA

GIOTTO. DEPOSITION (FRESCO DETAIL), 1303-1305. SCROVEGNI CHAPEL, PADUA

GIOTTO. NOLI ME TANGERE (FRESCO DETAIL), 1303-1305. SCROVEGNI CHAPEL, PADUA

THE TRECENTO IN SIENA

DUCCIO DI
BUONINSEGNA,
c. 1260-1318.
VIRGIN IN MAJESTY
(RUCELLAI
MADONNA),
1285.
UFFIZI, FLORENCE

DUCCIO.
ST CATHERINE OF
ALEXANDRIA
(DETAIL FROM
THE MAESTA),
1308-1311.
MUSEO DELL'OPERA
DEL DUOMO, SIENA

DUCCIO.
ADORATION
OF THE MAGI
(PANEL FROM
THE PREDELLA
OF THE MAESTA),
1308-1311.
MUSEO DELL'OPERA
DEL DUOMO, SIENA

It has become customary to compare Cimabue's *Madonna Enthroned with Angels* (now in the Uffizi) with the *Rucellai Madonna* which in 1285 the Florentine Brotherhood of Santa Maria Novella commissioned from a Sienese painter now known to be Duccio di Buoninsegna. The two works share a basic Byzantinism adapted to suit contemporary taste; but it is surprising that they should ever have been attributed to the same artist. Duccio lacks the solidity of Cimabue; he aims at lightness and grace in composition, a nervous linear elegance (the gold hem on the Virgin's robe) and brilliance in the light and jewels rather than convincing spatial representation of objects or figures.

This, the first known work by Duccio, was apparently followed by cartoons for a stained-glass window in Siena Cathedral (1287-1288) and a *Madonna with Three Kneeling Franciscans* (1290). There are no documents or paintings to throw light on the following years, but in 1308 the city of Siena commissioned Duccio (with detailed specifications) to paint a large altarpiece of the Virgin, the *Maestà*. It took a long time to finish; not until 9th June 1311 was it carried in a triumphal procession to the cathedral, honoured both as an object of piety and an emblem of the patriotic pride of the Sienese citizens who had caused this miraculous masterpiece to be painted.

Duccio seems, like many Renaissance artists, to have been a difficult person, who cared greatly about his position in the town; he died in 1318.

Only one 'modern' artist seems to have influenced him, the sculptor Nicolo Pisano, who executed a famous pulpit in Siena Cathedral. Was Duccio ever at Assisi, as has been thought? Whether or no, his art seems to have derived from traditional Byzantinism by way of an original and autonomous evolution.

His masterpiece, the *Maestà*, shows the Madonna enthroned and

32

THE TRECENTO IN SIENA

surrounded by saints; on the back are forty small panels narrating the story of Christ. (Apart from a few fragments which have gone to London and Washington, they are all in the Opera del Duomo at Siena.) Basically this painting, so superior in technique and spirit to the average italianized 'Greek manner', combines the best qualities of great Byzantine art: the splendid colour, the intensity, the subtle effects.

The composition in the narrative panels is simple and clear, as well-balanced as Giotto's; it would be monumental if the size were not so small and the lines and movements so taut. Some figures recall the sculpture studied by Duccio; on the other hand, he shows his sense of the tragedy of the New Testament scenes and reproduces it with the moving simplicity of folk tales.

He is mainly preoccupied with colour. The gold background demands an extreme purity and intensity which heighten the refinement of the colour-harmonies: salmon pink with red or red with green and mauve. His arrangement of volumes in space has little significance in itself: the overwhelming gold sky reduces the forms to accidents within a flow of light. It is the delicious harmony of the pale or dark tones which is most immediately striking.

There is something Gothic about Duccio; certainly his elegance, sensitivity, gracefulness and mannerisms have certain analogies with contemporary developments in French art—Parisian miniatures and stained-glass windows. Thus it was Duccio who ensured that the future Sienese school (Siena was a Gothic town *par excellence*) would be linked with the West of Europe.

But behind Duccio's 'modernity' was a sort of Eastern background which disappeared from the much more transparent art of his successors. If Giotto had a counterpart in Siena it was probably Simone Martini rather than Duccio di Buoninsegna.

DUCCIO. CALLING OF THE APOSTLES PETER AND ANDREW (PANEL FROM THE BACK OF THE MAESTA), 1308-1311. NATIONAL GALLERY OF ART, WASHINGTON

DUCCIO. THREE MARIES AT THE TOMB (PANEL FROM THE BACK OF THE MAESTA), 1308-1311. MUSEO DELL'OPERA DEL DUOMO, SIENA

DUCCIO. TRANSFIGURATION (PANEL FROM THE BACK OF THE MAESTA), 1308-1311. NATIONAL GALLERY, LONDON

THE TRECENTO IN SIENA

SIMONE MARTINI,
1284-1344.
BLESSED AGOSTINO
NOVELLO RESCUING
A CHILD BITTEN
BY A WOLF.
S. AGOSTINO,
SIENA

SIMONE MARTINI.
ANGEL AND VIRGIN
OF ANNUNCIATION
(DIPTYCH).
MUSÉE ROYAL DES
BEAUX-ARTS,
ANTWERP

SIMONE MARTINI.
MUSICIANS
(DETAIL FROM
ST MARTIN
BEING MADE
A KNIGHT).
LOWER CHURCH OF
S. FRANCESCO,
ASSISI

If Giotto's art is reminiscent, to a certain extent, of thirteenth-century sculpture, Simone's has more in common with miniature-painting. The first known work by him, the *Maestà* of 1315 (Palazzo Pubblico, Siena) is still Duccian but rather more decorative; the position of the huge ornamental baldachin sets the new tone. In his *Portrait of the Condottiere Guidoriccio da Fogliano* of 1328 (also Palazzo Pubblico) the curve of the rider on his caparisoned mount lingers in the memory; this strange work has an epic atmosphere.

With Simone, Italian painting took a definite Gothic turn. He travelled widely; from 1317 he was probably in Naples painting a panel of St Louis of Toulouse; 1330 is given as the date of his stay in Assisi, where he decorated the St Martin Chapel of the lower church. One has only to compare his work with the Giotto frescoes nearby to see how much taste has changed: painters have become more descriptive, more eager for subtle effects and less chary of confusion, Giotto's *bête noire*.

Simone returned to Siena in 1333 and there produced his finest work—probably the most 'Sienese' ever painted—*The Annunciation* (Uffizi). The Virgin draped in blue turning shyly away, the graceful white curves of the angel who is hailing her, the vase of lilies and shimmering gold background make up a moving and unforgettable poetic study. It was no mere accident that Petrarch wrote two sonnets to Simone, just as Dante had celebrated Giotto.

Simone met Petrarch in Avignon where the artist went in 1339. He painted a portrait (now lost) of Laura and decorated Petrarch's copy of Virgil with a miniature: a strange and beautiful evocation of the classical world as seen by the first Humanists. Simone died in Avignon leaving various works (the *Madonna* of the Church of Notre Dame des Dons) which had a decisive influence on the future artistic alliance between Siena and the Gothic West.

THE TRECENTO IN SIENA

PIETRO LORENZETTI,
c. 1280 ?-1348.
THREE PANELS
FROM THE
ALTARPIECE
OF THE BLESSED
HUMILITY.
UFFIZI, FLORENCE

Not until the fifteenth century did it become clear how profoundly Sienese art had been marked by Simone's manner; in his own lifetime there had still been room for Pietro Lorenzetti, who followed a completely different trend. His career (of which we catch glimpses between 1316 and 1348) was interrupted by the plague in the mid-fourteenth century: little is known of its details.

The altarpiece of *The Blessed Humility* (Uffizi) seems almost Florentine; the small narrative panels composing the wings are painted with an assurance and organisation which suggest the influence of Giotto. Pietro may have studied in Florence but he spent the rest of his life in Siena apart from a few visits to Assisi where he painted some frescoes in the lower church. There is no Sienese lyricism in the *Arezzo Polyptych,* commissioned in 1320, in which the powerful figures are splendidly balanced.

He shows the full extent of his powers in the Assisi church frescoes. The taut expression of *The Madonna between St Francis and St John the Evangelist* and the masterly composition of the six scenes of the Passion establish them as mature works (1326-1329); but his *Crucifixion,* full of movement yet with every detail well in hand, is assigned to a still later period.

PIETRO LORENZETTI.
CRUCIFIXION
(FRESCO DETAIL).
LOWER CHURCH OF
S. FRANCESCO,
ASSISI

PIETRO LORENZETTI.
NATIVITY OF
THE VIRGIN
(DETAIL),
1342.
MUSEO DELL'OPERA
DEL DUOMO, SIENA

35

THE TRECENTO IN SIENA

AMBROGIO LORENZETTI, ACTIVE 1319-1348. CITY BY THE SEA. PINACOTECA, SIENA

AMBROGIO LORENZETTI, MADONNA DEL LATTE. SEMINARY, SIENA

AMBROGIO LORENZETTI. CITY BY A LAKE. PINACOTECA, SIENA

After the solemn Sienese *Altarpiece of the Carmelites* (1329), the triptych of *The Nativity of the Virgin* (1342), his last dated work, seems nearer the calmer, more intimate style of his brother Ambrogio. The beautiful recumbent figure of St Anne and the two visitors on the right herald the Classical masterpieces of the Renaissance.

Ambrogio was a complex character with many interests. He painted Eastern motifs and exotic themes, copied a figure from a Roman medal, drew an Antique statue whose discovery had just caused a great stir in the city, designed a (lost) 'revolving map of the world' and produced the first 'pure landscapes', which were no doubt parts of a decorated piece of furniture.

It has been wrongly suggested that he had discovered the vanishing point in perspective; he has even been put forward as the author of the 'Aristotelian' programme of the allegorical frescoes in the Palazzo Pubblico. Whether or no, he was certainly a personage of distinction, a member of the town council of Siena and one of the first artists possessed of enormous intellectual curiosity.

None of his youthful works are known, apart from the enigmatic, archaic *Madonna* of Vico l'Abbate (1319); probably he began work at Florence, which would explain his initial affinities with Giotto. After the frescoes of *St Francis* at Siena (1330-1331), he became more and more independent of Giotto's influence, developing an acute observation which was governed by the deep emotions of the colourist and a very individual poetic sensitivity. He has little in common with Pietro, with whom he collaborated only once, in 1335, on some frescoes (now lost).

His series of Virgins set the tone of his art: the *Virgin and Child Frightened by a Bird* (Siena, San Agostino), the idyllic *Madonna del Latte,* after a sculpture by Niccolo Pisano (Siena, Seminary), the *Virgin of Rapolano,* in which a vague anxiety seems to draw the mother

THE TRECENTO IN SIENA

and child close together; the rich colour of the *Madonna in Majesty* at Siena, the tenderness of the one in Massa Maritima. But despite his lyricism, Ambrogio is far from being a 'minor' artist. The composition of his huge-seeming narrative panels is admirable (*Story of St Nicholas of Bari*, Uffizi, 1332). He achieves a calm linear harmony in his altarpiece of *St Petronilla* and in his *St Michael of Badia* at Rofano presents a strange ornamental fantasy: the figure of a golden warrior on the complicated coils of the dragon. The two famous 'landscapes' are, in fact, urban views (of Montepulciano and perhaps Talamare); despite his evident topographical preoccupations, they are outstanding chiefly for their beautiful colouring, due, no doubt, to inspiration aroused by new subjects. They probably date from the same period as the frescoes in the 'Sala dei Nove' in the Palazzo Pubblico (1336-1339): *Allegory of Good Government and Bad Government* and *Effects of Good Government*. These were a sort of manifesto of a faction which had just taken power in Siena, the so-called *Nove*.

The *Allegory* is a complicated picture, filled with figures of different sizes, inscriptions scattered everywhere, and ropes which are literally threads linking the various figures. But without being symmetrical the whole is ingeniously balanced and the Antique figure of Peace in the centre of the wall sets the tone of monumental harmony. The *Effects*, illustrated with obvious relish, occupy a long wall and take the form of a huge panorama impossible to take in at one glance and swarming with enchanting details, both landscapes and genre scenes.

The *Presentation at the Temple* (Uffizi, 1342) belongs to Ambrogio's last period. In the vigorous unity of the composition it resembles Pietro's *Nativity of the Virgin*, of the same date. In 1344 Ambrogio painted *The Annunciation* (Siena, Pinacoteca), embodying a new and deep conception of the religious significance of the scene.

AMBROGIO LORENZETTI. PEACE (DETAIL FROM THE 'GOOD GOVENRMENT' FRESCO), 1337-1339. PALAZZO PUBBLICO, SIENA

AMBROGIO LORENZETTI. FORTITUDE (DETAIL FROM THE 'GOOD GOVERNMENT' FRESCO), 1337-1339. PALAZZO PUBBLICO, SIENA

AMBROGIO LORENZETTI. (DETAIL FROM THE 'GOOD GOVERNMENT' FRESCO), 1337-1339. PALAZZO PUBBLICO, SIENA

37

INTERNATIONAL GOTHIC

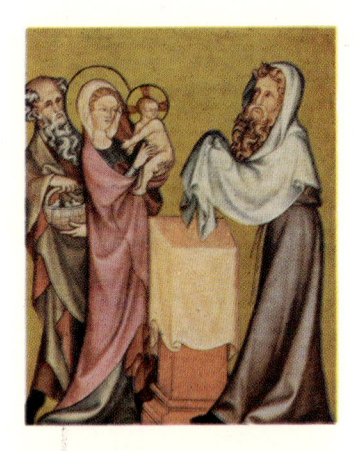

COLOGNE SCHOOL.
PRESENTATION AT
THE TEMPLE,
c. 1330.
WALLRAF-RICHARTZ
MUSEUM,
COLOGNE

MASTER BERTRAM.
CHRIST'S ENTRY
INTO JERUSALEM
(PANEL FROM
ALTERPIECE OF
CHRIST'S PASSION),
c. 1379.
HANOVER MUSEUM

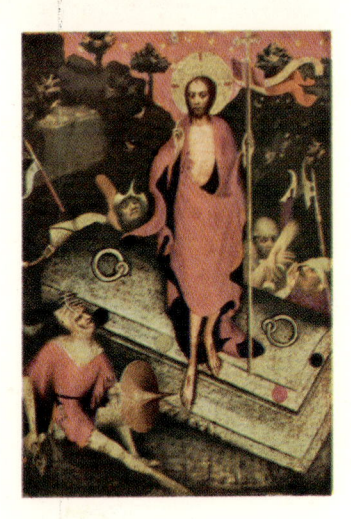

MASTER OF THE
TREBON
ALTARPIECE.
RESURRECTION,
c. 1380.
NATIONAL GALLERY,
PRAGUE

The Gothic approach to pictorial art is best illustrated by the tapestries, stained-glass windows, polychrome statues and, especially, illuminations of the age, rather than the frescoes or painted panels, which developed late. In the field of easel-painting distinctions between local or national schools are often artificial; in the fourteenth century artistic centres influenced and moulded each other to an unparalleled extent, owing to the influence of the Courts. Like mediaeval novels in literature, Gothic painting was mainly courtly, even in the religious sphere. Art-loving kings or lords commissioned illuminated books, fine altarpieces, splendid chapels for their castles. These patrons had contacts throughout Europe and often summoned artists from a distance. Novelties gained currency and travelled from place to place; taste was both refined and delicate. Hence the 'international' character of some works of 1360-1400.

The Valois kings were particularly fond of art. John the Good had no less than two hundred and thirty-nine tapestries made for his castles; the painter Girard of Orleans (active between 1344 and 1362) was a member of his Court and the probable author of his portrait, admittedly a still rough and hasty work. All the King's sons, princes with apanages, Charles V, Philip the Hardy of Burgundy and John, Duke of Berry, were patrons on a large scale. In John of Berry (died 1416) the collector's passion reached a peak. There is no more 'French' work in this period than the *Wilton Diptych* made for Richard II of England, possibly by an English artist; the delicate charm of this refined, precious and ornamental painting is characteristically 'Continental'.

From the reign of Charles IV onwards (King in 1333, Emperor in 1346), Bohemia became another important centre of Gothic painting. Its very swift artistic upsurge is not sufficiently accounted for by the fact that it assimilated influences from France and, later, Italy. The

38

INTERNATIONAL GOTHIC

King set on foot enormous activity: the great Cathedral of Prague alone contained some sixty altarpieces. In the cycle of the *Life of Christ* at Vyšší Brod there is a sensitivity to colour and nature rarely found in the fourteenth century; the long lines of powerful portraits with large heads and flowing drapery which flank the walls of the Chapel of Karlstyn (1367) are by one Theodoric of Prague who seems also to have been very active in Hamburg. But the masterpiece of Gothic art in Czechoslovakia is the *Trebon Altarpiece* (now in Prague) which includes the famous *Resurrection*: Christ, slender, straight and rigid, wrapped in a black and red cloak, stands on the massive tomb surrounded by rustic, menacing guards and stretches up towards a red sky sprinkled with golden stars. This work heralds the most striking and profound productions of the Renaissance in Central Europe.

Bohemian art filtered into southern Germany and Austria where the rich monasteries used it for their decorations, although they also drew inspiration from Italy and Paris: in the Hanseatic towns, Bertram, a sturdy 'popular' artist with a sculptor's rather than a painter's temperament, continued along the lines of Theodoric (*Grabow Altarpiece*, 1379, *Buxtehude Altarpiece*, c. 1390).

The flourishing towns along the Rhine developed a culture of their own in an empire otherwise disorganized. Cologne, a centre of mystical theology and sentimental asceticism, produced a school of gentle, mannerist painting, specializing in the themes of the Virgin and Childhood of Christ. Its finest representative was Stephan Lochner who lived in the second quarter of the fifteenth century. Until about 1450 paintings remained wedded to embossed gold backgrounds, decorative outlines and flowers and near to miniatures and metalwork; only Tuscany and Flanders were able to shake off (1420-1430) the spell cast by gold, colour and prettiness.

AUSTRIAN SCHOOL. HOLY TRINITY, END 14th- BEGINNING 15th CENTURY. NATIONAL GALLERY, LONDON

FRENCH SCHOOL (GIRARD D'ORLÉANS). PORTRAIT OF KING JOHN THE GOOD. c. 1360. LOUVRE, PARIS

FRENCH OR ENGLISH SCHOOL. WILTON DIPTYCH: RICHARD II OF ENGLAND PRESENTED TO THE VIRGIN BY HIS PATRON SAINTS, c. 1395. NATIONAL GALLERY, LONDON

INTERNATIONAL GOTHIC

GENTILE DA
FABRIANO.
1360?-1427?
VIRGIN AND CHILD,
c. 1420.
NATIONAL GALLERY
OF ART,
WASHINGTON

GENTILE DA
FABRIANO.
ADORATION OF
THE MAGI
(DETAIL),
1423.
UFFIZI, FLORENCE

PISANELLO.
c. 1395-1455/56.
PORTRAIT OF
LIONELLO D'ESTE,
c. 1441.
ACCADEMIA
CARRARA,
BERGAMO

Apart from the Sienese artists, International Gothic is principally represented in Italian art by the Umbrian painter Gentile da Fabriano. Vasari wrote that his name described his painting; the 'gentle' painter left a long-lasting mark on two centres of Italian art, Venice and Florence. His early life had been spent in the north; at Verona and Padua he learned the florid art of the Gothic Courts and in Venice he caught a last glimpse of the Byzantine splendour. Out of the two he developed a charming style—a little too charming, perhaps—which shows careful attention to detail and a certain amount of naturalism, although he was not much interested in reality: painting was now concerned only with romance and paradise.

None of Gentile's frescoes are still in existence; his works at Venice (Palazzo Ducale, 1408-1409), Brescia and Rome (San Giovanni in Laterano, 1427-1428) are all lost. To us of the present day his masterpiece is *The Adoration of the Magi* (1423), painted, like the *Quaratesi Altar,* during the few years when he was living in Florence. This visit coincided with the renaissance of Sienese painting and the apparent eclipse of Giotto's city; Lorenzo Monaco had just introduced the new fashion. Gentile therefore found ready-made admirers; on the other hand, Masaccio, who at the same period was challenging this florid, overloaded art with his own more powerful and incisive painting, remained an outsider. And for a long time after the city had been converted to Masaccio, a precious, romantic, courtly and 'curious' current still flowed through Umbrian art.

The alliance between Gothic and Byzantine art seen in Gentile's work was, of course, even more successful in Venice; as a formula it might have been specially devised for this city of spectacular palaces and exotic treasures. It was adopted by Jacopo Bellini and several exquisite minor artists. But Gentile's true successor, Pisanello, came from Verona, not Venice.

40

INTERNATIONAL GOTHIC

Antonio di Puccio di Cerreto, known as Pisanello, was born at Pisa but brought up at Verona. Like Gentile and numerous other International Gothic artists, he travelled widely, notably to Mantua (1424), Venice (with Gentile, 1425), Rome (where he completed Gentile's frescoes, 1431-1433), Verona (c. 1436), Mantua again and Milan (1440), Venice again (1442), Naples and Ferrara. Some of the Verona works are still close to Gentile; one thinks of *The Madonna with the Quail* or the fresco of *The Annunciation*, of which there remains only the angel—a figure of an overwhelming splendour and strange grace. The extraordinary *St George rescuing the Princess* (1436) combines all the elements of Gothic romance— Oriental figures, dream-architecture, a gallows on the horizon, unbelievable costumes. The essential formula of Gothic in its final period —a mixture of minute observation and fantastic imagination—remained valid for Pisanello, but did not account for the whole of his personality. He was a splendid animal-painter *(Vision of St Eustace)* and a tireless inventor of sartorial extravagances—the two themes recur often in his admirable drawings. He was also, like Gentile, a penetrating portraitist.

But his intellectual interests were more extensive than Bellini's and owed more than a little to Humanism: for instance, he copied motifs from ancient sarcophagi and used Greek characters in his medals. One of his drawings indicates that he took an interest in perspective. He was unequalled as a medallist.

But he stands out from his Gothic forerunners chiefly because of his gift and taste for design. Perhaps it was his work as a medallist which sharpened his sense of the relations between spaces and masses and showed him how to heighten silhouettes. At any rate, his pictures never appear crowded, however luxuriant the details. His work seems to contain the germs of a 'grand style'; it lacks only the talent for synthesis which the Florentines were to develop.

PISANELLO. PRINCESS OF TREBIZOND (DETAIL FROM THE STORY OF ST GEORGE: FRESCO), 1436. S. ANASTASIA, VERONA

PISANELLO. VISION OF ST EUSTACHE (DETAIL). NATIONAL GALLERY, LONDON

PISANELLO. PORTRAIT OF A PRINCESS OF THE ESTE FAMILY. LOUVRE, PARIS

THE QUATTROCENTO IN SIENA

SASSETTA, 1392-1450.
MYSTIC MARRIAGE OF ST FRANCIS.
MUSÉE CONDÉ, CHANTILLY

SASSETTA.
ST FRANCIS AND THE POOR MAN (DETAIL OF THE DREAM OF ST FRANCIS).
NATIONAL GALLERY, LONDON

SASSETTA.
JOURNEY OF THE MAGI (DETAIL).
METROPOLITAN MUSEUM, NEW YORK

Fifteenth-century Sienese art never completely abandoned the International Gothic style which was at its height in about 1400. Therefore it came to be considered reactionary; it accepted the new ideas of the great Florentine innovators, from Masaccio onwards, only with important modifications. But in Siena this reticence was due to originality, rather than inertia.

This originality can be seen in its purest form in the work of Sassetta (Stefano di Giovanni di Consolo). He deliberately looked back towards Simone Martini, who inspired his interest in formal rhythm: but he also quested after 'modernity' (the inscription of his polyptych of 1416 boasts of the 'novelty' of the work) and adopted full volumes with smooth surfaces such as he might have learned from a Florentine artist (say Masolino). From this date the buildings he painted had 'modern' semicircular arches. In his work the foreshortening and perspective, in which he was always interested, do not jar with the frailty of the figures and lavish ornaments and embroideries, owing to the light and elegant composition (altarpieces of *The Virgin of the Snow,* Florence, private collection, 1430-1431; *St Dominic,* Cortona).

Sassetta painted his masterpiece, the polyptych of *St Francis* at Borgo San Sepolcro, between 1437 and 1443. The altarpiece (for which he was well paid) is exceptionally lavish; its various parts (the Virgin surrounded by saints, scenes from the life of St Francis on the back) are now dispersed. The whole was precise, polished, extremely refined, full of touching details, strongly, almost nobly, constructed. Its dominant quality was the harmony between colour, light and volume; Piero della Francesca could have studied it, but not until he was already pursuing the same path himself—which at least proves that Siena was not 'backward'.

Sassetta's last work, a *Coronation of the Virgin,* was completed after the artist's death by Sano di Pietro on whom, as it were, his mantle

THE QUATTROCENTO IN SIENA

descended. Sano, without being a genius, was a conscientious, skilful artist, very representative of the average Sienese taste of the day. Little is known of his career: none of his works painted before 1444, when he was thirty-eight, are still extant. Some art-historians have considered that all the works of the anonymous artist known as the Master of the Osservanza (after his main work, dated 1436, in the convent of that name) are in fact early productions of Sano di Pietro. The former master was even more faithful to Gothic 'decorative' feeling.

Sano di Pietro produced many pictures, assisted no doubt by apprentices in his *bottega*. Hence the unevenness of quality and the often schematic uniformity of manner: round, flabby faces with slender, semicircular eyebrows, black eyes, a limited gamut of gay colours evenly applied—steel-blue sky, pink walls and pavements. Contemporaries praised Sano's piety; in his serial works he seems to have aimed mainly at satisfying his clients' demand for sentiment. In general his best works are his earliest, such as the polyptych of *The Jesuati* (Siena, apart from the *predella* with the story of St Jerome which is in the Louvre). Description and narration suited his temperament best. His most famous work is the *St Bernardino preaching in the Campo at Siena* which is in his best vein; he is happiest as a str ightforward narrator of miracles and martyrdoms.

Like Sassetta and the Master of the Osservanza, Sano was affected, to a certain extent, by the influence of Gentile da Fabriano who had worked in Siena in 1426. The inventive but slightly disordered art of Vecchietta (frescoes in the sacristy of the Hospital, 1436-1449) provided Sienese painters with another source of inspiration; he may be called the father of the fantastic, elaborately imaginative painters of the following generation: Neroccio de' Landi, Benvenuto di Giovanni and the amazing Francesco di Giorgio.

SANO DI PIETRO, 1406-1481. MADONNA WITH CALIXTUS III, 1456. PINACOTECA, SIENA

SANO DI PIETRO. ST BERNARDINO PREACHING IN THE CAMPO AT SIENA (DETAIL). c. 1444. SIENA CATHEDRAL

SANO DI PIETRO. ST PETER CURING PETRONILLA, 1479. PINACOTECA, SIENA

THE QUATTROCENTO IN FLORENCE

GIOVANNI DI FIESOLE KNOWN AS FRA ANGELICO, 1387-1455. ANNUNCIATION (FRESCO), AFTER 1437. CONVENT OF S. MARCO, FLORENCE

FRA ANGELICO. CORONATION OF THE VIRGIN (DETAIL), BETWEEN 1430-1440. LOUVRE, PARIS

FRA ANGELICO. LAMENTATION, 1440-1445. CONVENT OF S. MARCO, FLORENCE

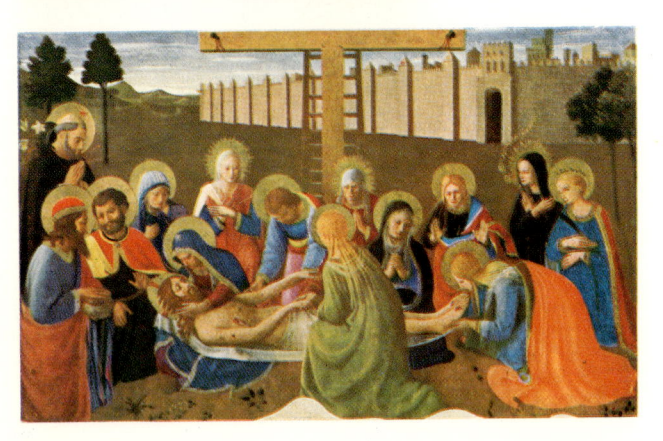

Fra Giovanni of Fiesole, who soon acquired the nickname of 'Angelico', still clung to the traditional Sienese art practised by his master, Lorenzo Monaco, and Gothic colour; but he was not indifferent to the new developments filtering through to Florence between 1420 and 1435: the airy treatment of Domenico Veneziano and the new ideas of the 'draughtsman' school which derived from Masaccio. However, in the main he remained faithful to the leading principles of the Trecento and may be called a conservative artist —a fact which by no means reduced his popularity during his lifetime.

He poured out a huge number of works, but the earliest known, the Fiesole altarpiece, seems to have been painted in 1428 when the painter would have been forty. What had he painted before? For what reason did he cling faithfully, during the next twenty-seven years, to artistic ideas which were already going out of fashion when (apparently) he began to paint?

The answer is bound up with the fact that he was a monk and with the conservatism of monastic traditions. He belonged first to the Dominican monastery at Fiesole and then to San Marco at Florence (where he was Prior); both were reformed communities. The rigourism of the second had its effect on the cultural life of Florence; on several occasions the monasteries launched violent and sometimes perspicacious attacks on the Humanist 'avant-garde'. The painting of the fourteenth century, with its gold and blue, its sentimental preciosity and figures without substance was held to be more pious than the naturalistic, monumental art of the innovators. No doubt the Gothic manner held more attractions for the Prior of San Marco, who was said to weep while painting the Crucifixion and never to take up his brush without first offering up a prayer.

Nevertheless he took over from the moderns whatever features suited his conception of religious art: clear, precise composition

THE QUATTROCENTO IN FLORENCE

(quite different from Gentile's confusion), an accurate feeling for space, light-handed modelling (Angelico avoided grey and painted shadows with darker tones). He sometimes showed classical architecture, in imitation of the contemporary palaces or churches of, say, Michelozzo (*The Annunciation*, Cortona; Chapel of Nicholas V, Vatican).

The chronology of his works shows up a surprising feature; they became progressively less 'modern' as he grew older. Indeed, some Gothic characteristics—a wealth of costly materials, opaque golden haloes, etc.—appear only in the later works; in them too the schemes of the Trecento begin to make themselves felt. The feeling for space in *The Virgin with Angels* (Vatican), the modelling in *The Virgin of the Linaioli* (Uffizi) and *The Deposition* (museum of San Marco) have no parallel in his later work. The frescoes in San Marco are uneven in quality, owing to the fact that too many collaborators assisted him.

The Coronation of the Virgin (Louvre) shows Fra Angelico's qualities in their best light. This Paradise has all the facility, beauty and preciosity of Gothic; there is no lack of gold and blue, 'flat' colours of great richness, but they do not prevent the volumes from being given their full value. The work succeeds through its freshness of inspiration, well served by a painterly grace which is not insipid.

So great was his popularity that he received commissions from outside Florence. His work at Perugia inspired several artists of great refinement; in Rome, to which he went twice, he decorated the Chapel of San Lorenzo in the Vatican for Nicholas V, dexterously manipulating decoration in the Antique manner. In Orvieto he began to decorate the vaulting of the Chapel of San Brizio but the work was finished by Signorelli. The miniatures often attributed to him are, probably, by one of his closest collaborators, Zanobi Strozzi.

FRA ANGELICO. CHRIST MOCKED (FRESCO), AFTER 1437. CONVENT OF S. MARCO, FLORENCE

FRA ANGELICO. NOLI ME TANGERE (FRESCO DETAIL). CONVENT OF S. MARCO, FLORENCE

FRA ANGELICO. SCENES FROM THE LIFE OF CHRIST: ANNUNCIATION, AFTER 1450. CONVENT OF S. MARCO, FLORENCE

THE QUATTROCENTO IN FLORENCE

TOMASO MASACCIO,
1401-1428.
VIRGIN AND
CHILD WITH
ST ANNE,
1420-1424.
UFFIZI, FLORENCE

MASACCIO.
CHRIST AND
THE APOSTLES
(DETAIL FROM THE
FRESCO OF THE
TRIBUTE MONEY),
1426-1428.
BRANCACCI CHAPEL,
S. MARIA DEL
CARMINE,
FLORENCE

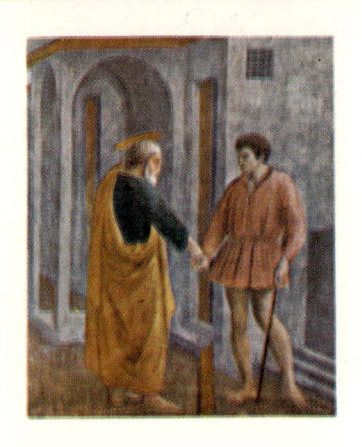

MASACCIO.
ST PETER
PAYING THE
TRIBUTE MONEY
(DETAIL FROM THE
FRESCO OF THE
TRIBUTE MONEY),
1426-1428.
BRANCACCI CHAPEL,
S. MARIA DEL
CARMINE,
FLORENCE

There is something dramatic about the way in which Masaccio appeared in the Florence of the 1420s, still preoccupied with the Gothic graces. There is no other example in the entire history of painting of such a radical and long-lasting transformation being brought about in such a short time (Masaccio died in 1428 at the age of twenty-seven). The principles laid down in the few works he had time to create were never forgotten; whenever Florentine artists felt a deep need to return to the old traditions deriving in a direct line from Giotto, young painters made their way towards the Brancacci Chapel to copy its Masaccio frescoes. It was Leonardo da Vinci who first coupled the names of Giotto and Masaccio, the two artists who had set painting on the right road—the road towards strong, powerful modelling and monumental greatness.

For his forerunners one can look only to the sculptor Donatello and the architect Brunelleschi, the inventor of scientific perspective. As far as painting was concerned, he had no antecedents. On the contrary, his master Masolino, was more than a little influenced by his pupil. One can follow this development in Masolino's work —the strengthening of the drawing, the progressive interest in problems of space—but he never completely lost the Gothic taste for rich variety, and although he handled perspective with skill and discretion, it never amounted to much more than a decorative asset. Masolino collaborated with Masaccio on the Brancacci Chapel (1426-1427), and it was he who completed the cycle of frescoes begun by Masaccio in San Clemente at Rome when the younger man died. Despite the numerous travels which took him on occasion as far as Hungary, Masolino never managed to come to grips with the new style even in the very interesting decorations for the Baptistery of Castiglione d'Olona.

It has never been possible to establish the dating of the two

THE QUATTROCENTO IN FLORENCE

painters' works with any certainty; nor is it always possible to make out who painted what in their collaborations. In the *Virgin and Child with St Anne* (Uffizi, 1420-1424), the Madonna, Jesus and right-hand angel, all modelled with great authority, are usually attributed to Masaccio. The influence of Donatello's prophets can be recognized in the dense, strongly lighted and firmly arranged figures of the saints in a polyptych of 1426 (now dispersed). The whole conception of a fresco in Santa Maria Novella showing *The Trinity with two Patrons* was revolutionary; all the figures are placed within a *trompe-l'œil* framework—a Brunelleschi-type structure whose perspective is calculated to take full effect when the spectator is on the other side of the nave. It is this new conception of 'reality' in painting, rather than the geometrical virtuosity (in which he is thought to have been helped by Brunelleschi) that is of importance here. The grave, solemn presence of objects and figures, both sacred and profane, is far removed from illusionism.

Apart from a fragment of a polyptych, nothing remains of Masaccio's last works, painted in Rome. The real Masaccio is to be found in the Brancacci Chapel. His hand can be distinguished from those of Masolino and Filippino Lippi by the 'weight' of his figures. Just as he avoided Gothic 'charm', so he abandoned the false nobility of Classical-type poses: his figures, seen on a level (their heads are all the same height) have a peasant reality which imparts a mysterious solemnity to their ultra-simple but forceful gestures. The strict concentration is never relaxed; he avoids all dramatic effects, except the intense lighting in the scene of *The Alms-Giving*. The foreshortening of volumes, an achievement of which fourteenth-century artists were so proud, is executed with a new consistency (it is applied even to the saints' haloes) but without ostentation. For two centuries it remained the embodiment of Florentine artistic consciousness.

MASACCIO. ST PETER HEALING THE SICK (FRESCO DETAIL), 1426-1428. BRANCACCI CHAPEL, S. MARIA DEL CARMINE, FLORENCE

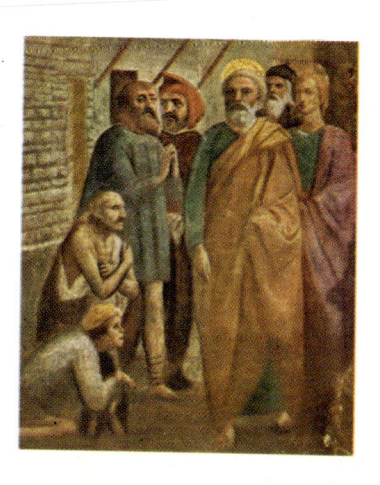

MASACCIO. ST PETER DISTRIBUTING ALMS (FRESCO DETAIL), 1426-1428. BRANCACCI CHAPEL, S. MARIA DEL CARMINE, FLORENCE

MASACCIO. PORTRAIT OF A YOUNG MAN. NATIONAL GALLERY OF ART, WASHINGTON

THE QUATTROCENTO IN FLORENCE

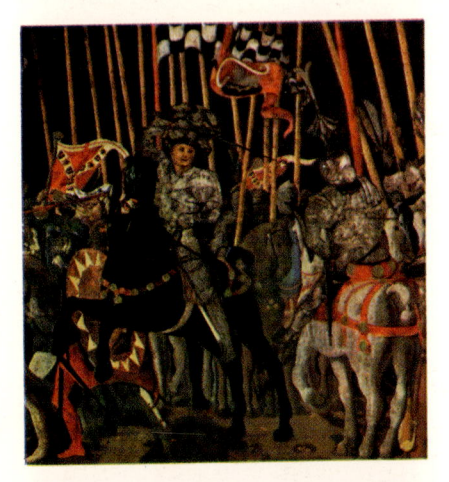

PAOLO DONI KNOWN AS UCCELLO, 1397-1475. BATTLE OF SAN ROMANO, *c.* 1456-1458. NATIONAL GALLERY, LONDON

UCCELLO. BATTLE OF SAN ROMANO (DETAIL), *c.* 1456-1458. LOUVRE, PARIS

UCCELLO. HUNT BY NIGHT (DETAIL). ASHMOLEAN MUSEUM, OXFORD

The traditional view was that Paoli Doni, known as Uccello, was a man obsessed by the problems of perspective, as much a geometrician as a painter. As a visionary he was viewed somewhat ironically by his follow-artists and given few commissions; he spent his nights studying 'that sweet thing', the art of foreshortening such subjects as a faceted rings or a *mazzochio*, later used by the ornamentalists of the Quattrocento.

This rather Balzacian character, as given in Vasari's biography, is not completely remote from the truth. It is true that his painted works are full of both virtuoso tricks with perspective and *mazzochi*, that his drawings reveal his preoccupations with this subject, that he was not very successful. Vasari said that, indifferent to everything that did not bear on perspective, he applied colour completely haphazardly, and it is true that he sometimes painted horses blue and fields red. But the anecdotes about Uccello given by his first biographer are not enough to explain him, or explain him too much.

There can be no doubt that in some ways Uccello associated himself with the movement started by Brunelleschi and Masaccio: the importance he attached to volumes and space, and his indifference towards 'beautiful' colours are anti-Gothic. But this does not mean that he was either a realist like Massaccio or a geometrician like Brunelleschi. He served his apprenticeship in the workshop of the gold- and bronze-smith Ghiberti; in 1425, when he was twenty-eight, he was summoned to Venice to make mosaics for St Mark's. Nearly twenty years later, in 1443-1445, he designed cartoons for the windows of Florence Cathedral (notably a *Resurrection*). He was, therefore, basically a practical artist, seeking to apply and extend the innovators' theories.

Uccello cannot be regarded as an out-and-out enemy of Gothic; such an attitude would be inconceivable in an artist of his lowly

48

THE QUATTROCENTO IN FLORENCE

status, almost a craftsman. His minor works unexpectedly show him as a descriptive painter, charming and romantic (*The Hunt by Night,* the two *St Georges,* etc.). Probably this vein of fantasy, inseparable at that period from the minor genres, accounts for the tricks which Vasari put down to perspective-madness.

The large-scale paintings are more in keeping with the Uccello legend. His first dated fresco, the equestrian *Portrait of Sir John Hawkwood* (1436), was, like Masaccio's *Crucifixion,* designed to be seen from close up. But the colossal monochrome figure was not attractive in this form and Uccello was ordered to repaint the work, sacrificing scientific truth to visual charm. Little of the cycles of frescoes executed in the following years still exists: some scenes from *Monastic Life* in San Miniato (1439-1440), *The Creation* and *The Flood* in the 'Green Cloisters' of Santa Maria Novella (1445-1460), *The Nativity* in San Martino alla Scala. The remains hint at strange compositions with very beautiful details and complicated networks of perspective-lines used in an experimental manner to obtain unexpected effects. Even in the *predella* of Urbino, which gives a straightforward account of *The Legend of the Jew and the Host,* one of these strange demonstrations is introduced into the second scene. The three episodes of the *Battle of San Romano* (Uffizi, Louvre and National Gallery, London), huge panels painted in about 1456-1460, reveal the hand of a highly original painter who has not completely forgotten the art of mediaeval tapestries but is aiming principally at a strange imitative magic conjured up by unreal geometrical volumes, rhythmically grouped and contrasted by dream-colours. In old age he produced little. The Florentine public would have no truck with fantastic Gothic painting which lacked elegance and charm, or with a 'modern' treatment of volumes and space without realism or *trompe-l'œil.*

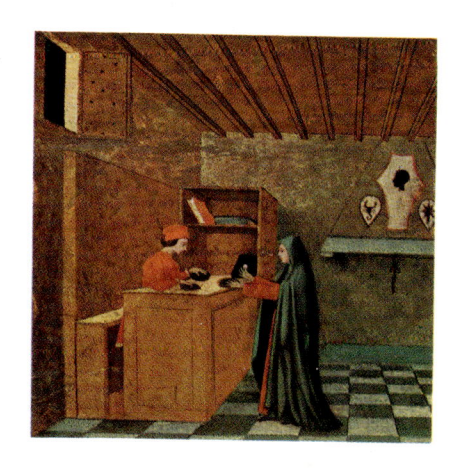

UCCELLO. LEGEND OF THE JEW AND THE HOST (PREDELLA, DETAIL OF FIRST PANEL), 1465-1468. PALAZZO DUCALE, URBINO

UCCELLO. LEGEND OF THE JEW AND THE HOST (DETAIL OF SECOND PANEL), 1465-1468. PALAZZO DUCALE, URBINO

UCCELLO. LEGEND OF THE JEW AND THE HOST (DETAIL OF SECOND PANEL), 1465-1468. PALAZZO DUCALE, URBINO

49

THE QUATTROCENTO IN FLORENCE

DOMENICO
VENEZIANO,
c. 1400-1451.
ST JOHN IN
THE WILDERNESS,
c. 1450.
NATIONAL GALLERY
OF ART,
WASHINGTON

DOMENICO
VENEZIANO.
PORTRAIT OF A
YOUNG WOMAN,
c. 1460.
STAATLICHE MUSEEN
BERLIN

FRA FILIPPO LIPPI,
1406-1469.
ANNUNCIATION.
ALTE PINAKOTHEK,
MUNICH

It was almost certainly Domenico Veneziano who prevented Florentine painting from falling wholly under the influence of Masaccio; this Venetian painter lent a new dignity to colourism by introducing the technique of oil-painting and the art of using colour to organise space. We know that he was in Florence in 1439 working in the Church of Sant' Egidio with his disciple Piero della Francesca. Unfortunately, this work has disappeared, so that we cannot tell exactly what his artistic character was at this date; nor do we know whether this was his first visit to Florence. Perhaps his *Adoration of the Magi* (Berlin) should be attributed to an earlier period (1435?). It is still Gothic in tendency but provided the starting-point for a development which would lead eventually to a broad, clear treatment of space, defined by light as much as by perspective, as in the *Madonna of Santa Lucia dei Magnoli* (Uffizi) and the frescoes of 1460 in Santa Croce, in which the Florentine influence is best assimilated.

In a letter of 1438 offering his services to the Medici family Domenico incidentally names two monks, Fra Angelico and Fra Filippo Lippi, as the best Florentine painters of the day. The second, then thirty-two, caused much scandal because of his dissolute life. In painting he was an eclectic, seeking a middle way between Masaccio and the colourists. Though he acquired the arts of modelling and perspective, he never managed to restrain his prolific imagination enough to unify space, centralize his compositions and integrate his colour. His gifts lay in the direction of vivacity and lyricism; on occasion, as in the famous *Adoration* (Uffizi), he achieved a beautiful tonal unity. At first Lippi revived the post-Sienese sweetness of his master Lorenzo Monaco; later he assimilated the technique of Masaccio without his discipline (*Coronation of the Virgin*, Uffizi). The frescoes at Prato are inventive; in those at Spoleto Lippi quests for unity.

50

THE QUATTROCENTO IN FLORENCE

Benozzo Gozzoli might well be termed a sort of Gentile da Fabriano of the second half of the fifteenth century, a painter able to juggle off-handedly with all the skills of modern art for the sole purpose of diversifying works which covered huge surfaces but were nevertheless in the spirit of the French tapestries or miniatures. As an apprentice of Ghiberti and student and collaborator of Angelico, Gozzoli grew up in a conservative atmosphere. His first large-scale work was a fresco of *The Journey of the Magi* in the chapel of the Medici-Riccardi palace (1459) a theme treated by Gentile in Florence itself and providing ample opportunities for exoticism, sartorial inventiveness and amusing narrative details. This art suited the Medici taste. Later, Gozzoli's work on various enormous cycles of frescoes (*Life of St Augustine,* 1465) kept him in San Gimignano. At Pisa he painted frescoes in the Campo Santo (1468-1484). There was no reason why he should revive an artistic formula admired throughout the provinces; his richness, honest realism, disguised portraits in historical paintings and 'inventions' were as admired as the ornamental extravagance in his small *cassoni* paintings.

Alesso Baldovinetti, the purest and most refined of the Florentine colourists has much in common with Domenico Veneziano. Like Piero della Francesca, with whom he worked on the frescoes of Sant' Egidio (1439-1445), he studied under Veneziano: he shared Piero's serenity (*Virgin and Child,* Louvre) and sometimes his breadth of manner. Like Piero, he attempted a synthesis of form and colour. His horizons were wide; he took a new interest in landscape-painting (*Nativity,* Florence, Annunziata), in decorative arrangement (Chapel of the Cardinal of Portugal) and in mosaic, an art which he attempted to revive (Baptistery). It was only his lack of power which prevented him from being of capital importance.

FRA FILIPPO LIPPI. THE MADONNA AND CHILD, WITH SCENES FROM THE LIFE OF THE VIRGIN. PALAZZO PITTI, FLORENCE

BENOZZO GOZZOLI, 1420-1497. JOURNEY OF THE MAGI (FRESCO DETAIL), 1459. PALAZZO MEDICI-RICCARDI, FLORENCE

ALESSO BALDOVINETTI, 1425-1499. ANGEL (DETAIL FROM ANNUNCIATION). NATIONAL GALLERY OF ART, WASHINGTON

THE QUATTROCENTO IN FLORENCE

ANDREA DEL CASTAGNO, 1423-1457. VIRGIN, ST JOHN (DETAILS OF THE CRUCIFIXION). REFECTORY OF S. APOLLONIA, FLORENCE

ANDREA DEL CASTAGNO. CUMAEAN SIBYL, c. 1450. VILLA LEGNAIA, FLORENCE

ANDREA DEL CASTAGNO. PETRARCH, BOCCACCIO, c. 1450. VILLA LEGNAIA, FLORENCE

The most important of the confirmed Masaccio-followers of Florence was called Andrea del Castagno. Although born only five years before Masaccio's death, he seems so intimately linked with him that he might be taken for his pupil. Like Masaccio, Castagno enjoyed only a short career in Florence (to which he came in 1440) before his early death in 1457.

His art differs from that of his great predecessor in its brutal, shattering quality. This made such a profound impression that a legend grew up towards the end of the fifteenth century that he had treacherously assassinated the man who collaborated with him in decorating the Church of Sant' Egidio, the gentle Domenico Veneziano. So wrote Vasari: it was believed for three centuries.

Castagno painted his first frescoes in Venice, in the Church of San Zaccaria (1442); after returning to Florence, he showed his full powers in the frescoes he painted for the refectory of the Monastery of Sant' Apollonia (1445-1450), possibly the most monumental and certainly the most spectacular mural decorations in Florentine art; they were also the most strictly organized. Like Masaccio's fresco in Santa Maria Novella, the perspective, designed to be seen from the actual viewpoint, produces a striking 'scenic' effect. His is a heroic and violent art, with a deliberately aggressive side to its naturalism. It is as though he purposely avoids nobility, a quality which Masaccio possesses without striving after it.

About 1450 he was commissioned to produce a series of *Famous Men and Women* for the Villa la Legnaia near Florence. It comes as a surprise to find these extremely forceful decorations in the entrance-hall of a small suburban dwelling. The theme had been popular in Italy for more than a century and had just been treated by Uccello at Padua in a (lost) cycle so impressive that it was nicknamed 'The Giants'. Castagno worked in the same spirit. Each of his

52

THE QUATTROCENTO IN FLORENCE

figures—the admirably drawn Eve, the Tuscan poets, the *condottiere* Pippo Spano—is unforgettable, its 'presence' full of power. Castagno also pitted his strength against Uccello, Masaccio's most direct descendent, apart from himself; he painted the *Equestrian Statue of Niccolo da Tolentino* opposite Uccello's *Sir John Hawkwood*. But there is no comparison between his brutal, slightly theatrical, force and Uccello's magic unreality.

Antonio Pollaiuolo, who derived much from Andrea del Castagno, survived him by some forty years and so became the leader of the generation of the 1460s. He was basically an exceptionally fine sculptor in bronze, but his painting is not particularly sculptural; in general Pollaiuolo seems to have adopted only those traits of Castagno which distinguish him from Masaccio. Pollaiuolo's passions were many and contradictory: Antiquity, which he knew well, anatomy (he seems to have been the first to carry out dissections for purely artistic purposes), Flemish-type landscape, movement and expressions which verge on frenzy and grimaces. The inspiration for his strange dancers in the Arcetri frescoes may well have come from Antique, perhaps Etruscan, vases representing bacchantes; *The Labours of Hercules* (smaller copies in the Uffizi), *The Rape of Deianira* and especially the *St Sebastian* of 1475 (London) show how much importance Pollaiuolo attached to the panoramic landscape. One of his most successful achievements is the charming panel showing *Apollo and Daphne* (London); but often his minute detail, crisp execution and naturalistic programme border perilously on aridity. Everything was conducive to a sort of harshness at that time; the growing influence in the Florence of the 1460s of a northern type of painting, the ineradicable memory of Donatello, the fashion for engravings (Pollaiuolo was a great engraver). However, eventually there was a reaction in favour of linear elegance and softer colour.

ANDREA DEL CASTAGNO. PORTRAIT OF AN UNKNOWN MAN. NATIONAL GALLERY OF ART, WASHINGTON

ANTONIO BENCI KNOWN AS POLLAIUOLO, 1429-1498. DAVID AS VICTOR. STAATLICHE MUSEEN, BERLIN

ANTONIO POLLAIUOLO. PORTRAIT OF A LADY. POLDI-PEZZOLI, MUSEUM, MILAN

53

THE QUATTROCENTO IN UMBRIA

PIERO DELLA FRANCESCA, c. 1416-1492. STORY OF THE TRUE CROSS: PROVING THE TRUE CROSS (DETAIL). 1452-1459.

PIERO DELLA FRANCESCA. FINDING OF THE TRUE CROSS (DETAIL). 1452-1459.

PIERO DELLA FRANCESCA. SOLOMON RECEIVING THE QUEEN OF SHEBA (DETAIL). 1452-1459.

FRESCOES IN S. FRANCESCO, AREZZO

The central and dominating figure in the Italian painting of 1450-1470 belonged exclusively to none of the main artistic centres although he visited most of them. As a young man Piero worked with Domenico Veneziano at Florence on the frescoes of Sant' Egidio (1438-1440). Later he was invited to the Courts of Ferrara and Urbino, towns which were 'on the way up' but which could teach him little in the way of technique or formal skill. Many of his masterpieces were produced in the small towns of his native region, Arezzo and Borgo San Sepolcro.

While in Florence he acquired an intimate knowledge of the work of Masaccio and Domenico Veneziano. In his work Masaccio's monumental dignity is reproduced in a more hieratic and mysterious form; he also adopted Veneziano's bright, transparent colour — the colour which was ready to become part of the intensity of the light and the structure of space. From the theorists Piero learned geometry and perspective, *the* problems of the moment. But the fashions and interests which developed in Florence after he had left had no effect on him; after 1460 only Flemish painting enriched his own manner. While all the rest of artistic Italy was becoming more and more fascinated with movement, expression and archaeologically accurate reconstructions of Antiquity, Piero, quite alone, was developing his very different type of art — static, impersonal, far from temporal, quite contrary to the Florentine trend. In *The Baptism of Christ* (London) and *St Jerome* (Venice) he manages to effect a harmonious blend of Veneziano's colour and a type of landscape-painting in which he incorporates a touch of Tuscan Luminism. In *The Nativity* (London) he was to define more exactly this bucolic, Virgilian element; it seems to have been inborn in Piero, since it remained a constant factor in his art. His small *Scourging of Christ* (Urbino) derives from Uccello; despite some incredible geometrical

THE QUATTROCENTO IN UMBRIA

subtleties (the design of the pavement includes a demonstration of the squaring of the circle!) all is visually clear and organized.

From the time of *The Story of the True Cross* (frescoes in the Church of St Francis of Arezzo, 1452-1459), Piero's work acquired an aristocratic, legendary flavour which blended with his Eclogue-like quality. The *Legend* may have been painted as a result of Pope Pius II's crusade project. In it the artist exploits every possibility, shows battle-scenes, a night scene, a court ceremony, landscapes, '*istorie*'; but none of these disturbs the calm grandeur of his epic style. These frescoes and other works of the same period (the *Madonna of the Cloak*, the *Resurrection* at Borgo San Sepolcro) are probably the most individual expressions of his personality. In the polyptych of *St Augustine* (now dispersed: at Lisbon, London, New York . . .) the statuesque saints, derived from Masaccio, swim in a splendid light closely linked with the colour.

The works he painted for Federigo da Montefeltro of Urbino from 1465 are nearer the main currents of contemporary Italian painting. The portraits of the Duke and Duchess with allegories of the Triumphs on the back, show that Piero had studied miniature-painting and Flemish art, although his own individual poetry is as great as ever; the same influence can be seen even more clearly in the *Madonna of Sinigallia*, who is shown bathed in the soft, filtered light of an interior. Scholars have puzzled for centuries over an iconographical detail of the *Madonna* of Brera—an ostrich egg hung in the church; the picture is very carefully and minutely worked out but preserves the grandeur and strange Mallarméan 'absence' which is one of the secrets of Piero's power. His theoretical treatises on perspective and geometrical solids were disseminated by his disciples; in them he gave various formulae for geometrical construction, derived from the Pythagorean aesthetic of numbers.

PIERO DELLA FRANCESCA. STORY OF THE TRUE CROSS: COURTIERS OF THE QUEEN'S SUITE. S. FRANCESCA, AREZZO

PIERO DELLA FRANCESCA. BATTISTA SFORZA AND FEDERIGO DA MONTEFELTRO (DIPTYCH), 1465-1466. UFFIZI, FLORENCE

PIERO DELLA FRANCESCA. NATIVITY (DETAIL). NATIONAL GALLERY, LONDON

THE QUATTROCENTO IN UMBRIA

MELOZZO DA FORLI,
1438-1494.
PORTRAIT OF
PLATINA (DETAIL
FROM THE FRESCO OF
'SIXTUS IV
APPOINTING PLATINA
VATICAN
LIBRARIAN').
1474.
VATICAN MUSEUM,
ROME

MELOZZO DA FORLI.
ANGEL OF THE
ANNUNCIATION.
UFFIZI, FLORENCE

LUCA SIGNORELLI,
1441/50-1523.
SELF PORTRAIT
(DETAIL FROM
FRESCO OF THE
'STORY OF THE
ANTICHRIST'),
c. 1500.
ORVIETO CATHEDRAL

Piero della Francesca's work did not give rise to a new school of painting, but under his influence Umbrian art became more aware of the contemporary interest in problems of form and space. Melozzo da Forli, who specialized in the illusionist foreshortening of arches and ceilings, was Francesca's closest disciple, if not in spirit at least as regards technique. His fresco of *Sixtus IV Appointing Platina Vatican Librarian* (1474), with its severe figures shown in profile and the noble rhythm of the painted architecture, seems to stand halfway between Piero and Mantegna. Two years later we find Melozzo at Urbino, working in Federigo da Montefeltro's studio. He gave free reign to his talent for virtuoso perspective-work in the Chapel of the Casa Santa (Loreto, after 1477), the Church of San Biagio at Forli, where he took the young Palmezzano as collaborator, and above all in *The Ascension* in the apse of the Church of the SS. Apostoli in Rome (1480). The angels making music in *The Ascension* became enormously popular, partly owing to the Umbrian charm which was beginning to dominate Melozzo's work. But the chief merit of this slightly eclectic painter was his ability to organize space, in such a way that his figures move freely in every direction. This gift and his feeling for grandeur later enraptured Bramante whose earliest paintings show his influence.

Luca Signorelli, a pupil of Piero, threw off his influence to take up the 'modern' trends of Pollaiuolo: dramatism and the nude. In his *Scourging of Christ* (Milan, Brera), painted when he was less than twenty-five, he gave the first proof of his great originality; it led to violent gestures and effects. This style is more marked in the Sacristy of Loreto (c. 1480) and his inspiration becomes more clearly defined. At that time Signorelli was fascinated by symmetrical groupings, colour contrasts and fixed 'expressions' (*Madonna with Saints*, Perugia, 1484) but his work never lacked poetry. The splendid

THE QUATTROCENTO IN UMBRIA

School of Pan painted for Lorenzo de' Medici in about 1490 (destroyed in 1945) illustrates the relationship between rustic life and a life of study, the 'melancholy' of the philosopher and the pleasure of the sage, with a gravity and vigour that epitomize Humanist bucolicism. But Signorelli was above all a fresco painter. In 1481 he had worked side by side with the best Florentine artists on the decorations for the Sistine Chapel, and, in the years following 1497 he produced a cycle of *The Life of St Benedict* at Monteoliveto. But his main work was the decoration of the Chapel of San Brizio in Orvieto Cathedral (1499-1504) where he depicted the Last Judgment and its consequences in a tragic, noble style which inspired Michelangelo. The dramatic events connected with Savonarola had just taken place; Signorelli's work is a striking embodiment of the prophetic, apocalyptic spirit then haunting Italy. He himself was resolutely hostile to Savonarola and his fresco of Antichrist might well be an indictment of him, full of direct allusions to his career. The whole work is deeply impressive, with its violently agitated waves of powerfully modelled nude bodies; it is the first pictorial work which can bear comparison with Dante, and indeed seems to pay homage to Dante in the spirit of the Humanist commentators. This is quite clearly his intention in the painted dado, in which strange 'grotesques' surround small scenes from the *Purgatorio,* and in the portraits of visionary poets who have described the beyond. But Signorelli was born too late: his attachment to Florentine Humanism was already out of date, as was his hard, violent style. He ended his days, almost forgotten, as the head of a workshop in Cortona.

The University of Padua was famous for its legal and medical schools: for a long period the city remained one of the centres of astrology (a major preoccupation with Renaissance thinkers), but its art-lovers soon developed a taste for Antiquity which had a marked

SIGNORELLI. SCOURGING OF CHRIST (DETAIL), *c.* 1475. BRERA, MILAN

SIGNORELLI. END OF THE WORLD (FRESCO DETAIL), *c.* 1500. ORVIETO CATHEDRAL

SIGNORELLI. LIFE OF ST BENEDICT (DETAIL OF FRESCO OF 'TWO BENEDICTINES BREAKING THE FAST'). GREAT CLOISTER OF MONTE OLIVETO

57

THE QUATTROCENTO IN PADUA

ANDREA MANTEGNA, 1431-1506.
JUDITH.
NATIONAL GALLERY OF ART, WASHINGTON

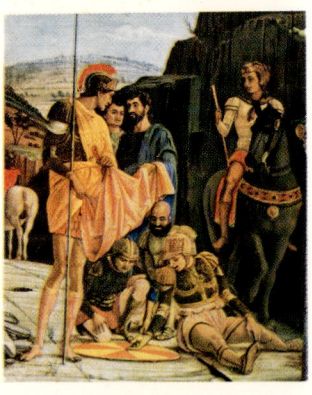

MANTEGNA.
CALVARY (DETAIL).
LOUVRE, PARIS

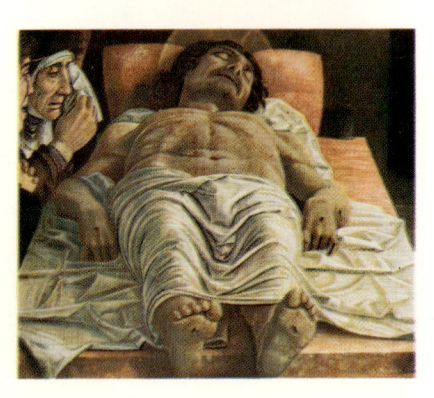

MANTEGNA.
THE DEAD CHRIST.
BRERA, MILAN

influence on local painting. Round about the 1450s the 'hard' style and 'scholarly' art were given an additional impetus by the visit to Padua of Donatello (1443-1452) and Uccello's fresco (now lost) of 'The Giants'. Squarcione, a passionate, capricious collector but a mediocre painter, organized a school where he seems to have instilled in his young, archaeology-stuffed disciples a romantic feeling for Roman grandeur.

Two of his disciples were outstanding: Niccolo Pizzolo (1421-1453) who died young, and Andrea Mantegna. From 1449 they worked together on the Eremitani Church in Padua; after Pizzolo's death Mantegna continued on the cycle of *The Life of St James* alone. The sculptural, impressively strong figures are carefully arranged against a background of restored Antique architecture on a sort of terrace corresponding with a horizon which is ingeniously lowered to facilitate the design: a cast of severe, strictly organized characters plays out the drama against a backcloth of rocks and ancient towns. In 1457 Mantegna executed a superb altarpiece for San Zeno, Verona—a manifesto of the new art in the stronghold of international Gothic. Instead of being composed of delicate open frameworks, the altarpiece takes the form of an aedicule with four columns, extended by means of perspective; it recalls Donatello's altar of the Santo in Padua. The three-panelled *predella* (the *Crucifixion* is in the Louvre) shows how the precision of the style eventually drove Mantegna into a sort of dryness, cold colour and purity of form which can resemble Uccello.

The Gonzaga family of Mantua gave Mantegna the opportunity to show his true mettle. In 1474 he decorated the Camera degli Sposi for the ducal pair. Considerable admiration was aroused by the *trompe-l'œil* dome enlivened by sportive mythological figures, and the mural frescoes showing scenes from Court life. These were set against a background of simulated architecture which made skilful use of the existing features of the real room. The perspective and architecture provided a basis for many imitations. Mantegna was invited to paint some allegorical panels, to a prohibitively complicated 'programme', for Isabella d'Este's cabinet; he managed to acquit himself creditably.

In general he was quite ready to sacrifice colour to monochrome, but the large *Madonna of Victory* (Louvre, 1496) is harmonious and fresh; in it he shows a stronger interest in the actual look and texture of objects. His style has become suppler but he is still fond of difficult foreshortenings (*The Dead Christ,* Milan), archaeological reconstructions (cartoons for *The Triumph of Caesar,* Hampton Court, 1482-1492), and fashionable 'Classicising' props, as in the splendid *St Sebastian* in the Louvre (1485). His forms remain clear, polished, often heavily scored with folds; they always appear to be cast in metal, or carved out of stone or crystal. In addition, they swim in a strange greyish-blue light, sometimes as though they were under water. One can sense the growing importance of engraving with its precise requirements.

Mantegna's influence had a decisive effect on all art in north-eastern Italy. Venice had its Mantegnesque period when Bartolommeo Vivarini and the Bellinis were working; the renaissance of the art of Ferrara owed almost everything to him, as did the art of Crivelli in the Marches. His engravings (*Battle of the Sea-Gods, Triumph of Caesar,* etc.) introduced a new world to the public and blazed the trail for the young Dürer. In time people grew tired of his broken forms, fluted drapes and ostentatious foreshortening; but his repertoire of medals, inscriptions, garlands and Antique arms found a lasting place in Renaissance art. And the man himself, the ardent collector who created a Classical frame for his life, the learned theorist, helped to create the new type of artist.

MANTEGNA.
VIRGIN AND CHILD
WITH ST JOHN
THE BAPTIST AND
THE MAGDALENE.
NATIONAL GALLERY,
LONDON

MANTEGNA.
PORTRAIT OF
A MAN.
NATIONAL GALLERY
OF ART,
WASHINGTON

MANTEGNA.
PRESENTATION
AT THE TEMPLE.
STAATLICHE MUSEEN,
BERLIN

THE QUATTROCENTO IN FERRARA

COSIMO TURA,
c. 1430-1495.
PORTRAIT OF A
MEMBER OF
THE ESTE FAMILY.
METROPOLITAN
MUSEUM,
NEW YORK

COSIMO TURA.
VIRGIN AND CHILD.
ACCADEMIA, VENICE

ERCOLE DE' ROBERTI,
c. 1456-1496.
POTRAIT OF
GINEVRA
BENTIVOGLIO,
c. 1480.
NATIONAL GALLERY
OF ART,
WASHINGTON

It was not until the middle of the century that Ferrara, the great and wealthy capital of the Este dynasty, developed a taste for art and luxury. But then palaces were built with great speed, castles provided ever-increasing opportunities for decorations, painters such as Pisanello, Piero della Francesca and Mantegna were invited, Flemish work became known in the town. Ferrara became a meeting-point for different styles, and developed a taste for brilliance and originality which made it an outstandingly important centre from 1460 to 1490. Cosimo Tura, the founder of the school, studied at Padua; he saw Donatello's works and probably knew Squarcione. Borso d'Este later gave him numerous commissions for decorations, which led him to concentrate on ornamental inventions. But in certain large works—*The Annunciation* and *St George,* 1496, the *Roverella Altarpiece,* 1474—the strange, whimsical forms and fairy-like colours must surely be put down to his personal taste. In them dream-landscapes, stiff draperies, improbable aedicules and symbols jostle each other; the treatment is glossy, the colours unreal. But in his portraits Tura could be as severe as a Pisanello and his small works are surprisingly delicate.

Together Tura and a team dominated by Francesco del Cossa (? 1436-? 1478) and Ercole de Roberti worked from 1469 on decorations for the Palazzo Schifanoia, including astrological frescoes and scenes of Court life. Although many parts are terrifying and even savage, there are also panels of a charming freshness. It is not always easy to distinguish one artist's work from another's. Compared with Cossa's energetic and almost monumental art, that of Roberti (the younger man) stands out for its brilliance and unbridled imagination: the *Griffoni Triptych,* Bologna (with Cossa), the *Lazarus Altarpiece,* Berlin, destroyed in 1945. His very original *Madonna* (Milan, c. 1480) is not unlike Venetian art.

THE QUATTROCENTO IN VENICE

Many art trends met in southern Italy. In the mid-fifteenth century, the kingdom of Naples had been more profoundly affected by Flemish painting than any other part of Italy. Antonello da Messina, a Sicilian, was undoubtedly acquainted with this art, well represented at Naples by works by Jan van Eyck and Rogier van der Weyden. He may have seen other Provençal and Spanish masters who used oils and were acquainted with the rich, costly manner of Bruges and Ghent. In the middle of the century an unknown Catalan or native of Ferrara painted the unforgettable *Triumph of Death* in the Palazzo Sclafani (Palermo), the last great masterpiece of International Gothic before it gave way to a stronger, broader art.

Messina studied under Colantonio in Naples; at first he was attracted by Van Eyck (*Crucifixion*, Sibiu, Rumania; *St Jerome*, Reggio di Calabria)—as can be seen from his oil technique, scrupulous detail, attention to outward appearance and composition. But owing to the linear perspective, the disposition and grouping of *St Jerome in his Study* (London) are more strict. The clarity of the spatial organization and the rigorous disposition of the figures are reminiscent of Laurana's sculpture (*Christ Blessing*, London, 1465) which shares the same spirit. Without abandoning his 'Flemish' qualities (the richness of the surface texture, the deep colour), Antonello worked towards large, simple and noble forms, becoming eventually a sort of southern Piero della Francesca (the *Annunciations* in Munich and Palermo). The authority of his famous portraits could not have been equalled by any Flemish painter. In particular two of his polyptychs (the altarpiece of *St Gregory*, Messina, 1473 and, especially, the altarpiece of *San Cassiano*, painted in Venice in 1476, now dismembered (a fragment is in Vienna) exerted a decisive influence on later Italian art and turned Bellini towards the future Venetian style.

ANTONELLO DA MESSINA, c. 1430-1479. PORTRAIT OF A MAN. NATIONAL GALLERY, LONDON

ANTONELLO DA MESSINA. VIRGIN ANNUNCIATE. ALTE PINAKOTHEK, MUNICH

ANTONELLO DA MESSINA. PORTRAIT OF A MAN. METROPOLITAN MUSEUM, NEW YORK

THE QUATTROCENTO IN VENICE

GENTILE BELLINI,
1429-1507.
PORTRAIT OF
A BISHOP.
MUSEO CIVICO,
FELTRE

GENTILE AND
GIOVANNI BELLINI.
ST MARK
PREACHING AT
CONSTANTINOPLE
(DETAIL).
BRERA, MILAN

GIOVANNI BELLINI,
1430 ?-1516
VIRGIN AND CHILD.
BRERA, MILAN

The Bellini workshop played a leading role in the transformation of Venetian painting during the crucial years. Its founder, Jacopo (1400-1470), still worked in a style similar to Gentile da Fabriano's Gothic; he was interested in Paduan art and in his large-scale designs, filled with architectural fantasies, he manipulated the new science of perspective so as to obtain some amazing effects. Jacopo was Mantegna's father-in-law and the artists who carried on the workshop, his sons Gentile and Giovanni, were inspired by Mantegna.

Gentile's temperament fitted him to paint agreeably picturesque narrative works. He was a good portraitist, skilful even in the pure profile (*Lorenzo Giustiniani*, 1465). In 1480 the Venetian Republic sent him to paint Sultan Mohammed II and after the journey he became an 'orientalist', content to amaze his compatriots with simple depictions of the wonders of 'abroad' (*St Mark preaching at Constantinople*). For the huge collective cycle of the Scuola di San Giovanni Evangelista he painted the immense *Procession of the Relic of the True Cross*; in it he shows complete mastery of the subject and achieves a perfect balance between the solemn tone and decorative character. Venice acquired a taste for these enormous official paintings; it lasted for three centuries.

Giovanni Bellini (Giambellino), Gentile's younger brother, dominated Venetian painting throughout his long and successful career. He was very receptive towards new ideas but could always assimilate them. A whole era of Venetian art bears the stamp of his personality.

In 1557 a fire broke out in the Palazzo Ducale and his history pictures, which had decorated the Sala del Maggior Consiglio (1480) were destroyed. Bellini is now known almost exclusively from his religious paintings, but even in this sphere alone it is easy to follow his unified development from his Mantegna-inspired beginnings to the point where he discovered Antonello da Messina

THE QUATTROCENTO IN VENICE

(1475-1476) and succeeded in creating a 'tonal atmosphere' which paved the way quite naturally for Giorgione and Titian.

His altarpieces illustrate this evolution. The four triptychs painted in about 1464 for the Church of the Carità are influenced by Mantegna, though they are less hard and less preoccupied with perspective than his work. The slightly later altarpiece of *St Vincent Ferrer* (Church of SS. Giovanni and Paolo) is already conceived in terms of light-effects; the Pesaro altarpiece (*c.* 1475) shows the preoccupation with space and Classical spirit of a Piero della Francesca; in the last and most mature altarpieces (*St Job*, 1486-1487, the *Frari Triptych*, 1488 and *Saint Zachariah*, 1505) the harmonious effect of the diffused light which modifies the colours is deepened. The same may be said of the half-length *Madonnas*—subjects which Bellini popularized and which were later repeated *ad nauseam* by his imitators. They too show Bellini's development—his growing Luminism, the way he falls under the (very considerable) influence of Antonello, and, above all, his landscapes. His skill in portraying the sympathy between nature and humanity was unrivalled. It was a matter of 'atmosphere' in both the literal and figurative senses. The sky in the Milan *Pietà* (*c.* 1470), the golden landscape cut off by the marble square in the Uffizi *Christian Allegory,* and the scene of plenty in the *St Francis* (Frick Collection, New York)—these are some of the finest examples of his unique feeling for the intimate harmony of the world, a universal 'grace' which reaches its apotheosis in the *St John Chrysostom* of 1513. It is no accident that religious themes are so frequent in Bellini's work; nevertheless he was a lively and sometimes inspired portraitist *(The Doge Leonardo Loredan)*. Moreover his *Feast of the Gods,* a witty and scholarly mythological picture—Titian completed the foliage—is a masterly rendering of a pagan view of nature.

GIOVANNI BELLINI. PORTRAIT OF THE DOGE LEONARDO LOREDAN (DETAIL). NATIONAL GALLERY, LONDON

GIOVANNI BELLINI. FEAST OF THE GODS (DETAIL), *c.* 1510. NATIONAL GALLERY OF ART, WASHINGTON

GIOVANNI BELLINI. PORTRAIT OF BARTOLOMEO COLLEONI. NATIONAL GALLERY OF ART, WASHINGTON

THE QUATTROCENTO IN VENICE

VITTORE CARPACCIO,
c. 1455-1526.
LIFE OF ST URSULA:
ARRIVAL OF
THE ENGLISH
AMBASSADORS
(DETAIL),
c. 1495.
ACCADEMIA, VENICE

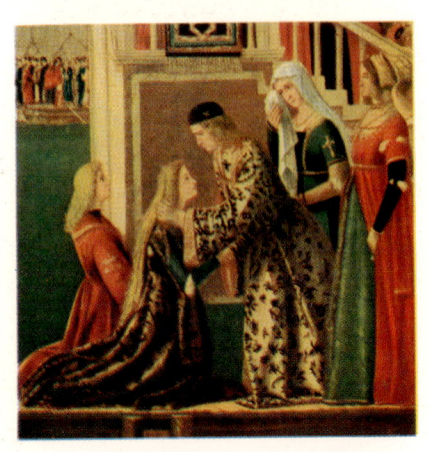

CARPACCIO.
LIFE OF ST URSULA:
FAREWELL OF
ST URSULA
(DETAIL),
c. 1495.
ACCADEMIA, VENICE

CARPACCIO.
LIFE OF ST URSULA:
ARRIVAL OF
THE ENGLISH
AMBASSADORS
(DETAIL),
c. 1495.
ACCADEMIA, VENICE

Vittore Carpaccio's art belongs to the trend determined by Gentile Bellini; from his teacher, Lazzaro Bastiani, a pleasant but somewhat shallow narrative artist, he took over only a few stylistic traits; he soon abandoned even these. The charming mixture of romantic, intimate and decorative elements that Memlinc was creating in Flanders at this period found in Carpaccio its best Italian exponent.

From panel to panel of his first great work, the *Life of St Ursula* (1490-before 1498), one can trace the stages of his development. The first of the series reveal the beginner trying to say too much and lacking the ability to coordinate the details, but later descriptive painting gains the upper hand and it is then that Carpaccio, the colourist and landscape-painter *par excellence,* shows the extent of his powers. The interior in *The Dream of St Ursula,* with its simple but splendidly proportioned cubes and dovetailed rectangles, is one of his most charming works. His treatment became more and more unfettered, his urban views more and more airy. He seems to communicate his delight in inventing landscapes, buildings, costumes and figures. In addition, Carpaccio produced one of the most lively and brilliant evocations of Venice in the background to the *Miracle* in his cycle of *The Legend of the Cross.*

Carpaccio's methods of composition were rather individual; particularly in his youth, he managed to give details and isolated portions all the independence of perfectly balanced pictures. He avoids diagonals in depth; each person or object is shown full-face or in profile so that its outline defines it and shows it in its entirety: nothing could be more suitable for narrative painting. The narrative style remains a constant in his work: on it he works a series of variations, from intimate poetry to exoticism, from a Mantegna-like, metallic hardness to the luminosity of a Bellini.

The strange *Dead Christ in a Landscape* (Berlin) is the first

64

THE QUATTROCENTO IN VENICE

example of an unusual macabre quality which recurs in the two pictures of *St George Killing the Dragon* and, in a more poetic, pensive and mysterious form, in *The Lamenting of Christ* (New York). All the elements of his art are brought into play in the *Legends of St George, St Jerome* and *St Triphon* painted for the Scuola di San Giorgio dei Schiavoni where it still remains. In it landscape and figures are intimately bound together, the whole is bathed in a warm, amber light and various oriental details create a fairytale atmosphere very unlike the documentary tone of Gentile Bellini's work. The setting of the famous *St Jerome in his Study* (in reality St Augustine bathed in the light emanating from St Jerome) is the most beautiful Italian recreation of a scholar's study. The room looks exactly as one would imagine a Humanist's study to have looked, with its manuscripts, its statuettes and instruments.

Carpaccio had a vast reputation as a painter of narrative cycles; and was constantly besieged with commissions for them. The members of his workshop helped in the painting of a *Life of the Virgin* for the Scuola degli Albanesi in about 1504. The *Life of St Stephen* (1511-1520), now dispersed, is more mature: each scene is better arranged in space, the landscape more immediate in effect. Obviously in the intervening years Carpaccio had learned much from Giovanni Bellini, with whom he had decorated the Sala del Maggior Consiglio. His altarpieces in particular show the influence of Bellini (altarpiece of *San Vitale*, 1514).

The undated—and now incomplete—picture which is wrongly called *Two Courtesans* (c. 1510?) is probably one of the first examples of what has come to be known as 'genre painting'. It is easy to read a 'genre' meaning into much of Carpaccio's work—a fact which has contributed not a little to his popularity—but to do so is to ignore and distort some of the finest qualities of his painting.

CARPACCIO.
TWO COURTESANS,
c. 1510?
CORRER MUSEUM,
VENICE

CARPACCIO.
MIRACLE OF THE
RELICS OF
THE TRUE
CROSS (DETAIL).
ACCADEMIA, VENICE

CARPACCIO.
PRESENTATION
OF CHRIST
AT THE TEMPLE
(DETAIL).
ACCADEMIA, VENICE

65

THE QUATTROCENTO IN FLORENCE

ANDREA DI CIONE KNOWN AS VERROCCHIO, 1435-1488.
VIRGIN AND CHILD.
METROPOLITAN MUSEUM, NEW YORK

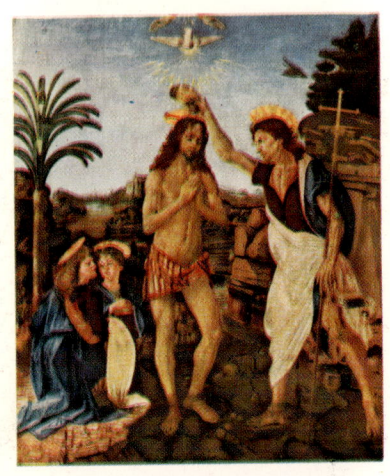

VERROCCHIO AND LEONARDO DA VINCI.
BAPTISM OF CHRIST.
UFFIZI, FLORENCE

VERROCHIO SCHOOL.
TOBIAS AND THE ANGEL.
NATIONAL GALLERY, LONDON

The generation of painters that lived under the rule of Lorenzo il Magnifico steered Florentine art into new channels. It was an age, if not of aesthetes, at least of 'artists'—an entirely new concept. No longer a mere practitioner, the painter was beginning to be a 'man of culture' coping with problems not apparently connected with his art.

The two main Florentine workshops centred round Pollaiuolo and another painter and bronzesmith, Verrocchio. The latter was, both as a man and as an artist, the leader of the new class of painters. Leonardo da Vinci, Lorenzo di Credi and Perugino frequented Verrocchio's workshop; it produced not only paintings, but sculptures in bronze, marble and terra cotta, decorative work and armour. Music was played and composed, all kinds of scientific, technical and aesthetic problems were discussed; in short it provided an all-round education, as well as teaching its apprentices the finer points of painting as a craft and imbuing them with certain stylistic habits. In general they worked as a team—the best-known illustration of this is Verrocchio's *Baptism of Christ* in which Leonardo painted the angel—which explains why it will never be possible to make an accurate inventory of Leonardo's earliest works or to decide how much the teacher and pupil influenced each other.

Verrocchio was not among the greatest painters. He favoured a polished style of execution, clearly defined forms (a sculptor's taste inherited by Lorenzo di Credi and given a personal interpretation by Leonardo); he was interested in Flemish naturalism but his composition displays an almost Classical spirit. The hard reflections on his delicate modelling make chiaroscuro impossible. It is his sculptures, in particular, with their grace, tendency towards caricature, and famous Verrocchian smile, which recall Leonardo's art. One can see the limits of his manner in the altarpiece of Pistoia

THE QUATTROCENTO IN FLORENCE

Cathedral, in which the figures stand out like painted statues.

Compared with Verrocchio, Domenico Ghirlandaio may be called a 'conscientious craftsman'. His love of work was a legend; it was said that he would have been happy to cover all the fortifications in Florence with frescoes. Eclectic by temperament, he supplemented Baldovinetti's teachings with gleanings from Verrocchio and Rome (he worked on the Sistine in 1481) and Flanders (Hugo's *Portinari Altarpiece,* which had arrived in Florence, made a profound impression on him). These contacts lent maturity to his art and determined the character of the series of great works that he painted after returning home from Rome: the decorations for the Sassetti Chapel in the Santa Trinità in Florence (1483-1486), the fresco of *The Story of St John the Baptist* in Santa Maria Novella (1485-1490), *The Adoration of the Magi* in the Spedale degli Innocenti (1488). In the Sassetti Chapel frescoes the miracles of St Francis are less important than the anecdotal tone and reminiscences of Rome, but at bottom he was indifferent to Antiquity and happier as a chronicler, as in the *Story of John the Baptist* which is enlivened by many portraits of people of the day. His calm, unstressed manner, precise draughtsmanship and clear composition were particularly suited to this kind of descriptive painting. For him the theme of the Adoration of the Magi, whose Humanist undertones he stressed, was chiefly a pretext for a broad landscape and a variety of human types.

Ghirlandaio's workshop, carried on by his brother David, who attempted to revive the art of mosaic in Florence, is of extreme historical interest. It marks the beginning in Florence of the decorative and commemorative painting which was to be exploited later in so many different ways; it shows the high level of literary and artistic culture demanded of even this minor genre; it was there that Michelangelo first studied.

DOMENICO GHIRLANDAIO, 1449-1494. PORTRAIT OF GIOVANNA TORNABUONI. THYSSEN COLLECTION, LUGANO

GHIRLANDAIO. ADORATION OF THE SHEPHERDS, 1485. ACCADEMIA, FLORENCE

GHIRLANDAIO. OLD MAN AND HIS GRANDSON. LOUVRE, PARIS

THE QUATTROCENTO IN FLORENCE

SANDRO BOTTICELLI,
1444/45-1510.
JUDITH AND
HOLOFERNES,
1470-1472.
UFFIZI, FLORENCE

BOTTICELLI.
ANNUNCIATION,
1489.
UFFIZI, FLORENCE

BOTTICELLI.
PORTRAIT OF A
MAN WITH A
MEDAL,
c. 1475.
UFFIZI, FLORENCE

Nowadays Sandro di Mariano Filipepi, called Botticelli after the goldsmith with whom he first studied, is usually considered to be the representative artist of the age of Lorenzo il Magnifico. But to his contemporaries he was a somewhat isolated genius. Though protected by the younger branch of the Medici family, he had little of Pollaiuolo's or Verrocchio's intellectual curiosity, exerted no influence outside Florence and ended his life in almost complete solitude; his individuality then became even more marked.

Some elements of this style were obviously due to his training as a goldsmith and his lasting taste for the minor arts (marquetry, embroidery, narrative panels on *cassoni*): the free play of lines which became more and more of an end in itself and the tense, nervous dramatic quality of the 'stories'. At the beginning of his career Botticelli had more in common with Filippo Lippi and Verrocchio; in his *Fortitude* (Uffizi, 1476) and *Judith and Holofernes* the treatment of the volumes and the richness of the colour are in the manner of those artists. But he lost interest in the irregularities of forms and landscape, pushing to the point of Mannerism a poetry based on graceful contours and sober modelling—the antithesis of Pollaiuolo's art. Early in his career he was given official commissions; he was, for instance, asked to paint the hanged anti-Medici conspirators in 1478. But the true extent of his powers did not emerge until the following years when he painted the series of mythological allegories which includes the famous *Primavera, Mars and Venus* and *Birth of Venus*. The Antique world of the Humanists is given an intense dream-like quality: the 'sacred' character of the subjects is never belittled, the decorative curves and dance-poses never lessen the mysterious, suggestive power. It has been proved that they convey allusions to the Platonic concepts of Love and Beauty.

By 1480 Sandro Botticelli had

68

THE QUATTROCENTO IN FLORENCE

produced the magnificent *St Augustine* in perspective in the Church of the Ognissanti. In 1481 he adopted a 'modern' style (luxuriant and stuffed with archaeological details) in *Scenes from the Life of Moses* on the walls of the Sistine Chapel in Rome. But on his return to Florence his art became more exquisite, less interested in spatial depth and scenic effects (frescoes of the Villa Lemmi, 1485-1486). In his *Madonnas* painted on circular panels *(tondi)* we can trace his evolution towards a style based on taut lines, enriched by deep colours, glossing over the problems of perspective (*Madonna of the Magnificat*, 1485, *Madonna with the Pomegranate*, 1487). The altarpiece of *St. Barnabas* (Uffizi, 1485-1486) and the *Coronation of the Virgin* (Uffizi, 1488) are further steps towards his later archaizing mannerism, with its strange, almost Byzantine effect.

In the following years, even before the advent of Savonarola, the painter's calm melancholy gradually gave place to an exasperated and often dramatic anxiety (*The Annunciation*, 1489); even in a non-religious work such as *Calumny*, after a description by Lucian of a work by Apelles, the feverish movement rises to a great crescendo, without disturbing the admirable clarity of the design (Uffizi, 1495). Some works, such as the *Pietà* in Munich and Milan, the *Crucifixion* in Cambridge, Massachusetts, and the *Nativity* in London, are deliberately visionary and discordant; their tragic feeling is closely linked with the Savonarola crisis which cast a doubt on all the ideas the artist had cherished. In a man of his extreme sensitivity this was bound to cause a profound inner reaction. But the taut, almost contorted, form and nervous style of this period not only owe something to the wave of neo-Gothic expressionism then sweeping over Ferrara and Venice. At the end of his life Botticelli spent many years illustrating Dante's *Divine Comedy* with designs of a strange, mystical, pared-down beauty.

BOTTICELLI.
BIRTH OF
VENUS (DETAIL),
c. 1486.
UFFIZI, FLORENCE

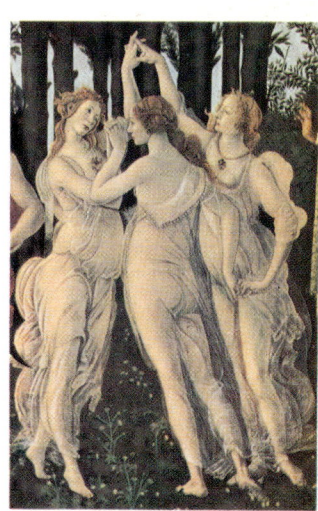

BOTTICELLI.
PRIMAVERA
(DETAIL),
c. 1478.
UFFIZI, FLORENCE

BOTTICELLI.
MARS AND VENUS,
c. 1485.
NATIONAL GALLERY,
LONDON

69

THE QUATTROCENTO IN FLORENCE

FILIPPINO LIPPI,
c. 1457-1504.
SELF-PORTRAIT
(PAINT ON
TERRACOTTA).
UFFIZI, FLORENCE

FILIPPINO LIPPI.
AN ANGEL ADORING
(FRAGMENT).
NATIONAL GALLERY,
LONDON

FILIPPINO LIPPI.
PORTRAIT OF
A YOUNG MAN.
NATIONAL GALLERY
OF ART,
WASHINGTON

Fra Filippo Lippi's son was the only Florentine painter to be profoundly influenced by Botticelli. He went so far in imitating the master that for a very long time several paintings of doubtful authorship (now known to be his) were assigned to an 'Amico di Sandro'. Filippino received his artistic training in Botticelli's workshop; it is by no means surprising that the young, highly receptive artist should have begun by attempting to improve on his master's manner. But one of his first important works, *The Virgin appearing to St Bernard* (Florence, Badia) already explores a field which was foreign to Botticelli: landscape. While he was still a young man Lorenzo de' Medici commissioned him to decorate his villas with paintings. A little later he was given the dangerous honour of being asked to continue Masaccio's frescoes in the Brancacci Chapel; he managed to leave the unity of Masaccio's work intact (perhaps because he worked from his original cartoons), although one can sense his feeling of constraint. In 1488 Lorenzo sent him to Rome with a highly adulatory testimonial; there he acquired a knowledge of archaeology which he was later able to put to good use.

His versatility was outstanding: when he was asked to finish an *Adoration of the Magi* sketched by Leonardo da Vinci, he produced work of a Leonardesque flavour; in the same year he was commissioned by one of Savonarola's supporters to paint a *Crucifixion* and this time he used an archaizing gold background. Temperamentally he inclined towards strange, bizarre invention best deployed in allegory (*Music*, Berlin, frescoes in the Caraffa Chapel in Santa Maria sopra Minerva, Rome). The Strozzi Chapel in Santa Maria Novella is his masterpiece; it embodies an extraordinary mixture of fantastic ornaments and buildings, complex symbols and picturesque details. This exhibition of scholarship and romanticism provided full scope for his boundless eclecticism.

THE QUATTROCENTO IN FLORENCE

Both Lorenzo di Credi and Piero di Cosimo have much in common with Verrocchio. Lorenzo was one of his disciples—a disciple more faithful than original; like Leonardo, he collaborated in the Madonnas of the workshop. His meticulousness was almost a neurosis; he favoured polish and in his drawings on coloured paper stressed delicacy of modelling. Verrocchio and Leonardo once gone, he was not great enough to be able to carry on their traditions. He became one of Savonarola's first supporters. There was no need for him to make any changes in his sound, conventional manner, beyond abandoning such pagan subjects as Venus.

Piero di Cosimo had not profited directly from Verrocchio's teaching, but derived more benefit from it. He became very eccentric, living alone and working frenziedly amid hideous squalor. It was said that he had a religious respect for nature and a neurotic fear of bells, fire and all non-vegetarian food. The Vespucci and Pugliese families employed him to decorate their villas; for them he produced *Bacchanales* in cold colours and strange re-creations of the life of primitive man (*Hunting, Prometheus* and *Vulcan* cycles) and the fables of Greece and Rome (*Perseus and Andromeda*). Like Leonardo, from whom he learned a great deal, he was one of the first to succeed in integrating figures and extremely varied landscapes. His strange, clear, cold art gives a foretaste of Mannerism.

LORENZO DI CREDI, 1458/59-1537.
VENUS.
UFFIZI, FLORENCE

PIERO DI COSIMO, 1462-1521.
PORTRAIT OF SIMONETTA VESPUCCI.
MUSÉE CONDÉ, CHANTILLY

PIERO DI COSIMO.
A MYTHOLOGICAL SUBJECT.
NATIONAL GALLERY, LONDON

FIFTEENTH-CENTURY FRANCE

ATTRIBUTED TO
JEAN MALOUEL (?),
ACTIVE 1396-1419.
THE 'GRANDE
PIETÀ RONDE',
c. 1400.
LOUVRE, PARIS

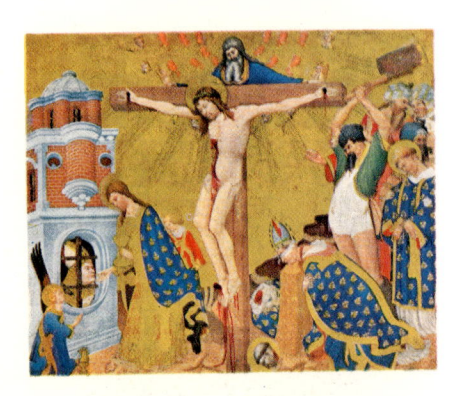

HENRI BELLECHOSE,
ACTIVE
c. 1415-c. 1444.
LAST COMMUNION
AND MARTYRDOM
OF ST DENIS,
1416.
LOUVRE, PARIS

ANONYMOUS
(FORMERLY
ATTRIBUTED
TO PISANELLO).
PORTRAIT OF A LADY,
1410-1415.
NATIONAL GALLERY
OF ART,
WASHINGTON

The cabinet picture (or—more comprehensively—the easel picture) first appeared in France in the mid-fourteenth century. Previously artists had responded in other ways to man's need to adorn the setting of his life. The decorators of Merovingian buildings imitated Byzantine mosaics, which in Romanesque art were replaced by a less troublesome substitute: fresco painting. When the supporting walls of Gothic cathedrals were whittled away, fresco fields became windows, and frescoes stained glass. Detaching themselves from the walls of private rooms, frescoes also became tapestries—paintings in wool, which were warmer and more mobile than their predecessors. The last stage in this evolution, the easel picture, does not actually derive from wall painting but from a movable element, the altarpiece-wing, secularized when the portrait of the donor, who would have himself depicted looking on at some holy scene, grew to fill the entire panel—which then became independent. This is how the earliest surviving picture of the French school, the portrait of King John the Good, came into being (see page 39).

The birth of the easel painting in the middle of the Hundred Years' War was made possible by the long line of artists who had brought fame to the Paris school of illumination. It was facilitated by the accession to the throne of the Valois dynasty. Starting with Charles V and his brothers—Philip the Bold, Duke of Burgundy, Louis of Anjou, and, above all, John, Duke of Berry—they were all passionate lovers of art. The artists who worked for them were still artisans in the sense that they illuminated books as well as providing decorations for festivities or painting altarpieces. However, through being attached to a particular family or Court, they also became courtiers, and moved from castle to castle and from country to country, as all the nobility of Europe was linked together by blood. The mobile and cosmo-

FIFTEENTH-CENTURY FRANCE

politan character of this art does not make it any easier to trace the genealogy of works, especially as one can only reckon on examples that have survived by chance.

The part played by Flemish artists seems overwhelming to begin with. Jean de Bandol of Bruges and André Beauneveu of Valenciennes came to work for Charles V. Philip the Bold summoned Melchior Broederlam of Ypres to paint four scenes from the life of the Virgin on the wings of an altarpiece for the Chartreuse de Champmol (Dijon); they combine Flemish solidity with French elegance and Italian freshness (*c.* 1394-1399). The same patron employed Jean de Beaumetz of Hainault, Jean Malouel of Gelders, probable author of the '*Grande Pietà Ronde*' in the Louvre, and, above all, Henri Bellechose of Brabant, to whom is ascribed *The Last Communion of St Denis*, still close to illuminations with its figured gold background. However, at this period it is a mistake to infer the national characteristics of an artist's *œuvre* from his birth-place. Jan van Eyck and Rogier van der Weyden were both styled *gallicus* by the Italians, because the Count of Flanders owed allegiance to the French throne. At the same time Burgundy, the natural link between Flanders and Italy, was providing employment for Italian artists. Valentina Visconti, who married the Duke of Orleans, did not leave Milan empty-handed or without a retinue. Art-lovers competed for *ouvrages de Lombardie*, the latest fashion in about 1400. Even in England the *Wilton Diptych* is considered the work of a Frenchman; and French, too, was the unknown artist who illustrated the '*Livre de Chasse*' of Gaston Phœbus, Count of Foix, with such delightfully rustic and racy scenes.

Thus, the modern picture-form came into being through the conjunction of many circumstances; for, during the same period, the invention of engraving was to kill illumination. If the painting of this date seems international,

POL MALOUEL KNOWN AS POL DE LIMBOURG, ACTIVE *c.* 1402-1416. MINIATURE FROM THE 'TRÈS RICHES HEURES' OF THE DUKE OF BERRY: THE MONTH OF JUNE, THE PALACE AND THE SAINTE-CHAPELLE (DETAIL), *c.* 1416. MUSÉE CONDÉ, CHANTILLY

POL DE LIMBOURG. MINIATURE FROM THE 'TRÈS RICHES HEURES' OF THE DUKE OF BERRY: THE MONTH OF AUGUST, THE CHÂTEAU D'ÉTAMPES (DETAIL), *c.* 1416. MUSÉE CONDÉ, CHANTILLY

ANONYMOUS. MINIATURE FROM THE 'LIVRE DE CHASSE' OF GASTON PHOEBUS: BETWEEN FIELD AND FOREST, 1405-1410. BIBLIOTHÈQUE NATIONALE, PARIS

FIFTEENTH-CENTURY FRANCE

JEAN FOUQUET,
1420?-1480?
SELF-PORTRAIT
(ENAMEL),
c. 1450.
LOUVRE, PARIS

JEAN FOUQUET.
PORTRAIT OF
CHARLES VII,
1444-1445.
LOUVRE, PARIS

JEAN FOUQUET.
MINIATURE FROM
THE BOOK OF HOURS
OF ÉTIENNE
CHEVALIER:
THE STONING OF
ST STEPHEN,
1452-1460.
MUSÉE CONDÉ,
CHANTILLY

it is because nations did not yet exist; they were born of the conflict between England and France, and emerged at the same time as national schools of art. While still serving religion, painting freed itself from the aesthetic ideas of the Middle Ages, and shook off the ascendancy of architecture and the book. Instead of being an adornment, it became complete in itself; instead of sacred, profane; instead of international, national. But this evolution took 200 years; the masterpieces of the fifteenth century were still religious works.

During this period the patron was all-important. The most distinguished Maecenas was John, Duke of Berry. He amassed magnificent works of art in each of his seventeen residences, but especially in his favourite castle at Mehun-sur-Yèvre. His library contained some twenty manuscripts (illuminated books of hours), and included three masterpieces: the *'Grandes Heures'* (Paris, Bibliothèque Nationale, 1409) by Jacquemart de Hesdin, successor to Jean Pucelle; the psalter adorned with delicate *grisailles* by André Beauneveu (Paris, B.N., c. 1380-1385); and the finest painted work before 1420, the *'Très Riches Heures'* illuminated by the three brothers Pol, Hennequin, and Herman de Limbourg. In the twelve pictures accompanying the 'calendar', scenes from Court life alternate with scenes from the life of the countryside. The February picture shows a snow-covered village, which—with its donkey carrying a load of fire-wood, sheep in the fold, peasant-women warming themselves by the fire, and birds scratching about in the snow—recalls Bruegel. Others evoke the daily round—haymaking, the wine-harvest, sowing—and show buildings later defaced or destroyed. Most attractive of all are the scenes showing the life of the corpulent and pleasure-loving Duke himself, on the eve of the disasters. One watches him enjoy a pantagruelian meal at Mehun, on a country outing at Dourdan, hunting with falcons at Étampes, with a group

74

FIFTEENTH-CENTURY FRANCE

of elegant horsewomen and gallant knights out riding at Riom. It was here that courtly life found its last testimony and last poet. Nothing even faintly suggests religion in this prayer-book, whose purpose is to glorify a completely artificial way of life that sought to imitate the romaunts of chivalry.

The assassination of John the Fearless, occupation of Paris, and death of Charles VI provoked a crisis in the Parisian art-world. Artists migrated to 'unoccupied zones': on the Loire with the exiled King and his cousin the Duke of Anjou; the peaceful havens of Avignon and Provence; the Flemish Courts of Philip the Good. In Anjou the tradition of patronage was maintained by Louis II, of whom a profile portrait in brocaded garments has been preserved (Paris, B.N., *c.* 1412). His wife Yolande d'Aragon, the daughter of the queen of the troubadours, Violante de Bar, commissioned a book of hours from an outstanding artist known incorrectly as the Master of the '*Heures de Rohan*' (Paris, B.N., *c.* 1245).

The Loire school found its first and greatest painter in the person of Jean Fouquet. Born at Tours, he learned his craft working with the Flemish artists attracted by the Duke of Berry to his enchanted palace at Mehun, which his nephew Charles VII used while he remained 'King of Bourges'. As a young man, Fouquet was one of the first artists to travel to Italy; and at Rome he was privileged to paint Eugenius IV with two dignitaries of the Church. Unfortunately this picture has been lost, though for a long time it could be seen in Santa Maria sopra Minerva. Raphael drew inspiration from it for his portrait of Leo X between two cardinals; and Titian, in his turn, imitated Raphael when he depicted Paul III between his nephews. On returning to Touraine, Fouquet was engaged to paint portraits of high officials of the Court. They included the royal treasurer Étienne Chevalier, Chancellor Guillaume Juvénal des

JEAN FOUQUET. ÉTIENNE CHEVALIER PRESENTED BY ST STEPHEN (LEFT PART OF MELUN DIPTYCH), *c.* 1450. DEUTSCHES MUSEUM, BERLIN

JEAN FOUQUET. VIRGIN AND CHILD (RIGHT PART OF MELUN DIPTYCH), *c.* 1450. MUSÉE ROYAL DES BEAUX-ARTS, ANTWERP

JEAN FOUQUET. MINIATURE FROM THE BOOK OF HOURS OF ÉTIENNE CHEVALIER: THE BIRTH OF ST JOHN THE BAPTIST, 1452-1460. MUSÉE CONDÉ, CHANTILLY

FIFTEENTH-CENTURY FRANCE

GUILLAUME DOMBET
OR THE MASTER OF
THE AIX
ANNUNCIATION,
ACTIVE *c*. 1414-1460.
THE PROPHET
JEREMIAH (RIGHT
WING OF
ANNUNCIATION
TRIPTYCH).
1445.
MUSÉE D'ART
ANCIEN, BRUSSELS

GUILLAUME DOMBET.
ANNUNCIATION
(CENTRAL PANEL
OF TRIPTYCH),
1445.
ÉGLISE DE LA
MADELEINE,
AIX-EN-PROVENCE

MASTER OF 1456.
PORTRAIT OF A MAN,
CALLED THE
PORTRAIT
OF 1456.
LIECHTENSTEIN
COLLECTION,
VADUZ

Ursins, and the King himself. Perhaps the earliest likeness is that of *'le très victorieux roy de France'* posing stiffly in his surcoat. Here, the old-fashioned profile has been abandoned in favour of a three-quarter view of the King's red face, set in a look of sulky surprise. The finest portrait is of Étienne Chevalier with his patron saint; this formed the left half of the *Melun Diptych,* of which the other panel is a Virgin and Child. This Madonna has the features of Agnès Sorel, which is explained by the fact that the treasurer was Agnès' executor. Besides giving the figure the childlike forehead, short nose and tiny mouth of the King's mistress, the artist has bathed her skin and celebrated bosom in an unrealistic pearly whiteness which stands out against the background of angels' wings. Although he retained an earthy Gothic quality, Fouquet made a thorough study of the new perspective of the Tuscan artists, using it in his series of illuminated books: the *'Heures d'Étienne Chevalier',* the *'Grandes Chroniques de France'* (Paris, B.N., *c*. 1458), the Munich 'Boccaccio' (*c*. 1459), and the *'Antiquités Judaïques'* (Paris, B.N., *c*. 1470). In these he emerges as a universal artist, both a Court and a landscape painter, able to represent the life of peasants as well as of courtiers, scenes from the Bible as well as from contemporary life. The subject of the *'Heures d'Étienne Chevalier'* is the life of Christ, the Virgin and the saints. While still giving due attention to the illuminated initial, Fouquet's quest for accurate representation led him to make several innovations. St Margaret spinning and watching her sheep in the presence of armed horsemen reminds one irresistibly of St Joan at Domrémy. The martyrdom of St Apollinaris takes place before a platform that recalls the theatres of the miracle-plays. In the *'Grandes Chroniques de France',* probably executed for Charles VII, the artist revealed his progress in the grouping of crowds, the variation of his compositions, and the precise

FIFTEENTH-CENTURY FRANCE

rendering of details. He suppressed everything that still bound the image to the book. These illuminations seem more like miniature easel paintings. Jean Fouquet, like all his contemporaries, had no historical sense and dressed the ancient world in the fashions of the fifteenth century. His scenes from the life of his times, however, do have an eye-witness quality (scene of Charles IV entering St Denis on a litter drawn by four white horses, while the citizens watch with interest from their windows). The Munich 'Boccaccio', executed for the King's secretary Laurens Gyrard, is even more realistic; in its *Trial of the Duke of Alençon in 1458*, a piece of story-telling becomes a page of history. Fouquet produced his only documented work for Jacques d'Armagnac, Duke of Nemours. It is a series illustrating Josephus' *Jewish Antiquities:* his study of perspective bore fruit in the masterly representations of battles, marching soldiers and crowds. Fouquet became painter to the King in 1475, and until he died his status was almost dictatorial. He freed painting from the book and founded the French school, characterized by its vigour, finesse and modesty.

Meanwhile, Provence was still a centre of attraction for cosmopolitan art. Under Benedict XII, Sienese artists worked at Avignon, which for seventy years was the capital of Christendom. When the Curia had to leave, it was not without regret. Avignon did, however, remain Church property and the seat of a papal legate. On retiring to Aix to live the life of a voluptuary and a dilettante, René of Anjou, the chimerical King of Sicily, put new life into the market provided by religious establishments, wealthy middle-class patrons and the guilds. Nevertheless, the Provençal centre was too unstable to be called a school; and though an Avignon painter, Jacques d'Iverny, was active early in the century, one has to go to the Castello della Manta near Saluzzo (Piedmont) to see the

NICOLAS FROMENT, *c.* 1435-1484/90. THE BURNING BUSH (CENTRAL PANEL OF TRIPTYCH), 1476. CATHÉDRALE SAINT-SAUVEUR, AIX-EN-PROVENCE

ENGUERRAND CHARTON (OR QUARTON), ACTIVE *c.* 1447-1461. CORONATION OF THE VIRGIN, 1454. HOSPICE DE VILLENEUVE-LÈS-AVIGNON

AVIGNON SCHOOL. PIETÀ, *c.* 1460. LOUVRE, PARIS

FIFTEENTH-CENTURY FRANCE

MASTER OF MOULINS, KNOWN c. 1480-1500. THE NATIVITY AND A DONOR, CARDINAL JEAN ROLIN (DETAIL), c. 1480. MUSÉE D'AUTUN

MASTER OF MOULINS. ST MARY MAGDALENE AND A (FEMALE) DONOR, c. 1490-1495. LOUVRE, PARIS

MASTER OF MOULINS. PORTRAIT OF A YOUNG PRINCESS, c. 1490. LEHMAN COLLECTION, NEW YORK

elegant decorations attributed to him, in which members of the local ruling family are shown as nine heroes and nine heroines of antiquity (c. 1420). If one keeps to works actually in the *comté*, the masterpiece that heads the list — the altarpiece of *The Annunciation* in Ste Marie-Madeleine at Aix (1445) — is still so Gothic that even before M. Jean Boyer identified its author as Guillaume Dombet, trained at Dijon but active in Provence, it was possible to associate him with the Burgundian school. The chief attraction of the altarpiece lies in the magnificent still-lifes composed of books, ink-stands, manuscripts and boxes of dried preserves, which fill the niches above the prophets. Another still unidentified artist is the creator of the famous *Pietà* of Villeneuve-lès-Avignon (c. 1460), an awkward and simplified work, but intense and majestic.

The difficulty involved in tracing lines of artistic dependence at this period, when the test was not where an artist was born but where he worked and what his patron wanted, is shown by the fact that two pictures claimed for the Provençal school were painted by Enguerrand Charton (or Quarton) from Laon and Pierre Villatte from Limoges. These are the *Madonna of Mercy* (Chantilly, 1452), executed for the Celestine church at Avignon, and the *Coronation of the Virgin* which Charton produced for the Carthusian of Villeneuve. The masterly *Coronation* is magnificently French in its scholastic severity, excellent balance and soft colouring. Here one particularly admires the light-toned Provençal landscape spreading out below the elated throng of the elect, made up of wonderful portraits. Charton's artistic heir, Nicolas Froment, was a real Provençal, born at Uzès. He painted the triptych of the *Virgin in the burning Bush* for the church of the Grands Carmes at Aix; but, being susceptible to all the prevailing tendencies and without the genius to combine them into a new whole, he was unable to

78

FIFTEENTH-CENTURY FRANCE

avoid a composite effect—even in the subject laid down for him. On the wings appear the two donors: good King René with his gourmand's nose and self-indulgent jowl and, opposite him, his second wife Jeanne de Laval. The princely aesthete devoted his spare time to writing a *'Traité des Tournois'* (Paris, B.N. 1460) and an allegorical romance, *'Le Livre du Cœur d'Amour épris'* (Vienna, c. 1460), of which he supervised the illustration. In the miniatures accompanying the account of the tournament, the colouring and boldness of effect are dazzling. Those of the novel (an account of a dream) seem to be bathed in moonlight, like a foretaste of romantic chiaroscuro.

The latter work was dedicated to Jehan of Bourbon, brother of the Lord of Beaujeu, who employed the last of the French 'primitives' —the mysterious and anonymous author of the *Moulins Triptych*, sometimes identified with Jean Perréal. The altarpiece, which represents the Triumph of the Virgin, was donated to the collegiate church at Moulins by its founders, who are represented on the wings: Pierre II of Bourbon, Lord of Beaujeu, and his wife Anne of France, daughter of Louis XI, who was deservedly known as 'Madame la Grande'. By turning their seats at Moulins and Chantelle into centres of artistic activity, the illustrious pair remained true to a family tradition. The resplendent charm of the Triumph is almost too perfect. It displays the most truly French virtues of Fouquet and Charton in its strict economy, relaxed sweetness and pleasing realism, all combined with a judicious regard for the final result that marks the highest artistic taste.

Scholars have associated several comparable works with the unknown author of the *Moulins Triptych*, beginning with the Autun *Nativity*, which was donated by Cardinal Jean Rolin, son of the famous chancellor of Burgundy. Naturally enough, some admirable portraits have also been ascribed to him, including the *Young Princess*

MASTER OF MOULINS. VIRGIN AND CHILD WITH ANGELS (CENTRAL PANEL OF MOULINS TRIPTYCH), 1498-1499. MOULINS CATHEDRAL

ATTRIBUTED TO THE MASTER OF MOULINS. PORTRAIT OF A PRAYING CHILD, c. 1495. LOUVRE, PARIS

MASTER OF MOULINS. PORTRAIT OF CHARLES II DE BOURBON. ALTE PINAKOTHEK, MUNICH

79

SIMON MARMION, KNOWN 1449-1489. MATER DOLOROSA AND MAN OF SORROWS. STRASBURG MUSEUM

ANONYMOUS. PORTRAIT OF MARGARET OF YORK, WIFE OF CHARLES THE BOLD, c. 1468-1470. LOUVRE, PARIS

ANONYMOUS. MAN WITH GLASS OF WINE, c. 1455. LOUVRE, PARIS

in her violet velvet surcoat, and the more unconventionally beautiful *Praying Child*. This probably represents Charles VIII's son Charles-Orland, who died in 1495 at the age of three. If, to round off this survey of French fifteenth-century art, one turns to the Burgundian centre, one observes that it had moved so far northwards as to merge with that of Flanders, where the amazing adventure started by Jan van Eyck was under way. Moreover, it is within the sphere of Rogier van der Weyden that Simon Marmion (active at Valenciennes) must be placed. He is thought to be the author of the wings of the rich altarpiece once in the Abbey of St Bertin at St Omer (c. 1459). These reveal the same strict perspective and minute precision in the detail as the miniatures Marmion painted for the '*Grandes Chroniques de St Denis*' (Toulouse, 1449-1455).

Other anonymous artists are: the Master of St Sebastian, in Provence, with his naive sense of drama; the Master of St-Jean-de-Luz, in Burgundy, with his portraits of Hugues de Rabutin and Jeanne de Montaigu; the Master of St Giles, who worked in the North, and whose scenes from French national history have such fascination; and Jean Bellegambe, with his altarpiece for Anchin Abbey. But next to nothing is known about all these painters. Moreover, even Simon Marmion was irresistibly drawn by the splendour of Northern art; in 1459 he joined the Tournai guild. It is better to conclude with two portraits that are linked by their style as well as by the fact that they were both once in Viennese collections. The first is the famous *Man with a Glass of Wine*, which, if the hunt for its author was not still ranging from Flanders to Portugal, could be called the first proletarian portrait in French art; the second is a fine figure of a young man, dated 1456. Both reveal the new raising of the individual's status within pre-Reformation Christendom.

NETHERLANDISH SCHOOL IN THE FIFTEENTH CENTURY

The year 1432 is outstandingly important in the history of painting. On 6th May the altarpiece of the *Adoration of the Lamb,* by the brothers Hubert and Jan van Eyck, was formally exposed to view in the church of St Jean-Baptiste (now the cathedral of St Bavon) at Ghent. It was becoming clear to the whole Western world that artists were feeling and painting in a new way.

What exactly was the new contribution of the Flemish painters? It took the form of a novel technique and a fresh attitude of mind —though there has been much discussion as to the technique. Vasari maintained that Jan invented oil painting, but this is not borne out by any of the documents that have come to light. Others have held that the Van Eycks' innovation consisted in the use of volatile oils. At all events, the new process, which made it possible for artists to give their colours unparalleled depth, luminosity and brilliance, and which provided a stable and permanent paint-structure, was evolved in the Flemish workshops. It lent itself to minute detail and the most subtle gradations of tone, so that easel pictures became 'the chamber music of painting'.

The new attitude was made up of a sense of objectivity, a thirst for knowledge about the world and a love for everything in it: it has come to be known, crudely, as 'realism'. A kind of serenity usually reigns over paintings produced by this method, which seems in general much less suited to the representation of tragic events—martyrdoms or battles—than peaceful ones. It tends to transform emotion into contemplation, through which the spectator enjoys the colour harmonies and the rendering of distance by means of a skilful gradation of light.

These are the qualities of the altarpiece of the *Adoration of the Lamb,* whose subject, stated in the broadest terms, is the Redemption. When closed, it shows the *Annunciation* taking place in the Virgin's

MASTER OF FLÉMALLE (OR ROBERT CAMPIN 1375/79-1444)?
PORTRAIT OF A WOMAN.
NATIONAL GALLERY, LONDON

MASTER OF FLÉMALLE (OR ROBERT CAMPIN?)
ANNUNCIATION.
MUSÉE ROYAL D'ART ANCIEN, BRUSSELS

MASTER OF FLÉMALLE (OR ROBERT CAMPIN?)
VIRGIN AND CHILD BEFORE A FIRESCREEN.
NATIONAL GALLERY, LONDON

NETHERLANDISH SCHOOL IN THE FIFTEENTH CENTURY

JAN VAN EYCK,
c. 1390-1441 ?
MAN IN A TURBAN,
1433.
NATIONAL GALLERY,
LONDON

JAN VAN EYCK.
VIRGIN
AND CHILD WITH
CHANCELLOR ROLIN,
c. 1435.
LOUVRE, PARIS

JAN VAN EYCK.
THE MARRIAGE OF
GIOVANNI (?)
ARNOLFINI
AND GIOVANNA
CENAMI (?)
1434.
NATIONAL GALLERY,
LONDON

chamber, with glimpses of a townscape through the windows. Above are the prophets Zechariah and Micah and Sibyls who predicted the coming of Christ; below, in *grisaille,* are imitation statues of the Baptist and the Evangelist, flanked by the donor and his wife.

The altarpiece only reveals its splendours when it is open. In the upper tier the two nude figures of Adam and Eve, represented with almost ruthless precision, flank angels who, clad in black and gold, and red and gold, are making music; next come the Virgin and, again, the Precursor; in the centre sits God, with the attributes of Father and Son.

In the lower tier the focal point is the Altar of the Lamb set, before a clear fountain, in a paradisean landscape. It is a green paradise, its mood that of nature in the springtime. In the background rise the towers and steeples of a city. Monks, popes, and bishops are coming from the right to adore the Lamb; beyond them, are the holy virgins. From the left come Doctors and prophets; and, beyond them, leaders of the Church. On the wings—which seem to continue the subject of the central panel, because they prolong its skyline— the warrior saints arrive in a manycoloured group overtopped by banners; and opposite them, on a more severe note, the hermit and pilgrim saints. An inexpressible sense of holy joy emanates from this work: from the landscape, in which one can recognize the species of both native and exotic trees; and from the faces of the figures, which, though transfigured by their innocence, have all been made quite different from each other. Strongly individualized, the Adam and Eve introduce a note of vigour without sensuality.

An inscription on the altarpiece states that Hubert van Eyck ('who was surpassed by none') began it, and that his brother Jan completed it. The authenticity of this inscription has been contested— wrongly, it would seem. There are quite a number of documentary

82

NETHERLANDISH SCHOOL IN THE FIFTEENTH CENTURY

references to Jan, whereas those concerning Hubert are very rare; and this has led some critics to maintain that he never existed, except as a legendary figure.

Jodocus Vyd, who commissioned the altarpiece, was only an alderman. However, during the period of the Van Eycks this sometimes rather niggardly middle-class clientèle was reinforced by the princely patronage of the magnificent Burgundian Court. The adventurous spirit of an aristocracy devoted to luxury, tournaments and warlike pursuits joined forces with the more matter-of-fact spirit of the middle class, and sometimes even contended with it—to the advantage of the artists who had to portray princes as well as paint religious subjects. Moreover, the Court contributed to the unification of the Low Countries. This process, along with the fact that the towns were all very close together and therefore in constant, active communication with each other, produced a really homogeneous school of painting, whether the artists came from French- or Flemish-speaking areas. So there are no signs of the provincialism and sub-schools that hampered German art.

Jan van Eyck profited greatly by the patronage of the Dukes of Burgundy. Not later than 1425 he was appointed Court painter and *valet de chambre* to Philip the Good, who on several occasions entrusted him with diplomatic missions, notably to Portugal. Like his brother Hubert, he began as a miniature-painter, and their joint style always showed signs of this. Their true forerunners are the Limbourg brothers and the Master of the '*Heures du Maréchal de Boucicaut*', though in the pages of the '*Heures de Turin*', which there are good grounds for ascribing to Jan, he was already painting real pictures. Several carefully signed and dated works mark the stages of his career: the *Man in a Turban*, which, with its shades of vermilion and black, is one of the boldest portraits ever painted

JAN VAN EYCK. PORTRAIT OF MARGARET VAN EYCK, 1439. MUSÉE COMMUNAL, BRUGES

HUBERT AND JAN VAN EYCK. POLYPTYCH OF THE ADORATION OF THE LAMB: WINGS SHOWING 'KNIGHTS OF CHRIST' AND HOLY HERMITS, 1432. ÉGLISE SAINT-BAVON, GHENT

HUBERT AND JAN VAN EYCK. POLYPTYCH OF THE ADORATION OF THE LAMB: ANGELS MAKING MUSIC, 1432. ÉGLISE SAINT-BAVON, GHENT

83

NETHERLANDISH SCHOOL IN THE FIFTEENTH CENTURY

ROGIER VAN DER WEYDEN, 1399?-1464. ST MARY MAGDALENE (WING OF THE BRAQUE TRIPTYCH), c. 1451-1452. LOUVRE, PARIS

ROGIER VAN DER WEYDEN. VIRGIN AND ST JOHN; CHRIST ON THE CROSS. PHILADELPHIA MUSEUM

ROGIER VAN DER WEYDEN. SACRAMENT OF MARRIAGE (DETAIL OF THE ALTARPIECE OF THE 'SEVEN SACRAMENTS'), c. 1449. MUSÉE ROYAL DES BEAUX-ARTS, ANTWERP

(1433); the picture of the artist's wife Margaret wearing a cinnabar dress, softly modelled in subdued tones. Among Jan's major works is the portrait of Arnolfini and his wife standing together in a room (1434). The chandelier, convex mirror, bed, pattens are minutely rendered, and soft light bathes the thin-, almost foxy-faced man and his wife, who is wearing a long, green dress. Trustingly they join hands—a touching image of matrimony, in which the feeling prevents the picture from suggesting genre painting too forcibly. The *Virgin and Child with Canon van der Paele* (1434-1436), one of the treasures of the museum at Bruges, is perhaps less moving. In the undated *Virgin and Child with Chancellor Rolin,* the two principal figures face each other to left and right of a triple-arched opening through which can be seen an exquisite town- and riverscape.

However decisive Jan van Eyck's influence on the early growth of Flemish painting, another painter must be assigned an equally important place in art-history. This is the author of a group of works that have been assembled under the undoubtedly ill-chosen pseudonym of the Master of Flémalle: the *Virgin and Child before a Fire-screen;* the Virgin of the *Mérode Altarpiece* (New York, Met. Mus.); and that of the Brussels *Annunciation.* All these figures have inexpressive faces without grace or charm but possessing unusual plastic force. The painter had a special gift for surrounding them with domestic objects rendered with a vigorous feeling for relief. The most admired of his works is a fragment preserved in the Staedel Institute at Frankfurt that shows the Good Thief, looking like a sculpture, on the cross.

Is this highly individual artist identical with the painter Robert Campin, whose activities are well documented? He was Rogier van der Weyden's teacher, and became a citizen of Tournai in 1410. But many scholars doubt whether the Master of Flémalle ever existed,

84

NETHERLANDISH SCHOOL IN THE FIFTEENTH CENTURY

and attribute the works ascribed to him to the young Rogier van der Weyden.

Born at Tournai but active in Brussels by 1345, Van der Weyden is closer to the Master of Flémalle than the Van Eycks. Little is known about him from documents, though they establish that he paid a visit to Rome in 1450; not a single signed work has survived. Nevertheless, his fame and influence are fully demonstrated by the large number of surviving copies of his paintings: pictures based on them went on being produced right into the sixteenth century. Even though his temperament was very different from that of the Van Eycks, he was strongly influenced in his *St Luke painting the Virgin,* of which the best versions are at Boston and Munich, by the *Virgin and Child with Chancellor Rolin.* He excelled in creating lucid compositions with tragic overtones, as in his Vienna, Madrid, and Philadelphia *Crucifixions,* and, above all, in his *Pietà* panels with the rigid body of Christ resting in his mother's arms (e.g., Berlin Museum). This can also be seen in his representations of the *Descent from the Cross;* the most moving is the one at Madrid, even though it is probably a very early work. Against the gold background the figures form a pathetic bas-relief, and the Magdalene wrings her hands in a convulsive movement. Rogier's *Entombment* (Florence, Uffizi), with Christ, seen full face, supported under the arms on both sides, is one of his most original compositions; the *Adoration of the Kings* in of his Munich triptych is beautifully composed and gloriously coloured. For the town hall at Brussels he executed a series of wall-paintings showing examples of justice being done, so that the magistrates would have them permanently before their eyes: Dürer admired them during his visit to the Netherlands, but today they are only known very incompletely from tapestries. The altarpiece of *The Seven Sacraments,* in which the

ROGIER VAN DER WEYDEN. PORTRAIT, THOUGHT TO BE OF ANTOINE, 'GRAND BÂTARD' OF BURGUNDY, *c.* 1456. MUSÉE ROYAL D'ART ANCIEN, BRUSSELS

ROGIER VAN DER WEYDEN. PORTRAIT OF A LADY, *c.* 1455. NATIONAL GALLERY OF ART, WASHINGTON

ROGIER VAN DER WEYDEN. PORTRAIT OF LAURENT FROIMONT. MUSÉE ROYAL D'ART ANCIEN, BRUSSELS

ANONYMOUS. PORTRAIT OF JOHN THE FEARLESS, *c*. 1415. MUSÉE ROYAL DES BEAUX-ARTS, ANTWERP

MASTER OF THE VIRGO INTER VIRGINES. ANNUNCIATION. D. G. VAN BEUNINGEN COLLECTION, VIERHOUTEN

PETRUS CHRISTUS, ?-1472/73 PORTRAIT OF A CARTHUSIAN. METROPOLITAN MUSEUM, NEW YORK

sacraments have been represented as a series of little scenes all taking place inside a church, still shows the influence of miniature painting, and its chief attraction lies in its colour. During the latter part of his career, between 1450 and 1452, he painted the Beaune *Last Judgment*, with nude figures that recall those carved round cathedral doorways; and the *Braque Triptych*, in which the Magdalene, dressed with the elegance of a Burgundian Court lady, stands out against a landscape background more like stage scenery than the Van Eycks'.

Rogier's portraits form an important part of his *œuvre*. Although adequately individualized, they nevertheless tend to conform to types and have a lordly, stiff air, as in *The Man with the Arrow*, presumed to be Antoine, 'Grand Bâtard' of Burgundy. In another, Laurent Froimont is shown praying with intense devotion. Furthermore, several of these portraits originally formed one half of a diptych, of which the other showed a Madonna. Although the woman in the Washington portrait possesses a distinctive feature in her full lips, even she has been somewhat 'standardized'. Friedländer has written that whereas Jan van Eyck was a discoverer, Rogier was an inventor whose observations lacked the subtlety of his predecessor's, but whose talent for composition and sense of drama made him easier to appreciate.

Among the painters who preceded Rogier in working for members of the Burgundian Court, it is appropriate to include the anonymous artist who portrayed John the Fearless as a swarthy, long-nosed figure in a tall hood decorated with a jewel. He is shown against a blue background that grows paler in the vicinity of his silhouette.

At first the work of Petrus Christus, whose documented career extends from 1444, when he became a citizen of Bruges, to his death in 1472-1473, was influenced by the Van Eycks. He produced an amazing masterpiece of delicacy in the portrait of a young woman

NETHERLANDISH SCHOOL IN THE FIFTEENTH CENTURY

in the Berlin museum. The smooth, rounded forehead, the face with only a hint of modelling, and the slanting eyes put one in a reflective mood as do Vermeer's works. Two portraits of a donor and his wife, dominated by reds and blacks, are amongst the finest works preserved in the National Gallery of Art, Washington; but they are less well-known than the picture in the Lehman collection: *St Eligius weighing the Wedding Rings of a Bridal Couple*. However, in some ways this work is almost too flawless: even though in the representation of accessories—metal vases and a jewel-case on the display shelves of the shop; people and objects reflected in a convex mirror like the one behind the Arnolfini couple—one again finds the virtuosity of a Jan van Eyck, the work as a whole lacks warmth, unlike the Arnolfini double-portrait. The poetic quality of the London picture eluded Christus, who, now more influenced by Rogier than the Van Eycks, came near to lapsing into genre painting—one of the dangers besetting Flemish art.

The slightly facile charm of the young Christus recurs in an *Annunciation* in the Van Beuningen collection attributed to the Master of the Virgo inter Virgines, who is so named after a picture in the Amsterdam museum showing the Virgin and her companions surrounded by the fence of a *hortus conclusus*.

Born at Haarlem and obviously a contemporary of Petrus Christus, Dieric (Dirk) Bouts settled in Louvain in about 1450. Though he did not lack skill, and was indeed almost ostentatious in his representations of paved floors in perspective, his work has a certain awkwardness: there is something touching about the thin, stiff-limbed Christ in his Louvre *Pietà*. This stiffness marks the tidy rows of figures in the *Last Supper* (altarpiece of *The Sacrament*). It was painted for the Church of St Pierre, Louvain, during 1464-1468, and has the unusual distinction of never having been moved. However, despite the awkwardness,

PETRUS CHRISTUS.
PORTRAIT OF
A DONOR
AND HIS WIFE,
c. 1446.
NATIONAL GALLERY
OF ART,
WASHINGTON

PETRUS CHRISTUS
PORTRAIT OF
A LADY,
c. 1446.
STAATLICHE MUSEEN,
BERLIN

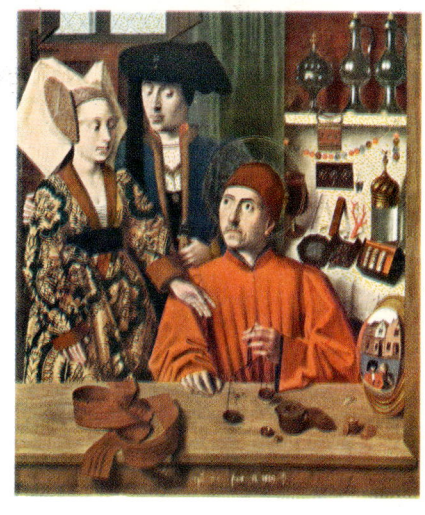

PETRUS CHRISTUS.
ST ELIGIUS
WEIGHING THE
WEDDING
RINGS OF A
BRIDAL COUPLE,
1449.
LEHMAN
COLLECTION,
NEW YORK

87

NETHERLANDISH SCHOOL IN THE FIFTEENTH CENTURY

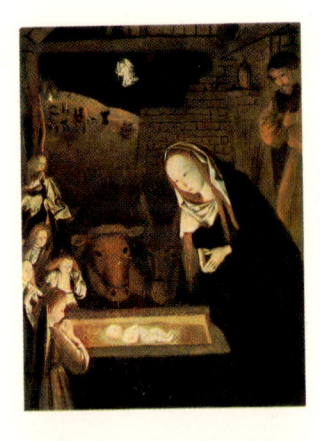

GEERTGEN TOT SINT JANS, 1460/65-1490/95. NATIVITY. NATIONAL GALLERY, LONDON

GEERTGEN TOT SINT JANS. ST JOHN THE BAPTIST IN A LANDSCAPE. STAATLICHE MUSEEN, BERLIN

DIERIC BOUTS, 1415/20-1475. DEPOSITION. LOUVRE, PARIS

the general effect is one of deep feeling. Some of the faces bear comparison with the wonderful portrait in the Metropolitan Museum, New York, of a man with a tall cap and a long face marked by the signs of a strenuous life, or with the male portrait in the National Gallery, London. Bouts became town painter at Louvain, and undertook a number of official commissions, including the two *Justice of Emperor Otto* panels now in the Brussels museum. One represents the execution of a nobleman who was sentenced to death as a result of a false accusation by the Empress; the other shows how he was posthumously cleared by his wife, who submitted to ordeal by fire. The artist ran the danger here of lapsing into mere storytelling; but he was saved by the quality of his colouring, which is rich in warm reds. Nevertheless, the inability of the Netherlanders to depict martyrdoms becomes obvious in Bouts' *Martyrdom of St Erasmus* (Louvain) and *Martyrdom of St Hippolytus* (Bruges): both have the coldness of an official report.

In a sense, the art of Christus and Bouts cashed in on that of their great predecessors, the Van Eycks and Rogier. There is much more novelty and invention in the work of a painter who must have been born some fifty years later, at Leyden, but about whom very little is known from documentary sources, namely, Geertgen tot Sint Jans. He seems more or less to have led the life of a monk in the community of the Brethren of St John, at Haarlem, where he died in 1495. Two of his works set him among those artists who were independent-minded enough to introduce new ideas. In his *St John the Baptist in a Landscape* (Berlin museum), the actual figure of the saint has nothing special to recommend it: it is triangular and bulky, and the painting of the hands and feet is accomplished and dry. What is new, however, is the way the figure is literally submerged in a very green, well-watered landscape with fine trees,

88

NETHERLANDISH SCHOOL IN THE FIFTEENTH CENTURY

which extends very high up the panel. This is no longer just a picture of St John the Baptist, but of a landscape *with* St John. Geertgen conceived his *Nativity* as a night-piece in which, as with Correggio, the main light emanates from the Infant Christ.

Those Italians who, in the fifteenth century, knew of 'Giovanni da Bruggia' and 'Ruggiero da Brusselle' were far from forgetting 'Ugo d'Anversa' or, in other words, Hugo van der Goes. When Tommaso Portinari, the Medici agent in Bruges and a very important person, wanted to send a Flemish work to his own country, it was to Hugo that he turned; and the resultant *Portinari Altarpiece,* originally in Santa Maria Nuova, Florence, but now in the Uffizi, was much admired by his compatriots. Completed round about 1475, the altarpiece is the key work of the artist, who was probably born at Ghent, and entered the guild there in 1467. Moreover, its attribution to Hugo is the only one confirmed by documentary evidence; critics have been able to group numerous panels round it, and trace the course of a dominant influence. Hugo's *œuvre* contains none of the elegant but trifling pictures that most of the Netherlanders enjoyed painting. He had a sense of grandeur, movement and energy. The main composition of the *Portinari Altarpiece,* showing the Nativity, is most wonderfully balanced. To the left is Joseph and, in the middle-ground, the ox and ass, with the Virgin, in a dark blue dress, on the left of the central area. Also in the middle-distance —but on the right—are the shepherds with their ill-shaven peasant faces. Behind them one glimpses a landscape in which the angel brings the glad tidings to shepherds amid their flock. A link between the two groups, and a note of gaiety, is provided by two angels. Angels in heavy copes or white robes occupy the foreground, and beyond them lies the Infant Christ. There is nothing to distract the attention: none of those charming

DIERIC BOUTS. THE LAST SUPPER (CENTRAL PART OF THE ALTARPIECE OF THE HOLY SACRAMENT), 1468. ÉGLISE SAINT-PIERRE, LOUVAIN

DIERIC BOUTS. PORTRAIT OF A MAN, 1462. NATIONAL GALLERY, LONDON

DIERIC BOUTS. JUSTICE OF EMPEROR OTTO: THE ORDEAL BY FIRE (DETAIL), 1471-1473. MUSÉE ROYAL D'ART ANCIEN, BRUSSELS

89

NETHERLANDISH SCHOOL IN THE FIFTEENTH CENTURY

HUGO VAN DER GOES, c. 1440-1482. PORTRAIT OF A MAN. METROPOLITAN MUSEUM, NEW YORK

HUGO VAN DER GOES. FALL OF MAN (WING OF A DIPTYCH), c. 1470. KUNSTHISTORISCHES MUSEUM, VIENNA

HUGO VAN DER GOES, THE PORTINARI CHILDREN (DETAIL FROM THE PORTINARI ALTARPIECE), 1475-1476. UFFIZI, FLORENCE

traditional figures, such as midwives giving assistance at the birth. Hugo van der Goes' conception no longer has the purely narrative quality of that of the earliest Flemish painters. On the wings, the gaunt-faced, hollow-cheeked donor and his wife are accompanied by their patron saints and by their children, whom the artist has represented with amazing realism for a period when children were all too often made to look like miniature adults. Van der Goes' hand can sometimes be discerned in the works of fellow-artists: for example, he quite obviously painted the donors on the wings of Dieric Bouts' altarpiece with the *Martyrdom of St Hippolytus*. In his Vienna *Fall of Man,* he took up the Adam and Eve motif from the Van Eycks' *Adoration of the Lamb,* with a more elegant use of line but less realism. The Berlin *Adoration of the Kings* and Brussels *St Anne* are nearest to the Flemish tradition.

Round about the time when he was working on the *Portinari Altarpiece,* he retired as a lay brother to the Roode Clooster monastery near Brussels, but went on painting there. In 1480 he became mentally ill, though he continued to have moments of lucidity up to his death in 1482. His *Dormition of the Virgin* is undoubtedly datable to this last phase of his life. Although its composition and the movement of the figures are very skilfully handled, the colouring is disappointing: it lacks body, and the juxtapositions are sometimes harsh.

Both at home and abroad, he had enormous influence; it is very conspicuous in the work of artists such as the Master of Moulins.

After discussing Hugo, mention must be made of his associate Joos van Wassenhove, who became a Master at Antwerp in 1460. He is much better known through the works that he executed in Italy where he was called Giusto da Guanto (Justus of Ghent)—for the study and library of the Duke of Urbino. Although profoundly influenced by the Italians, in portraiture he kept his Flemish virtues.

NETHERLANDISH SCHOOL IN THE FIFTEENTH CENTURY

To preserve the chronological sequence, Hans Memlinc has to follow hard on the heels of Hugo, but their gifts are widely different. Memlinc was born round about 1433 in Germany, probably at Seligenstadt near Frankfurt-am-Main. Did he remain long enough in the Rhineland to acquire the excessive softness characteristic of Rhenish art? Very probably he was a pupil of Rogier van der Weyden. He became a citizen of Bruges in 1465, and remained there until he died in 1494, leaving many works. These seem to have met with huge success during his lifetime, though this was nothing compared with their popularity during the Romantic period, when Memlinc became *the* 'primitive' painter, and the personification of Bruges. Around his life there then grew up a legend of which little has withstood critical investigation. However, as always, the reaction has gone too far. Undoubtedly Memlinc was no innovator. He appears to have learned hardly anything from contemporaries such as Hugo, and added nothing to the art of his teacher Rogier. This he smoothed down, sometimes making it lifeless, and his portraits have nothing like the energy of those of the Burgundian princes. On the other hand, from the *Niccolo di Sforzore Spinelli* in the Antwerp museum to the *Martin van Nieuwehove* (1487) in the museum of the Hôpital St Jean at Bruges, they all display an affected refinement in their harmonies. In the Bruges work, a violet jerkin combines with a brownish-grey sleeve; while, behind, a stained-glass window representing St Martin adds variegated accents of colour, which are sufficiently subdued, however, not to stand out. As for Memlinc's portraits of women — the one dated 1480 and known as the *Sibyl Sambetha* or *Persian Sibyl* after an inscription added later; the one of *Maria Portinari* in the Metropolitan Museum, New York; the old woman in the Louvre — they benefit by the very shortcomings of the artist,

HUGO VAN DER GOES. VIRGIN AND CHILD, ST ANNE AND A DONOR. MUSÉE ROYAL D'ART ANCIEN, BRUSSELS

HUGO VAN DER GOES. DORMITION OF THE VIRGIN. MUSÉE COMMUNAL, BRUGES

HUGO VAN DER GOES. SHEPHERDS (DETAIL FROM THE PORTINARI ALTARPIECE), 1475-1476. UFFIZI, FLORENCE

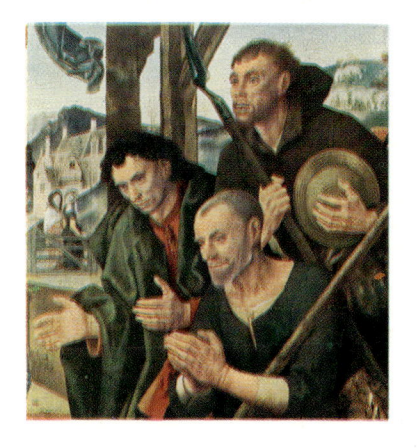

91

NETHERLANDISH SCHOOL IN THE FIFTEENTH CENTURY

HANS MEMLINC,
1433 ?-1494.
SHRINE OF
ST URSULA:
ARRIVAL AT
COLOGNE,
c. 1489.
HÔPITAL
SAINT-JEAN, BRUGES

MEMLINC.
PORTRAIT OF
MARIA PORTINARI.
METROPOLITAN
MUSEUM,
NEW YORK

MEMLINC.
MARTYRDOM OF
ST SEBASTIAN,
AFTER 1470.
MUSÉE ROYAL
DES BEAUX-ARTS,
BRUSSELS

and there is little in the whole Early Netherlandish school to equal their candid charm. Memlinc's Danzig *Last Judgment* is a very close imitation of Rogier van der Weyden's altarpiece at Beaune; in his *Martyrdom of St Sebastian,* he approaches Dieric Bouts' elegance. Two of his best altarpieces—the one he did for Jan Floreins, dated 1479, and the one with the two St Johns and the *Mystic Marriage of St Catherine,* which was completed in 1479—are preserved in the Hôpital St Jean at Bruges. Perhaps Memlinc's most attractive feature is his great gift for telling stories. Two works—the Turin *Passion of Christ* and Munich *Lives of Christ and the Virgin*—incorporate a series of little scenes with minute, lively figures, which have many of the characteristics of miniature painting. However, Memlinc's greatest success in this field is the famous *Shrine of St Ursula,* a mixture of naivety and florid imagination, and the testament of a world that would soon be no more. In the six side panels (the two end ones are devoted to separate subjects), the artist has represented the story of the saint and her eleven thousand companions, from their arrival at Cologne to their martyrdom there when they returned from their pilgrimage to Rome. Throughout the series, St Ursula wears a white mantle over a blue dress; and her hair is arranged in coils over the ears. The virgins are dressed in red, green, and mauve. Decorously they expire beneath the blows of the Huns; and the variegated harmonies of the paint-pattern are so charming that one cannot take the massacre completely seriously. This cycle had such a success that towards the end of the century an anonymous artist working at Bruges painted a less refined version of it for the Black Sisters.

Memling died in 1494, on the threshold of the new century. In just over sixty years Flemish painting had developed into something completely new. It was quite unlike that of any other school, and in

NETHERLANDISH SCHOOL IN THE FIFTEENTH CENTURY

its fertility equalled the art of Italy.

There is no point in looking for a bridge between the seraphic quality of Memlinc's world and the sinister burlesque of Hieronymus Bosch's vision; it just does not exist. Moreover, it is not only in relation to Memlinc that Bosch seems like a product of spontaneous generation, but in relation to *all* the art of his times, and of the preceding period too. Next to nothing is known about him. He was probably born in about 1450 at s' Hertogenbosch, not a notably active artistic centre, and died there in 1516. His real name was Van Aken; and he is known to have joined the Illustrious Brotherhood of Our Lady, whose members were tonsured and performed miracle-plays. Nevertheless, Hieronymus Bosch was famous even in his own day, as can be seen above all from the number of the replicas that exist of his great altarpieces. Don Felipe de Guevara, a Spanish nobleman and gentleman-in-waiting to Charles V, acquired six of his works, and also wrote about him. Guevara passed on his taste to Philip II, who, in his sullen seclusion, meditated on Bosch's pictures. Friedländer has said of them, that the first thing to interest the spectator is their 'what' (in other words, the subject); the 'how' is a secondary matter. As regards the 'what', Bosch has left a series of riddles. In my opinion it is a mistake to see him as the representative of a current of popular art. At times he did no doubt illustrate the proverbs of his country, as in *The Cure for Madness*. The subject of *The Hay Wain* has also been connected with a Flemish proverb: 'The world is a mountain of hay; everyone takes what he can grab.' All the same, he drew far less on popular sources than Pieter Bruegel the Elder was to do nearly a century later. As to Bosch', sense of fun, it clearly exists, and the solemn twentieth century pays far too little attention to an element that undoubtedly contributed to the artist's success. However, it is too jarring, too disturbing just

MEMLINC. PORTRAIT OF MARTIN VAN NIEUWENHOVE (WING OF A DIPTYCH), 1487. HÔPITAL SAINT-JEAN, BRUGES

MEMLINC. THE THREE KINGS AND THEIR SUITE (DETAIL FROM THE 'SEVEN JOYS OF THE VIRGIN'), 1478-1480. ALTE PINAKOTHEK, MUNICH

MEMLINC. THE 'SIBYL SAMBETHA', 1480. HÔPITAL SAINT-JEAN, BRUGES

HIERONYMUS BOSCH, c. 1450-1516.
THE PEDLAR.
BOYMANS MUSEUM, ROTTERDAM

BOSCH.
TRIPTYCH OF THE HAYWAIN (CENTRAL PANEL), c. 1490.
PRADO, MADRID

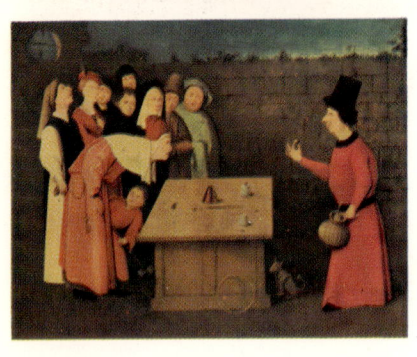

BOSCH.
THE CONJUROR.
MUSÉE DE SAINT-GERMAIN-EN-LAYE

to be called 'fun'. Gevaert saw Bosch as a preacher and moralist, while Combe has dwelt on his links with the Flemish mystics. The universe that Bosch created was certainly one of monsters, but not those bred (according to Goya) by the sleep of reason. Bosch's monsters have a kind of inverted logic and his world belongs to Satan, the ape of God—not to the minor demons. He disdained the elegant colour-harmonies and smooth finish typical of the school; and the general effect of his colouring is much paler, with a predominance of pinks. Spheres are made to look three-dimensional by an almost schematic method of modifying the local colour. Bosch's work contains a great many nudes, but despite some very suggestive poses, there is absolutely nothing sensual about these slender figures, with their non-naturalistic colouring. They are differentiated only by their contours; and even these seem not so much to have been observed from nature as arbitrarily chosen, once for all, without being individualized. One of Bosch's characteristics is his taste for acute angles, points, and thinness.

The chronology of his works remains very uncertain. For convenience, one can make a distinction between his relatively small panels representing a single scene, and the large triptychs, which involve, so to speak, the construction of a topsy-turvy world. Among the first group one finds several pictures that are openly comic: *The Cure for Madness* (Prado); *The Conjuror,* which seems to be free from any hidden meaning; *The Ship of Fools* (Louvre), which is connected with a subject very popular in the literature of the period, and, above all, with Sebastian Brant's work bearing the same title; the ragged *Pedlar ;* the *St John on Patmos* (Berlin), based on a print by Master E. S.; and even the ring of scenes representing the *Seven Deadly Sins* on the table-top in the Escorial. The *Christ carrying the Cross* in the

NETHERLANDISH SCHOOL IN THE FIFTEENTH CENTURY

Ghent museum is an assemblage of hideous, bloated faces, like the ones by Leonardo: Bosch was his contemporary, and could just possibly have known examples of his work.

In the second group come the three *summae* : *The Garden of Delights, The Hay Wain,* and *The Temptation of St Anthony*. Merely to describe one of these works, without any reference to the technique, would take many pages. Contemptuous of perspective, Bosch has piled up his figures, which fill the panels from top to bottom, as in a scene from a medieval play. In *The Garden of Delights,* which is scattered with symbolic eggs and fruit, and in which a man and woman are about to make love in a crystal globe, the most striking passage is the pool in which naked women are bathing. Round it parade figures mounted on a variety of animals, including a pig. Two lovers sit on the hay in *The Hay Wain*. They seem to represent courtly love, but by their side an obscene monster joins them in their music-making. As in the case of *The Garden of Delights,* one wing represents Hell (here the most prominent figure is mounted on an ox and transfixed by a hunting-spear), and the other Paradise. Of the three works, *The Temptation of St Anthony* (Lisbon) seems the least constricted: air circulates in it. The hermit himself is not much in evidence, but Bosch has had a wonderful time creating monsters: a man with a pig's head; a fish, with a barred window, imprisoning a swimmer; another fish with sword and sword-belt; a four-footed pot. It is not so much St Anthony's virtue that is being tried as the credulity of the spectator.

In the Netherlands of the fifteenth century, where painters were so calm and confident, Bosch was the Fool present at all gatherings, to whom all is permitted: he holds up a distorting mirror to the faces of supposedly rational men, who are appalled to recognize themselves in it.

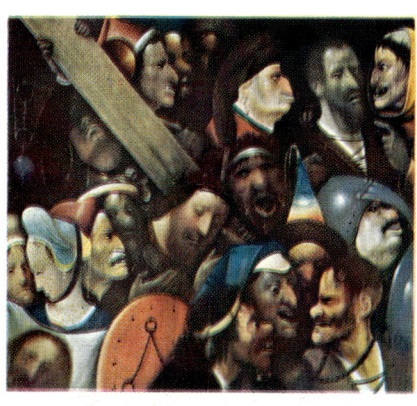

BOSCH. CHRIST CARRYING THE CROSS, *c.* 1505. MUSÉE ROYAL DES BEAUX-ARTS, GHENT

BOSCH. TRIPTYCH OF THE GARDEN OF DELIGHTS (DETAIL OF CENTRAL PANEL), AFTER 1500. PRADO, MADRID

BOSCH. TRIPTYCH OF THE GARDEN OF DELIGHTS (DETAIL OF CENTRAL PANEL), AFTER 1500. PRADO, MADRID

FIFTEENTH-CENTURY SPAIN

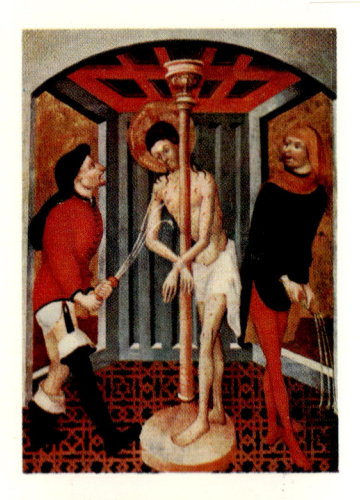

LUIS BORRASSA. SCOURGING OF CHRIST, BEGINNING OF 15th CENTURY. MUSEU GOYA, CASTRES

JAUME HUGUET, 1414?-1492. HEAD OF A WOMAN (DETAIL FROM THE 'MIRACLE OF ST VINCENT'). MUSEU DE ARTE CATALAN, BARCELONA

JAUME HUGUET. ST GEORGE (DETAIL OF 'ST GEORGE AND THE PRINCESS'). MUSEU DE ARTE CATALAN, BARCELONA

From the Gothic Age onwards it became clear that Catalonia had a very original culture and native genius. The country had links with other Mediterranean powers; Valencia and Aragon were her allies, the Balearic islands her possession, Italy (especially Siena) her cultural foster-mother. The characteristic features of Catalan painting were gold backgrounds and stucco reliefs—these lingered on much longer than elsewhere—and a charming atmosphere of mild melancholy. In about 1400 Luis Borassa was the head of a famous workshop in Barcelona. The finest work to come out of it was the huge altarpiece at Vich—one of a type that Catalan communities frequently commissioned. A *Scourging of Christ* in the Castres museum shows how violent Catalan art, though basically gentle, could become.

Later, Franco-Flemish influences dominated the school. The Valencian artist Luis Dalmau, in particular, travelled widely in Flanders; his altarpiece of *The Councillors of Barcelona* is completely in the style of Van Eyck. Nevertheless Italy continued to exert a certain influence and its links with Valencia were strengthened by the active hegemony of the Borgia family, which originated from Aragon, had settled in Valencia and eventually produced Pope Alexander VI.

In the middle of the fifteenth century an artist with a very clearly defined personality, Jaume Huguet, emerged in Barcelona. The intensity and truth of his panels of *St Vincent* are quite outstanding. His famous picture of *St George* is dominated by the same qualities, and a sort of romantic, chivalric poetry. The story of St George rescuing the princess from a dragon was a favourite theme with Catalan artists. It was presented with great dramatic brilliance by the so-called Master of St George. Jaume Huguet shows his St George after the fight; his passion is only to be discerned through a dignified, serious, meticulously drawn and infinitely graceful exterior.

FIFTEENTH-CENTURY PORTUGAL

It was not until the middle of the fifteenth century that Portugal began to play a part in the history of European painting. At this time there occurred an event which was of importance not only to the Portuguese school, but also to the Hispano-Flemish school of Castille: this was the visit of Jan van Eyck, Philip the Good's painter, to Portugal in 1429. He was one of the ambassadors sent to ask for the hand of the Infanta, Isabella of Portugal. There is undoubtedly a Van Eyck-like quality in the polyptych of *St Vincent*, but there is also a very individual poetry and atmosphere which have little to do with Flemish realism.

This polyptych, one of the finest masterpieces of world painting, is by Nuño Gonçalves, who was appointed Royal Painter in 1450. It was painted between 1460 and 1467. In the centre is St Vincent, the patron saint of the kingdom and of Lisbon, and round him the whole of Portuguese society, from the highest (King Alfonso V, the future John II, Henry the Navigator as a child) to the lowest (the humble fisherfolk who made up the commons of Portugal). In fact this huge composition must be read as a sea- or adventure-poem — in other words, a poem of Portugal. For Portugal, tucked away in the furthest corner of Europe, opens on to the seas which, as a later poet, Camoens, sang, 'had never been sailed by man.' Nets and ropes appear in this picture as later they would appear, with other maritime attributes, in Manueline art, and one feels sure that the minds of the men shown are occupied with great exploration-projects. The drawing is strict, the colours brilliant, particularly the white, and the composition grandiose; but even the smallest details are precise. In Gonçalves' painting there is a strength, skill and purity which one can hardly avoid comparing with the perfection of the Flemish primitives. But equally striking is the very different and very specific spirituality of this dense, serious, lyrical and truly Portuguese art.

NUÑO GONÇALVES, ?-1471. KING ALFONSO V (DETAIL FROM THE ST VINCENT POLYPTYCH). MUSEU DE ARTE ANTIGA, LISBON

NUÑO GONÇALVES. PRINCE JOHN, THE FUTURE KING JOHN II (DETAIL FROM THE ST VINCENT POLYPTYCH). MUSEU DE ARTE ANTIGA, LISBON

NUÑO GONÇALVES. PRINCE HENRY THE NAVIGATOR (DETAIL FROM THE ST VINCENT POLYPTYCH). MUSEU DE ARTE ANTIGA, LISBON

GERMAN SCHOOL OF THE FIFTEENTH CENTURY

MASTER OF THE UPPER RHINE OR MIDDLE RHINE. PARADISE GARDEN. STÄDELSCHES KUNSTINSTITUT, FRANKFURT

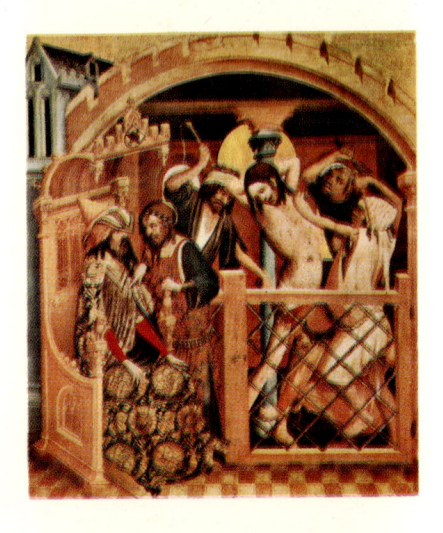

MASTER FRANCKE, ACTIVE *c.* 1400-1430. SCOURGING, *c.* 1425. KUNSTHALLE, HAMBURG

MASTER OF THE VIRGIN OF BENEDIKTBEUREN, ACTIVE *c.* 1400. VIRGIN AND CHILD. ALTE PINAKOTHEK, MUNICH

The beginnings of German panel-painting—approximately at the start of the fifteenth century—were closely linked with the political and social condition of the country. There was little unity of development. Through trade, the German towns had become prosperous with astonishing rapidity. They were practically independent and their wealthy inhabitants were often eager to make a grand show. On the other hand, there was hardly any princely patronage and no Court to give a direction to art. Thus Germany was made up of a number of neighbouring but independent centres which held little communication with each other. Often the schools which grew up in these regions looked for guidance to other countries—Flanders, Burgundy or Italy.

In general, artists painted on single panels, but the most important vehicle for expression was the altarpiece made up of a number of panels grouped in ensembles which became more and more gigantic and often contained painted sculpture as well as pure painting. At the height of its development, the altarpiece comprised a central part, usually with sculpted decoration, a crowning panel over it, a *predella* below and wings on both sides; these last were often double and painted on both back and front. Thus one altarpiece could produce a variety of effects according to whether the wings were closed or open.

One of the first German schools was Cologne, which produced a style distinguished for its rather affected sweetness—a quality which some, and notably the Romantics, have been pleased to admire as mysticism. The Master of St Veronica, active about 1410-1420, is the first of the Cologne artists to reach a really high standard.

It must have been at about this time that a charming picture, *The Paradise Garden,* attributed to a master of either the Upper or Middle Rhine, was painted. It shows a walled garden in which, protected from the world outside,

98

GERMAN SCHOOL OF THE FIFTEENTH CENTURY

saints, angels, youths and a child (in fact, they all look like children) are reading, making music, plucking fruit, drawing water—all on a smooth greensward sprinkled with flowers. The work is still very close to miniature-painting.

Because of their international trade, the Hanseatic towns were particularly susceptible to foreign influence and new ideas. In the second half of the fourteenth century one Master Bertram was working in Hamburg; he painted, sculpted and produced several altarpiece-panels in which the forms stand out boldly against gold backgrounds. But Hamburg's greatest painter was Master Francke, who in 1424 produced an altarpiece for the Johanniskirche; it had been commissioned by merchant-mariners who traded with England. In all probability he was not himself a native of Hamburg since his style seems to derive directly from Burgundian art. His colour is lively and charming, his imagination fertile enough for him to be able to invent episodes and scenes with supreme ease. Thus in the *Scourging*, Christ and the soldiers are shown behind a metal grating which pushes them into the background. His inventions are many; he also takes an interest in landscape and stresses tree-silhouettes.

The Abbey of Benediktbeuren in Upper Bavaria produced at least one enigmatic work which is probably not Bavarian at all—a *Virgin and Child*. The background is gold and the blues and reds of the garments blend together subtly. In one hand the Virgin holds an apple with which she is amusing the Child. The subject was, of course, often used, particularly in sculpture, but here the Child's movement is much more natural than was usual at that period.

Historians have often discussed the probable influence of the Councils held at Constance (1414-1418) and Basle (1431-1443) on south-west German art; they have even, with a certain amount of over-emphasis, coined the term 'Council painters'. In 1431 Lucas

CONRAD WITZ, c. 1400-1444/47. SYNAGOGUE (PANEL FROM THE HEILSPIEGEL ALTARPIECE), c. 1435. KUNSTMUSEUM, BASLE

CONRAD WITZ. SABOTHAI AND BENAJA (PANEL FROM THE HEILSPIEGEL ALTARPIECE). KUNSTMUSEUM, BASLE

CONRAD WITZ. DELIVERANCE OF ST PETER (WING OF ST PETER ALTARPIECE), c. 1444. MUSÉE D'ART ET D'HISTOIRE, GENEVA

99

GERMAN SCHOOL OF THE FIFTEENTH CENTURY

MASTER OF WERDEN
OR MASTER OF THE
LIFE OF THE VIRGIN,
ACTIVE 1460-1480.
CONVERSION OF
ST HUBERT.
NATIONAL GALLERY,
LONDON

MASTER OF THE LIFE
OF THE VIRGIN.
ANNUNCIATION.
ALTE PINAKOTHEK,
MUNICH

MASTER OF THE
LIFE OF THE VIRGIN.
VISITATION.
ALTE PINAKOTHEK,
MUNICH

Moser, a painter from Rottweil, added a despairing inscription to his altarpiece at Tiefenbronn, evidently feeling that there was no longer any place for him in a small town where Conrad Witz (who was born there) was already painting— and was to produce his master pieces. However they were interested in similar things: but whereas Witz was a great innovating genius in painting, Moser never succeeded in conveying a truly three-dimensional effect, although he painted still-lifes with great poetry and was bold enough to show Mary Magdalene and her companions in a boat cradled in crimped waves. As far as we know today, Witz's work comprises only two altarpieces—the one called the *Heilspiegel Altarpiece* (Mirror of Salvation), whose main portions are in the Basle museum (*c.* 1435), and the altarpiece of *St Peter* in the Geneva Museum (*c.* 1444). There is also a fragment of an altarpiece probably painted for a Basle convent, now in the Strasburg museum.

Witz is chiefly interested in depth and relief; to suggest it he uses heavy shadows and incorrect but energetic perspective. He breaks up the drapery to heighten the relief of the more prominent parts of the figures. And, in particular, he is fond of showing weapons with their simplified volumes which he stresses almost to the point of *trompe-l'œil*.

The 'realist' revolution triggered off by Witz and a few other painters, such as Multscher, had very little effect on Cologne, where artists were still pursuing an ideal of sweetness. The leading painter of the school, Stephan Lochner, came in fact from Meersburg on Lake Constance, the Swabian region from which Witz himself originated, but he is known to have been in Cologne from 1422 and seems to have settled there. In his masterpiece in Cologne Cathedral, the *Dombild* which Dürer went to see during his journey to the Netherlands, and in his *Adoration of the Magi*, the figures seem to be at ease and the folds of the

100

GERMAN SCHOOL OF THE FIFTEENTH CENTURY

drapery, though not so boldly emphasised as Witz's, show that the artist knew how to use shadow to bring out depth. But the figures themselves are childlike, though not without great charm.

The *Virgin of the Rose-Bower* is much like the Virgin in *The Adoration of the Magi*, but here the quest for prettiness is even more marked: witness the flowery arbour behind the Virgin and the multicoloured *putti* who swarm round her playing musical instruments.

From about 1460 the Cologne school was entirely under Netherlandish influence. The Master of the Life of the Virgin was obviously so much affected by Rogier van der Weyden and Bouts that one wonders if he was not trained in a Netherlandish workshop. As an anecdotal painter he is charming; his figures are supply posed and the wasp-waisted women wear their costumes with a coquettish air. He was extraordinarily prolific and it is now generally thought that in many cases the Master of Werden (several pictures in the National Gallery, London) has been confused with him; the Werden works would date from his youth, while the panels of the *Life of the Virgin*, once part of an altarpiece in St Ursula's in Cologne, would date from his full maturity, about 1470.

The Netherlandish influence lived on in Cologne in the work of two artists who worked there at the turn of the fifteenth century. The Master of St Bartholomew improved on the coquetry of his predecessors. In the panel showing St Bartholomew flanked by SS. Agnes and Cecilia, Agnes is a lady of high society, splendidly dressed in costly materials and holding a book and a palm in her long, tapering fingers with an affected air. The Master of the Ursula Legend painted a cycle of panels on the theme of St Ursula's life (now dispersed). One of the most charming shows the saint lying down against a background of flowers: a tall angel with multicoloured wings stands at the foot of her bed.

Oddly enough the great master

MASTER OF THE
ST URSULA
LEGEND,
ACTIVE *c.* 1490-1510.
THE ANGEL
APPEARING
TO ST URSULA,
WALLRAF-RICHARTZ
MUSEUM, COLOGNE

STEPHAN LOCHNER,
1400 ?-1451.
VIRGIN OF
THE ROSE-BOWER.
WALLRAF-RICHARTZ
MUSEUM, COLOGNE

MICHAEL PACHER,
c. 1435-1498.
ST WOLFGANG
AND THE DEVIL
(PANEL FROM THE
ALTARPIECE OF 'THE
FATHERS OF
THE CHURCH'),
c. 1483.
ALTE PINAKOTHEK,
MUNICH

101

GERMAN SCHOOL OF THE FIFTEENTH CENTURY

MASTER OF THE
ST BARTHOLOMEW
ALTARPIECE,
c. 1450-1510?
ST BARTHOLOMEW
BETWEEN
ST AGNES AND
ST CECILIA.
ALTE PINAKOTHEK,
MUNICH

MARTIN
SCHONGAUER.
THE NATIVITY.
ALTE PINAKOTHEK,
MUNICH

MARTIN
SCHONGAUER,
1430/35-1491.
NOLI ME TANGERE.
UNTERLINDEN
MUSEUM, COLMAR

of the other side of Germany remained largely impervious to what is usually understood by the spirit of the Renaissance. Michael Pacher came from the Tyrol, a region open to Italian influences, and it is quite obvious that he studied Mantegna closely. He borrowed the density of Mantegna's wood-carvings, probably particularly attractive to him since he himself was a very great sculptor in wood. But he does not seem to have been influenced by Antique art. The whole of the altarpiece of *St Wolfgang* on the shores of the Abersee was painted by him. It was commissioned in 1472 and dates from 1479 and 1481; by good fortune it has remained intact. Not long afterwards he painted the panels of another altarpiece, that of *The Fathers of the Church*, now in the Munich Pinakothek. There are also a few portions of an altarpiece dedicated to Thomas à Becket in Vienna and Graz. Pacher's large, solid figures are set against architecture whose perspective effects bear a certain resemblance to those of Conrad Witz.

Towards the end of his life there is evidence that Pacher was at Salzburg. The best known master of the Salzburg school, Frueauf the Elder, divided his time between that town and Passau from 1470 to 1507. His work is more archaic and banal than Pacher's, though the nude figure in *The Man of Sorrows* has a certain dry elegance.

At about the same time various other towns were becoming prominent, often only because of the work of a single artist. In about 1475, for instance, Friedrich Herlin, an artist much influenced by Rogier van der Weyden, was working in the small Imperial town of Noerdlingen. The inside of the wings on his altarpiece show the *Female Donors* in their pews; their starched veils are almost as rigid as the wooden pews which divide the picture into compartments.

The Imperial city of Nuremberg, on the other hand, virtually formed a State. Its first painter of note, Pleydenwurff, brought to his work

GERMAN SCHOOL OF THE FIFTEENTH CENTURY

a great sense of harmony and a refinement heavily influenced by the Netherlandish manner.

He was followed by the man who married his widow. Wohlgemut was a business-like artist and organized the painting of many altarpieces; these verge on the commonplace, though they have a certain force, but would hardly merit attention if Wohlgemut had not been Dürer's teacher.

But the man through whom German painting finally attained a position of dignity was the Alsatian painter Schongauer, the 'fair Martin' who was born in Colmar in the middle of the fifteenth century, founded a workshop which acquired a tremendous reputation, and died in 1491. In fact, it was his copper-engravings rather than his paintings which aroused the greatest admiration—so great that Michelangelo made a coloured copy of one of his prints. The birth and development of engraving were events of capital importance to Germany. Schongauer was not the first engraver but his were the first works to penetrate everywhere because of their elegance, even their mannerism. The only paintings known to be by him are *The Virgin of the Rose-Bower* in the Church of St Martin at Colmar and, it is almost certain, the little *Nativity* in the Alte Pinakothek at Munich. There is no mistaking the influence of the Netherlands, especially Rogier van der Weyden—it was almost universal at this period—but it has been perfectly assimilated. The Virgin wears a vermilion dress; her fingers are extremely slender, almost emaciated; and the large-bellied Child is treated in a highly realistic fashion. The Mother and Child sit on a stretch of grass strewn with little flowers. The Dominicans of Colmar had commissioned Schongauer to paint an altarpiece which when open would show scenes of the Passion. Most of the panels were painted by a pupil under Schongauer's direction and in them his weaknesses are emphasised, but even this work has some of the master's charm.

FRIEDRICH HERLIN, 1435 ?-1500. GROUP OF FEMALE DONORS, 1462. STADTMUSEUM, NÖRDLINGEN

RUELAND FRUEAUF THE ELDER, 1440/50-1507. MAN OF SORROWS. ALTE PINAKOTHEK, MUNICH

HANS MALER, ACTIVE 1500-1529. POSTHUMOUS PORTRAIT OF MARY OF BURGUNDY, c. 1510. LEHMAN COLLECTION, NEW YORK

THE HIGH RENAISSANCE IN ITALY

LEONARDO DA VINCI,
1452-1519.
VIRGIN
(DETAIL FROM
THE ANNUNCIATION),
c. 1475.
UFFIZI, FLORENCE

LEONARDO DA VINCI,
UNFINISHED
PORTRAIT
OF A MUSICIAN,
c. 1485
AMBROSIANA
LIBRARY,
MILAN

LEONARDO DA VINCI.
PORTRAIT OF
GINEVRA BENCI,
c. 1478.
LIECHTENSTEIN
COLLECTION,
VADUZ

All the problems and achievements of fifteenth-century Florentine art were epitomized and expressed in their noblest form in the work of that century's most striking genius, Leonardo da Vinci. With the aid of chiaroscuro he was able to reconcile all the opposing demands raised by painting: expressiveness and proportion, perspective and anatomy, strict geometrical composition and the rendering of detail, the need to make figures stand out and the need to integrate them with the landscape. In his work light and shade create space, envelop forms, suggest distance, lend harmony to colour and, sometimes, constitute the true subject of the picture. But it is difficult to deal with Leonardo only as a painter, for he was equally important in architecture and sculpture—fields in which we can judge his achievements only from sketches and unreliable imitations. The key to his painting and his whole activity lies in his literary, scientific and theoretical writings.

He was born in the village of Vinci, the son of a lawyer who in 1469 apprenticed him to Verrocchio. By 1475 he had set up as an independent painter; in 1481 he left Florence to serve Lodovico il Moro, Duke of Milan. From his Florentine period dates *The Annunciation* in the Uffizi, subtle and charming but bearing only too evidently the marks of Verrocchio's workshop—the careful execution and profusion of ornament. His fascinating *Portrait of Ginevra Benci,* bathed in chiaroscuro, is a step towards greater individuality. The unfinished *Adoration of the Magi* gives a foretaste of all his future characteristics: the pyramid of figures, extended landscape, subtle use of lighting, crowd effects and facial expressions. As in the later *Last Supper,* the whole is imbued with a feeling of spiritual revelation.

During his years in Milan (1481-1499), he painted *The Madonna of the Rocks,* which might be called the manifesto of Luminism and the new principles of composition, and *The Last Supper* (1499), a monu-

104

THE HIGH RENAISSANCE IN ITALY

mental work on Masaccioesque lines but with an infinite richness of movement and emotion disciplined by strictly symmetrical composition. From 1500 to 1506 he again lived in Florence and this time painted *The Virgin, Child and St Anne* (not completed until later)—a masterly solution of the problem of integrating figures and landscape. A whole world of subtle relationships is built up between the human figures—tenderness, indulgent wisdom—set against a background of theology. *The Battle of Anghiari,* begun at the same time (it was later abandoned and fell into ruins because of a technical error), was a dispassionate analysis of the pictorial aspect of the 'very bestial madness of war', showing the grimaces of fury and physical effort, strange armour and weapons, the effects of light in the smoke. After the rather different Milan portraits *(Lady with the Ermine, Portrait of a Musician),* that of Mona Lisa, now usually thought to have been painted while Leonardo was living in Rome (1513-1515), returns to the formula of *Ginevra Benci* but imparts a striking new depth to it. Long before it won a facile fame through its strange landscape and celebrated smile, it was admired for its masterly and delicate chiaroscuro, its tactile qualities and harmonious composition. In *John the Baptist* in the Louvre, much disfigured by over-painting, the qualities of Leonardo's art are shown in their most extreme form; it is essentially a play of light and shade on a fragile figure which suggests an elusive spiritual meaning.

The story of Leonardo's life is obscured by the many works which are now lost, in ruins or incomplete. It could hardly be otherwise with an artist for whom painting was nothing less than the synthesis in concrete terms of all knowledge and who thought it essential to rebuild that knowledge from its very foundations so as to be able to capture life itself, the struggle of the elements, the omnipresent flow of water, the universal light.

LEONARDO DA VINCI. LA GIOCONDA (MONA LISA), 1513-1515. LOUVRE, PARIS

LEONARDO DA VINCI. HEAD OF AN ANGEL (DETAIL FROM THE VIRGIN OF THE ROCKS), 1483-1487. LOUVRE, PARIS

LEONARDO DA VINCI. THE VIRGIN, CHILD AND ST ANNE, c. 1506-1510. LOUVRE, PARIS

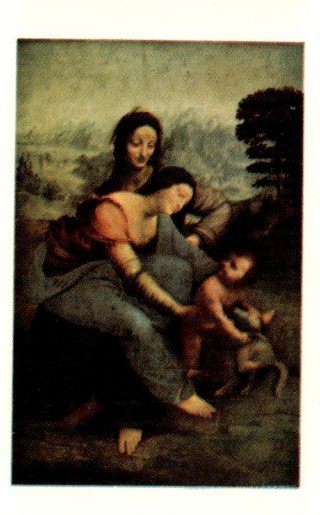

THE HIGH RENAISSANCE IN ITALY

PIETRO VANNUCCI
KNOWN AS
PERUGINO,
c. 1445-1523.
ST MICHAEL.
NATIONAL GALLERY,
LONDON

PERUGINO.
APOLLO AND
MARSYAS.
LOUVRE, PARIS

PERUGINO.
ST MARY
MAGDALENE,
1496-1500.
PALAZZO PITTI,
FLORENCE

It is difficult to account for the origins of the art of Pietro Vanucci, known as Perugino. His city, Perugia, situated in 'la dolce Umbria', had close artistic links with Siena and favoured such Florentine artists as Fra Angelico, Domenico Veneziano, Gozzoli: thus everything predisposed the local school to a facile art, a softening of the grand manner of Piero della Francesca, a taste for spacious, open landscapes, balanced scenes, light, clear colours. The young Perugino has been suggested as the author of certain panels of the *Life of St Bernardino* (Perugia, dated 1473) which are in a delicious version of this 'Umbrian' style. But in about 1475 the painter seems to have frequented Verrocchio's workshop; Piero della Francesca's influence, of which Perugino's first biographer speaks, can be seen in the Sistine Chapel frescoes (painted in 1481) in which the treatment of space is open, clear and airy.

Despite his gifts and the successes of his early years, his art soon burned itself out. With the aid of his large workshop he produced a number of pious compositions filled with monotonous figures symmetrically arranged (*Madonna with John the Baptist and St Sebastian,* Uffizi, 1493). Their rather sickly charm attracted an undemanding clientèle and ensured Perugino a success which grew ever larger towards the end of the century. Nevertheless the *Apollo and Marsyas* in the Louvre proves that he was still capable of fresh, unhackneyed inspiration on occasion. The frescoes in the Collegio del Cambio of Perugia which he executed in 1500 to a very 'up-to-date' Humanist programme worked out by a local scholar, include some figures so graceful and spontaneous that they have even been mistaken for early work by Raphael's hand. In 1505 Perugino was invited to Mantua where he ended his life docilely painting super-subtle allegories for Isabella d'Este. But the success of his manner left a lasting mark on the art of central Italy even as far as Ferrara.

106

THE HIGH RENAISSANCE IN ITALY

For several years, between the decline of Florence and the rise of Rome under Julius II, Umbrian artists held the centre of the stage in Italy. Signorelli, Perugino and his pupil Pinturicchio were the most sought-after artists in the country. The first two were already working in the Sistine Chapel in 1481; from 1492 to 1494 Pinturicchio decorated the apartments of Pope Alexander Borgia in the Vatican. In 1500 Perugino was at work on the Collegio del Cambio in Perugia; from 1500 to 1504 Signorelli was completing the frescoes in the Chapel of San Brizio in Orvieto Cathedral. In 1508 Perugino, Pinturicchio and the Sienese artist, Sodoma, began to decorate the Vatican 'Stanze'—a task finally carried out by their young compatriot, Raphael.

Later generations all agreed that Pinturicchio (his real name was Bernardo di Betto) deserved his reputation least. He was an ostentatious, archaizing painter who crammed his works with gold ornament, patterns and damascening which later became a standard joke with Florentine purists. His drawing was feeble and his composition non-existent; there can be no doubt that he deliberately aimed at his pseudo-archaic effects. However, his decorations in the Borgia apartments are historically important for two reasons. They are the first works to make great play with 'grotesques' (fantastic ornaments in 'the Classical style' with which Signorelli was later to achieve such striking effects) and with Egyptian motifs: Giovanni Nanni of Viterbo (incidentally a notorious literary forger) who had devised the programme, had been inspired to associate the bull of the Borgias with the Apis of Egypt.

Pinturicchio worked in Siena from 1503 to 1508 (frescoes in the Biblioteca Piccolomini, paintings for the Palazzo Petrucci), sobered down and cultivated an archaism of greater charm *(Penelope Weaving)*. But the great Classicism of Rome condemned his art to oblivion.

PERUGINO. PORTRAIT OF A YOUNG MAN. HERMITAGE, LENINGRAD

BERNARDINO PINTURICCHIO, 1454-1513. ELEONORA OF PORTUGAL (DETAIL OF FRESCO). PICCOLOMINI LIBRARY, SIENA CATHEDRAL

PINTURICCHIO. PORTRAIT OF A BOY. GEMÄLDEGALERIE, DRESDEN

THE HIGH RENAISSANCE IN ITALY

RAPHAEL SANZIO,
1483-1520.
PORTRAIT OF
AGNOLO DONI,
c. 1506.
PALAZZO PITTI,
FLORENCE

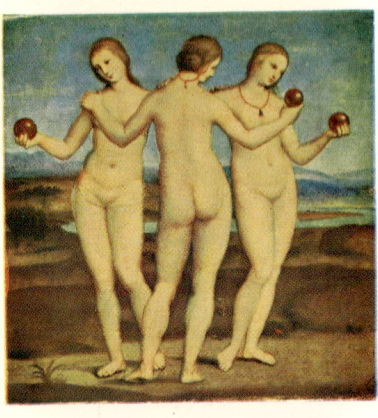

RAPHAEL.
THE THREE GRACES,
c. 1500
MUSÉE CONDÉ,
CHANTILLY

RAPHAEL.
PORTRAIT OF
BINDO ALTOVITI,
c. 1513
NATIONAL GALLERY
OF ART,
WASHINGTON

It was Raphael who defined the outlook of the Italian Renaissance towards Classical Antiquity and so gave it a centre of gravity. A number of contradictory influences contributed to his make-up but he was no inconsistent eclectic. Though he rapidly acquired a tremendous background of knowledge, his art never lost its spontaneity. For him Classicism was merely fitting expression of his natural genius, as one can see from his splendid drawings.

He grew up in the Umbrian tradition; his first master was Perugino. But he was deeply influenced by the nobler cultural ideas of the Court of the Montefeltres which devised the concept of the 'universal man', the Renaissance ideal. Though bounded by the formal limits of Perugino's style, he nevertheless showed from the beginning an incomparable freshness of feeling which made use of the better qualities of his master's easy harmony (*The Three Graces*, Chantilly, *Vision of a Knight*, London). In *The Marriage of the Virgin* (Milan), a variation of a similar picture by Perugino, his master's rather stiff, formal version is unified and animated by a sublime, spiritual quality. In Florence (1504-1508) he turned towards Leonardo, as did so many others, imitating his 'pyramid' composition (*La Belle Jardinière*, Louvre), his chiaroscuro (*Madonna del Granduco*, Florence, Pitti), his type of portraiture. But his conviction always subdues the formula. In 1508 he was invited to Rome through the influence of his uncle, Bramante, and found the city undergoing a transformation. Julius II, the most 'imperial' Pope since the Middle Ages, wanted art which would measure up to the grandeur of his dreams. As the centre of a European rebirth, Rome needed monuments which would proclaim her noble mission: St Peter's and the Vatican. Like Bramante and Michelangelo, Raphael felt qualified to produce such works. He was commissioned to paint the Vatican 'Stanze' (Julius II's apartments) and managed

THE HIGH RENAISSANCE IN ITALY

to hit on the necessary 'grand style' almost at his first attempt. In the Stanza della Segnatura (1509-1511) the groups symbolizing Theology, Philosophy, Poetry and Law, complemented and explained by the allegories on the ceiling, show the building-up of the new scholarship and faith, the Creation and daily life as recast by Humanism. These grandiose and serene paintings, a vision of a Golden Age, were followed by the dramatic narratives in the Stanza del'Eliodoro (1511-1514) with their allusions to the main events of Julius II's pontificate. Raphael was already expert conveying the feeling of Antique art; here he is stimulated by Michelangelo's art, Venetian colour and Luminism. But his overwhelming success and many commissions forced him to delegate an ever-increasing part of his work to his workshop. The two last rooms, painted for Pope Leo X (1514-1525) are largely by other artists. In the Vatican 'loggias', the dome (mosaic) of the Chigi chapel and, above all, the Villa Farnesina which created a new type, *(Galatea, Story of Psyche),* he forged a closer bond between painting and architecture.

While continuing to assimilate new ideas — Roman Antiquity and echoes of Flanders are admirably synthesized in the tapestries showing *The Story of the Apostles* — Raphael extended the scope of religious painting in his *Madonnas* (from the essentially human and charming *Madonna della Sedia* to the supernatural *Sistine Madonna),* and in his *Vision of Ezekiel, Vision of St Cecilia,* and *Transfiguration;* these radiate a feeling of divinity never before expressed.

His portraits are in a different category again: they are often fascinating artistic achievements (the subtle scale of grey shades in *Baldassare Castiglione,* the grouping of the figures in ceremonial portraits like *Pope Leo X).* But they are chiefly masterpieces of the art of evoking the atmosphere of a society which declared that after the death of such an artist life was hardly worth living.

RAPHAEL. PORTRAIT OF POPE LEO X WITH THE CARDINALS LUIGI DE' ROSSI AND GIULIO DE' MEDICI. UFFIZI, FLORENCE

RAPHAEL. MADONNA DELLA SEDIA. PALAZZO PITTI, FLORENCE

RAPHAEL. THE MASS OF BOLSENA (DETAIL OF FRESCO), 1511-1514. STANZA DEL' ELIODORO, VATICAN, ROME

THE HIGH RENAISSANCE IN ITALY

MICHELANGELO
BUONARROTTI,
1475-1564.
THE HOLY FAMILY,
1503.
UFFIZI, FLORENCE

MICHELANGELO.
ADAM (DETAIL OF
'THE CREATION
OF EVE'),
1507-1512.
FRESCO IN THE
SISTINE CHAPEL,
ROME

MICHELANGELO.
ORIGINAL SIN
(DETAIL),
1508-1512.
FRESCO IN THE
SISTINE CHAPEL,
ROME

In the early years of the sixteenth century Leonardo met Michelangelo in Florence; the older man, a passionate lover of nature and the natural sciences, comparatively indifferent to religious and literary questions, quarrelled with the young sculptor, saturated with Humanism and poetry, and a prey to moral and religious crises since adolescence. Later, in Rome, Michelangelo fell out with Raphael, whom he had known in Florence. This time the conflict was between a powerful, wilful artist, glorying in his misanthropy, and an artist whose guiding principle was to give pleasure, who was accessible to all influences. But the solitary genius who hated to owe anything to anybody and took no pupils (for which he was much criticized), became the idol of sixteenth-century artists and art-lovers.

He learned the rudiments of his craft from Ghirlandaio, the last master one would associate with him. But his real teachers were the Antiques (in the Medici collection), Donatello and the Platonic Humanists, whose society he cultivated. They led him to conceive beauty as an insight into spirituality, a manifestation of divinity; to believe that the artist possessed by a 'passion' for beauty was inspired and that in its way the poetic beauty of Antiquity revealed the same truth as the Christian religion. Michelangelo never accepted these optimistic doctrines unreservedly: after the advent of Savonarola his grave scruples made him see beauty as a fatal trap for the soul and seek salvation in remorse and asceticism. (Even this guilt-feeling had been anticipated by Platonism which saw it as 'Saturnine melancholy', a mark of genius.)

Michelangelo began as a sculptor and while still young became more famous than any artist before him. It was not until 1503 that he tried his hand at painting. The city of Florence commissioned him to paint *The Battle of Cascina* for one of the rooms in the Palazzo Vecchio. It was to show soldiers surprised while bathing and to

THE HIGH RENAISSANCE IN ITALY

serve as a counterpart for Leonardo's proposed *Battle of Anghiari*. However the fresco was never painted and the cartoon, a miracle of pictorial invention, was torn to pieces by enthusiastic artists. In 1503 he also painted *The Holy Family* whose grouping shows Leonardo's influence, though the sculptural treatment and cold colours are Michelangelo's alone.

Five years later, in Rome, Michelangelo was commissioned to decorate the huge ceiling of the Sistine. He approached it as a sculptor. He uses an impressive, semi-illusionist series of thrones, socles and openings as a setting for countless figures of all sizes, representing the faculties and destiny of the soul. These are arranged in three superimposed tiers (the world of the darkness before Christ, the prophets who predicted the light to come, scenes from Genesis). The nude figures and regal draperies owe something to both Florentine design and Antique monumentality; their varying relationships to the framework give the whole work its richness, tension and powerful organization.

Much later, after Michelangelo's most cherished artistic projects had fallen through and the Florentine republic which he had defended had perished, he returned to the Sistine Chapel to paint the immense *Last Judgment* (1536-1541). This time there is no architectural framework, no principles of organization —only a blue vacuum through which rise and fall naked bodies. Underlying the mastery of form is a note of private anguish and despair which cannot be ignored. The work aroused much controversy; never before had an artist expressed himself with such liberty. Apart from the violent, discordant frescoes in the Pauline Chapel, this was his last painted work. His drawings and incomplete sculptures still showed his art in transformation: the hand which had been so assured could now only produce a hesitant and tragic evocation of an unforgettable expressive power.

MICHELANGELO. DANIEL, 1508-1512. FRESCO IN THE SISTINE CHAPEL, ROME

MICHELANGELO. DELPHIC SIBYL (DETAIL), 1508-1512. FRESCO IN THE SISTINE CHAPEL, ROME

MICHELANGELO. JUDITH, 1508-1512. FRESCO IN THE SISTINE CHAPEL, ROME

THE HIGH RENAISSANCE IN ITALY

ANDREA DEL SARTO,
1486-1531.
PORTRAIT OF A
YOUNG MAN, CALLED
'THE SCULPTOR'.
NATIONAL GALLERY,
LONDON

ANDREA DEL SARTO.
PORTRAIT OF
LUCREZIA,
THE WIFE OF
THE PAINTER.
PRADO, MADRID

JACOPO CARRUCCI,
KNOWN AS
PONTORMO,
1494-1556.
PORTRAIT OF
UGOLINO MARTELLI.
NATIONAL GALLERY,
WASHINGTON

After its three greatest masters had left, almost simultaneously, for Rome, Florentine art degenerated into a sort of local, minor Classicism. Fra Bartolommeo, a supporter of Savonarola, combined the traditions of Perugino and Leonardo and a few Venetian touches with his own academic art. This is sometimes noble but always perilously near insipidity, particularly when he worked in collaboration with Albertinelli. His drawings are remarkable for their refinement.

Andrea del Sarto's nervous power got Florentine art out of this impasse. He retained only the externals of Raphael's tranquillity and Leonardo's wisdom. Only his very earliest frescoes (in the Church of the Annunziata) are relaxed: the *Life of John the Baptist* in the Carmelite monastery, with its deliberately Classical *grisaille*, nevertheless has touches of intimacy and pathos; the strange Leonardesque *Madonna with the Sack* (1525) is in a refined, delicate style which heralds the anxiety of *Charity* (Louvre, 1528) and *The Assumption* (Florence, Pitti, *c.* 1530). In his portraits, always moving and almost too 'interesting', his personality proclaims itself without reserve.

In fact this ambiguous artist was paving the way for Tuscan Mannerism, which his pupils developed to the full. Today Mannerism is taken to mean a complex trend which emerged between 1520 and 1600 and was therefore contemporary with a series of critical events: the Reformation, the Counter-Reformation, the establishment of authoritarian governments in Italy linked with Spain and the Empire. The general feeling of artistic decadence, the ascendancy of political and religious power over the arts, the excessive production, the international levelling of taste brought about by the academies and the publication of engravings—all these things caused a major crisis in art. Its symptoms were, on the one hand, the birth of an 'official' art, pompous and pedantic, and, on the other, escape into fantasy, preciosity, 'rustic' works, virtuosity.

THE HIGH RENAISSANCE IN ITALY

The first generation of Mannerists, the so-called 'Anti-Classicists', attempted to blow up the enclosing walls of Classicism from within. In a deliberate quest for discordance, they systematically used the traditional forms in an anti-traditional way, distorted proportions and elongated figures. Pontormo, who began as an elegant decorator, a delicate, slightly shrill, painter like his master Andrea del Sarto, suddenly submitted first to the influence of Dürer and then to that of Michelangelo, although neither was particularly suited to his personality. In no other painter is the Mannerist frenzy so evident (*The Deposition of the Cross,* Florence, Santa Felicità ; *The Passion,* Monastery of Val d'Ema). His portraits, with their strange proportions and striking intensity, and his fluent drawings suggest a tortured, wounded sensibility. Pontormo ended his life on the brink of madness; he spent ten years working on a fresco of St Lawrence in which he emphasised the stridency and refinement of his art to such a point that the public refused to countenance it; the work was destroyed.

Like Vasari, the biographer of the Renaissance artists, Angelo Bronzino, a pupil of Pontormo, is one of the most typical figures of the second phase of Mannerism, when Academicism and Court art triumphed. He is best known as the portraitist of the Florentine Court, given a Spanish flavour by the Grand Duchess Eleonora, Cosmo I's wife. His paintings are polished in execution; the robes and drapes are vitally important. Expressiveness is strictly excluded; their chief merits are the very refined colour-harmonies, the carefully studied and elegant design, the firmness of volumes and contours and ceremonial severity. Bronzino also painted crowded allegories, masterly in technique, a *Holy Family* which is a manifesto of Academicism and cartoons for tapestries stuffed with learned allusions. Similar trends are only to be found in Flanders, France or Spain.

ANGELO BRONZINO, 1503-1572. PORTRAIT OF ELEONORA OF TOLEDO AND HER SON FERDINAND. UFFIZI, FLORENCE

BRONZINO. ALLEGORY OF TIME AND LOVE. NATIONAL GALLERY, LONDON

BRONZINO. PORTRAIT OF A YOUNG MAN. METROPOLITAN MUSEUM, NEW YORK

THE HIGH RENAISSANCE IN ITALY

ANDREA SOLARIO,
c. 1460-1520.
VIRGIN WITH THE
GREEN CUSHION,
c. 1500.
LOUVRE, PARIS

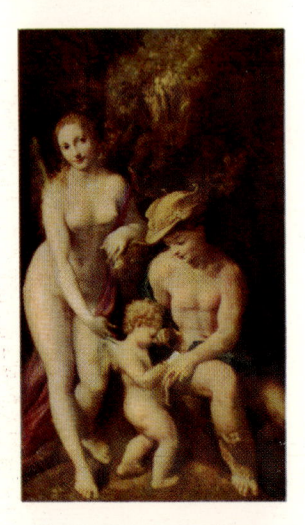

ANTONIO ALLEGRI,
KNOWN AS
CORREGGIO.
BEFORE 1489-1534.
VENUS, MERCURY
AND CUPID.
NATIONAL GALLERY,
LONDON

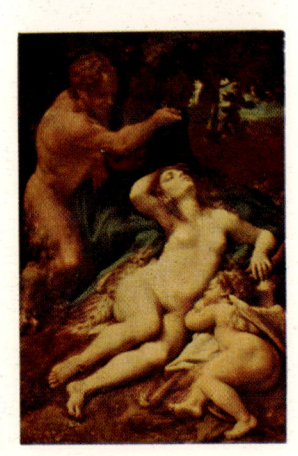

CORREGGIO.
ANTIOPE ASLEEP,
c. 1525.
LOUVRE, PARIS

At the start of the sixteenth century the fate of Lombard art was determined by Leonardo's sojourn in Milan and (to a lesser extent) the nearness of Venice. Leonardo's school, in the strict sense, produced no great masters; the best known of them, Luini, had not studied in the workshop itself and never renounced his links with earlier Lombard artists. Andrea Solario, another unorthodox disciple, had worked in France and learned from Transalpine art; he owes his fame to the *Madonna with the Green Cushion,* with its traditional Lombard colourism.

There is nothing to account for the phenomenon of Correggio — no local school, no master's influence. Apparently he never saw either Venice or Rome. The Mantegnas in Mantua may have inspired his illusionist frescoes, though they are treated in a spirit quite alien to the hardness and plasticity of the 'Bridal Chamber'; in Mantua he also came in contact with Lorenzo Costa, who followed in the footsteps of Perugino. However this does not account for his art; his work is only partially reminiscent of the Leonardesque school, for which grace and sweetness were the supreme virtues. His voluptuous, uncontrolled style is unique.

The altarpiece of *St Francis,* painted when he was twenty, recalls Costa's work. But from 1519, when Correggio settled in Parma, he experimented with new ideas. The decoration on a dome of the Convent of San Paolo are an experiment parallel to that of the Farnesina, but with a freedom of imagination and movement never before seen at Rome. In the dome of the Church of San Giovanni Evangelista he painted an extraordinary *Ascension;* round the edge a ring of foreshortened apostles encircles Christ in glory, while the pearly clouds, mauve figures with their frenzied gestures, and feeling of complete liberty create an almost Baroque atmosphere. The *Assumption of the Virgin* in the dome of the cathedral (1526-1530) goes even further in this direction; the

THE HIGH RENAISSANCE IN ITALY

trompe-l'œil of the drum heralds the vast display of light and colour, merged in a sky swarming with angels, the Blessed, and tangled clouds. In the series of *Loves of Jupiter* (for the palace of Mantua, about 1530), he carried this hazy, sensuous, charming painting, this mingling of colourism and chiaroscuro to extremes. Some of his religious paintings are more baffling: *The Marriage of St Catherine* in the Louvre; '*Day*' and '*Night*' in Parma and Dresden. His tendency to combine delicacy with frenzy, contrasting shapes with subtleties of light, makes a strange impression which is increased by the way the composition is based on sweeping diagonal lines. But however unexpected this art is, in its internal coherence and lack of caprice it almost rivals the greatest work of the High Renaissance.

But Mannerism was on the way in. Francesco Mazzola, called Parmigianino, used certain features of Correggio's style as the basis for a highly cerebral, elegant, refined art. This art could be reduced to basic formulae which were imitated throughout Europe — long, thin figures with very narrow heads, fingers delicately parted, abrupt transitions from large figures in the foreground to tiny ones in the background, graceful S-curves — all the delicate, refined grace of the famous *Madonna with the Long Neck*. In his amazing portraits this grace is supplemented by a taut nervosity and tortured sensibility. Parmigianino is the Mannerist *par excellence*. The shock-effect his pictures produced is illustrated by an anecdote in Vasari's life of him: when, during the sack of Rome, soldiers went to pillage his studio, they saw him painting the *Madonna of the Rose* and withdrew in silence. A model Mannerist, Parmigianino finally devoted himself to alchemy and went insane.

At the same time in Ferrara Giovanni Luteri, known as Dosso Dossi, who was a friend of Ariosto, was reviving romantic art, with the aid of the exotic colour of Venice and Flemish 'extravaganzas'.

FRANCESCO MAZZOLA, KNOWN AS PARMIGIANINO, 1503-1540. 'LA BELLA' (DETAIL). PINACOTECA, NAPLES

PARMIGIANINO. LA MADONNA DEL COLLO LUNGO, 1534-1540. UFFIZI, FLORENCE

DOSSO DOSSI, c. 1480-1542. CIRCE (DETAIL). NATIONAL GALLERY OF ART, WASHINGTON

THE HIGH RENAISSANCE IN ITALY

GIORGIO
BARBARELLI,
KNOWN AS
GIORGIONE,
1478?-1510.
CONCERT
CHAMPÊTRE.
LOUVRE, PARIS

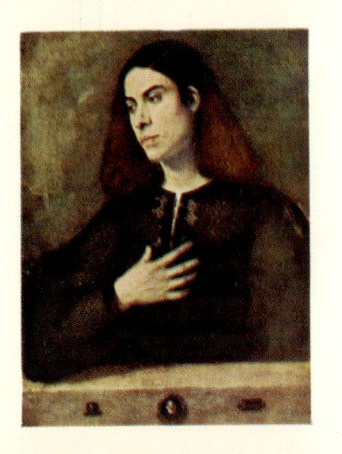

GIORGIONE.
PORTRAIT OF A MAN.
MUSÉE MAGYAR.
BUDAPEST

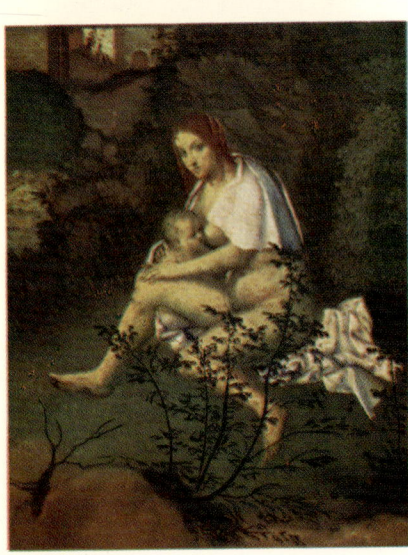

GIORGIONE.
TEMPEST (DETAIL),
c. 1505.
ACCADEMIA, VENICE

The classical era of Venetian painting began with Giorgione. He is considered to have been largely responsible (along with the elder Bellini, who died in 1516, and Titian in his earliest years) for the decisive change in 1505-1515. Giorgione died in 1510, little more than thirty years old; but without his work Bellini would never have attained his last manner, nor Titian his earliest inspiration. This revolution (exactly contemporary with the sudden emergence of Roman Classicism) might be described as a deepening of Bellini's 'tonal' vision: instead of the forms being modelled by means of the diffused light which links them with space, the starting-points seem to be space and light themselves. Vasari said that Giorgione did not work out the drawing on the canvas before applying the paint, but sketched out the work by laying on patches of colour. This disposes of the idea which has occasionally been put forward, that Leonardo's visit to Venice in 1501 was the main inspiration of Giorgione's *sfumato* and, therefore, of Venetian art in general; for Leonardo, who was essentially a 'draughtsman', modelling and volume were the main aims of painting. His *sfumato* serves the purposes of form rather than colour.

Little is definitely known about Giorgione's life and work. The success of his manner stimulated many imitators, often of high quality; Titian completed many of his unfinished paintings, probably including *The Concert*. Precise attributions are thus difficult. Giorgione seems to have frequented the company of the cultured art-lovers of Venice. The catalogue of the main collections, compiled in 1525-1545 by Michiel, indicates a demand for his works. Their subjects often remain mysterious, but various unusual iconographical details suggest that, even if he was not himself a Humanist, he at least moved in circles where music, the philosophy of love and the secrets of the 'harmonious' numbers were matters of constant interest.

THE HIGH RENAISSANCE IN ITALY

Although superficially a regular composition in the Bellini manner, the *Madonna of Castelfranco* (1504), one of the first great works definitely known to be by Giorgione, is entirely novel in its poetical treatment of light. The landscape echoes and envelops the dreamlike quality of the figures. The enigmatic *Tempest* (Venice) may represent a mythological scene after Ovid, but its greatest innovation is the lightning and its effect on the colours of the landscape: it is, as it were, a 'snapshot' in paint. It was realised very early on that Giorgione was the first painter to reject the idea that all objects must be rendered 'eternal' and to attempt, instead, to capture their 'fleetingness'. His 'melancholy' is a product of this. Nothing remains of the frescoes he painted with Titian in 1508 for the Fondaco de' Tedeschi: contemporaries were puzzled by the fact that they seemed to have no definite 'subjects'. It has been suggested that Giorgione was interested in esoteric ideas and proof of this theory has been vainly sought in the *Three Philosophers* at Vienna. But although X-rays have shown that he altered the plan of the picture (as in the *Tempest*) this proves only that he brooded over his compositions for a long time.

The famous *Sleeping Venus* in Dresden is the most perfect expression of one of Giorgione's favourite themes, the nude figure set in a landscape; the generous fulness of the light and the curves creates a feeling of complete harmony. In the *Concert Champêtre* in the Louvre, the last work that can definitely be attributed to him, this theme is enriched by all the things Giorgione loved: music, twilight, the gentle, soft countryside. The picture captures a single moment saturated in beauty, insurpassable. In a few 'Giorgionesque' works the originality and subtle interpretation of faces suggest that they are by him: *The Concert* (Florence, Pitti), finished by Titian; *The Old Woman* (Venice), embodying a realism inspired by the Northern art; *David* (Berlin, a self-portrait (?)).

GIOGIONE. THREE PHILOSOPHERS (DETAIL), *c.* 1508. KUNSTHISTORISCHES MUSEUM, VIENNA

GIORGIONE. PORTRAIT OF A YOUNG MAN. STAATLICHE MUSEEN, BERLIN

GIORGIONE. SLEEPING VENUS. GEMÄLDEGALERIE, DRESDEN

THE HIGH RENAISSANCE IN ITALY

TIZIANO VECELLIO,
KNOWN AS TITIAN,
c. 1485-1576.
MAGDALENE,
c. 1530-1540.
PALAZZO PITTI,
FLORENCE

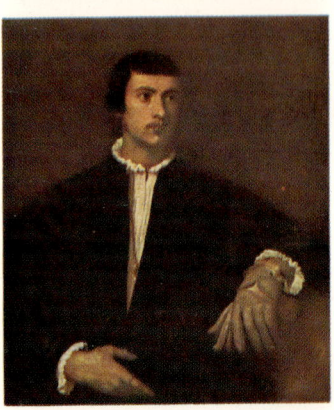

TITIAN.
MAN WITH A GLOVE,
c. 1522.
LOUVRE, PARIS

TITIAN.
VENUS OF URBINO,
1538.
UFFIZI, FLORENCE

According to an old document, Titian was born in 1477. However, everything contradicts this. Were it true, he would have been as old as Giorgione and died at the age of ninety-nine. Nevertheless the legend fits the character of 'patriarch of Venetian painting' which Titian acquired and guarantees its continuity from Bellini to Tintoretto. He became a sort of institution; to Florence and Rome 'the Venetian school' meant chiefly Titian. Charles V, Philip II, Pope Paul III, Francis I, the Dukes of Ferrara and Mantua—all flattered him, invited him, showered him with commissions. Although the 'draughtsmen' of central Italy opposed him on principle, his influence was felt everywhere, his disciples multiplied; Venetian art became, thanks to him, an integral part of the heritage of Italy, and, later, an inspiration to all Europe.

He was born in Pieve di Cadore in the Dolomites. As soon as he arrived in Venice at the beginning of the century he chose his position: side by side with Bellini, whom he imitated, and Giorgione, with whom he worked in 1508. His work stood out on account of its robust quality: the forms were full and rounded, the colours strong and balanced by means of simple contrasts. If, as in *Sacred and Profane Love* (Rome, Borghese Gallery, 1514) he chose a Platonic theme—naked beauty representing the nobler form of love, the spiritual or Uranian Venus, as opposed to the more earthly beauty surrounded by the riches of this world —the noble grouping of the figures (which for a long time were interpreted wrongly) contradicts the sentiment he is, superficially, expressing. From this early period onwards, Titian was by vocation a portraitist; he strove to convey the actual presence of a person and, with this in view, took certain 'liberties', such as using large empty areas so that the presence should make itself felt.

His large-scale religious paintings, such as *The Assumption of the Virgin* (Venice, Santa Maria dei

Frari, 1518), are monumental but not heavy. Simple structures, a few screens and breaks in chiaroscuro, give the scenes a broad foundation. *The Entombment* (Louvre, *c.* 1525) is further enhanced by the remarkably poetical treatment of light and landscape. The mythological series commissioned by Alfonso d'Este *(Bacchanals)*, with their magnificent *joie de vivre*, date from 1518-1523. Portraits like *La Bella* and compositions like the *Venus of Urbino* (1538) prolonged this Classical peak. But in about 1535-1545 Titian was infected by the epidemic of Mannerism than raging throughout Italy. His *Christ Crowned with Thorns* (Louvre, 1542) has something of the Mannerist anguish; the technique is loosened, the foreshortening exaggerated. But his visit to Rome in 1545-1546 stimulated him, as though in reaction, to heighten his burning, luminous colour, and imbue his portraits with a new and completely objective dramatic intensity (*The Aretino*, Pitti, 1545; *Paul III*, Naples, 1546). His manner became ever freer and more masterly *(Danaë)* and, particularly in the religious works, full of sparkling and visionary richness (*Martyrdom of St Lawrence*, *c.* 1567).

This freedom astounded Titian's contemporaries. Before him nobody had dared to exhibit such 'unfinished' works, with such broad brush-strokes and visible smudges. Many other artists attempted feats of virtuosity in the same style. But Titian was still adding more depth and pathos to his art (*Christ Crowned with Thorns*, Munich): he reached a new serenity in his last *Pietà*, completed by Palma Giovane.

He had covered an immense field, passing from the polished finish and meticulous outlook of his early works, through the superb triumphs of his twenties and the Mannerist anguish that followed, to the sumptuous intensity of his old age and finally the supreme inspiration of the very end of his life. Each of these stages influenced a whole generation of painters.

TITIAN.
BACCHANAL
(DETAIL),
c. 1518.
PRADO, MADRID

TITIAN.
LA BELLA,
c. 1536
PALAZZO PITTI,
FLORENCE

TITIAN.
DANAË,
1552.
PRADO, MADRID

THE HIGH RENAISSANCE IN ITALY

PALMA VECCHIO,
1480-1528.
PORTRAIT OF
A LADY,
c. 1520.
POLDI-PEZZOLI
MUSEUM, MILAN

SEBASTIANO DEL
PIOMBO,
c. 1485-1547.
DOROTHEA.
STAATLICHE MUSEEN,
BERLIN

PARIS BORDONE,
1500-1571.
VENETIAN LOVERS.
BRERA, MILAN

Inevitably, Titian's influence affected almost all the Venetian painters of his age; nevertheless within this general trend there were various divergences. A stubborn 'Giorgionesque' streak persisted in, amongst other places, Bergamo, a Venetian possession in Lombardy. Palma Vecchio was a native of Bergamo itself and stood half-way between Titian and Giorgione. One of the most memorable features of his work is the female type which he invented and reproduced in all his pictures (*Portrait of a Lady,* Milan, Poldi-Pezzoli Museum): buxom, fair-haired, with a broad face and white, gold and crimson drapery. His art is unstudied and fairly lively (altarpiece of Santa Maria Formosa), but it does not make a deep impact.

At an early age Sebastiano Luciano, known as del Piombo after Pope Clement VII had given him the much-desired sinecure of Frate del Piombo (1531), left Venice for Rome (1511). Thus he stayed in his native town long enough to know Giorgione, but hardly Titian. He was profoundly impressed by the frescoes in the Fondaco de' Tedeschi with their huge, monumental figures, and immediately adopted their 'grand manner' (*Saints* in San Bartolommeo on the Rialto, 1508). With this feeling for monumentality he was quite at home in Rome, although there he was considered, not altogether correctly, as an exponent of Venetian colourism and Luminism. Michelangelo, whose protégé he was, gave him the designs for his great *Resurrection of Lazarus* (London) and *Pietà* (Viterbo). This collaboration between a 'draughtsman' and a 'colourist' raised expectations of an ideal synthesis. But Sebastiano over-played his manner. His portraits, which aim at a Raphael-like effect (*Dorothea ; Portrait of a Woman,* Uffizi) lack Raphael's ease.

The work of Paris Bordone of Treviso represents the Mannerist branch of the Titian school. His portraits, in which he yields to the fascination of colour and

THE HIGH RENAISSANCE IN ITALY

materials, are rich and spontaneous; but a sort of affectation mars his large compositions. In them his aims remain uncoördinated.

Lorenzo Lotto is often quoted as the almost unique example of a Venetian painter who was not bewitched by the art of Titian. He paid for this intransigeance by a lasting lack of success which forced him to wander about northern Italy seeking clients in the smaller towns. In the end he was forced to admit failure; he sold his workshop and became a laybrother at Loreto. His ledger, begun in 1538, gives the details of his hopeless struggle.

His artistic personality is interesting; in part he looks back towards the archaic style, in part he anticipates Baroque. Though simple almost to the point of banality, his works are strangely disquieting. The numerous portraits, which are among the most original of his works, show how faithful he was to the Venetian manner of the preceding century, to its uniform lighting, showing up the details and the cold colour. Towards the end of his career Lotto's painting became more intimate, but it never had the nobility and psychological drama which Venice demanded of its portraitists.

He was no more at home in the atmosphere of Rome, which he visited in 1509. Raphael had only a fleeting influence on him. In fact the only real influence on his painting was that of northern Europe. His very moving landscapes show the inspiration of Germany (*St Jerome*, Louvre, 1506; the altarpiece of *St Nicholas*, Venice, 1529); the agitated figures, confused groups and details which reveal the burlesque humour of the common people suggest that he had studied German or Netherlandish engravings (altarpiece of *St Bernardino*, Bergamo, 1521; *Crucifixion*, Monte San Giusto, 1531). To this day some of the finest works by this curious artist, often particularly moving in his directness, are still in the small villages and chapels for which they were created.

LORENZO LOTTO,,
1480-1556.
PORTRAIT OF A
YOUNG MAN,
c. 1525.
STAATLICHE MUSEEN,
BERLIN

LOTTO.
PORTRAIT OF A
YOUNG MAN,
c. 1526.
CASTELLO
SFORZESCO,
MILAN

LOTTO.
PORTRAIT OF
BERNARDO DE' ROSSI,
1505.
MUSEO NAZIONALE,
NAPLES

121

THE HIGH RENAISSANCE IN ITALY

JACOPO ROBUSTI,
KNOWN AS
TINTORETTO,
1518-1594.
MERCURY AND THE
THREE GRACES,
1578.
PALAZZO DUCALE,
VENICE

TINTORETTO.
SUSANNA AND
THE ELDERS
(DETAIL),
c. 1560.
KUNSTHISTORISCHES
MUSEUM, VIENNA

TINTORETTO.
ORIGIN OF THE
MILKY WAY.
NATIONAL GALLERY,
LONDON

It was mainly through Parmigianino that Mannerism reached Venice. To a certain extent Venetian art was also influenced by the ideas of Giulio Romano, a decorative genius who had studied under Raphael, and from afar the overwhelming mastery of Michelangelo left its mark on the city, but his art was accepted only with radical modifications of its spirit. Venetian originality remained as strongly marked as ever.

Tintoretto, the leading spirit of the school which aimed to 'out-Titian Titian', was insular by birth and by choice. He left his birthplace only twice; once, in his youth, to visit Rome and again, in old age, to go to Mantua. It was Schiavone, the Venetian forerunner of Parmigianino, who first encouraged him to cultivate a free, capricious, wilfully unreal manner. By the age of twenty-one he had set up as an independent painter, but it was only after the visit to Rome (in about 1545) that his genius for scenic effect really came into its own (*The Last Supper*, 1547; *St Mark Freeing the Condemned Slave*, 1548).

Tintoretto's art is dramatic and complete in every respect. Everything adds to the intensity of expression—the picture-size, the point from which the scene is viewed, the distribution of figures and objects and accessories, the rapid, nervous treatment, the brilliant or glowing colours and, above all, the lighting, manipulated with extreme ingenuity. His imagination stops at nothing; nothing seems beyond his powers. His figures, twisted by the helical movement so characteristic of Mannerism and arranged along bold diagonal or oblique lines, are violently foreshortened and reach out in every direction; great jets of pale or golden light streak the canvas; bars of shadow are laid on with apparent arbitrariness. Tintoretto never seems to run out of ideas or energy, and worked at a speed which astonished his contemporaries. Sometimes he uses a more Titian-like manner (*Adam and*

THE HIGH RENAISSANCE IN ITALY

Eve, Venice, Accademia); sometimes he turns in the direction of Veronese (*Susannah and the Elders,* Vienna); sometimes he relieves any mechanical quality which may have crept into his painting by concentrating, unexpectedly and with great ingenuity, on detail. In the huge works commissioned from him, which he tackled without any feeling of constraint or inadequacy, the qualities and defects of his very individual style became more and more marked.

The *Miracles of St Mark* (1562-1566) show his technical skill; he distributes the figures one above the other, overlapping, lit from the front, with their backs to the light. Also in 1564 he began on the enormous cycle of the Scuola di San Rocco, on which he worked for twenty-three years. This is an unforgettable work, visionary, heady in its brilliance; the impression of overwhelming richness is diversified and complemented by striking details, deployed with equal skill in the colossal, dramatic paintings (*The Bearing of the Cross, The Crucifixion*), the *Flight into Egypt,* with its lyrical landscape and *Christ before Pilate,* with its unusual use of colour. It was followed by various works for the Palazzo Ducale—paintings in the Sala del Collegio, the Sala del Senato and, in 1588, the *Paradise* in the Sala del Maggior Consiglio. In this last Tintoretto's feeling for excess has run riot and the work—rather schematic—is inferior to the original sketch (Louvre). He does less violence to the Venetian tradition in his portraits, in which the intense life of doges and senators shines out through their ravaged faces, in a uniformly dark, sober setting.

With all his drama and passion, Tintoretto still worked hard and regularly. His charcoal drawings were obviously made in the studio, from small clay models with exaggerated muscles, but they are indelibly marked with the fire and vigour of this most vigorous of artists.

TINTORETTO. PORTRAIT OF THE PROCURATOR, JACOPO SORANZO. ACCADEMIA, VENICE

TINTORETTO. CHRIST WALKING ON THE WATERS (DETAIL). NATIONAL GALLERY, WASHINGTON

TINTORETTO. PORTRAIT OF THE SCULPTOR JACOPO SANSOVINO, 1565-1570. UFFIZI, FLORENCE

THE HIGH RENAISSANCE IN ITALY

PAOLO CALIARI, KNOWN AS VERONESE, 1526-1588. UNFAITHFULNESS. NATIONAL GALLERY. LONDON

VERONESE. PORTRAIT OF DANIELE BARBARO. PALAZZO PITTI, FLORENCE

VERONESE. MARS AND VENUS. GALLERIA SABAUDA, TURIN

Like Tintoretto, Veronese remained on the fringes of Mannerism. But whereas the one transcended the limits of the style of the period because of his fiery excesses, the other was distinguished by his exceptional balance. There is no trace of restlessness in Veronese's rich, serene art; it means exactly what it says and derives directly from the 'beautiful' period of Titian's early years. Veronese was a decorative artist, like so many other Mannerist masters, but he never sacrificed the clarity of forms to the effect of the whole.

Paolo Caliari, or Veronese, lived in Verona until he was twenty-five (1553) when he moved to Venice. In Verona Mantegna and Bellini were still important, but the influence of Raphael had reached the city through Giulio Romano's work in Mantua, as had the suave art of Correggio, who was working not far away, at Parma. All this can be traced in Veronese's first works (the *Bevilacqua Altarpiece,* Verona, 1548; the altarpiece of *Cardinal Gonzaga,* Mantua, 1552). Paradoxically, only in Venice did he adopt some of the Mannerist formulae at the instance of Ponchino with whom he worked on the Sala dei Dieci of the Palazzo Ducale. During his first years in Venice Veronese received commissions for architectural decorations in which he showed great skill. After the ceiling of the Palazzo Ducale (1553) came the frescoes for the Convent of San Sebastiano (1555-1556); the walls show the life of the saint, the ceiling the story of Esther. From 1556 he decorated the Villa Barbaro at Maser, using amusing *trompe-l'œil* devices—false doors and balconies—which go to make up a masterpiece in an agreable, 'pleasing' style, perfectly suited to Palladio's architecture. After visiting Rome in 1560, Veronese obviously forced himself to imitate (successfully) the spirit of the decorations in Antique buildings.

The clear light in his work gives the pale tones their full value and allows contours to remain

THE HIGH RENAISSANCE IN ITALY

precise. He often depicted banquets and festivities, though without any feverishness or rhetoric (*The Marriage at Cana,* Louvre, 1563; *The Feast of Levi,* Venice, Accademia). The last overdid the secular spirit of genre painting; the Inquisition was incensed by its dogs, dwarfs and monkeys, but the painter defended himself adroitly, promised compliance, but left the work exactly as it was. Until about 1570 Veronese continued to develop this type of art — luxuriant but simply and soundly constructed (*The Family of Darius,* London), sometimes precious (*Mars and Venus,* Turin), even a little artificial (*The Annunciation,* Uffizi). At Rome he had learned to use Raphael as a corrective for Giulio Romano: for a while he moved towards the Giorgionesque (*St Menas and St John the Baptist,* Modena). Then, like almost everybody else, he too succumbed to Tintoretto (*St Helen: Vision of the Cross,* London; *Christ in the Garden,* Brera). The *Calvary* in the Louvre has a tragic quality of its own. Veronese's narrative talent had been enriched by a new dramatic force.

In the Palazzo Ducale he decorated the Sala del Collegio (1575) and, most important of all, the Sala del Maggior Consiglio, in which he painted the magnificent *Triumph of Venice* (1578). In these works his skilful illusionism was complemented by a certain official rhetoric which helped to make him one of the masters of Venetian Baroque. The gay, pleasing Venice admired by all Europe was, at least in part, created by Veronese.

There were other surprising artists in sixteenth-century Venice. Jacopo Bassano and his family were creating the European-wide fashion for 'pastoral nocturnes', of capital importance to art-history. The humble *madonneri* were carrying on Byzantine traditions. El Greco studied their work and learned much from it. But a decline was setting in; it was to last until the unexpected resurrection of Venetian painting in the eighteenth century.

VERONESE, CALVARY. LOUVRE, PARIS

VERONESE. FEAST AT THE HOUSE OF LEVI (DETAIL), 1573. ACCADEMIA, VENICE

VERONESE. RAPE OF EUROPA (DETAIL), c. 1580 PALAZZO DUCALE, VENICE

THE RENAISSANCE IN FRANCE

JEAN COUSIN,
1490-1560.
EVA PRIMA PANDORA,
c. 1550.
LOUVRE, PARIS

ANONYMOUS.
MARS AND VENUS.
PETIT PALAIS, PARIS

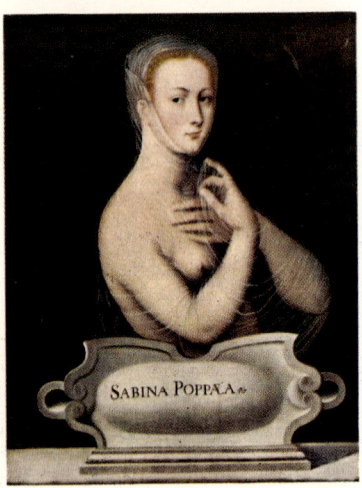

ANONYMOUS.
SABINA POPPAEA.
MUSÉE D'ART ET
D'HISTOIRE,
GENEVA

In art as in politics, the sixteenth century was split in two for France by the year 1559, which marked the end of the Italian wars and the beginning of the Wars of Religion. During the first period Italian influence held sway. As early as 1494 Charles VIII's first expedition allowed direct contact with a refined civilization that seemed a 'paradise' to the King. The French were spellbound by the Italian climate, elegant manners, women and art of living. Charles returned to Amboise with his coffers full of clothing, perfumes, bronzes, books and prints; but he did not know that the High Renaissance was over in the peninsula and that the style he was bringing back with him was that of the Mannerists — pupils of Raphael.

The same was true of Francis I, despite his express determination to acquire the services of the greatest Italian artists. It is true that he brought back Leonardo da Vinci, but he died three years later, having given nothing but advice. When, on returning from his Madrid captivity, the errant King decided to settle down at Fontainebleau and rebuild the old castle of his forefathers, his ideas were, unknown to him, one or two generations behind the times. He approached Michelangelo, who sent one of his pupils, Rosso; failing Raphael, who had died ten years before, he made overtures to Giulio Romano, who sent his pupil Francesco Primaticcio. Rosso died in 1540, Primaticcio in 1570, both loaded with honours and wealth. The style that the two Italians succeeded in creating was a compromise between their Mannerism and the structural solidity of traditional French craftsmanship. Little remains of this work. In the Francis I gallery, which was the King's own idea, only the original drawings and tapestries woven after them show how Rosso's marvellous compositions, framed by great nude figures in high-relief stucco, must have looked. The even more extensive work of Primaticcio has fared no better.

THE RENAISSANCE IN FRANCE

His key-work, the Ulysses gallery, has been destroyed; and though the stuccos and paintings executed for the Duchess of Etampe's apartment still exist, the room itself has been replaced by a staircase.

However, in return for his contribution to French art, Primaticcio absorbed enough French influence to refine the Mannerism he had inherited from Parmigianino, an effect that was intensified when Francis I had him produce casts after Antique models. To the French, these revealed an art stripped of all inessentials, and they admired its simplicity and grandeur. Classical Antiquity gave rise, outside Italy, to a new language of forms drawing on mythology, allegory and fable for its subject-matter. Hence the appearance in painting of the gods of Olympus—Mars and Venus, or Diana—and of figures from Roman history like Poppaea Sabina, the wife of Nero. From the reign of Henry II onwards, French artists felt able to take over from their masters. Among these innovators was Jean Cousin the Elder, who produced the first great nude in French painting. This is the *Eva Prima Pandora*, inspired by Cellini's *Nymph of Fontainebleau* and by Venetian pictures of Venus, but transfigured by an aura of gravity emanating from a hidden core that is more intellectual than erotic. The figures appear to be a record of a *tableau vivant* presented in honour of Charles V's entry into Paris in 1549, for which Cousin provided designs. Indeed, to the French, the nude was certainly the most attractive of the new formal motifs imported from Italy. As Brantôme testified, it is not that the morals of the period lacked freedom. But many centuries earlier Christian art had banished the nude, apart from representations of Adam and Eve or martyred saints, and when it was depicted in a state of heavenly glory. A pretext was required to enable artists to unclothe the human body outside the precincts of Paradise and glorify its profane beauty. They found

ANONYMOUS.
LA BELLE GABRIELLE AND LA MARÉCHALE DE BALAGNY.
c. 1596.
LOUVRE, PARIS

ANONYMOUS.
DIANA AS HUNTRESS,
SECOND HALF OF 16th CENTURY.
LOUVRE, PARIS

ANONYMOUS.
LADY AT HER TOILET,
1570-1590.
KUNSTMUSEUM,
BASLE

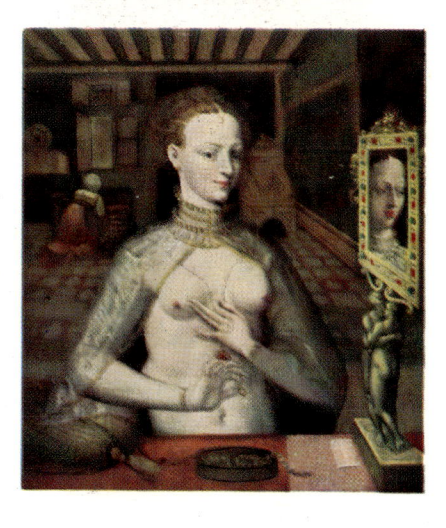

127

JEAN CLOUET,
1485 ?-1540/41.
PORTRAIT OF
FRANÇOIS I,
c. 1528.
LOUVRE, PARIS

FRANÇOIS CLOUET,
c. 1520-1572.
PORTRAIT OF
PIERRE QUTHE,
1562.
LOUVRE, PARIS

SCHOOL OF CLOUET.
PORTRAIT OF
FRANÇOIS DE
FRANCE, COUNT
OF ALENÇON,
c. 1568.
LOUVRE, PARIS

their excuse in pagan mythology, and, more simply, in scenes of dressing and bathing.

This transformation was facilitated by Henry II's mythological expressions of his devotion to his mistress Diane de Poitiers. On the King's entry into Lyon, the magistrates delighted Diane by presenting a tableau of Diana out hunting. The painters had only to copy the decorators, as did the unknown author of the beautiful *Diana as Huntress* (Louvre) with the features of the King's mistress. So often was the subject repeated that I mention the great Rouen *Bath of Diana* only because it is a variant inspired by the Judgment of Paris.

A series of half-length figures of ladies at their toilet (Dijon; Basle) or taking a bath (Washington, Kress collection) links up with the theme of the nude. No doubt the two subjects were intended for companion-pieces; Sterling thinks they derived from prototypes by François Clouet. The highly transparent veil covering the breast of these women gives their beauty an unobtrusively erotic flavour. In the oddest of the group, Diane d'Estrées and her sister Gabrielle are shown together in the same bath, with Diane pressing her sister's breast—a reference to the birth of the future Henry IV's son. The picture is probably by the Court painter Jean Brunel the Younger.

Francis I summoned famous Italian artists to work for him, but was sufficiently catholic in his taste to choose François Clouet, a Fleming by birth, as his favourite painter. François' father, Jean II (called Janet) Clouet, had been Court painter to Louis XII, and both became famous as portraitists. The outburst of individualism that is a feature of the sixteenth century, and that found literary expression in the many popular memoirs and 'lives', appeared in art in the guise of portraiture. This fashion for portraits was on a European scale, and there is no question of comparing the minutely realistic faces depicted by the two Clouets with the amazing psycho-

THE RENAISSANCE IN FRANCE

logical reconstructions of Holbein and Dürer. The Clouets' is a Court art, limited by its charm but exquisitely delicate, made the more striking by the way in which the artists remained emotionally detached from their work. There are believed to be eight authentic portraits by Jean Clouet in existence: those of the five so-called *Preux de Marignan,* the Dauphin, the Duke of Guise, and Francis I himself. The King is shown wearing the collar of the order of St Michael, puffed up and proud in his magnificent pourpoint. Like those of his son, the twenty-seven drawings ascribed to Jean were done simply in preparation for painted portraits. They had to make rapid chalk sketches, since their sitters soon tired of posing. Modern taste shows a preference for these simple chalk sketches and presumably they also appealed to the artists' contemporaries, for Queen Catherine filled an album with drawings of her children and family, and everybody followed her example. There was a demand for replicas, countertypes, and copies—which explains the uneven quality. Of no other period is the appearance of the leading figures better known, thanks to these portraits in black, white and coloured chalk, in which Brantôme's heroes live again: the men with their flat caps and spade-shaped beards; the women with their deep Medici collars. Perhaps the most appealing are those of children, who did not have to be flattered. François Clouet's vast output extends over four reigns. The state portraits of Henry II and Charles IX, and many drawings are attributed to him. His only signed portrait is that of the apothecary Pierre Quthe, his friend and very near neighbour. Through Clouet, the likeness has been preserved of François, the fickle Count of Alençon, who was jealous of his brother Henry III and then of Henry IV. He nearly became King Consort of England by marrying Elizabeth I, allowed his friend La Môle to be beheaded,

ATTRIBUTED TO FRANÇOIS CLOUET. PORTRAIT OF ELIZABETH OF AUSTRIA, 1571. LOUVRE, PARIS

CLOUET SCHOOL. PORTRAIT OF CLAUDE DE BEAUNE, 1563. LOUVRE, PARIS

ANONYMOUS. PORTRAIT OF CHARLES DE COSSÉ, FIRST COUNT OF BRISSAC, c. 1538. LOUVRE, PARIS

THE RENAISSANCE IN FRANCE

CORNEILLE DE LYON,
c. 1500-1574.
PORTRAIT OF
JACQUELINE DE
ROHAN GIÉ,
c. 1540.
LOUVRE, PARIS

CORNEILLE DE LYON.
PORTRAIT OF
CLÉMENT MAROT,
c. 1536.
LOUVRE, PARIS

CORNEILLE DE LYON.
PORTRAIT OF
MARGUERITE OF
FRANCE,
c. 1559.
MUSÉE CONDÉ,
CHANTILLY

and died at the age of twenty-nine. Then there is Elizabeth, wife of Charles IX and granddaughter of Charles V; she was the most virtuous princess of her times, but the King neglected her for Marie Touchet. Widowed at twenty-one, she retired to Vienna to live at the Court of her brother, Emperor Rudolf. There is the Count of Brissac, known to the ladies as 'le beau Brissac'; he was as bold and successful in war as in love.

Naturally enough, the Clouets had imitators in this field. Another masterly portrayer of faces, Corneille de Lyon, must be mentioned first. Though born at The Hague, he worked for forty years in his adopted city, always depicting his sitters on a small scale against a green or blue background. An example of his work is the portrait of Marguerite of France, sister of Henry II. Learned and pious, she was a patron of scholars and poets. Others are the picture of Jacqueline de Rohan-Gié, whose eyes are said to have aroused the passion of a kingdom; and that of the poet Clément Marot, protégé of Marguerite of Navarre and friend of Calvin. Yet another portraitist worth mentioning is Charles IX's Court painter Marc Duval; and before it gave way to engraved portraiture, French portrait painting could also boast the names of Jean Decourt, Dumoûtier, Lagneau, and François Quesnel, Court painter to Henry III.

So unsatisfactory is the state of research on French sixteenth-century painting, that various wedding scenes, or records of royal entries and the activities of the Catholic League may still be undiscovered. Artists dealt mainly with subjects related to such entries, tournaments and masquerades, which were extremely popular. Scholars have recently resurrected the most original witness of these scenes — Catherine de' Medici's painter Antoine Caron, whose drawings for the Artemisia tapestries were already known. His *Triumphs of the Seasons* series (c. 1570), which follows the same

130

THE RENAISSANCE IN FRANCE

allegorical pattern, has come to light; it looks to the future as well as the past. Pedantic reconstructions of Antique architecture and the fruit of a remarkably odd imagination combine to give the scenes a very real kind of unreality. Perhaps no-one has ever produced works less 'self-contained' or more full of literary allusions than those of this friend of the Pleiade. He was a fierce supporter of the League; following Appian's text, he depicted the blood-chilling events of the *Massacre under the Triumvirate* (Louvre, c. 1562-1566) in two compositions like ballets of death, which, for contemporaries, were clear references to the relentless struggles of the Catholic triumvirate, spurred on by the Guises. Caron's *Astrologers studying an Eclipse* is connected with the eclipse of 1574, which coincided with Charles IX's death and terrified the superstitious Catherine. In his *Augustus and the Sibyl* (Louvre, c. 1580), he made use of Virgil to predict the final triumph of his faith; and, lastly, his most beautiful work, *Melchizedek investing Abraham* (c. 1595) celebrates the Pope's absolution of Henry IV after his abjuration.

In art, Henry's reign prolonged the sixteenth century. His vast programme of renovation made its mark chiefly in decorative art bound up with architecture. This development is known as the Second School of Fontainebleau; its leaders were Toussaint Dubreuil, Ambroise Dubois, and Fréminet, who transformed Mannerism into Academicism. However, Henry IV's real painter was yet another Fleming, Frans Pourbus the Younger, who became a French citizen in 1618 and died in 1622. This was a crucial period for French art. In 1621, Marie de' Medici summoned Rubens to decorate the gallery of the Luxembourg Palace—the last great commission obtained by a foreigner in France up to the present day; Poussin arrived in 1624 at Rome, from whence Vouet returned to France in 1627.

CORNEILLE DE LYON.
PORTRAIT OF
MADAME DE
ROCHECHOUART.
MUSÉE CONDÉ,
CHANTILLY

MARC DUVAL (?),
c. 1530-1581.
PORTRAIT OF
A FLAUTIST,
1566.
LOUVRE, PARIS

FRANÇOIS QUESNEL,
c. 1544-1616.
PORTRAIT OF
HENRI III.
c. 1575.
LOUVRE, PARIS

131

THE RENAISSANCE IN GERMANY

ALBRECHT DÜRER,
1471-1528.
SELF-PORTRAIT,
1493.
LOUVRE, PARIS

DÜRER.
DÜRER'S FATHER,
1497.
NATIONAL GALLERY,
LONDON

DÜRER.
PORTRAIT OF
OSWALD KREL,
1499.
ALTE PINAKOTHEK,
MUNICH

The story of German painting in the Renaissance is curious in the extreme—a precocious blossoming followed by almost complete sterility. Between 1470 and the beginning of the sixteenth century there was born a galaxy of painters, some artists of genius and all of them outstandingly original: Albrecht Dürer, Mathis Neithardt, known as Grünewald, Hans Baldung Grien, Lucas Cranach the Elder, Albrecht Altdorfer and Holbein the Younger. By the middle of the century they were all dead, leaving behind them hardly any successors; with them died the great painting of Germany.

Of all the German Renaissance painters Albrecht Dürer is generally acknowledged to be the greatest and the equal of the great Italian masters. He was born in 1471 in Nuremberg; his father was a goldsmith who came from Hungary. At fifteen he was apprenticed to Wolgemut, the painter most firmly entrenched in Nuremberg. His formative years were dominated by two artists in particular: Schongauer, whose works he made a special pilgrimage to see in Alsace during his journeyman years, and the great Italian Renaissance masters, whose art he assimilated by copying Mantegna's engravings and, later, making two journeys to Italy where the strange painter Jacopo de' Barbari initiated him into the 'mysteries' of the mathematical construction of figures. In 1493, on the eve of his wedding-day, he painted a self-portrait in tempera on parchment; even at this early period the hard face set against the dark background suggests that he was a perfectionist in the use of line for whom approximations would never suffice.

In the year 1498 he came to full maturity as both painter and engraver, for his woodcuts of *The Apocalypse* and great copper-engravings are at least equal to his first altarpieces. From then onwards Dürer enjoyed a tremendous reputation in his own country—and the friendship of the Humanist thinker Pirkheimer. He painted several

THE RENAISSANCE IN GERMANY

portraits including that of Oswald Krel set against a rich red background and that of a young man in a beret who is traditionally supposed to be his brother Hans Dürer. On his second visit to Italy (1506) his compatriots at the Fondaco de' Tedeschi in Venice commissioned him to paint a large picture. After this he painted the harmonious, if slightly mannered, *Adam and Eve,* with its two large nude figures. In 1508 he produced one of the most famous pictures in his brilliant manner, *The Adoration of the Holy Trinity* (Vienna), after which he devoted himself principally to engraving, designing the most mysterious of his copperplates: *Melancholia I* and *The Knight, Death and the Devil*. Between 1515 and 1520 he executed woodcuts for Emperor Maximilian: after 1520 he made a tour in the Netherlands, where all the painters paid homage to his genius and he made some fine silverpoint drawings.

The last years of his life were a little clouded by religious events which troubled him, as a sincere Lutheran. Nevertheless in 1526 there was another spurt of activity and he painted some of his most accomplished portraits, and the dignified, monumental *Four Apostles* (Munich). In its noble treatment of the drapery, and the simplicity of its grandeur, this is his masterpiece; it is also, in a sense, his moral testament, marking the highest point of the evolution which had taken him from the Gothic, proliferating design of *The Apocalypse* to a masterly Classicism in which, without losing his German character, he became the equal of the greatest Italians of his century.

Nobody could be more different from Dürer than Grünewald, whom A. M. Vogt has called a master of anti-classical painting. The man himself remains a mystery. First of all, his name was certainly not Grünewald: he was called Mathis Neithardt and assumed the additional name of Gothardt. In 1509 we know that he was painter to the Court of the Elector and Arch-

DÜRER.
PORTRAIT OF
A YOUNG MAN
(HANS DÜRER?),
1500.
ALTE PINAKOTHEK,
MUNICH

DÜRER.
ADAM AND EVE
(DIPTYCH),
1507.
PRADO, MADRID

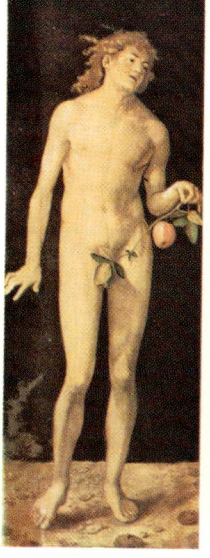

DÜRER.
VIRGIN AND CHILD
WITH ST ANNE,
1519.
METROPOLITAN
MUSEUM, NEW YORK

133

THE RENAISSANCE IN GERMANY

MATHIS GOTHARDT-NEITHARDT, KNOWN AS MATHIAS GRÜNEWALD, c. 1475-1528. ST JOHN THE EVANGELIST, THE VIRGIN AND ST MARY MAGDALENE; DETAIL FROM THE CRUCIFIXION (ISENHEIM ALTARPIECE), c. 1515. UNTERLINDEN MUSEUM, COLMAR

GRÜNEWALD. ST JOHN THE BAPTIST; DETAIL FROM THE CRUCIFIXION (ISENHEIM ALTARPIECE), c. 1515. UNTERLINDEN MUSEUM, COLMAR

GRÜNEWALD. VIRGIN; DETAIL FROM THE ANGEL CONCERT (ISENHEIM ALTARPIECE), c. 1515. UNTERLINDEN MUSEUM, COLMAR

bishop of Mainz, Ulrich of Gemmingen; later he entered the service of Archbishop Albrecht of Brandenburg who was created cardinal in 1518. Although Albrecht showed great tolerance towards members of the Reformed Church, it was probably for religious reasons that Mathis sought refuge at Frankfurt and later at Halle, where he was employed as supervisor of the town's waterworks and died in 1528. The inventory taken after his death shows that he was not rich in worldly goods apart from a very sumptuous wardrobe and a large number of Luther's works. His date of birth is the greatest mystery of all: some authorities suggest a date around 1460, in which case he would have been more than fifteen years older than Dürer; others suggest about 1480, which means that he would have been more than five years younger. Both theories present problems.

His masterpiece is the enormous altarpiece which he painted from 1512 to 1516 for the Antonites of Isenheim, whose abbot was a Sicilian, Guido Guersi; it is now at Colmar. The sculptured part had already been executed by Nikolaus of Hagenau at the order of Jean Orliac, Guido Guersi's predecessor. The altarpiece comprises no less than nine pictures by Grünewald, epitomizing his genius. *The Crucifixion* is a paroxysm of violence. The body of Christ, lacerated, covered all over with bleeding wounds, looks as though it has been rolled in thorns. His hands, with their thin fingers, are curling in agony; on the left the Virgin, in a white mantle with stiff folds, is fainting, supported by John the Evangelist, while at her feet Mary Magdalene, providing the only note of theatricality in the picture, is convulsively twisting her interlaced fingers. On the right John the Baptist is pointing out Jesus.

In *The Annunciation*, *The Incarnation* and *The Resurrection* Grünewald shows his skill in making light serve his visionary gifts. The Virgin, her face merging into a cloud of glory, listens to a choir of

THE RENAISSANCE IN GERMANY

angels standing beneath a Gothic aedicule. Christ rises up into heaven in a circular blaze of light like a rainbow; his head fades into the divine brilliance.

The two panels devoted to *St Anthony and St Paul* and *St Anthony* show Grünewald's power of heightening reality: they contain landscapes filled with strange vegetation, horrible grovelling monsters, and, at St Anthony's side, a man covered with hideous abscesses — no doubt symbolizing the ergotic poisoning that Anthony cured.

Grünewald's work is at one and the same time archaic in spirit and very advanced in technique. But although he may have known Italian works and certainly knew those of Dürer, he was not interested in art which had no religious content or aims. Innumerable scholars have given their explanations of the altarpiece. We know that the artist or his adviser must have been familiar with the *Revelations* of St Bridget but only one of the greatest geniuses in German art could have interpreted them so forcefully.

His other *Crucifixions* have much in common with that of the Isenheim altarpiece. One of the works of his maturity showing St Erasmus clad as a bishop conversing with St Maurice, depicted as a negro in armour, is much more calm than is usual with Grünewald; he seems principally interested in conveying the cope and the embossed armour. When he wanted he could be a great virtuoso, but in general his mood is tragic.

Albrecht Altdorfer of Ratisbon, on the other hand, painted with the detailed care of a miniaturist; his life, moreover, seems to have been an easy one. In 1505 he acquired the rights of citizenship in Ratisbon where his fellow-townsmen wanted to make him a burgermaster in 1528.

His most striking feature is his imaginative gift for landscape. A tiny St George equably slays a dragon in the heart of a great, luxuriant forest, whose foliage is shown in the greatest detail with-

GRÜNEWALD. ST JOHN THE EVANGELIST; DETAIL FROM A CRUCIFIXION, *c.* 1519. NATIONAL GALLERY OF ART, WASHINGTON

GRÜNEWALD. SS. ERASMUS AND MAURICE, *c.* 1524. ALTE PINAKOTHEK, MUNICH

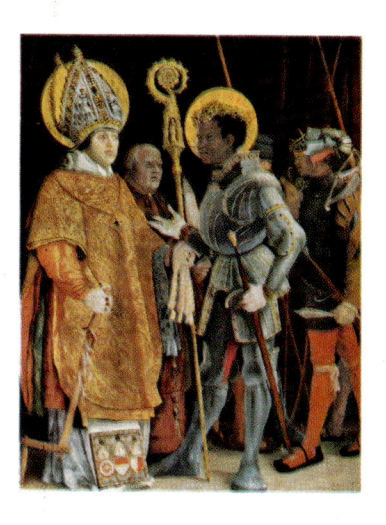

ALBRECHT ALTDORFER, 1480 ?-1538. PORTRAIT OF A WOMAN. THYSSEN COLLECTION, LUGANO

135

THE RENAISSANCE IN GERMANY

HANS BALDUNG,
CALLED GRIEN,
1484/85-1545.
DEATH AND
THE LADY,
c. 1517.
KUNSTMUSEUM,
BASLE

HANS BALDUNG.
THE THREE GRACES
(DETAIL).
PRADO, MADRID

HANS BALDUNG.
VANITAS,
MUSIC,
1529.
ALTE PINAKOTHEK,
MUNICH

out the overall effect being at all weakened. He too worked for the Emperor Maximilian. In 1529 he painted an extraordinary picture — *The Battle of Arbela* (Munich); within a comparatively small area is a host of soldiers, squadrons galloping, flags flying . . . All this was typically Humanist in outlook, but the sun burning away into a fiery crater above the scene gives a hint of Altdorfer's visionary qualities, which would hardly be suspected from his other works.

Hans Baldung was born in about 1484-1485 in the neighbourhood of Strasburg. He followed the lead given by the great Albrecht Dürer and even went to Nuremberg in his journeyman years. In 1509 he was granted the rights of citizenship in Strasburg for the first time; he then spent five years in Freiburg where he was commissioned to paint the main altarpiece of the cathedral. This was finished in about 1516 and proved to be his greatest painted work. Later he returned to Strasburg, where he spent the rest of his life; it was disturbed, since he was a confirmed Lutheran, by religious difficulties.

Despite the pupil-teacher relationship, his art is very unlike Albrecht Dürer's — in its colour, feeling for light, and spirit. He was a more subtle and unusual colourist than Dürer. Apparently this was noted even by his contemporaries since, as it seems, they nicknamed him Grien after the quality of his greens *(grün)*. He ventured on colour-combinations which at first strike the eye as discordant, or even painfully jangling, but later offer an equally sharp pleasure. In his altarpiece at Freiburg he still made considerable (and successful) use of white. But his feeling for light is best seen in his night scenes and remarkable chiaroscuro woodcuts

He was a sensual man; there is no lack of female nudes in his work. Olympus, fables and allegories all provided him with suitable themes. In one picture a buxom woman is being held by Death in a voluptuous embrace. Various others show a hell peopled with equally

136

THE RENAISSANCE IN GERMANY

nude witches which, in certain drawings, even verge on obscenity. But, like the engravings of *The Bewitched Varlet* they all show that Baldung had a strong tinge of the grotesque humour and this rather surrealistic quality has its own fascination.

The two Swiss painters, Urs Graf and Niklaus Manuel Deutsch, were almost exact contemporaries of Baldung and probably knew his work. They both enlisted in the ranks of the Swiss guards for several campaigns in Italy — an act almost without parallel in art-history. One can understand why the soldier's life could have appealed to Urs Graf, who was 'a bit of a lad'; all his engravings (he painted very little) smell of blood, sweat and women. But Niklaus Manuel Deutsch was a man of an entirely different stamp: he made a thoroughly respectable marriage, was a member of the Grand Council at Berne for sixteen years and was entrusted with various diplomatic missions. What made him decide to go to the wars in Piedmont in 1522? Some of his works do suggest a certain preoccupation with women and death but there is nothing of either in two entrancing tempera panels (Basle Museum, 1523). Although their dimensions are comparatively large they are painted with great delicacy. In *The Judgment of Paris,* the Venus is pale of flesh, covered only with a transparent drape; she has the bulging belly modish at the end of the century. She and Minerva have voluminous, completely incredible feather headdresses; Juno is a respectable, decently dressed bourgeois lady. The landscape in *Pyramus and Thisbe* is full of poetry; Thisbe, her drapery revealing her body as does Venus', is shown in the act of stabbing herself through the heart with a sword. Both pictures are noteworthy for their charming relish and mixture of boldness and mediaeval design. The colour is exquisitely fresh.

Although German painters had no monopoly of ambiguity, they certainly cultivated it eagerly.

HANS BALDUNG. PORTRAIT OF A MAN. NATIONAL GALLERY, LONDON

NIKLAUS MANUEL DEUTSCH, 1484-1530. JUDGMENT OF PARIS, *c.* 1523. KUNSTMUSEUM, BASLE

NIKLAUS MANUEL DEUTSCH. PYRAMUS AND THISBE, *c.* 1523. KUNSTMUSEUM, BASLE

137

THE RENAISSANCE IN GERMANY

LUCAS CRANACH
THE ELDER,
1472-1553.
PORTRAIT OF
A SAXON
PRINCE,
c. 1517.
NATIONAL GALLERY
OF ART,
WASHINGTON

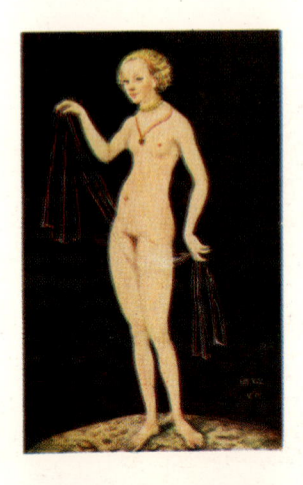

CRANACH THE
ELDER.
VENUS,
1532
STÄDELSCHES
KUNSTINSTITUT,
FRANKFURT

CRANACH
THE ELDER.
PORTRAIT OF A
LITTLE GIRL
(LUTHER'S
DAUGHTER?),
BETWEEN 1520
AND 1540.
LOUVRE, PARIS

Cranach the Elder is a case in point. He was born at Cronach in Franconia one year after Dürer.

Little is known about his early years but his first pictures and the earliest of his engravings to have survived augur the emergence of an artist of Dürer's calibre. The composition of his *Crucifixion* of 1503, now in the Munich Pinakothek, is daring, even revolutionary. Contrary to all tradition, Christ on the cross is shown almost in profile on the edge of the picture, instead of occupying the centre, while the Virgin and St John seem to attract all the attention to themselves. The landscape heralds Altdorfer.

In 1504 Cranach was summoned to Wittenberg by Frederick the Wise, Elector of Saxony, and from then onwards he remained in the service of the Saxon rulers, towards whom he showed himself touchingly faithful. (At the age of seventy-eight he chose to be imprisoned with John Frederick the Magnanimous after the disastrous battle of Mühlberg.) However, in art Saxony was rather backward and many critics have maintained that this accounts for the strange turn taken by his artistic development.

He was a sincere Lutheran, in fact a personal friend of Martin Luther himself. His workshop, organized after the old fashion, was prosperous; it is hard to tell which of the pictures marked with its winged dragon are by him.

His genius for portraying rough, coarse-grained men and irritatingly sharp women never weakened. One sees it at work in the series of portraits of Saxon rulers and related princely houses: the museum at Rheims possesses whole series of excellent sketches, very complex in technique, which show several of them in all their hideous ugliness (probably stressed on purpose). These sketches were probably intended to serve as patterns from which the workshop could make replicas. Then there are portraits of Lutheran notabilities; a contemporary claimed that Cranach's workshop produced over a thousand portraits of Luther himself.

THE RENAISSANCE IN GERMANY

It was Cranach too who painted the child portrait in the Louvre which is traditionally held to be of Luther's daughter, although the dates belie this identification: it shows a girl with a round head, pale, almost wan face, and fair curls falling on to her black bodice.

But it was also Cranach—Cranach the respected citizen, the owner of a pharmacy, the devout Christian—who painted a plethora of nude nymphs, Lucretias and Venuses, very uneven in quality but all slender, with small, high breasts and narrow eyes and all holding an excessively transparent drape over the part of the body most in need of concealment, thus drawing attention to it. His first Venuses, (Leningrad, 1509) still have a certain Classical quality. But gradually they become slimmer and slimmer; the sinuous curves of their outline lends them an undeniable charm. In his *Judgment of Paris,* an even stranger work than Deutsch's, there is something quite disconcerting about the huge hat of one of the nude goddesses and the extraordinary dislocation of Paris, shown as a knight in armour.

One of the most surprising examples of Cranach's later style is the picture in Vienna, dated 1529, in which he shows the Elector Frederick the Wise taking part in a stag-hunt. Documentary evidence tells us that he went hunting with his master so as to be able to draw such scenes from life. Therefore we may assume that the clumsiness of both men and animals is deliberate—coming from an artist of Cranach's stamp.

After his death at the age of eighty-one, his son Lucas Cranach the Younger kept the workshop going. (The eldest son, Hans, had died in 1537 during a visit to Italy.) The works produced varied little from those of the father's lifetime and it is only possible to distinguish the paintings of the two Lucases by their dates; the father died in October 1553.

In the work of Hans Holbein the Younger there is no longer any trace of the conflict between the

CRANACH THE ELDER. THREE GIRLS, *c.* 1530. KUNSTHISTORISCHES MUSEUM, VIENNA

CRANACH THE ELDER. THE JUDGEMENT OF PARIS, 1529. METROPOLITAN MUSEUM, NEW YORK

LUCAS CRANACH THE YOUNGER, 1515-1586. PORTRAIT OF A LADY. MUSEUM OF FINE ARTS, BOSTON

139

THE RENAISSANCE IN GERMANY

HANS HOLBEIN
THE YOUNGER,
1497/98-1543.
PORTRAIT OF
MADDELENA
OFFENBURG AS
LAÏS OF CORINTH,
1526.
KUNSTMUSEUM,
BASLE

HOLBEIN THE
YOUNGER.
THE ARTIST'S
WIFE WITH
THEIR TWO
CHILDREN, 1528.
KUNSTMUSEUM,
BASLE

HOLBEIN THE
YOUNGER.
PORTRAIT OF
HERMANN WEDIGH,
1532.
METROPOLITAN
MUSEUM, NEW YORK

spirit of Gothic and the spirit of the Renaissance which had torn each of the other German painters, with varying results. He is the last of the great, and belongs to a later generation, since he was twenty-five years younger than Dürer. Another difference was that he came from Augsburg, an easy target for all Italian influences and the native town of Burgkmair, Maximilian's chief collaborator in his enterprises. His father, known to us as Holbein the Elder, had made no bones about introducing Antique decoration into his works.

In 1515 the son was to be found at Basle, but although his portraits, decorations for buildings and engravings for book-illustrations earned him a fair amount of prestige, he made little money and found the environment stultifying. From this period date his famous *Christ Entombed* (1521), a pitiless and masterly testament of faith, and the *Meyer Madonna* (Darmstadt Museum, *c.* 1526).

A little later Holbein became friendly with Erasmus, and in 1523 he painted his first and possibly most expressive portrait of him; this is the weasel-faced profile in the Louvre. Shortly afterwards the famous Humanist gave Holbein a recommendation to friends in England and in 1526 he made his first visit to that country. Before going he painted the female figure known as *The Courtesan Laïs of Corinth* which, according to tradition, shows a lady of the Offenburg family. Her regular, vacant features stand out against a green curtain and her slashed bodice is of a garnet shade. The pose suggests that Holbein had studied Leonardo da Vinci. As in all his figures, the hands are supremely well drawn.

In 1528 he was once again in Basle, but this time better supplied with money. It was then that he painted the splendid family group which marks the climax of his art and feeling; it shows his wife with their two children in her arms. Her face is severe, regular, rather unattractive: the profile of one of the children recalls Italian medals,

140

THE RENAISSANCE IN GERMANY

while the other has the dimpled chubbiness of babies of that age.

But the Reformed Church was becoming ever more iconoclastic. Holbein left Basle and, after a short stay in Antwerp, returned to London in 1532.

He was received with open arms and was very successful as an artist. First he was commissioned to do a series of portraits of merchants for the Hanseatic representatives in London. Then came one of his most famous works: the full-length picture of two French ambassadors — Jean de Dinteville and Georges de Selve. In this official portrait the two men stand on either side of a two-tiered table loaded with characteristic attributes, each of which is a masterpiece of still-life. For some extraordinary reason the artist has placed in front of them a distorting mirror reflecting a skull, made quite unrecognizable by the odd perspective.

Usually Holbein preferred to let his sitters speak for themselves. There is, for instance, the portrait of Henry VIII himself, shown as a suspicious voluptuary clad in a sumptuous costume of gold brocade. Holbein was honoured with commissions to paint most of Henry's female favourites, both his victims and those he thought of marrying. There are also a large number of drawings of Court ladies which have an elliptical power and impact vastly superior to Clouet's rather careful crayons. As for the painted portraits, they can only be described as perfect. Each sitter's character is brought out with such intensity, and the details are subordinated to the whole with such power, that they probably produce a more telling effect than the sitter would have done in real life. The skill is so great that it is not apparent.

Holbein died of the plague in 1543 at the height of his fame. With him died a great period of German painting; from then onwards it produced only imitators and men of talent, and long ceased to figure prominently in European art-history.

HOLBEIN THE YOUNGER. HENRY VIII, 1539. GALLERIA NAZIONALE, ROME

HOLBEIN THE YOUNGER. PORTRAIT OF ERASMUS (CIRCULAR), 1530-1532. KUNSTMUSEUM, BASLE

HOLBEIN THE YOUNGER. JEAN DE DINTEVILLE AND GEORGES DE SELVE, FRENCH AMBASSADORS AT THE ENGLISH COURT, 1533. NATIONAL GALLERY, LONDON

GERARD DAVID, 1450/60-1523. REST ON THE FLIGHT INTO EGYPT. NATIONAL GALLERY OF ART, WASHINGTON

GERARD DAVID. VIRGIN ANNUNCIATE. METROPOLITAN MUSEUM, NEW YORK

GERARD DAVID. VIRGIN WITH THE SOUP BOWL. MUSÉE ROYAL D'ART ANCIEN, BRUSSELS

The ways in which the Renaissance penetrated into the Netherlands are barely detectable. In the work of Gerard David, they still amount to nothing more than a few inconspicuous touches. David was born in about 1460 at Oudewater, near Gouda. In 1483 he settled at Bruges, where he admired Memlinc more than any other painter. Like Memlinc—though to a lesser extent—he tended to be rather backward-looking. He quickly made a name for himself, and in 1496 married a wealthy girl. In 1498 he was commissioned to paint scenes representing justice, like those executed at an earlier date by Bouts—whose example he did, in fact, follow. His subject was the story of the corrupt judge whom Cambyses condemned to be flayed alive. These are 'old-fashioned' pictures, with the heads all on the same level, the figures too bunched together, and the execution represented in a callous and brutal way. Nevertheless, in the scene that shows Cambyses passing judgement on Sisamnes, one is surprised to see two medallions in the Antique style and some garlands held up by *putti*—not far from arched openings that give on a thoroughly Flemish square. David was much more at home in a soft, gentle vein, as can be seen from the delightful *Rest on the Flight into Egypt,* in which heavenly peace prevails. While the landscape is yellowish green in the middle distance, the blue horizon may indicate a knowledge of Lombardic art. The picture seems to have been painted shortly after 1509, which is the date of David's masterpiece in the Rouen museum, the *Virgo inter Virgines,* with the Infant Christ holding up a bunch of grapes. This is the most brilliant phase of the artist's career, for in 1502-1507 he painted the sumptuous altarpiece with the *Baptism of Christ,* for Jan de Trompes.

In 1515 Gerard David joined the guild at Antwerp, where he met Quentin Massys. However, it does not seem as though the

NETHERLANDISH SCHOOL OF THE SIXTEENTH CENTURY

Antwerp school, which was much more lively-minded than that of Bruges, had an appreciable influence on him, to judge from the insipidity of his *'Soup' Madonna*. The same sort of affectation marks the pretty picture of a *Girl with a dead Bird* (see page 146).

Thus, at the beginning of the sixteenth century, it is to Antwerp —then in full vigour—that one has to turn, not to Bruges, whose trade had suffered greatly through the silting up of her port. There, the Haarlem painter Isenbrandt was almost the only one to continue the tradition; but at Antwerp were to be found the three artists who, for different reasons, deserve most attention: Massys, Patenir, and Jan Gossaert, known by the name of Mabuse.

Quentin Massys, a blacksmith's son, was born at Louvain in 1465. The eldest of the trio, it was he who had most in common with the earlier Netherlandish painters. In some respects—as in his gift for calm observation—he continued the art of Jan van Eyck; but, having settled at Antwerp in 1491, he had close ties with Erasmus. Massys' portrait of the famous Humanist is a pendant to one of another Humanist, Pieter Gilles; the two works are now separated. They must have made a splendid pair. Further, Sir Thomas More extolled Massys in a poem. These men were interested in art chiefly in relation to their sociological and philosophical ideas, and tended to direct it towards *genre* and satire. Massys' *Money Changer and his Wife* includes elements of both; while, at the same time, the stillness of the figures and minute detail of the objects are reminiscent of earlier Flemish painting.

However, his satire goes further and he shows Leonardo's interest in grotesque faces. One is conscious of the influence of Hieronymus Bosch in some of his works, particularly *The Temptation of St Anthony* for which he provided the figures and his friend Patenir the landscape. Nevertheless, Massys, the friend of the great Human-

GERARD DAVID.
VIRGIN AND CHILD,
ST MARY
MAGDALENE
WITH THE DONOR
MADELAINE
CORDIER;
WINGS OF THE
ALTARPIECE OF
JAN DE TROMPES,
c. 1502-1507.
MUSÉE COMMUNAL,
BRUGES

JOACHIM PATENIR,
1475/80-1524.
FLIGHT INTO
EGYPT,
c. 1520.
MUSÉE ROYAL DES
BEAUX-ARTS,
ANTWERP

JOACHIM PATENIR
AND QUENTIN
MASSYS.
TEMPTATION
OF ST ANTHONY,
c. 1520.
PRADO, MADRID

JAN GOSSAERT,
KNOWN AS MABUSE,
c. 1478-1533/36.
TWO PORTRAITS
OF DONORS.
MUSÉE ROYAL D'ART
ANCIEN, BRUSSELS

JAN GOSSAERT.
PORTRAIT OF
ISABELLA
OF AUSTRIA,
SISTER OF
CHARLES V, AS
THE MAGDALENE.
MUSÉE ROYAL D'ART
ANCIEN, BRUSSELS

JAN GOSSAERT.
DANAË,
1527.
ALTE PINAKOTHEK,
MUNICH

ists was always much more down to earth than Bosch.

In the works of Jan van Hemessen and Marinus van Reymerswaele this social satire takes on a new bitterness. It is known from documentary sources that Reymerswaele was, oddly, sentenced for joining in the iconoclastic riots. With him one is far removed from the temperate spirit of Erasmus: religious fanaticism is combined with a sense of human injustice to produce a vehement style. *The Two Tax-gatherers* in the National Gallery, London, is a cruel caricature; and it is made very strange indeed by the fantastic head-gear. Joachim Patenir was not very good at painting figures: since he usually made them very small, he did not need to be. But this Walloon from Bouvignes was a very remarkable landscape artist. Like Massys, he settled at Antwerp, joining the guild there in 1515 and dying there in 1524. It is true that in the Dinant area, where he was born, one comes across rocks of strange and fantastic shape. However, even if one accepts that he may have gained inspiration from this source, he condensed and intensified it. His pictures overflow with houses and pierced, sharp-pointed rocks, generally all arranged in planes parallel to the bottom of the panel, as if Patenir was always afraid of not putting enough in. The result is that, though the landscapes never look natural or like real country-side, they make a strong impression on the viewer. Towards the front of these compositions the greens are intense. The far distance may be very blue, or else marked at the horizon by the line where the sky meets a strip of water, which, between two banks, reflects the light. This occurs in *Charon crossing the Styx*, on the right of which flames pierce the darkness.

Massys and Patenir were not seriously diverted from their course by the impact of the Italian Renaissance. It was a very different story with the group known as the Antwerp Mannerists, whose leader

NETHERLANDISH SCHOOL OF THE SIXTEENTH CENTURY

was Gossaert. Probably born at Duurstede and not, as has long been supposed, at Maubeuge, he was a member of the Antwerp guild in 1503. Commissioned to copy Antique statues and monuments, he accompanied Philip of Burgundy, one of the illegitimate sons of Philip the Good, to Italy. He remained in his service until his master's death in 1524, when he transferred his allegiance to Philip's nephew, Adolph of Burgundy. Gossaert, who was very highly regarded by his contemporaries and had enormous influence, developed a style with a great many Italian features. His pictures are loaded with Antique-type architecture, and sometimes give the impression of a world made of marble. Among the best is the painting in the Munich Pinakothek of Danaë seated in a colonnaded apse with one breast bared, receiving the shower of gold. She has charm, despite the deliberately unnatural pinkness of her complexion; and the gleaming metal and bright blue dress have been boldly juxtaposed. Gossaert turned out a large number of nudes which, with their involved poses and intertwined limbs, possess the cold but rather obtrusive erotic quality peculiar to the Mannerists. In his *Neptune and Amphitrite* (Berlin) he was not content just to rehash the composition of a copper engraving by Dürer, whom he actually met during the latter's visit to the Netherlands. Like all the painters of his country, he was always an excellent portraitist, and could give warmth to his female figures, such as Charles V's sister, Isabella, whom he depicted as the Magdalene, or Jacqueline of Burgundy, with her youthful sparkle. In this field he was the equal of his forerunners. Mention must be made of Joos van Cleve, now identified with the Master of the Death of the Virgin, and, in the succeeding generations, Frans Floris, known, pretentiously, as the Flemish Raphael, and Bartholomeus Spranger.

Bernard van Orley (1492-1542), on the other hand, was a Brussels

JAN GOSSAERT.
PORTRAIT OF
A GIRL
(JACQUELINE
DE BOURGOGNE ?)
NATIONAL GALLERY,
LONDON

QUENTIN MASSYS,
1465/66-1530.
THE MONEY
CHANGER
AND HIS WIFE,
1514.
LOUVRE, PARIS

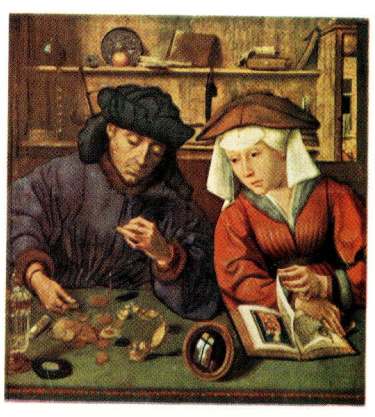

MARINUS VAN
REYMERSWAEL,
1495 ?-1567.
TWO TAX
GATHERERS.
NATIONAL GALLERY,
LONDON

145

NETHERLANDISH SCHOOL OF THE SIXTEENTH CENTURY

MARTIN VAN HEEMSKERCK, 1498-1574. PORTRAIT OF ANNA CODDE, 1529. RIJKSMUSEUM, AMSTERDAM.

LUCAS VAN LEYDEN, c. 1494-1533. LOT AND HIS DAUGHTERS. LOUVRE, PARIS

ANONYMOUS (JUAN DE FLANDRE?). GIRL WITH A DEAD BIRD. FIRST QUARTER OF 16th CENTURY. MUSÉE ROYAL D'ART ANCIEN, BRUSSELS

painter. His special claim to fame is that he produced wonderful cartoons for tapestries, in which perfect harmony exists between the painting process and the finished work as a whole. The designs are the best of their period, and include, among others, those for the twelve scenes of the *Hunts of Maximilian*. This genius for composition does not appear at all in his subject pictures; but however incompatible the requirements of portraiture may seem to be with the decorative aims of tapestry-designing, Van Orley was yet another Fleming to excel as a portrait painter, whether representing Dr Georg van Zelle at his work-table or his patroness Margaret of Austria, Regent of the Netherlands. Margaret's not very beautiful face is framed by the severe lines of her head-dress and by a collar with geometrical pleats, which makes her look like a nun.

In the northern Netherlands, the artist chiefly responsible for introducing Italian motifs was Jan van Scorel, who had studied under Gossaert during the latter's Utrecht period. Born round about 1495 near Alkmaar, Van Scorel died at Utrecht in 1562 after travelling to Italy and even to the Holy Land. His portraits are often hard to tell apart from those of several closely related artists; the one of a schoolboy in dark grey clothing and a red cap against a light green background has a youthful air which lends it a certain charm, and it includes, along with the date 1531, a Humanist-style inscription. Van Scorel's Italianate manner was continued at Haarlem by Martin van Heemskerck, who spent three years in Rome, and whose drawings are a valuable source of information about the topography and antiquities of the Eternal City. The same difficulty exists over identifying his portraits as over Van Scorel's. He has been rejected as the author of the beautiful picture in the Amsterdam museum of Anna Codde, the wife of Pieter Bicker, by a connoisseur of Hoogewerf's standing, who attributes it to a

146

NETHERLANDISH SCHOOL OF THE SIXTEENTH CENTURY

'Master of the Bicker Portraits'.

Amid the flood of sometimes poorly assimilated Italian motifs, the most original artist, and the one who most successfully preserved his own identity, is probably Lucas van Leyden, a pupil of Cornelis Engelbrechtsz, himself a by no means insignificant painter. When Lucas was at Antwerp in 1521, Dürer did a drawing of him there; but this meeting made no great difference to the Netherlander, as he had already long been an admirer, and sometimes an imitator, of the great German artist. He died in Leyden in 1533, leaving a corpus of engravings that shows dazzling mastery of the burin and etching-needle, and in which he managed on the whole to preserve his originality with respect to both the German and Italian Schools. As for his paintings, the few that exist are of remarkably high quality. Among others, they include a *Last Judgment* (still at Leyden) which is without the disturbing hidden meanings of a Bosch; a number of genre subjects; and *Lot and his Daughters,* an extremely mannered history picture with colouring based on a combination of blues and vermilion.

Both in regard to Italian influence and to local developments, the spreading of the new style through the Low Countries was greatly facilitated by the trade in prints. The man who played the decisive rôle here was Hieronymus Cock. After a stay in Rome, he returned to Antwerp round about the middle of the century, setting up there as a print publisher; and in 1550 the young Pieter Bruegel began working for him as a designer. Bruegel had been trained by an artist of great historical importance, Pieter Coeck van Aelst, who spent long periods in Italy and at Constantinople, and translated Serlio and Vitruvius. After becoming a master in the Antwerp guild in 1551, Bruegel left for Italy. *En route,* he made drawings of Alpine scenery, which, though he was under thirty, already show complete mastery. On his return, he

BERNARD VAN ORLEY. 1488 ?-1542. PORTRAIT OF THE DOCTOR GEORG VAN ZELLE, 1519. MUSÉE ROYAL D'ART ANCIEN, BRUSSELS

BERNARD VAN ORLEY. PORTRAITS OF MARGARET OF AUSTRIA. MUSÉE ROYAL D'ART ANCIEN, BRUSSELS

JAN VAN SCOREL, 1495-1562. PORTRAIT OF A STUDENT, 1531. BOYMANS MUSEUM, ROTTERDAM

147

NETHERLANDISH SCHOOL OF THE SIXTEENTH CENTURY

PIETER BRUEGEL
THE ELDER.
c. 1525-1569.
HUNTERS IN
THE SNOW
(JANUARY),
1565.
KUNSTHISTORISCHES
MUSEUM, VIENNA

BRUEGEL THE ELDER.
THE NUMBERING
OF THE PEOPLE
AT BETHLEHEM,
1566.
MUSÉE ROYAL D'ART
ANCIEN, BRUSSELS

BRUEGEL THE ELDER.
PARABLE
OF THE BLIND,
1568.
MUSEO NAZIONALE,
NAPLES

was again engaged by Cock, who employed a lot of draughtsmen and engravers working in a variety of styles to copy drawings by a very mixed group of artists. It was at this period that Bruegel became familiar with the works of Bosch.

No securely dated painting by Bruegel survives from before 1558 —which is rather late; but from then on there is a rich succession of signed and dated works, right up to his death in 1569.

For a long time his reputation was based on a partial misunderstanding, to which his two old nicknames—'Peasant Bruegel' and 'Bruegel the Droll'—bear witness. Undoubtedly most purchasers bought his works for their sense of fun, but this certainly does not apply to Peter Paul Rubens, who, according to his inventory, owned twelve pictures by Bruegel, including the *grisaille* representing the *Dormition of the Virgin*. This is not to say that Bruegel's comic sense does not appear in many of his works. However, there are exceptions, such as *Dulle Griet* (*Mad Meg*, Antwerp, Musée Mayer van der Bergh), which is an almost unmistakable reference to the tragic events of the artist's times; for one has to remember that Bruegel was still alive at Antwerp under the Duke of Alba's campaign of repression. With Bruegel the popular element is more prominent than in the work of Bosch; it was he who more often depicted proverbs.

Compared with Bosch, Bruegel was far the more 'painterly', in the subtle sense in which the word is understood today. His eye was sensitive to almost musical colour harmonies: a pink, a white, and a black in *The Land of Cockaigne*; a brown, a grey, and a vermilion in *The Peasant and the Bird-nester*. Sometimes he adopted a form of open composition, with a lot of figures arranged in separate groups united only by the colour-scheme. These works need to be 'read' slowly and in the greatest detail, and they include *The Massacre of the Innocents* (Vienna); *The Number-*

NETHERLANDISH SCHOOL OF THE SIXTEENTH CENTURY

ing of the People at Bethlehem and *The Battle between Carnival and Lent.*

This type of composition had already been favoured by Hieronymus Bosch, who made similar use of a very high sky-line in order to get everything into the picture. Bruegel, however, employed it in a much less naive form; by introducing a very high view-point, he was able to prevent figures from overlapping in almost every case. At the same time he paid scrupulous attention to their perspective, and through tricks of foreshortening that make the head and bust seem large in relation to the lower part of the body, he increased the comic effect. Rubens remembered this in his *Kermesses*.

Bruegel's genius probably reached its highest point in his landscapes. It will suffice to mention three in Vienna: *Hunters in the Snow, Gloomy Day,* and *The Return of the Herd.* All are dated 1656, and no doubt they formed part of a series representing the months. In *Hunters in the Snow,* the sky is a leaden grey of the same hue as the frozen ponds that reflect it, and the snow is not completely white, but tinged with cream; shown with their dogs against the light, the hunters are keyed to the general tonal effect by their sombre clothing; the leafless trees in the foreground stand out almost pure black, though not such a pure black as the crows sitting on the branches or skimming through the air; farther off, other trees form patches of pale grey.

Thus, the story of Netherlandish painting in the sixteenth century ends with a very distinguished name indeed. Pieter Bruegel the Elder had a few imitators, such as Grimmer, and some highly skilled copyists, like his son Pieter the Younger, known as 'Hell Bruegel'; to find another painter in the same class, however, one has to wait for Rubens. By then, however, there was, strictly speaking, no longer an art of the Netherlands in general, but an art of the Catholic Netherlands and a very different art of the Protestant Netherlands.

BRUEGEL THE ELDER.
LAND OF COCKAIGNE,
1567.
ALTE PINAKOTHEK,
MUNICH

BRUEGEL THE ELDER.
PEASANT WEDDING,
c. 1568.
KUNSTHISTORISCHES
MUSEUM, VIENNA

BRUEGEL THE ELDER.
PEASANT DANCE,
1568.
KUNSTHISTORISCHES
MUSEUM, VIENNA

BREUGEL THE ELDER.
HEAD OF AN OLD
PEASANT WOMAN,
c. 1568.
ALTE PINAKOTHEK,
MUNICH

SIXTEENTH-CENTURY SPAIN

ANTHONIS MOR
VAN DASHORST,
KNOWN AS
ANTONIO MORO,
1519-1575.
PORTRAIT OF
A NOBLEMAN, 1561.
MAURITSHUIS,
THE HAGUE

ANTONIO MORO.
PORTRAIT OF THE
DUKE OF ALBA,
c. 1549.
MUSÉE ROYAL D'ART
ANCIEN, BRUSSELS

ANTONIO MORO.
PORTRAIT OF
HUBERT GOLZIUS,
CHRONICLER OF
PHILIP II,
1576.
MUSÉE ROYAL D'ART
ANCIEN, BRUSSELS

The Catholic Kings attracted many Northern artists to Spain. Charles V and Philip II, on the other hand, tended to favour the Italians. Nevertheless the country remained closely linked with Flanders, one of the most prosperous states of its huge empire. Thus Anthonis Mor van Dashorst, a Batavian, created the Spanish type of portrait. His patrons, Cardinal Granvelle and the Duke of Alba, presented him to Charles V and Prince Philip when these royal personages went to Brussels in 1549. In the following year he was sent to Portugal where he painted numerous portraits, as he did in Spain, which he visited then.

During a visit to London he saw various portraits by Holbein which enabled him to sharpen his artistic perception still further. Mor and Holbein may well be called two of the most penetrating portrait-painters of all time. Mor's discernment is at its zenith in his portrait of *The Duke of Alba,* the man who had shown such cruelty in subduing Flanders; in it the painting is dour, sombre, ferocious — altogether worthy of the sitter. It bears comparison with that other masterpiece of implacable truth, the portrait of Mary Tudor.

Finally Mor entered the service of the young Philip II and painted him in armour after his victory at Saint Quentin in 1557. Philip gave him a studio in the Alcazar in Madrid and from this period onwards he became known as Antonio Moro. Nevertheless the fact that he came from a northern country set the Inquisition on his trail. He returned to the Netherlands where he found a patron in the new Regent, Margaret of Parma. Antonio Moro figures in art-history as a master of the Netherlandish and Spanish schools; in the end he is perhaps best described as cosmopolitan, a typical product of an essentially royal Europe, crossed and re-crossed by international cultural currents. His successors in Spanish Court-portraiture were Coelho, a Portuguese, and Pantoja de la Cruz, a Castilian.

SIXTEENTH-CENTURY SPAIN

It is hard to distinguish a truly Spanish note in the Renaissance art of Spain, with its large proportion of foreign practitioners, its Italianate Flemings and the Italian Mannerism practised by the artists of the Escorial. Religious painters such as Juan de Juanes or Luis de Morales may seem characteristically Spanish, but in fact they look to Italy for inspiration. Morales came from Badajoz and worked his apprenticeship at Seville, the great port from which so many pious works of art were sent out to the Spanish missionaries in the Americas. He became so popular that he was even called 'the divine Morales'; the sweetness of his weeping Madonnas appealed to the popular taste in Spain.

His numerous variations on this iconographical theme were produced at the same time and in the same spirit as the great movement in mysticism; Morales, it may be observed, came from the same place as the famous ascetic of Estremadura, St Peter of Alcantara, besides being friendly with various divines and scholars. Thus his pious works are inspired by the popular religiosity of Spain, despite their vaguely Leonardesque appearance. Their softly shadowed contours, maternal tenderness and easy pathos are moving; they herald the *Purismas* of Murillo.

The Portuguese artist Coelho (or, in Spanish, Coello) studied under Moro at Brussels and then stepped into his shoes as official Court portrait-painter. One of his best works is the portrait of the Infanta Isabella Clara Eugenia (Philip II had two daughters by Isabelle de Valois—Isabella and Caterina). The King showed the tenderest affection towards both his daughters, in particular Isabella, as can be seen from the letters he wrote them. These reveal an unselfconscious, amused kindness which contrasts oddly with the commonly held beliefs as to Philip's character. Coelho's portraits bring to life the main figures at Philip II's Court where so much drama and mystery were enacted.

LUIS DE MORALES, 1500?-1586. MATER DOLOROSA. ACADEMIA SAN FERNANDO, MADRID

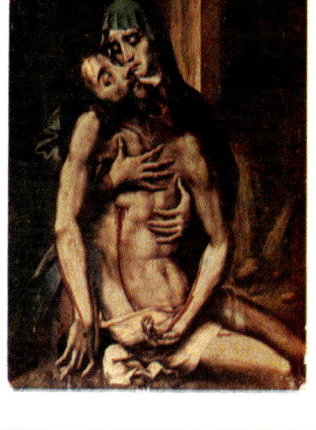

LUIS DE MORALES. VIRGIN AND CHILD, c. 1570. PRADO, MADRID

ALONSO SANCHEZ COELLO, 1531/32-1588. THE INFANTA ISABELLA, DAUGHTER OF PHILIP II, 1579. PRADO, MADRID

SIXTEENTH-CENTURY SPAIN

DOMENIKOS
THEOTOKOPOULOS,
KNOWN AS
EL GRECO,
1541-1614.
VIRGIN
(DETAIL FROM
THE 'HOLY FAMILY').
TAVERA HOSPITAL,
TOLEDO

EL GRECO.
PORTRAIT OF
THE CARDINAL
INQUISITOR
DON FERNANDO
NIÑO DE GUEVARA,
c. 1598.
METROPOLITAN
MUSEUM, NEW YORK

EL GRECO.
UNKNOWN MAN,
BETWEEN 1584
AND 1594.
PRADO, MADRID

Of the foreign artists who flocked to Spain when the Escorial was being rebuilt one of the strangest was a Cretan, Domenicos Theotocopoulos, later known as El Greco. His wanderings had taken him first to Venice and then to Rome. Thus he had sampled all the styles of the Mediterranean; he himself emerged as a Baroque artist, the bearer of a message from the East who, after his Odyssey, found in Toledo his ideal spiritual home and became one of the most penetrating interpreters of the Castilian spirit.

He often selected the theme of the Holy Family; his method of combining the holy figures, grouped attentively round the humble but divine babe, in various pictorial patterns is wholly Baroque, but one senses that the art of Byzantine icons was still fresh in his mind. In dealing with El Greco's work one should never lose sight of the different cultural influences which went to make up his art and, instead of remaining separate like geological strata, converged or conflicted with unending drama.

Although Philip II refused his work and Philip III ignored him, El Greco was popular with the nobility in Toledo, where he had settled, and painted portraits of most of its leading figures, including some of the most powerful, such as the terrible president of the Inquisition of Toledo, later the Grand Inquisitor.

The faces in El Greco's portraits are fascinating in the extreme. Those of his Madonnas or other women, whether holy or not, have an obsessional character. His male portraits penetrate deep into the psychology of the sitter and are sharply individualized. Nevertheless they are all marked by the subjectivity of the painter, who twists the features into painful asymmetry and fills the sitter's eyes with an enigmatic stupor, as of anguish and melancholy.

In 1586 the priest of Greco's parish, Santo Tomé, issued him with a detailed and precise commission. He was to paint a picture showing the miracle which

SIXTEENTH-CENTURY SPAIN

had occurred at the death of a saintly knight, Count Orgaz. St Stephen and St Augustine had come down from heaven to bury him with their own hands. The picture shows this scene being witnessed by the officiating priests and a number of noblemen who are all facing the spectator with hieratic solemnity. Above the world of the living the soul of the dead man is entering into glory. The steel-clad rigidity of death, the feeling of supernatural drama, the contemplative attitudes of the living and the rich splendours of the next world contrast in a way that makes this composition unique.

One always associates El Greco's personality with the personality of Toledo. The town, reduced to a symbolic form, appears in several of his works, as though it were the key and leitmotiv of his art in general. As he wrote in one of the few documents by his hand which are still extant, he made no attempt to portray the town as it stood but deliberately transplanted bridges and buildings to create a city of the imagination, which, in storm-scenes at least, takes on a fantastic air. In painting Toledo, he created our idea of the city.

Toledo is once again the background in *Laocöon* (El Greco's choice of this Antique subject is yet another of the surprises with which his art is studded). The Laocöon theme provided him with one more opportunity of showing his taste (it became increasingly marked through the years) for exaggerated distortion, extraordinary forms, for the pictorial storms first popularized by the Baroque, although he whipped them up to a peak of drama never attained by even the greatest Baroque artists.

There can be no doubt that Greco was popular in his day, but later he was forgotten, considered to be nothing but a madman. In a later age he has once again risen to favour and exerts a strong fascination. Thus in a way his fate as an artist was as capricious as his life and painting. Greco's is genius at its most arbitrary.

EL GRECO. BURIAL OF COUNT ORGAZ (DETAIL), 1586. CHURCH OF SANTO TOMÉ, TOLEDO

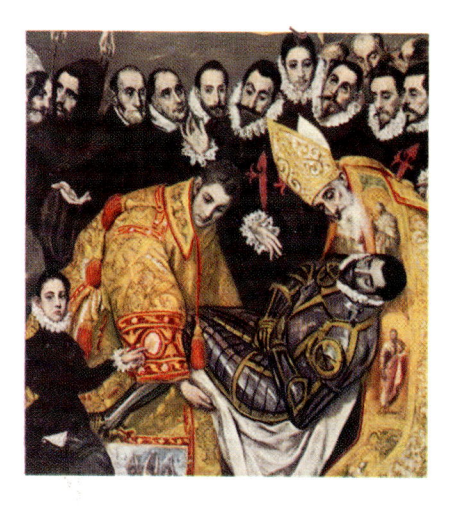

EL GRECO. VIEW OF TOLEDO, 1608. METROPOLITAN MUSEUM, NEW YORK

EL GRECO. LAOCÖON, *c.* 1610. NATIONAL GALLERY OF ART, WASHINGTON

CARAVAGGIO AND LUMINISM

MICHELANGELO MERISI, KNOWN AS CARAVAGGIO, 1573-1610. BACCHUS, c. 1589. UFFIZI, FLORENCE

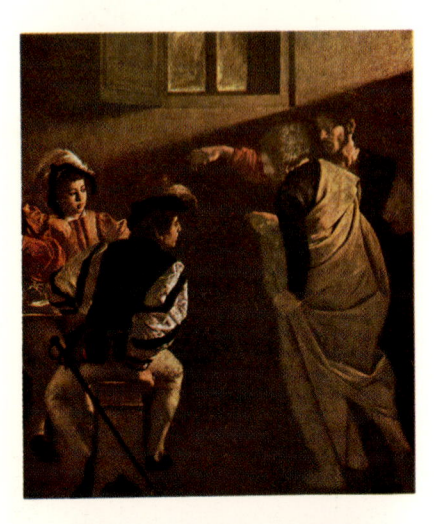

CARAVAGGIO. CALLING OF ST MATTHEW, c. 1597. S. LUIGI DEI FRANCESI, ROME

CARAVAGGIO. VIRGIN OF LORETO. (DETAIL). S. AGOSTINO, ROME

The emergence of Caravaggio was an event as unforeseeable in the history of European painting as Masaccio's career. Like Masaccio, Caravaggio died young and while still at the height of his career. During the short time when he was in Rome (c. 1590-1606) his work provided a stimulus and artistic shock which led to the birth of an important artistic movement—that of the *tenebrosi* or Luminists, to which belonged some of the greatest artists in the Europe of the seventeenth century.

None of Caravaggio's works from his early Milan period are definitely known; one can only conjecture that certain Lombard Luminists must have influenced him. At Rome he studied with the conventional d'Arpino, but soon broke away from him. A few art-lovers appreciated his own small pictures, often half-lengths, genre scenes or religious or mythological subjects painted in a 'naturalistic' spirit. In 1597 Cardinal del Monte got him a commission to decorate the Chapel of St Matthew in the Church of San Luigi de' Francesi; from that time Caravaggio concentrated almost exclusively on large-scale religious paintings. His works were refused again and again or returned for re-painting. He was a violent, choleric, intractable man; it was not long before he made enemies, became involved in brawls and duels and fell into the hands of the police. In 1603 he was thrown into prison; in 1606 he fled from Rome. The four last years of his life were spent in Sicily, Malta and Naples, always on the run, painting monumental altarpieces *(The Seven Works of Charity, The Scourging of Christ, The Beheading of John the Baptist, The Burial of St Lucy)*. This hectic life, his wounds and continual sufferings from malaria killed him in his thirty-eighth year. His tragic death took place at Naples; he left relatively few works but all were of immense suggestive power.

The small details which Caravaggio heaped up in his pictures, evidently with the aim of shocking

154

his viewers (the swollen corpse of the Virgin in the *Dormition* in the Louvre, the dirty bare feet of a peasant in the *Madonna of Loreto*), have led to the legend that he was a 'naturalistic painter' as have the subjects of his genre scenes *(The Card-Sharpers, The Fortune-Teller)* and the almost picaresque costume-pieces (*Bacchus, Narcissus, Eros,* etc.). But 'observation' interested him less than the reality of bodies, masses and volumes. His famous *Basket of Fruit'* (Milan, Ambrogiana), possibly a detail cut out of a larger work, is much more than a mere painted version of the objects: it is a composition of extraordinary weight and balance.

Yet, mainly by means of light, all this is transformed into poetry. In the religious pictures painted while he was in Rome, the hard, direct, side lighting, strongly contrasted with the zones of black shadow, creates a 'night world' which harmonises admirably with the religious emotion evoked. In the altarpieces of his last years the light is more diffuse and, as it were, unquiet; it seems to heighten their disrupted and anguished mood (*Resurrection of Lazarus,* Messina).

From the light pictures of his early years onwards his evolution was rapid and unparalleled. Caravaggio never accepted a conventional formula without questioning it; X-rays have shown that he made modifications to several religious paintings, no doubt at the request of those who had commissioned them, but his originality always shines out. Sometimes his tendency to make forms stand out boldly against space results in a rather heavy 'illusionism' *(Conversion of St Paul)* ; but this is only one aspect of an art centring on human reality, an art which is of the people, almost vulgar in its vigour, but endows faces, attitudes and things with such an individual dignity that, far from being irreligious, it reaches a plane where it illustrates, some have said, a religious attitude — that of the direct, human preaching of, say, St Philip of Neri.

CARAVAGGIO. LUTE-PLAYER, HERMITAGE, LENINGRAD

CARAVAGGIO. DAVID WITH THE HEAD OF GOLIATH, *c.* 1605. GALLERIA BORGHESE, ROME

ATTRIBUTED TO CARAVAGGIO. LUTE-PLAYER. GALLERIA SABAUDA, TURIN

CARAVAGGIO AND LUMINISM

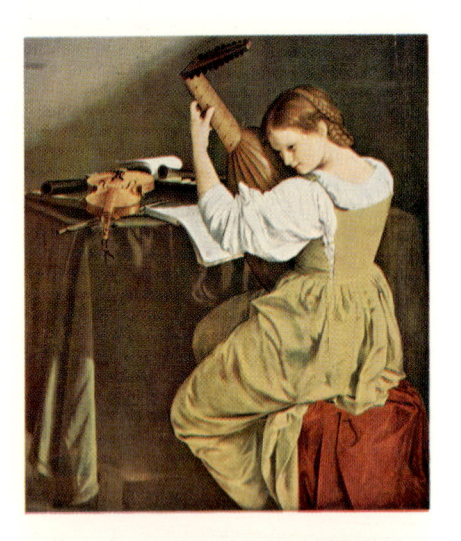

ORAZIO GENTILESCHI, 1563-c. 1640 (?) LUTE-PLAYER. GALERIE DU LIECHTENSTEIN, VADUZ

VALENTIN DE BOULLONGNE, 1591-1634. THE TAVERN, 1620-1625. LOUVRE, PARIS

HENDRIK TERBRUGGHEN, 1588-1629. THE FLUTE-PLAYER, 1621. GEMÄLDEGALERIE, KASSEL

There was no 'Caravaggio school', in the true sense of the term. Many of the artists said to be disciples of his never even knew him, or were older than he. The word Caravaggesque is variously used to describe the 'tenebrist' manner, a type of genre or still-life painting, a new feeling for volumes and a certain repertoire of motifs. But in one way or another, without being based on any distinct doctrine, the Caravaggio revolution left its mark on all the best European painting of the seventeenth century, indirectly influencing Velasquez, Rembrandt and Vermeer.

For a while the Tuscan painter Orazio Gentileschi was under the direct influence of the master. But though his training was essentially Mannerist, he never completely abandoned the light, chalky colour, linear precision and heavy drapery of the Florentines. After he had left Rome for the Marches (1617-1621), Genoa, Paris and finally London, the more conservative elements of his art gradually gained the upper hand.

Carlo Saraceni introduced Venice to a slightly devitalized, facile and conventional version of the Caravaggio manner. Neapolitan artists accentuated the 'tenebrist' style and the striking naturalism (Ribera: see p. 158) but also infused the Caravaggian still-life with a tincture of Spanish influence. In Rome itself Manfredi, his most faithful disciple, specialized in the anecdotal 'genre' and spread the gospel among young foreigners. Giovanni Serodine, a lively colorist with a vibrant touch, must be mentioned as one of the provincial products of the movement. It even spread to the Netherlands, through Van Honthorst's orthodox *tenebroso,* and Hendrik Terbrugghen who, though he died young, seemed likely to add a lively new sequel to the work of Caravaggio's early years. The German artist Adam Elsheimer, who produced many small-scale nocturnal landscapes, invented a sort of 'cabinet' Caravaggism which influenced Rembrandt a little.

There was an important group

CARAVAGGIO AND LUMINISM

of French artists in Rome at that time. Simon Vouet went through a brief Caravaggesque phase, but apart from Georges de la Tour (see p. 184) the most significant figure was Valentin de Boullongne, best known for his genre scenes showing half-length figures taking part in dramatic episodes (*The Card-Sharpers*, Dresden; *The Tavern*, Louvre). In one early picture, he rivalled Poussin (*Martyrdom of St Processus and St Martinian*, Vatican). His colour and manner found favour even with the academic experts and his works made their way into the King's collection.

It was Caravaggio's influence, too, which led to the first great upsurge of still-life painting as such. He had greatly shocked artistic opinion when he declared that a good still-life was as worthwhile, in his opinion, as any good figure-painting, but nevertheless he succeeded in raising the status of the genre to something more than mere decoration. Very early on, before 1600, first Neapolitan and then Spanish art devised a formula for a new kind of still-life — extremely uncluttered, symmetrical, strikingly noble (Sanchez Cotán, Zurbarán). There is something ascetic, even, according to some commentators, mystical, in the profound concentration and gravity of these pure compositions; space is barely indicated, the volumes of objects are shown stripped of all superficials but with the tactile qualities of their surfaces strongly suggested.

For two generations Netherlandish painters lavished all their virtuosity and great representational talent on genre scenes shown under an oblique light or pictures of tables heavily loaded with food and so on. There was no comparable painting in Italy, except perhaps the *bambocciate* of Rome and still-lifes of Naples. But in Bergamo, in Caravaggio's own region, Evaristo Baschenis, a man of warm sensitivity, painted groups of beautiful musical instruments rather in the spirit of his great fellow-countryman.

EVARISTO BASCHENIS, 1617-1677. MUSICAL INSTRUMENTS. ACCADEMIA CARRARA, BERGAMO

BAUGIN, ACTIVE *c.* 1630. WAFERS. LOUVRE, PARIS

BAUGIN. THE FIVE SENSES. LOUVRE, PARIS

FRANCISCO DE ZURBARÁN, 1598-1664. LEMONS, ORANGES AND ROSE, 1633. CONTINI-BONACOSSI COLLECTION, FLORENCE

157

SEVENTEENTH-CENTURY SPAIN

JOSE DE RIBERA, KNOWN AS LO SPAGNOLETTO. 1591-1652
ST. PETER.
HERMITAGE, LENINGRAD

RIBERA.
THE CLUBFOOT, 1652.
LOUVRE, PARIS

RIBERA.
ST AGNES WITH ANGEL, 1641.
GEMÄLDEGALERIE, DRESDEN

The great Caravaggesque and chiaroscuro movement which spread over the whole of Europe in the first part of the seventeenth century provided a splendid opportunity for the Spanish genius —essentially a genius for drama and realism—to express itself. Caravaggio, it may be remembered, was born in the Milan region, a Spanish possession. The great Valencian painters, Ribalta and Ribera, worked for most of their lives in Italy, in the Caravaggesque atmosphere which harmonized so well with the mixture of plebeian lyricism, naturalism and pathos of Counter-Reformation Spain.

Ribera, known as Lo Spagnoletto in Italy, settled in the Spanish viceroyalty of Naples and became one of the greatest masters of this school—at once completely European and strongly Spanish in flavour. In his painting the contrasts of light and shade, pronounced muscles and bleeding wounds add up to an eloquence which makes his pictures of saints and martyrs particularly striking. He also excelled in depicting ragged beggars, old and decrepit athletes and—a favourite subject with Spanish painters—human freaks.

It should not be forgotten that the reverse side of the spiritual mysticism of Spain at this time was a love of the picaresque. Don Quixote had just said a final farewell to his tales of chivalry, and real life, particularly its more sordid side, offered new adventures, more cynical, violent and horrible.

A completely new kind of religiosity began to triumph—a religiosity of the people, trivial and fierce. It needed pictures of tortures, pictures which would shout their meaning beyond possibility of mistake. This cult of images was the South's answer to the iconoclasm of the North; sometimes the images were princely, brilliantly sumptuous, at other times their realism was almost sadistic. But in Ribera's *St Agnes*, popular religiosity is garbed in an exquisite delicacy and splendidly simple, even passionate, modesty.

SEVENTEENTH-CENTURY SPAIN

The Valencian school, like the school of Seville, worked in a wholly Spanish spirit, free from all foreign influences. Murillo is one of its most brilliant masters. His work shows the typically Spanish contrast mentioned above, between extremely concrete naturalism and an idealism pushed to the point of dream and ecstasy. The idealism, as aforesaid, is at a level comprehensible to the people and on occasion it may seem to us of the present day over-sentimentalised, sloppy and facile.

Nevertheless Murillo is a great painter, gifted with a peculiarly Andalusian virtuosity which may not please those who never relax their severity but cannot fail to charm the majority. There is an undeniable fluent grace in this *Girl and Dueña*; the figures look as though they have stepped out of one of the *comedias* of the period.

But to us the strength of Murillo's art seems to lie in his naturalism. It is in his *Kitchen of the Angels* or his scenes of ragged children, beggars and street-life, with their sharp contrasts of light and shade, that we see the real, the great Murillo. It is quite easy to understand how these pictures of a picaresque, picturesque, plebeian Spain became as popular throughout Europe as his very different, over-sweet Madonnas.

It is also to see why this Spain should have exerted such a strong influence on the French Realists and Naturalists of the second half of the nineteenth century. One has only to look at *Boy with Dog* to see how it must have affected Courbet and, in his youth, Manet. Both these artists took over the Spanish conception of reality — the idea that the artist should not remain content with showing things as they actually look but accentuate them, set them in relief, underline their ugliness, blackness or insignificance. There is no question of making a moral judgment or giving a display of human compassion. But nevertheless one can discern a feeling of bitter satisfaction.

BARTOLOME ESTEBAN MURILLO, 1618-1682. GIRL WITH HER DUEÑA, 1665-1675. NATIONAL GALLERY OF ART, WASHINGTON

MURILLO. YOUNG BEGGAR, 1645-1655. LOUVRE, PARIS

MURILLO. BOY WITH A DOG, c. 1650-1660. HERMITAGE, LENINGRAD

159

SEVENTEENTH-CENTURY SPAIN

ZURBARÁN.
ST PETER
APPEARING TO
ST PETER
NOLASCO,
1629.
PRADO, MADRID

ZURBARÁN.
ST CASILDA,
1638-1642.
PRADO, MADRID

ZURBARÁN.
ST FRANCIS
OF ASSISI.
ALTE PINAKOTHEK,
MUNICH

Zurbarán's art contains elements of both Caravaggism and chiaroscuro, but it lacks the fire of Baroque. One remembers him above all for his style—its absence of pathos, its extraordinary feeling for line and volume, its grave, silent hieratic quality. With all its terrifying strangeness, the dramatic power in *The Apostle Peter Appearing to St Peter Nolasco* is singularly laconic. The picture contains Zurbarán's characteristic invention—the use of contrasted, intense, sculptural whites.

Inspired by the spirit of popular piety, Zurbarán painted a whole series of female saints who are in fact merely charming and lively Andalusian women in disguise—peasants or society-ladies, heroines out of comedies by Lope de Vega. Their various 'costumes' are full of grace, dignity, wit and sweeping line. The legend of St Casilda runs as follows: Casilda, the daughter of a Moorish king, was carrying bread to the Christians her father held captive; when she met her father by chance a miracle turned the bread to red roses.

In Spanish iconography the gentle St Francis of Assisi of Giotto's work became a tragic figure. When El Greco was a boy in Crete both Orthodox and Catholic Christians paid special homage to this saint; El Greco himself remained especially devoted to him and painted him in ecstasy in his retreat. For Zurbarán, too, he was a favourite subject. Zurbarán is the equivalent in painting of the great mystic and ascetic writers of Spain. Just as French ladies of the eighteenth century had themselves portrayed as goddesses out of Greek mythology, so ladies of fashion in the Spanish Golden Age had themselves painted in the guise of saints. There is something singularly attractive about the delicious sweetness and femininity (perhaps excessive femininity) of Zurbarán's saints; but there is also a hint of the reverse side of Spanish religious feeling—the meditation on death, the cry of solitaries calling on the divine absolute.

SEVENTEENTH-CENTURY SPAIN

Zurbarán painted one of his first series of conventual decorations for the chapel of the Fathers of Mercy in Seville. It dealt with the life of St Peter Nolasco and included *The Apostle Peter Appearing to St Peter Nolasco* and five other paintings, of which one has disappeared. Nothing could be more concrete, domestic and rustic than the vision which the young, graceful angel, himself extremely real, brings into the cell of the dreaming monk.

There are two versions of *St Marina,* with her coquettish hat. Like St Margaret, she carries on her arm a beautiful basket in many bright colours, which the spectator feels he could almost touch — yet another instance of the skill in super-real still-life, or *bodegon,* painting attained by so many Spanish painters of the period, including Zurbarán himself. Few have represented objects, materials and surfaces better than these 'mystics'. Their mastery of these two opposing qualities is one of the most extraordinary phenomena in Spanish painting.

Zurbarán's *Fray Jeronimo Perez* is another picture in which white plays an important part; the monk is exceptionally statuesque in his robe, with its long, hard folds. And yet, under his hood, his thin, silent face, with its terrified and half—delirious eyes, stares out with a peculiarly mystic quality. He is not reading the book resting horizontally on his hands; one feels that he *cannot* read it because his attention is entirely focussed on the other world, the world of the spirit. But quite apart from its significance the book is absolutely real as an object and one is made aware, here possibly more than anywhere else, of the extraordinary power of objectivity possessed by Spanish painters. They could, and did, recreate the actual presence of things in such a way that there is no room left for speculation or imaginative embroiderings on the part of the spectator. The book is a real object, *hic et nunc.* And yet all around it is fever and fire.

ZURBARÁN. VISION OF ST PETER NOLASCO: 'THE HEAVENLY JERUSALEM', 1629. PRADO, MADRID

ZURBARÁN. ST MARINA, 1630-1642. MUSEO PROVINCIAL DE BELLAS ARTES, SEVILLE

ZURBARÁN. FRAY JERONIMO PEREZ. ACADEMIA SAN FERNANDO, MADRID

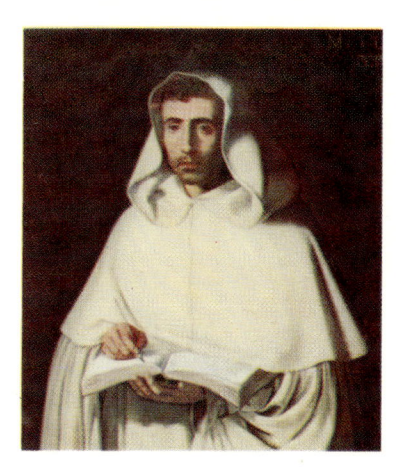

SEVENTEENTH-CENTURY SPAIN

DIEGO RODRIGUEZ
DE SILVA Y
VELASQUEZ.
1599-1660.
OLD WOMAN
COOKING EGGS,
1617-1622.
NATIONAL GALLERY,
EDINBURGH

VELASQUEZ.
LAS MENINAS,
1656.
PRADO, MADRID

VELASQUEZ.
SURRENDER OF
BREDA (LAS
LANZAS),
1634-1635.
PRADO, MADRID

For Murillo realism meant acknowledging that truth was more important than beauty. The same idea can be sensed underlying this early work by Velasquez, *Old Woman Cooking Eggs*. One feels the full force of the words with which Palomino, a very knowledgeable and valuable eighteenth-century art-critic, credits him: 'I would rather be the best rustic painter than the second-best painter of refinement.' Before long Velasquez' realism was to become as perfect as one could imagine. Eugenio d'Ors, the Spanish aesthetician, produced an ingenious pun on the two Spanish verbs 'to be' to describe this mastery: Velasquez painted objects, he said, *'como son y como están'*—that is, 'as they are in character and as they are now situated'.

This dual vision of objects—their quality and their position in space, this total reality, as it were, is presented more convincingly than ever before in *Las Meninas*, one of the two or three finest paintings in the world. In it a random point of time, a random arrangement of figures in space—actually, the painter's studio—are preserved for eternity. The artist himself was painting the royal pair visible in the mirror on the wall in the background. At that moment the Infanta came in with her dog, her clown, her maid and all her retinue. The door opens on to the sunlight outside and we, the spectators, are quite definitely within the room. Three walls are visible; the fourth is behind us. In this picture Velasquez solves all the technical and all the intellectual problems which had troubled artists before him.

However, another masterpiece, *The Surrender of Breda (Las Lanzas)*, takes place out of doors. Although the scene is supposed to be taking place in Holland, the distant deep blue sky is the sky of Madrid and the clear, luminous air of the high Castilian plateau. Most critics agree that this is a splendid evocation of the legendary chivalry of the nobility of Spain.

SEVENTEENTH-CENTURY SPAIN

Kings, infantas, noblemen, fools, freaks and idiots — Velasquez treated them all with the same artistic impartiality, the same lordly detachment, the same proud, assured style. The infantas were particularly rewarding subjects for his prodigious brushwork and palette; he brought into play all the resources of his art to convey the grandeur of their huge, unyielding Court dresses, their enormously artificial coiffures and headdresses and their vacant expressions.

The face of this *Woman with Fan* may have a shade more expression, although it would be a mistake to over-stress this aspect; her features are still restrained, fixed, immobile. Despite the seductiveness one could read into her eyes, mouth and body, they remain, basically, opportunities for the greatest of all technicians to show that his brush has not lost its skill.

The dwarf and Court Jester Antonio el Inglés had been dead for some time when Velasquez painted this portrait, so that it is doubtful whether he is in fact the man portrayed. This is one of Velasquez darkest canvasses and also one of his greatest successes — one of those in which the mysterious and almost insolent ease of his painting shows at its clearest. One cannot help feeling that the dog is more truly noble and alive than the sumptuously dressed midget who poses at his side.

This work is roughly contemporary with his last great masterpieces, *Las Meninas* and *The Spinners*.

Velasquez figures in art-history as the most painterly of painters. Everything supports this: his feeling for textures and his extraordinary brushwork, the miraculous sensitivity of his touch, the refinement of his tones (the greys and blacks just as much as the pinks and lighter shades), his rejection of everything which has no bearing on the painting and the impartiality with which he treats every aspect of the human figure and external world.

VELASQUEZ. INFANTA MARGARITA OF AUSTRIA, c. 1660. PRADO, MADRID

VELASQUEZ. WOMAN WITH FAN. WALLACE COLLECTION, LONDON

VELASQUEZ. DON ANTONIO EL INGLÉS, THE KING'S JESTER. PRADO, MADRID

FLEMISH SCHOOL OF THE SEVENTEENTH CENTURY

PETER PAUL RUBENS, 1577-1640. PORTRAIT OF MARIA DE' MEDICI, BETWEEN 1622 AND 1625. PRADO, MADRID

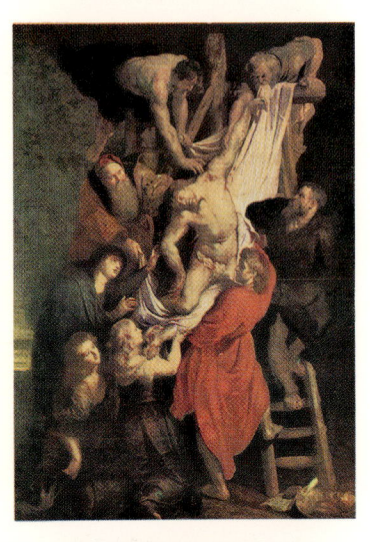

RUBENS. DESCENT FROM THE CROSS, 1612-1614. CATHEDRAL OF NOTRE-DAME, ANTWERP

RUBENS. CHAPEAU DE PAILLE. NATIONAL GALLERY, LONDON

In an unforeseeable way, Peter Paul Rubens set Flemish painting going again. It is almost as hard to connect him with his immediate predecessors as with the glorious Early Flemish school initiated by Van Eyck. He was born at Siegen, Westphalia, the son of a frivolous, exiled father and a capable mother. At Antwerp, he received the intellectual and social training that enabled him to meet both Humanists and princes on equal terms. He attended various studios, and had three successive teachers, though it is not clear what they passed on to him, other than a sound technique, which was traditional in Flanders. Then, in 1600, he left for Italy, returning only at the end of 1608. It was there that he learned all he had to learn—particularly from Titian. There was no other master whom he copied so diligently, or who inspired him more; but he always did so with the utmost freedom, puffing out in waves the simple lines of the bodies and transforming their golden flesh into milk warmed by blood. In 1609, he married Isabella Brandt, a girl of good family, and depicted himself with her in a touchingly intimate portrait. In 1610 and 1614 he painted for Antwerp Cathedral the great works that brought him fame: his *Raising of the Cross*; and, above all, his *Descent from the Cross,* in which a cascade of light, formed by the shroud, Christ's body, and the Magdalene's hair, extends from top right to bottom left. One of the figures who have detached the body is a riot of muscles; the other grips the shroud in his teeth. What makes one admire the Antwerp painters is the way they were not put out by these unwonted novelties, and at once accepted Rubens's superiority. Forthwith he began producing, at a seemingly unprecedented rate, religious scenes, martyrdoms, mythologies, battles, hunts—even landscapes; and his canvas was always full of forms in exalted movement. Not long elapsed between the *Descent from the Cross* and the *Rape of the Daughters*

164

FLEMISH SCHOOL OF THE SEVENTEENTH CENTURY

of Leucippus, which lights up a whole room in the Munich gallery. The two women's bodies trace complementary, shifting curves, while, against the sky, the silhouette of a horse with flowing mane spearheads the general movement, again along a diagonal.

As Rubens did not, strictly speaking, have different styles, it is extremely difficult to date his works on internal evidence; one must select a number of landmarks. In 1620, he was commissioned to produce forty paintings for the Jesuit church at Antwerp. From 1621 to 1625 he was engaged on the Maria de' Medici cycle, which he executed partly at Antwerp but completed at Paris. Now in the Louvre, it makes one marvel at both the fertility of his imagination and the ease with which he mixed mythology and history. For all these vast commissions, the procedure was nearly the same: Rubens himself painted small sketches, all movement and colour, in which his creative fire is beyond compare; then assistants executed the fullsized canvases, which he retouched.

He became very lordly, with a real palace containing his studios and a gallery for his collections. From 1627 to 1629, he carried out diplomatic missions to England, Holland, and Spain. At home, he led a well-ordered life, devoted to his art and to the permitted pleasures of the senses. He was very religious, attending Mass every day; and when, in 1635, the cardinal infante made a state entry into Antwerp, it was Rubens who supervised the entire decoration of the city. When Isabella died, her husband's grief was genuine; but he needed a woman's presence. So, at the end of 1630, he married a girl of sixteen, the buxom Hélène Fourment, one of whose sisters he had probably already represented in the *Chapeau de Paille.* The result was a new burst of activity: his most touching portrait is of Hélène with her children, while the most sensual shows her naked under a half-open fur-coat.

Rubens died in 1640, and was

RUBENS.
TOILET OF VENUS,
c. 1615-1618
GALLERY OF THE
PRINCE OF
LIECHTENSTEIN,
VIENNA

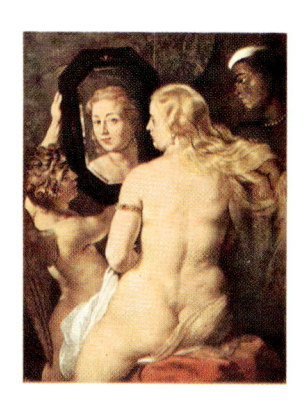

RUBENS.
RAPE OF THE
DAUGHTERS OF
LEUCIPPUS,
c. 1618.
ALTE PINAKOTHEK,
MUNICH

RUBENS.
HÉLÈNE FOURMENT,
c. 1630-1631.
KUNSTHISTORISCHES
MUSEUM, VIENNA

FLEMISH SCHOOL OF THE SEVENTEENTH CENTURY

FRANS SNYDERS,
1579-1657.
DOGS FIGHTING
FOR BONES.
MUSÉE ROYAL
D'ART ANCIEN,
BRUSSELS

CORNELIS DE VOS,
c. 1586-1651.
PORTRAIT OF
THE ARTIST
AND HIS FAMILY,
1621.
MUSÉE ROYAL
D'ART ANCIEN,
BRUSSELS

JUSTUS SUTTERMANS,
1597-1681.
PORTRAIT OF
MARIA MAGDALENA
OF AUSTRIA,
WIDOW OF COSMO II
DE' MEDICI.
MUSÉE ROYAL
D'ART ANCIEN,
BRUSSELS

buried in St Jacques, Antwerp, beneath the moving *Sacra Conversazione* that he had painted for his chapel there, and in which he probably figures as a knight.

The history of Flemish painting in Rubens' times is, to a considerable extent, the biography of his collaborators. Moreover, he made no attempt to conceal their help. In a famous letter of 28th April, 1618, to Sir Dudley Carleton, he specified what, in a number of works, came from his own hand, and what came from theirs. For the most part, it was not a question of followers or pupils, as this 'bandleader' succeeded in engaging artists of his own generation, several of whom were first class. Frans Snyders, the still-life and animal specialist, was barely two years younger than Rubens, who did not scruple to approach Snyders' mentor 'Velvet' Bruegel, either, even though Jan was Rubens' senior by some ten years. At all events, Snyders, who became a master at Antwerp in 1602, also made the journey to Italy, from whence he returned at almost the same time as Rubens. The two men were on very close terms, especially from 1611 to 1616. Snyders' pictures consist of tumbled heaps of fruit, vegetables, fish, poultry, and game with miraculously rendered fur.

Snyders married the sister of Cornelis and Paul de Vos. With a technique that was less rich and full, but with a livelier sense of the movement of animals, Paul did Rubens the same kind of services as his brother-in-law. As for Cornelis, he was the author of the peaceful and profound family portrait at Brussels, in which the children are painted with a freshness and sensitivity perhaps unequalled by Rubens. Until Van Dyck appeared on the scene, Justus Suttermans had great success with his portraits. He was the favourite painter of the Medici family at Florence, and his pleasant but rather superficial art became known at Vienna, Rome, Parma, Piacenza, Modena and Milan.

166

FLEMISH SCHOOL OF THE SEVENTEENTH CENTURY

Jacob Jordaens gives new point to the rebukes of those who are squeamish about Ruben's robust sensuality—which they call vulgarity—since he really did carry this tendency to extremes. With him, flesh became meat, fullness turned to fatness, an abundance of figures grew into congestion, and feasting degenerated into the hogging of grub. Moreover, he only collaborated with Rubens now and then, though he learned a great deal from these contacts. In particular, he assisted the older artist on the occasion of Ferdinand of Austria's state entry into Antwerp, and when, towards the end of his life, Rubens was commissioned to decorate the Torre de la Parada, near Madrid. Jordaens himself also took assistants, because his own studio was doing thriving business. Like Rubens before him, he had been a pupil of Adam van Noort, whose daughter he married. He possessed the most exuberant temperament of his period, and it is not easy to explain why, with his character and in the Catholic environment of his country, he should late in life have become a Calvinist. More admirable than the disorderliness of his banquets attended by big-bosomed hussies is his *Allegory of Fertility,* in which the heavy goddesses are superbly animal, as befits the subject. One of his most famous pictures, *St Peter finding a Stater in the Fish's Mouth* (Copenhagen), is also known as *The Antwerp Ferry;* the sailors, who together with the passengers fill the boat, arrogantly expand their muscles to manœuvre it. His more reflective *Four Evangelists* provides fine studies of three bushy-haired old men and of a young man —almost an adolescent—who has sometimes been mistaken for a Christ among the Docters. The works of Caravaggio obviously had an influence on Jordaens Like Cornelis de Vos, this master craftsman was capable of painting a moving portrait of his family, which also provides a faithful image of the Flemish middle class of his day.

JACOB JORDAENS,
1593-1678.
FOUR EVANGELISTS.
LOUVRE, PARIS

JORDAENS.
TWELFTH NIGHT,
c. 1638.
HERMITAGE,
LENINGRAD

JORDAENS.
HOMMAGE TO
POMONE:
ALLEGORY OF
FERTILITY
(DETAIL),
c. 1625.
MUSÉE ROYAL
D'ART ANCIEN,
BRUSSELS

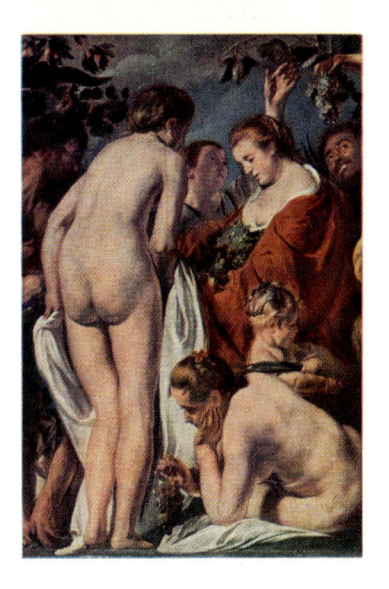

167

FLEMISH SCHOOL OF THE SEVENTEENTH CENTURY

ANTHONY VAN DYCK,
1599-1641.
SELF-PORTRAIT
(DETAIL),
c. 1621-1622.
ALTE PINAKOTHEK,
MUNICH

VAN DYCK.
PORTRAIT OF
TWO YOUNG MEN.
NATIONAL GALLERY,
LONDON

VAN DYCK.
PORTRAIT OF
MARCHESA
GERONIMA SPINOLA
(DETAIL),
c. 1623-1627.
KAISER-FRIEDRICH
MUSEUM, BERLIN

Anthony van Dyck, whom Rubens considered his best disciple, was too gifted to stay in anyone's shadow. Fromentin wrote of this 'young prince of royal blood, showered with every natural advantage . . . marked out for every success . . . dying as soon as the throne was empty, never to reign.' In the early self-portrait at Munich, his refined, aristocratic good looks and pink, rather too delicate, complexion beneath reddish-blond hair form a perfect contrast to the robust health of Rubens.

His precociousness is legendary. In 1616 or 1617, he joined the Rubens studio, became a master at nineteen, and absorbed Rubens' style so well, that he was given the hardest jobs. It is still debated to-day whether or not he was responsible for the negroes' heads in the Brussels museum. The contract of 1620 between Rubens and the Antwerp Jesuits provided for the master's designs to be executed by Van Dyck and other, un-named pupils. When, therefore, the young man set up on his own, he already showed his extraordinary gifts for portraiture, observing his sitters with more insight than Rubens.

In 1620, he paid his first visit to England. He did not stay long, however, and in 1621, on Ruben's advice, he headed for Italy, where he eagerly made drawings after Titian. First he stayed at Genoa, winning over its aristocracy; his Berlin *Marchesa Geronima Spinola,* so trimly elegant in her severe black dress relieved by a collar and cuffs of tulle, recalls this period. At Rome, where he was no less successful, he felt only scorn for his vulgar compatriots there, who spent far more time in taverns than in fashionable society. During this period, his works also included a considerable number of Old and New Testament subjects.

In 1627, he returned to Antwerp; but even though Rubens was then very busy with his diplomatic work, his personality still dominated the market, and Van Dyck did not achieve the success he consider-

168

FLEMISH SCHOOL OF THE SEVENTEENTH CENTURY

ed his due. Once more, he decided to try his luck, and in 1632 he was back in England. This time his success was complete. Highly favoured by Charles I, he blossomed out in the service of a prince who rightly passed for one of the leading connoisseurs of Europe. In the Louvre portrait, one sees him dismounted and every inch an aristocrat. The relationship of the grey satin to the brown-red breeches is enough to indicate the extreme refinement of the colouring. All the court passed before Van Dyck's easel, and a pre-ordained harmony existed between him and the English aristocracy, for whom he was *the* painter — so much so, that the eighteenth-century English school could do no better than follow in his wake. The artist had footmen and coaches, married the beautiful Marie Ruthven, and to entertain his sitters, he employed musicians. Apparently, he never spent more than one hour at a stretch on the same portrait. For his famous hands he sometimes used professional models, while for clothes he often called in assistants. One of his most wonderful pieces shows Lords George and Bernard Stuart, two almost femininely elegant cavaliers with long, curly hair; one of them casually holds a glove, painted with a virtuosity almost equal to that of Velasquez.

Rubens died at the end of May 1640, and, wanting once again to seek success in his homeland, Van Dyck left for Antwerp during the autumn of the same year. He hoped for employment by the French crown, but his propositions went unanswered. Though he was sounded about finishing the works of his master that were intended for Spain, his prices seemed so unreasonable that negotiations were broken off. In short, he met with nothing but disappointments, and so he returned to England — where more awaited him. In December 1641, he died, worn out by illness and perhaps by excesses; though glorious, he had never really reigned supreme.

VAN DYCK.
PORTRAIT OF LORD
PHILIP WHARTON,
1632.
NATIONAL GALLERY,
WASHINGTON

VAN DYCK.
CHARLES I
OF ENGLAND,
c. 1635.
LOUVRE, PARIS

VAN DYCK.
SUSANNA AND
THE ELDERS.
c. 1622-1623.
ALTE PINAKOTHEK,
MUNICH

FLEMISH SCHOOL OF THE SEVENTEENTH CENTURY

ADRIAEN BROUWER,
1605-1638.
THE SMOKER,
c. 1626.
LOUVRE, PARIS

ADRIAEN BROUWER.
DRINKERS SEATED
AT TABLE.
MUSÉE ROYAL
D'ART ANCIEN,
BRUSSELS

ADRIAEN BROUWER.
THE OPERATION.
STÄDELSCHES
KUNSTINSTITUT,
FRANKFURT

Rubens set Flemish painting in pursuit of a dynamic lyricism; his own *kermis* paintings and Jordaens' feasts are explosions of joy. But, far from having relinquished its claims, the tradition of naked, almost abject truth humorously and even comically observed—as Bruegel had understood it—was revived by two highly disparate artists: Brouwer and Teniers.

Adriaen Brouwer is the epitome of the unrepentant bohemian. He began painting at Antwerp, and one of his earliest known works, a *Temptation of St Anthony,* shows him engrossed in Bosch's fantasy. Then he moved to Amsterdam and to Haarlem, where he was influenced by Frans Hals, and seems almost at once to have achieved enviable successes. In 1631, he was back in Antwerp, where he became a master, after which not much more is known. He appeared cut out for success: his little pictures of noisy wrangles in taverns and smoking-dens sold well, and he attracted Rubens' attention—so much so that, at his death, the great man owned seventeen of his works. However, alcohol and tobacco absorbed all he earned, and an inventory of the property he pawned in 1632 reveals a pretty dismal situation. To crown it all, he went to prison in rather mysterious circumstances, but seems to have led a fairly tolerable life there—with access to his beloved poisons. In 1638, he died, in worse straits than ever, though he did receive a decent burial, thanks perhaps to Rubens, who had already helped to get him released.

Rubens was not one to misjudge the quality even of an artist so remote from him socially. In his small-scale works, Brouwer always painted broadly, sweeping the panel with his brush. His amazingly expressive faces are merely indicated without excessive precision, and softly lit. A certain contradiction exists between the more-or-less depraved subjects and very delicate colours: greys and browns, but also pale mauves, faint blues, burnt carmine, and

FLEMISH SCHOOL OF THE SEVENTEENTH CENTURY

blond tones. The Louvre *Smoker*, with his fat, red face, opens wide his mouth, from the depths of which escapes a thread of smoke. Brouwer also enjoyed the agonized grimaces of a patient being butchered by the village surgeon, while his brawls are no laughing matter: the participants grab each other by the hair. Yet he also painted a number of surprisingly sensitive landscapes, now mostly in Berlin. Usually, they are lit by the dim light of dusk or the moon. Their colouring is based on greys and bistres, and they are the work of a born painter.

Without doubt, Brouwer decisively influenced David Teniers the Younger. Our reversal of the accepted 'placing' would have amazed our ancestors; for whereas Brouwer was once almost unknown, Teniers had a European reputation. He married 'Velvet' Bruegel's daughter, who was also Rubens' god-child. When Archduke Leopold Wilhelm came to the southern Netherlands in 1646, he formed a great admiration for Teniers, attracted him to Brussels, and there put him in charge of his gallery, which the artist represented in a series of pictures of great documentary value. Teniers also founded the Antwerp Academy, and he acquired a property near the Château de Steen, where Rubens spent his last years. By and large, his repertoire was the same as Brouwer's—tavern scenes, card games, and doctors; but, in comparing the two artists, one may recall La Fontaine's fable about the wolf who preferred the hazards of freedom to the dog's comfortable bondage. This does not mean that Teniers lacked talent, for his colouring is delicate, without altogether being exquisite, and the treatment of his rather too mannerly figures is scrupulous and refined. He, too, made extensive use of landscape, and it was when it filled almost the entire picture that he produced his best work. This undoubtedly contains memories of Rubens, who, at the close of his life, perhaps influenced him.

ADRIAEN BROUWER. CARD-PLAYERS. ALTE PINAKOTHEK, MUNICH

DAVID TENIERS THE YOUNGER, 1610-1690. COUNTRY DOCTOR. MUSÉE ROYAL D'ART ANCIEN, BRUSSELS

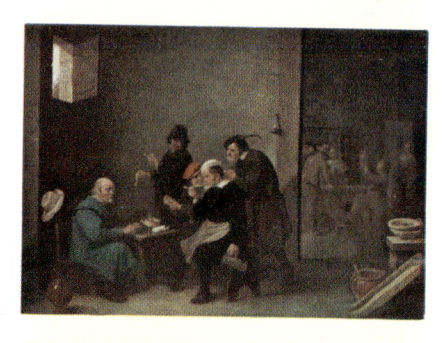

DAVID TENIERS THE YOUNGER. MAN IN A WHITE HAT. MUSÉE FABRE, MONTPELLIER

DAVID TENIERS THE YOUNGER. CARD-PLAYERS. MUSÉE ROYAL D'ART ANCIEN, BRUSSELS

DUTCH SCHOOL OF THE SEVENTEENTH CENTURY

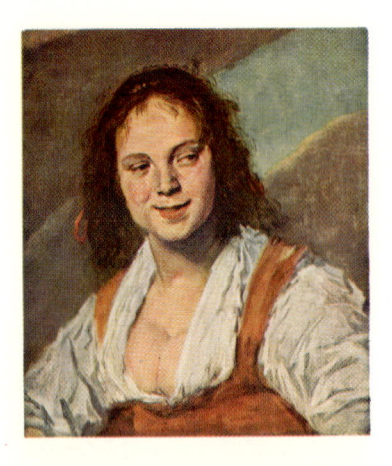

FRANS HALS,
1580/81-1666.
GIPSY GIRL
(LA BOHÉMIENNE),
1625-1628.
LOUVRE, PARIS

FRANS HALS.
'MALLE BABBE',
SORCERESS OF
HAARLEM,
c. 1640 or 1650 (?)
KAISER-FRIEDRICH
MUSEUM, BERLIN

FRANS HALS.
OFFICERS OF THE
KLOVENIERS
ARQUEBUSIERS
AT HAARLEM,
1633.
FRANS HALS
MUSEUM, HAARLEM

'Hals was only a practical craftsman...; but as such he is well above the most skilled and expert masters who have ever existed anywhere.' These are the words of a painter describing a painter; no portrait of the greatest virtuoso of the Dutch school will ever surpass the one created by Fromentin in *The Masters of Past Time*.

Van Dyck apart, who could evoke with more dash, gaiety and decisiveness the characteristic appearance, physical presence, and positive existence in space of a single figure or group of human beings? Still more than from his teacher Van Mander, it was from Rubens that the Haarlem painter (born in about 1580 at Antwerp) seems to have derived his life-giving power and his—in art—most rare exuberance and good humour. Even among the great Italians, ever present in the minds of the Dutch artists, portraiture almost always had a formal quality, but with Frans Hals it abdicated all its assumed nobility. The barriers of reserve between the painter and his sitters were removed, to be replaced by a close familiarity, although it hardly went beyond comradeship. Never mind about inner complexities and hidden secrets! This full-blooded optimist was closer in temperament to his harquebusier, or his buffoon than to a philosopher (although he did portray Descartes). He liked people to show as much vitality as he did, to laugh heartily, or to smile.

A born painter, he was a colourist through his love of light, of fabrics, and of every outward splendour that responds to the sun. Just as he liked to gather together all the members of a corporation or family, so he created a mutual understanding between all the details and the materials without, however, giving way to congestion or disharmony. So great were his candour and decisiveness, that he avoided—by a hair's breadth—the pitfalls that entrapped his rivals and his countless imitators, who possessed neither his

DUTCH SCHOOL OF THE SEVENTEENTH CENTURY

taste nor his instinctive awareness of the technical resources of painting.

Hals' eight huge 'official' group portraits, measuring from four to eight square metres, eclipse those of Bartholomeus van der Helst (1613-1670) and of all his predecessors. They do so through the ease and dispatch with which, aided sometimes by thin and sometimes by thick impasto, he was able to present ten or twenty figures on his stage, dressing them, lighting them, linking them together and deriving his pleasure from theirs. Similarly, in his individual portraits, he caught the characteristic expression, gesture and rhythm straight off, and was never guilty of the exaggerated effects or vulgarities of the Bolognese school and Caravaggio. All manner of success in the use of paint reveals his distinction in a field where the majority of artists appear stiff and awkward before an indomitable foe. With amazing richness and variety, he was able to make child's play of every technical problem, never aspiring after qualities that he did not possess, for he was aware of his limitations. All this can be seen in the *Gipsy Girl* and *Itinerant Painter,* and in the portraits of *Stephanus Geraerdts* (Antwerp), *Malle Babbe* or *Isabella Coymans* (E. de Rothschild collection). Yet, late in life, material difficulties and the threat of old age tinged his work with tragedy and shadows, as in *The Governors of the Old Men's Almshouse* and *The Women Governors of the Old Men's Almshouse.* These final masterpieces seem to have been influenced by an artist twenty-six years his junior. In his *Jan Six,* Rembrandt had had the work of Hals in mind; but now it was his turn to show the older man that there were unknown paths leading, by way of the body, straight to the soul.

Neither environment nor heredity explains the advent of Rembrandt. Whatever could have inclined this son of a Leyden miller to art? Of Protestant descent and therefore predisposed to reject all

FRANS HALS. PORTRAIT OF BALTHASAR COYMANS, 1645. NATIONAL GALLERY OF ART, WASHINGTON

FRANS HALS. PORTRAIT OF A MAN (DETAIL FROM 'GOVERNORS OF THE OLD MEN'S ALMSHOUSE'), 1664. FRANS HALS MUSEUM, HAARLEM

FRANS HALS. WOMEN GOVERNORS OF THE OLD MEN'S ALMSHOUSE, 1664. FRANS HALS MUSEUM, HAARLEM

REMBRANDT HARMENSZ. VAN RIJN, 1606-1669. 'NIGHT WATCH': THE COMPANY OF CAPTAIN FRANS BANNING COCQ, 1642. RIJKSMUSEUM, AMSTERDAM

REMBRANDT. PORTRAIT OF JAN SIX, 1654. SIX COLLECTION, AMSTERDAM

REMBRANDT. SELF-PORTRAIT, 1659. NATIONAL GALLERY OF ART, WASHINGTON

representations of Bible scenes, how did he come to be at once Hebraist and Catholic in his work? As a citizen of the materialistic United Provinces, which before him had thought about nothing but landscape, how did he manage to avoid commonplace to such an extent and in every field (portraiture, still-life, landscape, secular and religious subjects)? There is no valid explanation; we shall never know. What his work does teach us, however, is that this pupil of Pieter Lasterman and Jacob van Swanenburgh had already been set apart when, still under thirty, he painted the Amsterdam *Jeremiah* or the first *Supper at Emmaus* in the Musée Jacquemart-André, Paris.

What is it that already fills us with wonder in these very early works, and still more so in his drawings? It is what he could not have inherited from any master, even those from whom he often borrowed his general schemes: Mantegna, Dürer, Lucas van Leyden, Callot and Elsheimer. This comprises not only the fellowship with all mankind that he discovered within himself, but means of expression as fulgurant as those of the prophets, a vocabulary entirely new in painting, and a light that had nothing in common with ordinary daylight.

To say that light plays the leading role in Rembrandt's compositions is not to imply that he disregarded colour, poses, characteristic gestures or detail. What some have called his realism never paralysed his vitality. Paradoxically, it was always by way of the commonplace that he attained the sublime.

Rembrandt's light is most like that of Titian, who lacked his spirituality; it is a light that seems to emanate from the beings and objects represented. To speak of inner life, when discussing Rembrandt's portraits, is not just empty talk, since the form is modelled as much by the fires of the soul as by those of the external world. Even the inanimate — a flayed carcass of beef or hung game — is no less moving than the likenesses that

DUTCH SCHOOL OF THE SEVENTEENTH CENTURY

Rembrandt painted by the hundred, of himself, his mother, father, brother, son, and friends, as well as of his first wife Saskia and his second, Hendrickje Stoffels. If he preferred to subject these faces to effects of contrasted light, this was not to achieve a threatrical pathos, like the majority of his imitators, but to present an equivalent of the oppositions within every human being. It is not only the pictures that he drew, engraved or painted of biblical or legendary subjects that plunge us into an atmosphere of unreality. The fabrics, jewels and armour in which he loved to dress up are not so much ornaments as accessories of a certain inward enchantment. His choice of subjects is no more help in establishing a chronology of his works than is their handling. For him, a theme was never completely exhausted, and he returned, after an interval of several years, to the *Presentation in the Temple,* the *Adoration of the Shepherds,* the *Entombment,* or *Bathsheba,* as though the characters in these scenes had gone on growing inside him. He has often been accused of liking ugliness; but the fact is that he had been too thoroughly raised on the Scriptures not to feel the precariousness of everything here below, and respect even the flaws of mortal flesh.

Rembrandt was right when he advised people to stand back in order to contemplate his works: one thus avoided being alarmed by the peculiarities of an impassioned handling that contrasted with the smooth technique in which his age delighted. For long years he amazed and even offended. Misunderstood since his *Night Watch* and growing continually bolder after success had deserted him, he was never more exalted, despite frustrations and every kind of sorrow, than in the masterpieces of his mature and late periods: *David playing the Harp before Saul* (The Hague, Mauritshuis), *The Return of the Prodigal Son* (Leningrad, Hermitage), *The Syndics of the Drapers' Guild,* or *The Jewish Bride* (both Amsterdam, Rijksmuseum).

REMBRANDT.
BATHSHEBA,
1654.
LOUVRE, PARIS

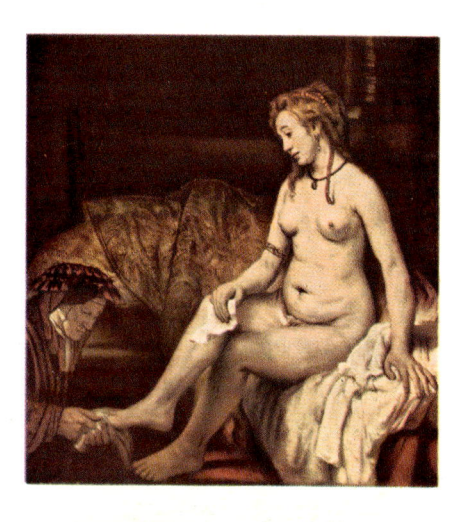

REMBRANDT.
PORTRAIT OF
A RABBI,
1657.
NATIONAL GALLERY,
LONDON

REMBRANDT.
THE JEWISH BRIDE,
c. 1665.
RIJKSMUSEUM,
AMSTERDAM

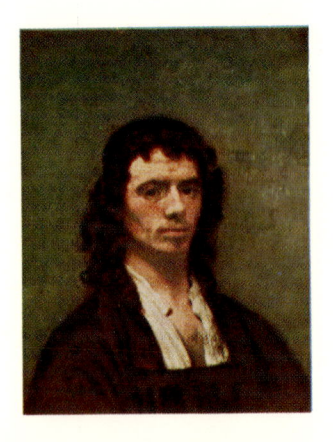

DUTCH SCHOOL OF THE SEVENTEENTH CENTURY

CAREL FABRITIUS,
1622-1654.
SELF-PORTRAIT,
1645.
BOYMANS MUSEUM,
ROTTERDAM

PIETER JANSZ.
SAENREDAM,
1597-1665.
THE OLD
TOWN HALL
OF AMSTERDAM,
1657.
RIJKSMUSEUM,
AMSTERDAM

SAENREDAM.
INTERIOR OF
ST BAVO, HAARLEM.
FRANS HALS
MUSEUM, HAARLEM

How delightful it is to pass from the overcrowded, spectacular still-lifes that made the reputation of such artists of the Italian, Flemish, and Dutch schools as Aertsen, Beuckelaer, Snyders, Jan Fyt, Heem, or Empoli, to the austere and purified compositions favoured by a few seventeenth-century Dutch painters, who specialized in what the twentieth-century calls realist painting! For the majority of compositions known so inexactly as 'still-lifes', the great stumbling-block has always been diffuseness, the refusal to leave anything out. Through exaggerated respect for detail, the picture tends to become a miniature, and one needs a magnifying glass to study it, whatever its size. In these assemblages, which entail chance juxtapositions of objects of different classes and from different spheres, too many reflections and gradations of colour run the risk of compromising the indispensable virtue of a picture: its unity.

Artists like Pieter Claesz, Willem Claesz. Heda, or Metsu avoided all promiscuity, every unseemly presence, and stressed the sympathy between the forms, materials, or planes of foreground and background. They were content with very simple, commonplace elements, the arrangement of which on a table or sideboard established a reciprocal action brought out as much by the character of the lines as by that of the colours. Whether they are a glass or metal goblet, a plate bearing two herrings or a cut lemon, or a pewter jug, the objects live. Instead of the lavish display of different multi-coloured substances with which we are assailed by artists who seemed to believe that their learning would be gauged by the number of materials juxtaposed, subtle organization directs a little concert limited to a very few instruments; and so sweet is the sound that it could be likened to chamber music. This organization is rather similar to that which we find at the same period in the work of the Alsace painter Stoskopff, the Frenchmen Linard and

DUTCH SCHOOL OF THE SEVENTEENTH CENTURY

Baugin, or the Spaniards Sánchez-Cotón and Zurbarán.

'Monochrome feasts' is what the Dutch called these high-class gatherings, in which cool tones predominate, as though, by contrast, to make clearer the vibration and brightness of a vivid hue, or the brilliance of a reflection. The spaces between the objects are almost as important as the objects themselves. Nothing could be more subtle than the mutual action set up by their proximity, and the way in which they play against uniform backgrounds — grey, ashen or golden — that help to unite them. In their still-lifes, as in their genre paintings, the seventeenth-century Dutch artists linked up again with the 'primitives' of the fifteenth-century, both as regards the quality of the execution and the sobriety and aptness of the feeling. It is this very tactfulness that makes them even more sought after today than a de Heem or a Kalf, who were for so long preferred.

The greatest of Rembrandt's followers, Carel Fabritius, to whom some attribute *The Good Samaritan*, produced a most unusual *trompe-l'œil* painting in his delicious *Goldfinch* on a small cupboard panel. It deserves its place in the Mauritshuis next to Vermeer's *Girl with a Turban*, and may be compared to certain works by Gerard Dou.

The economy and distinction of painters like Pieter Claesz or Heda reappear in the art of so-called architectural painters, such as Emanuel de Witte, whose subtle harmonies between stone and water sometimes foreshadow the eighteenth-century Venetians. It appears, too, in the work of one of the best painters of church interiors, Pieter Saenredam, whose delicate rigour, Protestant austerity, mystery in broad daylight, and palette made up almost entirely of whites and greys, have brought him back into favour. Without becoming dry, this artist (who heralded the Corot of *Sens Cathedral*) took to the economy of hues that also characterized the landscapes and still-lifes of the Haarlem school.

CAREL FABRITIUS.
THE GOLDFINCH,
1654.
MAURITSHUIS,
THE HAGUE

WILLEM CLAESZ.
HEDA,
1594-1680/82.
STILL-LIFE WITH
TOBACCO,
1637.
J. M. REDELE
COLLECTION,
DORDRECHT

PIETER CLAESZ,
1597 ?-1661.
STILL-LIFE
WITH FRUIT,
1649.
NATIONAL GALLERY,
LONDON

DUTCH SCHOOL OF THE SEVENTEENTH CENTURY

JAN VERMEER,
1632-1675.
WOMAN AT
THE WINDOW,
c. 1663.
METROPOLITAN
MUSEUM, NEW YORK

VERMEER.
THE LACE-MAKER,
c. 1664.
LOUVRE, PARIS

VERMEER.
THE STUDIO,
c. 1665.
KUNSTHISTORISCHES
MUSEUM, VIENNA

Of Jan Vermeer's early works, still influenced by the Utrecht Italianizers and particularly Terbruggen, all that remain are *Christ in the House of Martha and Mary* (Edinburgh), *Diana and her Nymphs* (Mauritshuis), and *The Procuress* (Dresden). At twenty-four he gave up painting mystic subjects, or ones from Antiquity, and began to specialize in a field in which he would have been just another minor master, had he not recalled the lessons he had learned from one of Rembrandt's only great pupils. This was Carel Fabritius, whose methods already foreshadowed the grainy technique that the enchanter of Delft would use to translate the caress of daylight on skeins, a bowl, a jug, rolls, a fabric or a rampart.

Restricted to interiors where only sea-charts, maps of the world, compasses, and books invite escape; faithful to one single female type, whose expression varies as little as her pose—by what sorcery did he succeed in making continual discoveries within so narrow a field? Never had chamber music been brought to such perfection. In the works of the other Dutch painters of indoor scenes, one can add or delete this or that detail, as one wishes. Here, however, the relations between the objects, the rhythms, and the colours are so exactly calculated, that it would be impossible to introduce the least modification into little masterpieces of refinement, such as *The Lacemaker*, *Woman weighing Pearls* (Washington), *Woman in Blue reading a Letter* (Amsterdam), *Woman at the Window with a Water Jug*, *Woman with a Pearl Necklace* (Berlin), or *Maid-servant pouring Milk* (Amsterdam).

How is it that such an atmosphere of peace and harmony emanates from little scenes so devoid of mystery that one might be tempted to compare their silence with the silence that reigns in the religious portraits of Philippe de Champaigne or the interior of Louis Le Nain? Here, as with Chardin a century later and then with Vuillard, the most workaday scene takes on a kind of unreality, and the moment seems eternal. Even when open, a window allows no sound to enter. The silence of a convent dwells in these middle-class homes, which are as cosy as the quilted, ermine-edged dresses of their occupants. The bareness of the walls allows them to become not opaque barriers, but mirrors in which gold, azure, pearl, and ivory blend. Just as Rembrandt created an ash-grey, gold, crimson, or night atmosphere around his figures, so Vermeer, by what seem like contrary means and in spite of his strictness, shielded his windows, tables, carpets and hanging lamps from ordinary lighting. Everything takes on a dream-like appearance, and this recreated, transfiguring light is the only active element remaining within an exquisite immobility.

Along with Watteau's *Embarkation for Cythera,* Renoir considered *The Lace-maker* to be the most beautiful canvas in the Louvre. The most precise details remain subject to a hidden logic, and unobtrusively play their part. Except for the *Girl with a Flute* and *Girl with a red Hat* (both Washington), the *Girl with a Turban* is just about the only Vermeer to possess the intensity of a portrait; and to find modelling of equal softness, one would have to go back to Titian, Giorgione and Correggio. One never tires of contemplating this bust-length figure with slightly protruding eyes. Voluptuously chaste, and as much a creature of the night as of the day, she belongs to neither country nor period. We know nothing about her, just as we know almost nothing about her portrayer. Much research has been needed to identify a total of thirty-five of his canvases. Vermeer was born in 1632, but we can only imagine what he looked like and how he lived. He really would have died the posthumous death that is an artist's cruellest test, if Reynolds and above all if, a century ago, Thoré Burger (who called him the Sphinx), had not

VERMEER.
THE GEOGRAPHER,
1669.
STÄDELSCHES
KUNSTINSTITUT,
FRANKFURT

VERMEER.
GIRL WITH
A TURBAN,
c. 1665 ?
MAURITSHUIS,
THE HAGUE

VERMEER.
LADY STANDING
BEFORE A
VIRGINAL,
c. 1671.
NATIONAL GALLERY,
LONDON

GERARD DOU,
1613-1675.
GIRL WITH
A LANTERN.
KUNSTHISTORISCHES
MUSEUM, VIENNA

JAN STEEN,
1626-1679.
BAD COMPANY.
LOUVRE, PARIS

GERARD TER BORCH,
1617-1681.
THE CONCERT.
KAISER-FRIEDRICH
MUSEUM, BERLIN

set about reviving him. Twenty female heads, a few conversation pieces, an allegory and two townscapes, all that remain of his works, have been enough to set him among the gods.

Through his familiarity and animation, Frans Hals (and after him his brother Dirk, who painted the *Country Feast* in the Louvre) had regenerated portraiture, making it evolve towards genre and, more particularly, the conversation piece. Stimulated by his prodigious powers as a colourist and life-instiller, exquisite minor masters, drawn to subjects so alike that their creators are often hard to tell apart, devoted not only the most refined technical qualities, but also their sentimentality, wit, or taste to little scenes taken from life.

A new intimacy reigns in these trim interiors, where all is dust-free and shining, and where the faces, like the fabrics and everyday objects, are exposed to the play of light. Nothing could be more unlike the solemnity still prevailing in France and Italy. An unaccustomed gaiety took possession of the painters' brushes; and the extreme care with which the most varied qualities are reproduced recalls that of the 'primitives' in gathering together all the offerings of the earth around the Virgin or a saint. Even if the spiritual quality has completely gone, and there is no longer anything beyond the picture itself, one finds the same powers of observation, meticulousness, and delight in forming a unified whole out of a hundred details and in giving an impression of depth on a surface which itself is flat.

Easel painting now engrossed artists as much as, formerly, the decoration of altars or public buildings had done. A well-to-do middle class liked to contemplate the reflection of its success in these little, jewel-like images, which look as though they have been copied from life. Once transposed, however, the scenes derive their merit chiefly from the delightful

DUTCH SCHOOL OF THE SEVENTEENTH CENTURY

understanding reached between the forms, the colours, the play of light, the open vistas, and the close-knit actions.

After Palamedesz, Codde, Leyster, Duyster, and Bruegel's heir Adriaen van Ostade, painters like Pieter de Hooch *(Interior of a Dutch House, The Card Players, The Courtyard)*, Gabriel Metsu *(Officer and Young Lady)*, and Gerard ter Borch *(Fatherly Advice, The Concert, le Galant Militaire)* excelled in those lively representations that, when vulgarized by the less witty approach of a Troost or a Gerard Dou, turned to empty displays of skill or to studio formulae, or else gave way to a triteness not always avoided by Jan Steen. Yet, this decline cannot obscure the exquisite tact with which, while other artists were rediscovering nature and the magic of the open air, the Haarlem and Leyden painters of domestic scenes applied their talents to the entente created by light between walls, human beings, and familiar objects.

It is surprising that the greatest, and today the most admired, of these 'Intimists' should for so long have remained unnoticed, though represented in the museums. Even if Vermeer of Delft did surpass them all, he cannot make us treat unjustly these minor masters, filled with wonder by the succession of little, trivial events in the rooms where people drank, supped, chatted, made love, or slept, and where everything seems new, shiny, and festive.

From J. B. Chardin to Renoir, Bonnard, and Vuillard, French artists have never ceased to learn from these enchanters. So long as silks, velvets, satins, jewels, flowers, the reflections of sunlight on wood, metal, or glass, and the softness and warmth of flesh still delight our eyes, craftsmen of genius like Ter Borch or Pieter de Hooch will continue to be esteemed and loved; and not just as clever wardrobe masters and skilled producers, but as friends wondrously intent on rediscovering all the pleasures of the daily round.

ADRIAEN VAN OSTADE, 1610-1684.
THE TOOTH-PULLER.
KUNSTHISTORISCHES MUSEUM, VIENNA

EMANUEL DE WITTE, 1617-1692.
INTERIOR OF DELFT CATHEDRAL.
LILLE MUSEUM

PIETER DE HOOCH, 1629-1683 (?)
THE MOTHER.
KAISER-FRIEDRICH MUSEUM, BERLIN

181

REMBRANDT,
1606-1669.
CASTLE AT
TWILIGHT,
c. 1650.
LOUVRE, PARIS

JAN VAN GOYEN,
1596-1656.
THE TWO OAKS,
1641.
RIJKSMUSEUM,
AMSTERDAM

SALOMON VAN
RUISDAEL,
AFTER 1600-1670.
RIVER,
1644.
MAURITSHUIS,
THE HAGUE

JACOB ISAACKSZ.
VAN RUISDAEL,
1628/29-1682.
WHEATFIELD.
METROPOLITAN
MUSEUM, NEW YORK

For a long time, Netherlandish artists believed it necessary to go to Italy for lessons in taste and the tricks of their trade. But at the start of the seventeenth century, 'non-migratory' artists appeared in Haarlem, Dordrecht, Delft, and Amsterdam. To earn a living, they often had a second occupation, and they realized that it is within our native horizons, among everyday sights, and above all inside ourselves, that we make the greatest discoveries.

Rejecting all the usual ennoblements, they made the sole object of their study what up to then had just been décor, subordinated all action to that of light, and found mystery outside the sacred. Along with Esaias van de Velde and Seghers, Van Goyen, that primitive of pure landscape painting, was the first to modify the age-old viewpoints. He lowered the horizon, giving up three-quarters of his canvas to depth and the movement of the skies, while his devotion to calm led him to make tonal effects predominate over those of colour.

The passion of Van Goyen, Jacob van Ruisdael, and Hobbema for nature was so all-consuming that they often gave the job of animating their foregrounds—by mingling little human adventures with those of the clouds and wind —to artists sometimes considered their superiors: Berchem, Jean Vermeer or Adriaen van de Velde.

Without Van Goyen, who in his *Oak Trees* came so close to Rembrandt, would we ever have known Ruisdael, Hobbema, Koninck, Cuyp, and so many others to whom he revealed how to evoke vast horizons? For nearly a century, these landscapists lent wings to Netherlandish art, which a certain native heaviness threatened to confine to slavish copying and inventions lacking grandeur. If this practical and courageous people succeeded in going beyond appearances, it was thanks to skies as ennobling as those of Venice or the Ile-de-France.

An unassuming craftsmanship, which in its lightness and finesse

DUTCH SCHOOL OF THE SEVENTEENTH CENTURY

recalls the technique of the 'primitives', was outstandingly well suited to conveying effects of what Théodore Rousseau, the disciple of these painters, described as 'aerial modelling'. There is nothing showy, and the artist kept in the background. Never before had such small frames confined so much space and skill as with these landscapes by Van Goyen, Seghers, Koninck, and Ruisdael.

Hobbema, despite his love of the vegetable kingdom, and the union that he created between the farm, the watermill, the avenue, and the spinney; Van der Meer, despite his receptiveness to all the transient effects of the sky; Wouwerman, Dujardin, Potter, and Cuyp, despite the precise control with which they combined the activities of man or beast with the rhythmic play of light—all, by comparison, seem at times to sacrifice too much to the picturesque. They fill our lungs with healthy air, but inside them a genre painter is waiting to be born.

Even to the countless artists who, after Porcellis, Willem van de Velde, and Bakhuysen, devoted themselves to the pomp of naval manœuvres and battles, it was, all things considered, the slow procession of the clouds and flashing mirrors of the sea that mattered most. While avoiding over-specialization, Van de Cappelle, Vlieger, and Willem van de Velde the Younger delighted in evoking the same atmospheric phenomena.

Rembrandt, and particularly Vermeer, only occasionally produced landscapes. No more than two outdoor masterpieces by Jan are known: *The Little Street* (Amsterdam) and *View of Delft*. In the first a small house with a crenellated gable, and in the second a line of fortifications, catch the eye, miraculously forcing space to condense in tiny iridescent drops on the stone, tiles, and window-panes. It was under the joint influence of Seghers, Rubens, and Van Goyen that Rembrandt painted some ten half-fanciful landscapes that display his supreme gift: giving the imaginary the fullness and relief of life.

JACOB ISAACKSZ. VAN RUISDAEL. THE MILL NEAR WIJK BIJ DUURSTEDE, 1665-1669. RIJKSMUSEUM, AMSTERDAM

MEINDERT HOBBEMA, 1638-1709. AVENUE, MIDDELHARNIS. NATIONAL GALLERY, LONDON

WILLEM VAN DE VELDE THE YOUNGER, 1633-1707. SUNSET. MAURITSHUIS, THE HAGUE

JAN VERMEER, 1632-1675. VIEW OF DELFT, c. 1658. MAURITSHUIS, THE HAGUE

SEVENTEENTH-CENTURY FRANCE

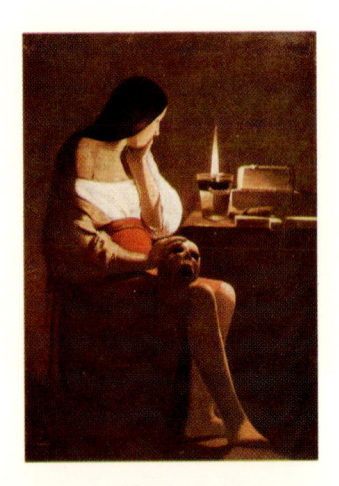

GEORGES DUMESNIL
DE LA TOUR.
THE MAGDALENE.
LOUVRE, PARIS

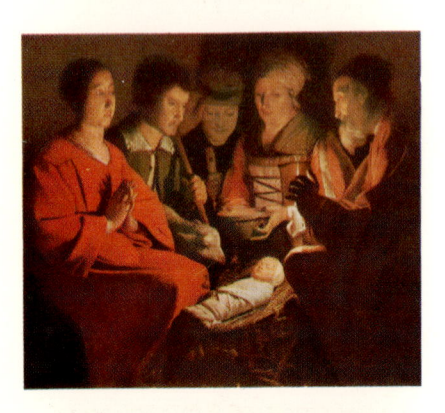

GEORGES
DE LA TOUR,
1593-1652.
THE NATIVITY.
LOUVRE, PARIS

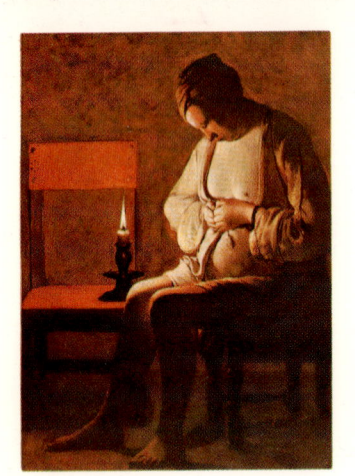

GEORGES DE
LA TOUR.
WOMAN WITH
A FLEA.
MUSÉE LORRAIN,
NANCY

French art of the seventeenth century divides into two periods. The first—also the longest and most fertile—corresponds to the era of Richelieu and Mazarin. It overflowed with original talent, which an antiquated tradition filched for the benefit of the second period, producing what is wrongly known as the Age of Louis XIV. One overlooks the fact that French Classicism first appeared under Louis XIII in a flood of creative variety and fantasy, later stemmed by the Academic discipline.

At the start of the century, Rome was still the hub of the artistic universe. Her Church, which, not unscathed, had triumphed over the Reformation among the Latin peoples, revelled in its victory; and its success was accompanied by an extraordinary upsurge of mysticism. The prestige of religion combined with the prestige of art to make Rome the rallying-point of a Catholic world renovated by the new religious orders and by the blood of recent martyrs. For the Jubilee of 1600, three million pilgrims thronged the Eternal City, and among them were painters of every nation. Having come for a few weeks, they stayed many years; Vouet spent fifteen years there from 1615, Mignard twenty-two from 1636, Poussin forty from 1624, and Claude his entire life. On their return to France, the influence of the peninsula lost its hold on these artists, who came again under the spell of their native surroundings, and of such a distinct spiritual atmosphere that each painter has been associated with one of the orders of the Counter-Reformation. La Tour is supposed to represent the Franciscan spirit of Pierre Fourier, Louis Le Nain that of Monsieur Vincent, Philippe de Champaigne that of Port-Royal, Le Sueur the theocentric outlook of Bérulle, Vouet of the Jesuits.

Though quite unknown until recently, Georges de La Tour meets certain requirements of modern taste so well that today he almost rivals Poussin for first place in the

SEVENTEENTH-CENTURY FRANCE

artistic hierarchy of the *grand siècle*. Yet his earliest works—which include genre scenes like *The Cheat, The Hurdy-gurdy Player* (Nantes), and *Woman with a Flea*—show his links with the Dutch Caravaggists, and contain nothing new. It is wonderful how he came to realize that truly dramatic qualities do not depend on subject-matter, but on light and shade, which can express feeling more intense and disturbing than that of the most explicit representations of violence. La Tour was born at Vic, but spent his life as a well-to-do citizen of Lunéville, taking good care of his worldly interests. The chronology of his few works is uncertain; and he kept to a limited range of subjects, which he repeated several times with the same models. All he cared about was the connection between style and feeling, but within this narrow field few artists have been greater. With Franciscan fervour, he accepted every minute of an ordinary life—as lived in the homes of his friends and acquaintances. But each scene from daily life became something exceptional through the power to radiate nobility and grandeur with which he endowed it. His figures have the serenity and tranquillity of statues, and the folds of their garments fall vertically, as though chiselled by Gothic sculptors. The silence that dwells within these works holds the spectator who has paused irresolutely before an indeterminate subject, diffusing an aura of mystery. A woman is looking at the tightly swaddled new-born child in her arms: is this a *Nativity*? A little boy is holding a candle to light a carpenter at his work: is the man St Joseph? One could quote many more examples. More than Caravaggio and Rembrandt, La Tour introduces an element of holiness into the life of each of us. He does so with the aid of a dim a candle that a figure shields with its hand; and this glimmer is also the lamp of the sanctuary, the light of the soul, the fire of inspiration, and the benediction of divine grace.

GEORGES DE LA TOUR. THE NEW-BORN CHILD. RENNES MUSEUM

GEORGES DE LA TOUR. ST JOSEPH THE CARPENTER, 1640-1645. LOUVRE, PARIS

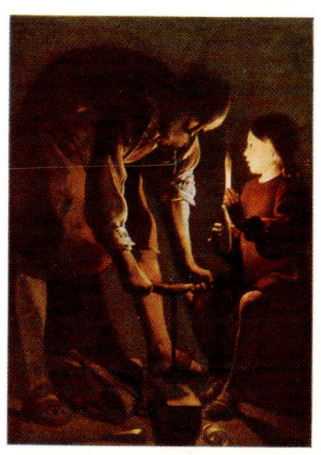

GEORGES DE LA TOUR. ST SEBASTIAN MOURNED BY ST IRENE. STAATLICHE MUSEEN, BERLIN

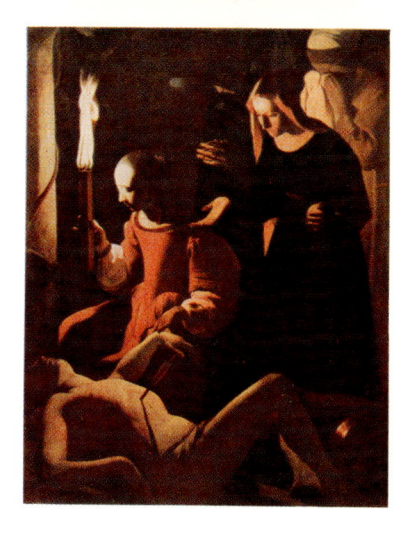

SEVENTEENTH-CENTURY FRANCE

LOUIS LE NAIN,
c. 1593-1648.
THE WAGON
OR PEASANTS HOME
FROM HAYMAKING,
1641.
LOUVRE, PARIS

LOUIS LE NAIN.
A SMITH IN
HIS FORGE.
LOUVRE, PARIS

LOUIS LE NAIN.
THE DAIRYMAID'S
FAMILY,
c. 1640.
HERMITAGE,
LENINGRAD

In the geography of art, La Tour in Lorraine had as neighbours Antoine, Louis and Mathieu Le Nain of Champagne. They too were poets, but of rustic life; instead of being screened by shadows, their holy mystery takes place in a fuller light. Every action of their subjects' uncomplaining lives, sanctified by sobriety, austerity, and dire poverty, seems to be accompanied by a prayer.

Only recently has it become possible to establish the approximate share of each of the brothers in their joint labours. None of them married and, though they owned a family estate in the Laon area, they worked at Paris, signing their pictures with a single name: Le Nain. Antoine, the eldest, remained a 'Flemish' artist, excelling—according to a contemporary biography—as a miniaturist and limner. The youngest, Mathieu, had social pretentions; he moved in Court circles, and painted groups showing people playing on the lute, at cards, or at backgammon. The greatest of the three was Louis, who was also the most religious. This appears not in his subjects, but in the spirit pervading scenes that, though as simple as La Tour's, lack their ambiguity of theme. A few masterpieces have been enough to establish his fame: *The Forge, The Wagon* or *Peasants home from Haymaking, The Christening Feast, Peasants at Supper, Four Figures at Table*. Strictly speaking, these pictures have no subject. The artist has caught his characters before or after their work or other activities, and while they are sitting peacefully at the end of the day. They drink or eat as if performing some ritual; while in their midst a cat dozes, a dog keeps watch, and a child plays softly on the flute. What distinguishes Louis from his brothers is his feeling for light. He is an outdoor painter, a painter of atmosphere, who directs his gaze to the distant countryside and horizon. A golden or silvery dusk envelops these peasants with their hollow cheeks and weary limbs.

SEVENTEENTH-CENTURY FRANCE

At Paris, where the young French school was coming to maturity in the shadow of the Court, the official posts and commissions went at first to Flemish artists, who formed a real colony at the Gobelins (called after one of them, Van Goblen). As already mentioned, Pourbus died at Paris in 1622. The previous year, Marie de' Medici had summoned Rubens to decorate her gallery in the Luxembourg Palace; and as he never did anything quite on his own, he collected the landscape artist Jacques Fouquières and portraitist Philippe de Champaigne *en route* at Brussels. Both stayed on in Paris after he had left. Richelieu did not like Rubens, whom he thought to be an agent of the King of Spain; but he made a protégé of Champaigne, and grew to appreciate his character and piety. He had him appointed Court painter, made him a French citizen, and commissioned works from him. Champaigne was a painter of religious subjects and an outstanding portraitist, whether of groups such as *The Aldermen of Paris* (Louvre) or of really individualized single figures like the official portraits of Louis XIII and the cardinals. Above all, the Louvre *Richelieu*, showing the chief minister in his grand cloak, with his commanding gaze and lordly air, greatly pleased its subject. In demand with religious houses, he had occasion to work for Port-Royal. He formed a friendship with these recluses, especially with the Arnauld family; of them he left some unforgettable portraits, such as *La Mère Angélique* and *La Mère Agnès*. His daughter Catherine, paralyzed since the age of two, was miraculously cured at the end of a novena. As an expression of gratitude, he painted a votive picture showing his daughter still stretched out on her chair, with Agnès Arnauld kneeling by her side (Louvre). Few paintings take one beyond appearances in the way that this does. It enables the onlooker to commune with the souls that once inhabited these robes.

LOUIS LE NAIN.
PEASANTS AT
SUPPER,
1642.
LOUVRE, PARIS

LOUIS LE NAIN.
OLD PEASANT
WITH A GIRL
(DETAIL FROM
PEASANT FAMILY),
c. 1643.
LOUVRE, PARIS

LOUIS LE NAIN.
FOUR FIGURES
AT TABLE
(SAYING GRACE)
(DETAIL).
LOUVRE, PARIS

SEVENTEENTH-CENTURY FRANCE

PHILIPPE DE
CHAMPAIGNE,
1602-1674.
PORTRAIT OF
A MAN,
1650.
LOUVRE, PARIS

PHILIPPE DE
CHAMPAIGNE,
LOUIS XIII
CROWNED
BY VICTORY.
LOUVRE, PARIS

PHILIPPE DE
CHAMPAIGNE.
PORTRAIT OF LA
MÈRE ANGÉLIQUE
ARNAULD.
LOUVRE, PARIS

At this time Philippe de Champaigne was not the leading light in the Paris art world. That place was occupied by Simon Vouet, a painter of brilliant and facile genius, who in Italy had been the favourite of the Popes. He had travelled as far afield as Constantinople, and lived long enough at Venice to learn the secret of Veronese's enchanting decorations. When, in 1627, he returned to Paris with a ravishing Italian bride, he quickly became its leading painter and was deluged with commissions. He opened a studio in which Le Sueur, Mignard and Le Brun all received their training, and was appointed first painter. Unfortunately, his best works—the great decorative schemes—have been destroyed. To justify his fame in this field there remain only the tapestries representing *Rinaldo and Armida* and *The Labours of Hercules,* woven after his cartoons; these reflect Venetian art, and sometimes evoke Titian.

His best pupil, Eustache Le Sueur, was the greatest religious painter of the day. He possessed an exquisite sensibility and a precocious gravity, which presaged a career that would be all too brief. For the small cloister of the Paris Charterhouse he painted scenes from the life of St Bruno, which do not retain the charm of his drawings. He was more successful with his *Life of St Martin,* for the abbey of Marmoutiers. In it he unaffectedly succeeds in matching up to the 'primitives' by means of his soft and shadowless technique and melodious colouring. Another 'Venetian', Jacques Blanchard, known as 'the French Titian', died too young to leave any evidence of his talent beyond a few nudes—the only seventeenth-century ones that dare to be really nude and sensual like Rubens'.

Despite all these talented painters, the top position at Paris was still waiting to be filled; and people were looking towards Rome, where two Frenchmen—both famous, but in different ways—were then living: Claude and Nicolas Poussin.

SEVENTEENTH-CENTURY FRANCE

Claude made a fortune out of his landscapes, while his compatriot and neighbour in the Via Paolina, Poussin, whom he used to meet in the evening at a near-by inn to talk about art, remained comparatively poor. Once a pastry-cook at Chamagne in the Vosges, Claude depicted ports bathed in light, in which tiny figures painted by his friends melt into the golden glow of the setting sun. He did not bother much about the subject of his canvases; no more do we — and still less did his noble clients. His spell consists in the richness of each vision, which lulls the intellect. One does not ask questions; one just gives way to rapture. His magic frees the spectator from the bonds of his surroundings, bringing him the bliss of oblivion, in the radiance of a nameless presence. That is why none have understood this classical painter better than the Romanticists. From Gœthe, who was so fond of him, to Turner, who imitated him, his glory has never ceased to be renewed — like the sun that casts the same spells at every dawn. Claude's art avoided the controversies of the period, whereas that of Poussin was so affected by them that, before approaching it, a few words of explanation are required.

In reaction against sixteenth-century Mannerism, two new aesthetic doctrines shared the favour of the young artists at Rome. They were personified by two artists, Anibale Carracci and Michelangelo Merisi da Caravaggio, who had started off by working together. Carracci, the famous decorator of the Farnese gallery, preached a return to the spirit of fresco painting, for which Raphael had provided the model in the Vatican *loggie*. He held that the requirements of decorative painting called for the use of light colours, which were conducive to the airy grace and charm that the princely owners of palaces demanded. On the other hand, Caravaggio — who, according to Poussin, was an evil-doer come with the intention of destroying painting — embodied the

CLAUDE GELLÉE
KNOWN AS
CLAUDE LORRAIN,
1600-1682.
SEA PORT,
1646.
LOUVRE, PARIS

CLAUDE LORRAIN.
ULYSSES RETURNING
CHRYSEIS TO
HER FATHER.
LOUVRE, PARIS

CLAUDE LORRAIN.
EMBARKATION
OF ST URSULA.
NATIONAL GALLERY,
LONDON

CLAUDE LORRAIN.
MARRIAGE OF ISAAC
AND REBECCA,
1640.
NATIONAL GALLERY,
LONDON

SEVENTEENTH-CENTURY FRANCE

NICOLAS POUSSIN, 1594-1665.
TANCRED AND ERMINIA.
c. 1630.
HERMITAGE, LENINGRAD

NICOLAS POUSSIN.
FINDING OF MOSES, 1645-1647.
LOUVRE, PARIS

NICOLAS POUSSIN.
POLYPHEMUS, c. 1649.
HERMITAGE, LENINGRAD

NICOLAS POUSSIN.
BACCHANAL.
NATIONAL GALLERY, LONDON

spirit of reformation. Instead of just imitating the masters, he aimed to get back to nature, the original fount of all art. As is natural, he had little success among his fellow-countrymen, who clung to the traditional craft of fresco painting. His true disciples were foreigners: the Dutch, who, with their taste for low-life and peasant subjects, saw him as the originator of a new art in which man had the status of an object; the French, on the look-out for a doctrine that would free them from Italian sway; and the Spanish, because of the sense of special kinship he aroused in them. Thus, before long, this adventurer of genius could lay claim to a dazzling progeny, including Georges de La Tour, Rembrandt, and Velásquez; Nicolas Poussin almost alone remained true to the old art.

Poussin had been in Rome since 1624; when news of his renown eventually reached Paris, the superintendent of building, Sublet des Noyers, saw him as God's gift to French art. As an inducement to return home, he showered him with gold and promises, and Louis XIII wrote to him personally. Reluctantly, Poussin made up his mind; and at the end of 1640 he arrived at Paris, where, in his own words, he received a 'splendid welcome'. Nothing shows the state of painting in France at this period better than the sudden change of fortune that marked this visit, which resulted from a misunderstanding. Poussin's art was intellectual; he painted only easel pictures, in which colour was subordinated to drawing. What the Court and art-lovers expected, however, was a decorator who would be able to provide a French counter-weight to the fame of Rubens. This comes out clearly in the words of Louis XIII, who, during his first interview with Poussin, declared that it would be 'one in the eye for Vouet'. Intrigues, criticism, and disappointing work combined to make Poussin disgusted with Paris. Within two years he was back in Rome, which he never left again.

SEVENTEENTH-CENTURY FRANCE

Poussin's work has no popular appeal, and there never was a more intellectual artist than this self-taught painter. His subjects come under the heading 'historical landscape', which, along with portraiture, seemed then the only field worthy of a painter who respected his calling. He found these themes in books on Roman history and in the Bible. Giving them prolonged thought, he composed his pictures like mimed psychological dramas. For this religious-minded artist, who set great store by orderliness, the order of nature constituted a language. When he measured the proportions of Antique statues, he was trying to establish the order through which each thing retains its essential character and the permanence of its laws.

Today, one has to admit to not being at home with these aims. One cannot, of course, remain unmoved by the perfect harmony of compositions such as the Dresden *Kingdom of Flora*, the *Finding of Moses*, the *Arcadian Shepherds*, the Louvre *Eliezer and Rebecca*, or the Louvre *Inspiration of the Poet*, in which the language of forms is wedded to that of thought. Yet one may still prefer the canvases, like the *Bacchanals* or the Cassel *Nymph carried by a Satyr*, that reveal a youthful feeling for naked beauty; and his landscapes even more. For, while his human figures follow Antique models, his view of nature stems from direct observation. Every morning he used to come down from the Pincian hill and go for a country walk, during which he would collect grasses and stones that he chanced upon and take them back to his studio. This was how he composed his cosmic visions with Diogenes (Louvre) and Polyphemus, and the *St Matthew and the Angel*; in them nature overruns the scene, and man disappears from sight and mind, like the hero of *The Funeral of Phocion*. One could say of Poussin that he, too, travelled back in time to the golden age in which he was really at home.

On his return to Rome in 1642,

NICOLAS POUSSIN.
ARCADIAN
SHEPHERDS,
1638-1639.
LOUVRE, PARIS

NICOLAS POUSSIN.
MIDAS AND BACCHUS,
c. 1630.
ALTE PINAKOTHEK,
MUNICH

NICOLAS POUSSIN.
ECHO AND
NARCISSUS,
c. 1624-1626.
LOUVRE, PARIS

SEVENTEENTH-CENTURY FRANCE

PIERRE MIGNARD, 1612-1695. PORTRAIT OF THE DUCHESS OF MAINE AS A CHILD. PALACE OF VERSAILLES

CHARLES LE BRUN, 1619-1690. CHANCELLOR SÉGUIER IN THE TRAIN OF QUEEN MARIA THERESA AT HER ENTRY INTO PARIS, 26 AUGUST 1660. LOUVRE, PARIS

ANONYMOUS. PORTRAIT OF A WOMAN. MUSÉE CONDÉ, CHANTILLY

he became mentor to a twenty-three-year-old artist on an allowance from Séguier, who was determined to elicit the secret of his ascendancy: Charles Le Brun. Back in Paris four years later, he began what, by dint of intelligence, will, tact and zeal, was to be his amazing career. First he put himself under Fouquet's wing, then under Colbert's, rising with his protector. He was the chief creator of the Academy. In 1622 he was appointed first painter. He did more than anyone to create the centralization that made art a means of enhancing the King's prestige. Every management requires a policy: this was the object of his lectures before the Academy during which he systematized Poussin's ideas. Its need for an executive organization was satisfied by the Gobelins factory, where all the craft guilds were united under his control; its need for a job to tackle, by Versailles. At the palace, where he designed everything from the pictures to the locks, Le Brun completed a truly superhuman undertaking. The result was more than the work of one man; it was the style of a reign, a style so well suited to its purpose that it conquered Europe. Set beside this triumph, Le Brun's portraits and his cartoons for the tapestries with the history of the King seem less important. Mention must be made, however, of his equestrian state portrait of Chancellor Séguier (see left); it is a beautiful page of history.

The portraitists were, indeed, the only artists who dared question Le Brun's ascendancy; for their fashionable clients required something more intimate than to be transformed into Olympian gods. Mignard, who, after Le Brun's fall from favour, took over from him, died shortly afterwards. He was chiefly a decorator and portrayer of women, whose vanity he flattered. On his recall to Paris from Rome, where he had painted Urban VIII, all the Court beauties sat to him, from Marie Mancini and Louise de La Vallière to

192

EIGHTEENTH-CENTURY FRANCE

Mmes de Sévigné and Montespan.
At the end of his reign, Louis XIV met Rigaud, who was to leave posterity its most spectacular image of the King. Faithful to the pomp and circumstance of the *grand siècle,* Rigaud continued to depict the young Louis XV in the same coronation robes as his predecessor; but, with his warm, Rubenesque palette and skilled use of glazes and reflections he also heralded a new era. His rival Largillière, trained at Antwerp, concentrated on a non-aristocratic clientèle; in the so-called *Belle Strasbourgeoise,* which was painted as though in homage to Van Dyck, he produced his masterpiece. The importance of speed in the seizing of a likeness helped to spread the fashion for rapid pastels. One of the first masters in this medium was Vivien, who, before going to work in Germany, produced an unforgettable portrait of Fénelon.

The reaction against Le Brun's authoritarian régime began, at the time of his decline from favour, within the Academy itself. It took the form of a dispute between the Rubenists, who favoured colour, and the Poussinists, who supported draughtsmanship. Rubens, who had been painter to the Duke of Mantua, had inaugurated in Italy a vigorous, heroic, and triumphal style—that of the Baroque; and it suited the Italian spirit so well that it conquered the peninsula, to the discomfiture of the followers of Carracci and Caravaggio. It did not, however, receive the same enthusiastic welcome from the French, who valued restraint, simplicity and balance. Nevertheless, it was Rubenism that won the day, but, once acclimatized to France, the Baroque became the charming Rococo style. It owed its success to a new clientèle; for though the Academy still lingered on, the Royal finances were in such a bad way that it was given nothing to do. At Versailles in 1736, François Lemoyne completed the ceiling of the Hercules Salon, the last great decorative project carried

NICOLAS DE LARGILLIÈRE, 1656-1746. LA BELLE STRASBOURGEOISE. PRIVATE COLLECTION, PARIS

HYACINTHE RIGAUD, 1659-1743. LOUIS XIV IN CORONATION ROBES, 1701. LOUVRE, PARIS

JOSEPH VIVIEN, 1657-1734. PORTRAIT OF FÉNELON, ARCHBISHOP OF CAMBRAI. ALTE PINAKOTHEK, MUNICH

EIGHTEENTH-CENTURY FRANCE

ANTOINE WATTEAU, 1684-1721.
MEMBERS OF THE COMMEDIA DELL'ARTE, 1719-1720.
NATIONAL GALLERY OF ART, WASHINGTON

WATTEAU. THE UNCONCERNED. LOUVRE, PARIS

WATTEAU. IL MEZZETINO. METROPOLITAN MUSEUM, NEW YORK

out in the palace. This shows 140 mythological figures set amid clouds that are breathtaking in their harmony. It is the swan-song of a dying art; hardly had its author been appointed first painter than he committed suicide, worn out by four years of such strenuous toil.

Painting in the grand manner was quite unsuited to the small rooms then in fashion. The artists whom the King had forsaken found a well-informed clientèle, who had been attending the Salons since 1737, in the middle-classes. This new public, more concerned with sensual enjoyment than the austere delights of the intellect, imposed on artists its taste for colour and genre subjects, hitherto a Flemish speciality. The advent of informed public opinion led to art criticism (pamphlets and reviews). The world of art took on the appearance that it has retained up to the present day.

In 1721, in the country house at Nogent of M. Le Fèvre, manager of the King's *menus plaisirs,* there died at the age of thirty-seven an artist who had anticipated the aspirations of the century. Born in French Flanders and an admirer of Rubens, his name was Antoine Watteau. He began by working for Gillot, a painter of scenes from the Italian theatre, from whom he acquired his taste for the characters of the *commedia dell'arte* who were to be the vehicles of his fantasy. Afterwards he went to live at the Luxembourg Palace, of which the then famous decorative painter Audran was the 'caretaker'— curator, that is. Watteau was able to take advantage there of the marvellous object-lesson offered by the Medici gallery. In the evenings, he strolled in the noble but lonely park, where the wonderful foliage of the trees and bushes was to provide a setting for his scenes. Thus, right from the start he was in possession of all the ingredients of his *fêtes:* theatrical fantasy, a park with beautiful effects of shadow, a virtuoso's technique and a Rubenesque palette.

EIGHTEENTH-CENTURY FRANCE

All the same, his earliest works were military subjects. Revisiting Valenciennes in 1709 to see his family, he found the town threatened by Imperial troops, after the capture of Tournai. He wandered through the suburbs, visiting military camps and amassing drawings. Back in Paris, he painted several pictures of the war seen from behind the lines: *The Temporary Camp* (Hermitage), *The Escort* and two pendants, *The New Levy* (Angers), and *The Halt,* which in 1712 won him entry to the Academy. He was than living as the guest of Crozat, the extremely rich owner of a matchless collection of Flemish and Italian pictures. At Crozat's house he executed *The Embarkation for Cythera* (Louvre, 1717), the masterpiece that he made his diploma work and that established him as a painter of *fêtes galantes* — a new term specially devised for him. The scene is not purely imaginary; it represents the final episode of Dancourt's comedy *Les Trois Cousines.* For Watteau painted from nature; when he wanted to compose a picture, he dipped into his sketch-books, which are crammed with drawings and poses taken from life.

What exactly is a *fête galante?* Although it can claim precedents in Giorgione's *Concert champêtre (Pastoral Concert)* and Ruben's *Garden of Love,* it is the new form that Watteau gave to mankind's abiding dream of a golden age, a refuge of happiness where time will pass in a perpetual carnival. Couples stroll and talk together; in the *Gamme d'Amour (Gamut of Love)* they sing or play the guitar; they dance; and above all, they just idle. Watteau has caught all the attitudes of relaxation, graceful detachment and nonchalance; the dresses with their folds broken over a knee or spread upon the ground; the poses that indicate whispered secrets, fond confessions, groundless anticipations and aimless departures. Readily but regretfully, these beauties turn their backs in order to show the spectator their pink, grey-lilac or

WATTEAU. 'LA GAMME D'AMOUR'. NATIONAL GALLERY, LONDON

WATTEAU. THE JUDGMENT OF PARIS, *c.* 1718-1720. LOUVRE, PARIS

WATTEAU. 'L'ENSEIGNE DE GERSAINT' (RIGHT HALF), 1720. CHARLOTTENBURG PALACE, BERLIN

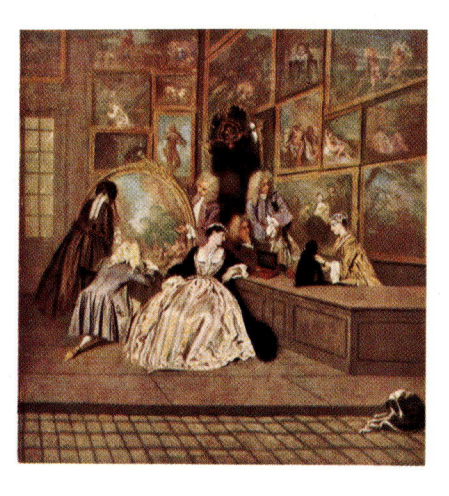

EIGHTEENTH-CENTURY FRANCE

NICOLAS LANCRET,
1690-1743.
THE MUSIC
LESSON.
LOUVRE, PARIS

JEAN-MARC NATTIER,
1685-1766.
PORTRAITS OF
MADEMOISELLE DE
LAMBESC AND THE
COUNT OF BRIONNE,
1732.
LOUVRE, PARIS

FRANÇOIS BOUCHER,
1703-1770.
ODALISQUE.
LOUVRE, PARIS

coppery satin dresses; but, tilting their heads on one side, they still remember to display their profiles. There is no action and no subject. Like the Louvre picture of that title, each is just a *Gathering in a Park* of elegant idlers dressed up as actors. They wear the costume, but do not play the part; and, as in a Shakespeare comedy, these disguises blend reality with make-believe. Could Watteau have had in mind the 'ballet of human life' that Poussin's idylls represent? In any case, he transposed this theme into a minor key; just as when, at the end of a beautiful day, one hears the bitter-sweet music of nostalgia. On returning from a trip to England, the consumptive wanderer, now at death's door, went to live at the home of his dealer and friend, Gersaint. Here he painted one last masterpiece, the famous *Enseigne* (sign-board), which was soon removed from Gersaint's shop, on the Pont Notre-Dame, where it had caused a riot of admiration. The new century admired its own image in Watteau's scene of enthusiastic purchasers and onlookers.

Watteau's influence was great but it required time to take effect. His immediate followers — Pater and Lancret — could do no more than borrow his themes and costumes. The best to be said for them is that they transformed the *fête galante* into a kind of genre scene. This has its moments of charm, as in Lancret's appetising *Ham Lunch* (Chantilly), which was intended as a pendant to de Troy's *Oyster Lunch* (Chantilly, 1735) in the King's small apartments at Versailles. For the new fashion for the middle-class way of life had reached the Court, and Louis XV refused to eat in public. This change of habits required a different, more adaptable setting, and artists responded perfectly to the call. It was above all in the designing of tapestries that they scored some brilliant successes, such as Desporte's *Indies,* de Troy's *Story of Esther,* and *The Loves of the Gods* by Boucher, who was, besides, the

EIGHTEENTH-CENTURY FRANCE

director of the Gobelins factory. François Boucher, Mme de Pompadour's favourite painter, is the best representative of a Court art that aimed only to please, to gratify the passing whim and jaded sensuality of its noble clientèle. In his works, all the female nudes — whether nymphs or goddesses, with chubby cheeks or plump behinds — look alike. He could never individualize his figures, even when painting his own wife.

To get a true account of how agreeable life could be, one must turn to other artists, like J. F. de Troy (1679-1752), himself a rich man. He painted *Reading in a Drawing-room, A Game of Handy-pandy, The Loose Garter;* all went to England or Germany to bear witness to the pre-eminence of French art and its popularity throughout Europe. For a breath of nature and reality, one must turn to the animal, landscape, and still-life painters such as Desportes, who executed pictures on the spot, like Corot, in the countryside around Beauvais; or Oudry, the amazing chronicler of the *Hunts of Louis XV* (Compiègne and Fontainebleau), whose handling of colour in *The White Duck* (1753) is a *tour de force*.

Portraiture followed the same stylistic movement from formality to informality, as a way of life dominated by ceremony gave way to one governed by social intercourse, in which women — naturally enough — played the leading part. When painting these women, artists were expected to produce flattering likenesses, and Nattier made a fortune by dressing up the ladies of the Court as Naiads, Sultanas, Flora, Diana or Aurora. Marie Leczinska was one of the few independent-minded enough to ask him to keep to the truth. Although he was Nattier's son-in-law, Tocqué continued the naturalistic style of Largillière, as can be seen in his superb *Comte de St Florentin* (Marseilles). He took great care over tone and colour values.

Maurice Quentin de La Tour,

FRANÇOIS BOUCHER.
DIANA RESTING
AFTER THE BATH,
1742.
LOUVRE, PARIS

MAURICE QUENTIN
DE LA TOUR,
1704-1788.
PORTRAIT OF
MADAME DE
POMPADOUR, 1755.
LOUVRE, PARIS

QUENTIN
DE LA TOUR.
PORTRAIT OF
KING LOUIS XV.
LOUVRE, PARIS

EIGHTEENTH-CENTURY FRANCE

JEAN-BAPTISTE
CHARDIN,
1699-1779.
THE YOUNG
SCHOOLMISTRESS,
c. 1739.
NATIONAL GALLERY
OF ART,
WASHINGTON

CHARDIN.
'LA POURVOYEUSE'
(YOUNG WOMAN
CARRYING
PROVISIONS), 1739.
LOUVRE, PARIS

CHARDIN.
BOY PREPARING
TO DRAW,
1737.
LOUVRE, PARIS

a sarcastic and querulous native of Picardy, held that nature was no longer open to improvement. However, he flattered himself in thinking he could probe the character of his sitters, for, like all the other portraitists of his times, he only depicted man's appearance as a social being. Conscious that they are under observation, his heads listen to and smile at their spectators. La Tour's technical brilliance was under the control of his intelligence; this he displayed by using pastel as his medium, since it is the only one that combines colour and drawing without any loss of freshness and spontaneity. The complete list of his portraits is like an image of his period. Let us single out *Mme de Pompadour* and *Louis XV* (Louvre), and the pictures of people he knew well: *Mlle Fel* (St Quentin), the adorable little *Nicole* (Louvre), and the portrait of *M. Duval de L'Épinoy*.

Continuing downwards in the hierarchy of picture types, one arrives at the level of middle-class life, to find there the still-life and its painter, Chardin. Chardin did not invent the still-life, and, before discussing him, it is customary to mention his forerunners: Italian *trompe-l'œil* painting, the Flemish *vanitas,* Dutch market scenes, Caravaggio's flowers and the Spanish *bodegón*. The reason why Chardin seems new, and even, to our eyes, the only 'modern' painter of his century, is that he invented a technique perfectly suited to his eye and mind. Not that one should accept uncritically his famous advice to make use of colour but to paint with one's sensibility; for, in a painter, sensibility is the power to see. What establishes a picture's value is no longer the 'social status' of its subject-matter, but the quality of the eye that directs the hand which is holding the brush.

Chardin made a closer study of tone values and the play of reflections than anyone before him. Whether depicting *Preparations for Lunch* (Louvre), *The Pipe, A Basket*

EIGHTEENTH-CENTURY FRANCE

of Peaches, or The Emblems of Music (Louvre), he would forget his subject and become sensitive only to a particular effect of reflected light, which his eye, like a diamond, would decompose, and his hand then recreate. Using tiny, variegated touches of pure, vibrant colour—like those that, later on, the Impressionists thought they had invented—he made a bottle, a cauldron, or a table-cloth appear out of the shadow; achievements such as these provoked Diderot to exclaim that Chardin's magic was completely baffling.

Although he later produced genre paintings, which, as in his *Young Schoolmistress, Pourvoyeuse, Boy blowing Soap-bubbles, Boy preparing to draw,* and *The Morning Toilet,* he brought to life with figures shown doing very ordinary, everyday things, Chardin continued to treat his subjects as objects—objects perhaps less pure than those of his still-lifes, even if they are more poetic. In so doing, he may have been wanting to compete with his friend Aved, whose *Mme Crozat before her Tapestry* and *Mme de Bacquencourt at her Toilet* come somewhere between genre painting and portraiture.

Story-telling was Chardin's concession to fashion but the very basis of Greuze's career. A good painter but a small-minded man, he was the victim of his own desire for fame, of the fashion for sentimental domestic comedy and edifying novels, and the advice of his friend Diderot. When the philosopher exhorted him to restore morality to art, he had an all too eager listener. In the mere five years separating his first Salon exhibit, *The Head of the Family reading the Bible to his Children* (1755), from *The Broken Pitcher* and *The Village Bride* (Louvre, 1761) Greuze won fame and a wide following. The success of these sham pastorals with their fake settings, which displayed the poor to suit the taste of the rich and villagers to please lords of the manor, can only be due to the undercurrent of sensuality. People doted on Greuze's

CHARDIN. BOY BLOWING SOAP-BUBBLES. METROPOLITAN MUSEUM, NEW YORK

CHARDIN THE MORNING TOILET. NATIONALMUSEUM, STOCKHOLM

CHARDIN. STILL-LIFE: PIPE. LOUVRE, PARIS

199

EIGHTEENTH-CENTURY FRANCE

JEAN-BAPTISTE GREUZE, 1725-1805. 'LA CRUCHE CASSÉE' (THE BROKEN PITCHER). LOUVRE, PARIS

JEAN-HONORÉ FRAGONARD, 1732-1806. THE SWING (LES HASARDS HEUREUX DE L'ESCARPOLETTE), 1768. WALLACE COLLECTION, LONDON

FRAGONARD. BATHERS, 1775. LOUVRE, PARIS

'head studies', which show the childlike faces of unmaidenly maidens with nothing artless about them except their expression. He himself became their chief victim; for the beautiful Gabrielle Babuti, whom he had been obliged to marry, was scandalously unfaithful to him. He had portrayed her in a splendid picture unexpectedly entitled *Philosophy asleep,* which shows his flighty spouse surrounded by books—perhaps because her father was a book-seller. Led astray by his urge to point a moral, Greuze achieved his least debatable successes in his portraits, like that of the witty *Sophie Arnould* or of the engraver *Georges Wille*.

A new generation of portraitists was now thronging the Salons, and among them women were to have an enviable position. Of these, the most famous is Mme Vigée Lebrun. As the daughter of an artist and wife of a picture-dealer, she had no difficulty in getting off to an early start; and as a close friend of the royal family, she executed many portraits of the Queen. Louis XVI's painter, Duplessis, can be represented by his *Gluck at the Harpsichord* (Vienna), The reason for mentioning Doyen here is that his masterpiece, *The miraculous Curing of St Anthony's Fire* (Paris, St Roch), is the only great religious painting between Rubens and Delacroix.

At the end of the century, Fragonard turned art into pyrotechnics. A southerner bursting with health and good spirits, he had been a pupil of Chardin, then of Boucher. He mastered every technique, and presented a summary of his times. His career began with a trip to Rome, where he got to know the charming Abbé de St Non and the worldly Hubert Robert. The Venetian painters—especially Tiepolo—attracted him, and so, naturally enough, did the life around him. He amassed sketches, and, on returning to Paris, composed a diploma work directly inspired by the opera *Callirhoé*. Amazingly lyrical, it is, however, his only large picture (Louvre, 1765). As he

EIGHTEENTH-CENTURY FRANCE

was very fond of money, he thenceforward worked only for the farmers-general. For the *receveur du clergé* he painted *The Swing* (1768), popularized by an engraving. This was the period of his delicately naughty works, of which several are now only known through sketches or prints; in *Women bathing*, *The Bolt*, *A Girl playing with a Dog on her Bed*, and *The stolen Shift*, one cannot deny the wit of his approach or the discretion that curbed his audacity. He decorated the boudoir of Mlle Guimard, who became his mistress, and five panels telling the story of a love affair from the first meeting to the final surrender were ordered from him by Mme du Barry for Louveciennes. In these exquisite works he showed that he could be as poetical as Watteau; but he was greedier than his forerunner, for, not content just to embark for Cythera, he landed and spent the night there.

At the age of forty, he married and became a father. This was when he painted his family scenes, like *The big happy Family* and *The Visit to the Foster-mother*. Though a born improviser, he also had great success in recording things actually seen. In *The Abbé de St Non clad in Spanish Costume*, the *Diderot* dressed as a doge, and the adorable fair-haired *Boy dressed as Pierrot*, he has left amusing impressions of his friends. He painted *The Communal Oven* while staying in Nègrepelisse at the home of Bergeret de Grancourt, with whom he paid a second visit to Italy, bringing back his famous sanguine drawings of the Villa d'Este gardens. Memories of Watteau still pervade the puppet-like figures in his *Fête at St Cloud* (Paris, Banque de France, 1775) for the Duke of Penthièvre.

In 1754, the Count of Stainville was created ambassador to the Papal Court; with him went Hubert Robert, his valet's son. As no one could deny the Count anything, the young Robert was given accommodation in the Villa Medici and became a *pensionnaire* at the School. Another stroke of luck

FRAGONARD. A BOY AS PIERROT. WALLACE COLLECTION, LONDON

ELISABETH VIGÉE-LEBRUN, 1755-1842. PORTRAIT OF MADAME MOLÉ-RAYMOND OF THE COMÉDIE-FRANÇAISE, 1786. LOUVRE, PARIS

LOUIS-LÉOPOLD BOILLY, 1761-1845. PORTRAIT OF GABRIELLE ARNAULD AS A CHILD. LOUVRE, PARIS

EIGHTEENTH-CENTURY FRANCE

JOSEPH VERNET,
1714-1780.
THE PONTE-ROTTO,
c. 1745.
LOUVRE, PARIS

HUBERT ROBERT,
1733-1808.
GARDEN OF A
ROMAN PALACE,
1769.
PRIVATE
COLLECTION

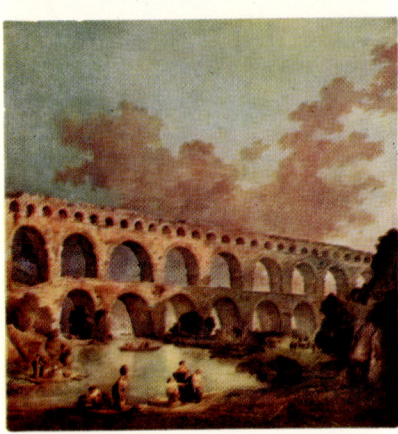

HUBERT ROBERT.
THE PONT DU GARD,
1787.
LOUVRE, PARIS

put him on friendly terms with St Non, as already mentioned; and thanks to the Abbé he was able to stay in Italy for eleven years. On his return, he married an elegant young lady from a good family, with whom he lived the fashionable life they both enjoyed so heartily. This did not prevent Robert from painting, and his experience in Italy of the work of Pannini and Piranesi had a decisive effect on him. It was the period of the return to nature and the fashion for Roman ruins, both of which crazes he took up in becoming a 'ruin painter'. He was not, of course, an archaeologist, and, treating monuments with the mind of an artist, he juxtaposed structures that were not in fact close together.

Today, however, Robert is most valued as a painter of naturalistic landscapes, such as his 'Roman Monuments of Provence' series, which includes *The Pont du Gard*. He became a 'reporter', recording events that changed the appearance of things in the Paris area: *Striking the Centering of the Pont de Neuilly, The Fire at the Opéra* (Carnavalet), *Replanting the Park at Versailles, Demolishing the Houses on the Pont-au-Change* (Carnavalet). Better still, he recorded such intimate scenes as Mme Geoffrin drinking chocolate or writing letters.

Hubert Robert's fantasy drew on reality; with Joseph Vernet, realism degenerated into the obvious. It is true that his early, Roman, works, like *The Ponte Rotto* and *The Castello Sant' Angelo*, possess a grace that heralds Corot. But later, when he was commissioned to paint fourteen pictures of the French ports, he repressed his imagination, to plot their exact topography, embellishing it only with the dresses of the pretty passers-by. His pre-Romantic bent, popular in England, led him to paint repetitive *Gusts of Wind, Storms* and *Tempests,* which for many years were the object of rivalry among art-lovers. No longer was landscape merely the framework of men's lives; it had become an end in itself.

EIGHTEENTH-CENTURY VENETIAN SCHOOL

By the eighteenth century Venice had become a city of pleasure and tourism, assured of a lasting, if slightly equivocal, prestige. Many of Italy's best writers (including Goldoni, the 'Molière' of a gaily cynical age) and almost all painters of importance came from Venice.

Officially, the *vedutista,* or painters of townscapes, who did a thriving trade, particularly with Englishmen making the 'grand tour', were considered minor artists. But although many *vedute* were merely churned out by competent craftsmen, some were exquisite masterpieces and extended the territory of painting. Often they were ornamental works, meant to be framed in fine woodcarving, or topographical series. In Venice and in Rome interesting etchings after *vedute* were produced.

While remaining a conscientious and correct *vedutista,* Canaletto was also, quite unconsciously and involuntarily, one of the great poetic painters of Venice. He began as a 'baroque' artist using strong light-contrasts, but gradually adapted his palette to the 'modern' light tones and eventually painted calm, almost crystalline views in which the atmosphere, saturated with pale light, transfigures and lends harmony to the clearly defined prisms of the buildings. The Grand Canal, St Mark's Square, the surrounding islands and various little squares or inner courtyards provided him with ever-new inspiration. A discerning art-lover, the consul John Smith, collected his works, sent them to London and instigated Canaletto's three visits to England. There he saw works by the Dutch landscape-artists and was influenced by the precious manner of Van der Heyden. He became colder, more artificial and turned, without a great deal of success, towards the *veduta ideale*. His nephew Bernardo Bellotto, named by him as his artistic successor, visited many European capitals in order to capture their charms in the now highly sought-after manner of his uncle; his panoramas of Warsaw, for instance, are quite irreplaceable.

GIOVANNI ANTONIO CANALE, KNOWN AS CANALETTO, 1697-1768. VIEW OF THE ISLAND OF SAN MICHELE. HERMITAGE, LENINGRAD

CANALETTO. THE BASIN OF SAN MARCO. BRERA, MILAN

THE PIAZZA IN FRONT OF THE CHURCH OF SAN GIACOMO OF THE RIALTO. GEMÄLDEGALERIE, DRESDEN

CANALETTO. VENICE: STONEMASON'S YARD. NATIONAL GALLERY, LONDON

EIGHTEENTH-CENTURY VENETIAN SCHOOL

FRANCESCO GUARDI,
1721-1793.
A VAULTED ARCADE
OF THE DOGES'
PALACE.
WALLACE
COLLECTION,
LONDON

GUARDI.
GONDOLA ON
THE LAGOON,
c. 1787.
POLDI-PEZZOLI
MUSEUM, MILAN

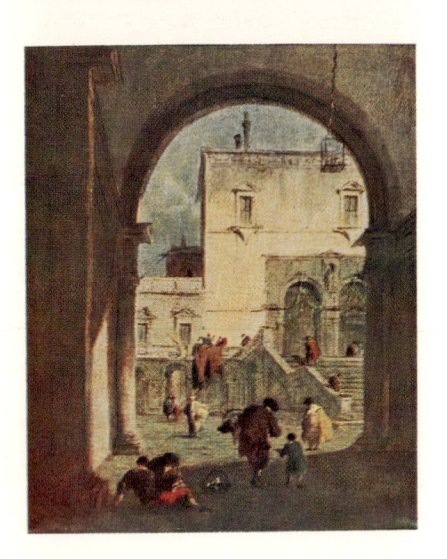

GUARDI.
VIEW OF VENICE,
c. 1780.
HERMITAGE,
LENINGRAD

Francesco Guardi demands comparison with Canaletto, although his training was different. He did not begin his career as a *vedutista*. In the modest surroundings of the family workshop he worked on all sorts of commissions and as the whole family collaborated it is hard to distinguish his individual contribution. In fact it is being suggested today that much of the credit for the 'Guardi revolution' should go to his elder brother Gianantonio (1699-1760). The word 'revolution' is no exaggeration and yet the Guardis caused so small a stir in the Venice of their day that at the height of his maturity Francesco became an assistant in the workshops of Canaletto and Marieschi. For a long time he painted from engravings by other artists and produced copies as and when they were asked for. It was only later, after Gianantonio's death, that he concentrated on *vedute*; he was old before he became known.

The question of identity—whether the artist was Gianantonio or Francesco—is most puzzling in connection with the paintings for the organ of the Church of the Archangel Raphael (*Tobias,* after 1753). They are painted in a perfected form of the free manner introduced to the Caravaggesque movement by Fetti and Lys and continued by Magnasco and Marieschi; it had never before achieved such a rich and animated effect as here. The forms melt into the extraordinary, vibrating light. This is no longer simply a sensitive, terse style, or a foretaste of Impressionism, but a move towards a new, exclusive, almost musical notation of tone-values and flashes of light which evokes an atmosphere of intense and sometimes visionary poetry. The calm *vedute* of after 1760 are totally different from Canaletto's art. His equable, careful, peaceful style and preoccupation with regular form-structure are replaced by evocations of fairyland (*Arcade of the Doges' Palace, Gala Concert,* Munich, *The Isola San Giorgio,* Bergamo, *The Piazzetta,* Venice, Ca' d'Oro, the

EIGHTEENTH-CENTURY VENETIAN SCHOOL

famous *Gondola on the Lagoon).* The composition is so new and bold, with its extreme economy of means, that Guardi's charming unreality cannot be explained by any particular formula. Moreover, at the late date when this picture was painted, Neo-Classicism was already reigning triumphant over the whole of Europe, spelling the doom of the qualities which had made Venetian painting so much admired — which adds to the solitary grandeur of the Guardis.

Paintings of everyday life, both in the country and the city, formed another minor genre, like the *vedute,* and had their own traditions and specialists in Italy. *Bambocciate* first derived from the Caravaggio tradition and the paintings of crafts from Caracci; later, Dutch painting also influenced them. But the best known of the 'painters of reality' was another Venetian, Pietro Longhi, who specialized in pictures of middle-class town life.

The success of these rather facile small pictures was no doubt due to their documentary, anecdotal character. Longhi only took up the genre after failing as a large-scale painter (decorations of the Palazzo Saguda, Bologna); by temperament he was not a 'realist' and in his work *mise en scène* always gains the upper hand over observation. Though he chronicled the activities of 'good society', he did not portray its faces. He was brilliant at suggesting the atmosphere of an interior (though less successful with landscapes: *Duck-Shooting),* skilful in arranging his figures within the very small area to which they are confined, not ungifted as a colourist; but on occasion he became stiff and almost mechanical. Like the comic dramatist Goldoni, he mirrored contemporary amusements *(The Family Concert),* occupations and manners *(The Dancing Lesson),* news items of the day *(The Black Ambassador* and *The Rhinoceros,* Venice, Ca' Rezzonico) but his figures are dressed-up puppets who would not have merited the close attention of a Chardin or the irony of a Hogarth.

GUARDI.
DEPARTURE OF
THE BUCENTAUR
(DETAIL).
c. 1763.
LOUVRE, PARIS

PIETRO FALCA
KNOWN AS
LONGHI,
1702-1785.
THE FAMILY
CONCERT.
BRERA, MILAN

PIETRO LONGHI.
THE RHINOCEROS,
1751.
CA' REZZONICO,
VENICE

EIGHTEENTH-CENTURY VENETIAN SCHOOL

GIAMBATTISTA TIEPOLO, 1696-1770. JUSTICE AND PEACE. CONGREGAZIONE DEGLI ARMENI, VENICE

TIEPOLO. TRIUMPH OF ZEPHYR AND FLORA. CA' REZZONICO, VENICE

TIEPOLO. NEPTUNE OFFERING VENICE THE TREASURES OF THE SEA, 1745-1750. PALAZZO DUCALE, VENICE

A less foreseeable development than the rise to favour of small-scale work was the renaissance of religious or decorative 'grand painting', in a baroque spirit. The last fresco-painters in the great tradition of the seventeenth century emerged in a city which had few large surfaces on which they could exercice their art.

Like Sebastiano Ricci (1659-1734), an eclectic virtuoso with a bright, vivid style, Giambattista Piazzetta made increasing use of light- and colour-contrasts, strong accents and twisted forms (*The Virgin Appearing to St Philip of Neri,* Venice, Church of La Fava, c. 1725). At the beginning he had drawn on the Caravaggesque tradition of *tenebroso*. Despite his love of the romantic and, sometimes, the intensity of his religious feeling, he was essentially a conservative. He specialized, with great success, in polished drawing and state portraits. When the Venetian Academy was founded in 1750 he was its first principal. For a while, in the thirties, he dallied with luminous painting (altarpiece of *The Jesuati,* Venice) and later he made a few concessions to genre painting (*The Fortune-Teller,* c. 1740), showing that he had decided to join the modernists. He influenced the strange Dalmatian painter Federico Bencovitch (1677-1753) and, for a while, Giambattista Tiepolo.

Tiepolo was a child prodigy. At nineteen he was already considered a master of his art; his tremendous prestige only began to diminish in the last phase of his life, with the advent of Neo-Classicism. Piazzetta and Bencovitch were the men who influenced his first *tenebroso* period (*Madonna,* Milan, Brera, c. 1721). After 1726 (the frescoes at Udine) his style became lighter, more airy; his dazzling and inventive virtuoso qualities found their true bent. The carefully calculated ceiling perspectives (Tiepolo often invoked the aid of the *quadraturista,* or geometrician, Mengozzi-Colonna) were undeniable triumphs (Venice: Church of

206

EIGHTEENTH-CENTURY VENETIAN SCHOOL

the Gesuati, 1737-1739, Church of the Scalzi, 1743-1744, the Pietà, 1754-1755; Milan: Palazzo Clerici, 1740; Würzburg: Residenz, 1750-1753; Escorial, Throne Room, after 1762). Often the scene on the ceiling seems to be viewed through a huge *trompe-l'œil* scroll or cartouche; the painting enters into the very fabric of the architecture and, with its pale pinks and mauves, seems to lose all materiality. The theatrical rhetoric of the baroque effects, as when the mural fresco seems to encroach on the space occupied by the spectator (Vicenza, Villa Valmarana, 1757, and, particularly, the *Story of Cleopatra*, Venice, Palazzo Labia, c. 1755) is, as it were, neutralized by the ironic ingenuity of the craftsmanship. Neither the cold, silvery light, the brilliantly free touch, nor the absence of rigidity in the composition (which is nevertheless carefully balanced) can be called a weakness: all these works are dominated by a kind of romantic grandeur which seems to place them at the end of the baroque period, rather than the beginning of Rococo.

Tiepolo painted so many huge works that, despite his incredible fertility, he was bound to run the risk of repeating himself or playing himself out. Sometimes his effects smack too much of the theatre some times they are too obvious, too dry, perhaps, compared with those of his great baroque predecessors. When he follows in the tracks of his masters, Veronese or Titian (*Danaë*, Stockholm, 1736), his excessive volubility can be irritating. For this reason some critics prefer his amazing drawings, sketches and etchings, of which he published several collections.

His son Giandomenico (1724-1804) was Tiepolo's assistant for a long time. He worked in a completely different spirit, with a sort of petty bourgeois meticulousness and a pleasing, unconventional realism, particularly in the rustic scenes with which he decorated several rooms in the Villa Valmarana.

TIEPOLO. PERFORMING DOGS. CA' REZZONICO, VENICE

TIEPOLO. APOLLO PURSUING DAPHNE, 1755-1760. NATIONAL GALLERY OF ART, WASHINGTON

GIANDOMENICO TIEPOLO, 1724-1804. PEASANTS RESTING, 1757. VILLA VALMARANA, VICENZA

207

SEVENTEENTH-CENTURY SPAIN

FRANCISCO DE GOYA Y LUCIENTES, 1746-1828. THE 3 MAY 1808 (DETAIL), 1814. PRADO, MADRID

GOYA. DOÑA GUMERSINDA GOICOECHEA Y GOYA, 1800-1804. PRIVATE COLLECTION, PARIS

GOYA. CLOTHED MAYA, 1796-1798. PRADO, MADRID

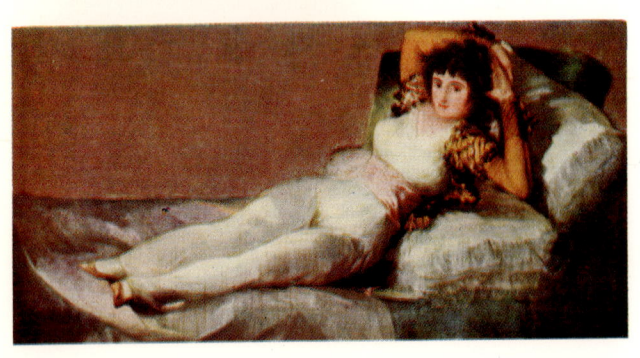

Goya is one of those figures in Spanish history who have no apparent antecedents and no immediate successors but who assert themselves with tremendous and absolute power. As a phenomenon, the philosopher Ortega y Gasset called this, collectively, 'Spanish Adamism'. Each figure is a new Adam, who, once again, begins from the beginning, emerges out of a complete void. Goya is one of these Spanish Adam-figures. But at the same time he symbolized Spain in another way—by giving expression to the distress and anger of her people during the War of Independence. The execution scene shown here is more terrible, in its tragic savagery, than any other Spanish outburst, apart from Picasso's *Guernica*.

Goya's agility, intellectual curiosity and fertility were truly amazing. He was also a great portraitist. Like Velasquez, he was a Court painter and depicted kings, princes, nobles and great ladies—a whole gallery of important personages, as well as his own friends and acquaintances. Sometimes he viewed them with irony or even cruelty, sometimes with graciousness and affection, but always with extreme penetration: whatever his mood, his brush was always able to echo it with perfect accuracy.

Which of the two *Majas,* the *Nude* or the *Clothed Maja,* is to be preferred? The second is, perhaps, the more attractive, and the more perverse. Certainly the two enigmatic portraits go to make up one of the most fascinating images of the conscious omnipotence of Woman. But, even so, the clothed girl expresses it with more emphasis—with less voluptuousness than the nude, but with the arrogant impertinence of those aristocratic women who amused themselves by playing the harlot and wearing the trousers of the *maja*. However, not all were moved by perverted snobbery: this taste for vulgarity owed something to a feeling for the Spanishness of Spain, a faith in what has been called 'casticity'.

SEVENTEENTH-CENTURY SPAIN

The *Woman with Fan* in the Louvre dates from 1817, when the sombre period of Goya's late life had already begun. He still painted portraits on occasion but he was soon to retire into a house in the countryside near Madrid, the Quinta del Sordo (House of the Deaf Man), cut off from the world by his infirmity and state of mind. There, in his last refuge before being exiled, he gave way to the nightmare visions of his delirium.

Death was bound to play a part in Goya's work: he shows it with the disconcerting sarcasm of Spain. He was a pitiless, bantering moralist who, in his *Capricchios,* revealed the most atrocious and at the same time the funniest aspects of the social comedy. One of the themes on which his ghoulish humour could embroider many variations was that of decaying beauty which continues to deck itself out in costly ornaments — a motif taken up by Baudelaire.

With one stroke he banishes from his universe the old academic allegories which had long ago lost all their immediacy. At the end of a note that he sent to a friend from Bordeaux in December 1825 is an airy postscript: 'Ah well, if we die, they will have to bury us!' It is as though from the depths of his last refuge the terrible ironist gives one final shrug of his shoulders before disappearing for good.

This must, of necessity, remain a very incomplete account of Goya's vast œuvre. I shall end it with a brief mention of the two *Maja* pictures. Although I may have expressed a preference for *The Clothed Maja,* as being the more subtle and disquieting depiction of the lures of women, its pendant is one of the finest nudes in all painting, the equal of the most brilliant feats by Rubens, Titian or Ingres. Manet was haunted by this picture during the early years of his career, as he was by Spanish painting in general, and its influence shows through his *Olympia,* another nude masterpiece with the same complete command of the brush but even greater ambiguity and acidity.

GOYA.
WOMAN WITH FAN,
1817.
LOUVRE, PARIS

GOYA.
OLD WOMEN.
LILLE MUSEUM

GOYA.
NUDE MAJA,
1796-1798.
PRADO, MADRID

EIGHTEENTH- AND NINETEENTH-CENTURY ENGLAND

WILLIAM HOGARTH.
1697-1764.
THE PAINTER'S
SERVANTS,
c. 1760.
NATIONAL GALLERY,
LONDON

HOGARTH.
CALAIS GATE:
'THE ROAST BEEF
OF OLD ENGLAND'
(DETAIL).
TATE GALLERY,
LONDON

HOGARTH.
MARRIAGE À LA
MODE:
THE COUNTESS'S
DRESSING ROOM,
1743-1745.
NATIONAL GALLERY,
LONDON

Painting in Britain never achieved a continuity comparable with that of France or Italy or the Lowlands. Nevertheless, certain characteristics can be said to recur, singly or in combination, throughout the centuries. English painting has always sprung more from the heart than from the head. It has more often depended upon line than upon a plastic sense of form; satire and anecdote have sometimes been its vehicle; its best portraiture, even at its most formal, is without pomposity; its lyric response to nature has been intense, at times to the point of mysticism.

At three moments in history, British artists have contributed to the European tradition as a whole. From the tenth to the fourteenth centuries, the English school of illuminators was of European stature, at times pre-eminent. Between 1750 and 1850, Britain evolved a portraiture that was bourgeois without being provincial, unaffected without being slight, and a landscape art that links the Dutch seventeenth century with Impressionism. Today, her painters have once again taken their place within the main stream of art in the Western world. Of these three periods of achievement, it is the middle one with its immediate antecedents and aftermath that concerns us here.

By the beginning of the eighteenth century the tender miniatures of Nicholas Hillyarde (c. 1547-1619) and the brilliant stage designs of Inigo Jones (1573-1652) were but memories. Van Dyck, Lely, Kneller were the names to conjure with. Joseph Highmore (1692-1780) and Arthur Devis (1711-1787) were painting portraits and 'conversation pieces' of delicacy and charm. Sir James Thornhill (1675-1734), however, a solitary English exponent of late Baroque, alone among his countrymen was in a position of power as a decorator of somewhat florid style. This was the scene into which William Hogarth (1697-1764) was born.

Hogarth was pugnacious and

210

EIGHTEENTH- AND NINETEENTH-CENTURY ENGLAND

prejudiced. He was also an upright man of simple tastes and unpretentious way of life. His training as a silver engraver brought him, via the world of engravers, into contact with French art, and possibly explains his love of intricate detail. Fired by Thornhill's influence and power, he set out to establish English painting on equal terms with that of other countries, and himself on equal terms with the foreign masters. Though he pillaged from all the sources available to him, it was indeed the Englishness of Hogarth's subject-matter that was so novel at the time. He was a Londoner, and London provided him with a seething, flamboyant gallery of types against backgrounds of squalor, violence and elegance.

The need for a regular income, after he ran off with Thornhill's daughter in 1729, led to the series of dramatic tableaux which he painted and subsequently engraved for popular consumption. 'I have endeavoured,' he wrote, 'to treat my subject as a dramatic writer; my picture is my stage, my men and women my players.' The six paintings of *The Harlot's Progress* (1731-1732), detailing the downfall of a simple country girl in the metropolis, were followed by *The Rake's Progress* (1735) and, in 1743-1745, the greatly superior *Marriage à la Mode*. From these episodic fables, with their strong satiric and moral bias, was to spring *la peinture morale* in France.

Their execution varies from the felicitous to the perfunctory: Hogarth's ambition too often out-ran such 'pot-boiling'. His incursion into art-theory, with his 'Analysis of Beauty' based on the serpentine line, still holds interest for historians, but of greater significance for painters was his portraiture. *Captain Coram* became the prototype for the following hundred years and such fresh and sympathetic works as *The Painter's Servants* and *The Shrimp Girl,* dating from his last years, show what might have been, had Hogarth's livelihood not depended on his engrav-

HOGARTH. PORTRAIT OF THE ARTIST WITH HIS DOG TRUMP, 1745, TATE GALLERY, LONDON

HOGARTH. THE RAKE'S PROGRESS: THE ORGY, 1734. SOANE MUSEUM, LONDON

HOGARTH. THE SHRIMP GIRL, c. 1760. NATIONAL GALLERY, LONDON

EIGHTEENTH- AND NINETEENTH-CENTURY ENGLAND

JOSHUA REYNOLDS.
1723-1792.
LORD HEATHFIELD,
1787.
NATIONAL GALLERY,
LONDON

REYNOLDS.
PORTRAIT OF
COUNTESS
SPENCER AND HER
DAUGHTER,
c. 1761.
EARL SPENCER
ALTHORP
COLLECTION,
NORTHANTS

REYNOLDS.
PORTRAIT OF
DR JOHNSON,
1788.
TATE GALLERY,
LONDON

ing. *The Shrimp Girl* was found in his studio when he died and has seemed irresistible ever since.

More fortunate in his period than Hogarth was Joshua Reynolds (1723-1792), the foremost portrait painter of his century. Yet, with equal truth, it could be said that his period, more particularly the classical age of English painting from 1760-1790, was in large measure his creation. Reynolds saw the need, if an English school was to be consolidated, for a stable basis on which to build. He spent two years, 1750-1752, in Italy. Having saturated himself in the work of the Italian masters he set himself, on his return to England, to marry the 'Grand Style' to the English portrait. At the same time he set out to raise the status of the artist. Choosing his circle from men of letters, among them Goldsmith and Dr Johnson, he methodically strengthened his own position in society. When the Royal Academy was founded, in 1769, it was Reynolds who was asked to become its first President. His fourteen Presidential 'Discourses' not only provide the theoretical background to the period but remain the best written material of their kind in the English language.

In his own work, Reynolds developed his resources steadily through his life. Technical deficiencies have left many of his pictures in physical ruin, but their pictorial architecture remains intact. He was marvellously inventive in reworking Italian formulae, and his grasp of character could be profound. *Lord Heathfield* surely epitomises the sterling qualities of his class, his calling, and his office.

What Reynolds did for English portraiture, Richard Wilson (1713-1782) did in large measure for English landscape painting. During some seven years in Italy he absorbed the language of classicism and applied its arcadian spirit, after his return to Britain, to the parks and houses of the nobility and to the mountain scenery of his native Wales. His achievement was to

EIGHTEENTH- AND NINETEENTH-CENTURY ENGLAND

invest this Italianate serenity at one and the same time with elements of naturalism and a Romantic sense of wonder in the face of nature. With Wilson, said Ruskin, 'the history of sincere landscape art, founded on a meditative love of nature, begins in England.' Worldly success eluded him, however, for his was a difficult and unaccommodating personality.

The contrast in prosperity between Reynolds and Wilson was marked; no less so was that in character between Reynolds and Thomas Gainsborough (1727-1788). Reynolds was clearly blessed with exceptional strength of will. He was careful, industrious, objective, urbane. Bored by high society, it was Gainsborough on the other hand who wrote: 'I'm sick of portraits and wish very much to take my viol-de-Gamba and walk off to some sweet village where I can paint landskips and enjoy the fag-end of life in quietness and ease.' His was a lyrical genius. The lightness of his touch and the charm of his colour give to even his routine portraits a seductive air and to the best of them an almost Renoir-like glow of happiness.

Gainsborough was without formal training but worked for a time as an assistant to Gravelot. To the influence of Gravelot and Hayman was joined the example of Ruisdael and the other seventeenth-century Dutch landscapists. Gainsborough's early work in Suffolk, where he painted the ever-enchanting *Mr and Mrs Robert Andrews,* is an earnest of the Constable he might have been and provides a link between seventeenth-century Holland and nineteenth-century France. The ingenuous note which lends to such works a kind of morning freshness, gave way, after he moved to Bath in 1759, to a more fashionably arcadian quality. Gradually, the direct observation of nature ceased and the backgrounds to his figures turned into theatrical backdrops. Gainsborough was, in fact, the one great English master of the

THOMAS GAINSBOROUGH. 1727-1788. PORTRAIT OF MR AND MRS ROBERT ANDREWS, *c.* 1748-1749. NATIONAL GALLERY, LONDON

GAINSBOROUGH. PORTRAIT OF MRS SIDDONS, 1785. NATIONAL GALLERY, LONDON

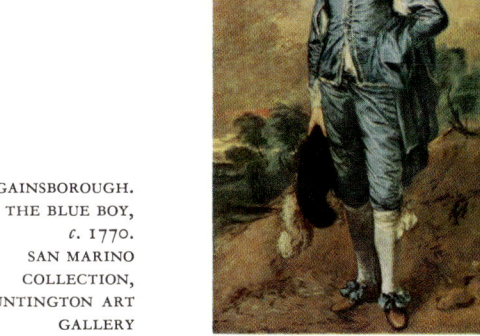

GAINSBOROUGH. THE BLUE BOY, *c.* 1770. SAN MARINO COLLECTION, HUNTINGTON ART GALLERY

EIGHTEENTH- AND NINETEENTH-CENTURY ENGLAND

GEORGE STUBBS.
1724-1806.
PHAETON AND PAIR,
1787.
NATIONAL GALLERY,
LONDON

GEORGE ROMNEY.
1734-1802.
PORTRAIT OF
MRS DAVENPORT,
1782-1784.
NATIONAL GALLERY,
WASHINGTON

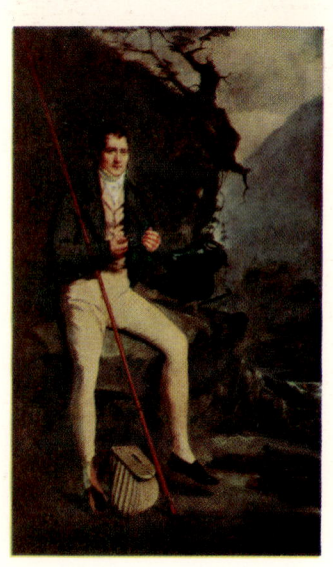

HENRY RAEBURN.
1756-1823.
PORTRAIT OF
LIEUT.-COLONEL
BRYCE MCMURDO,
c. 1810?
NATIONAL GALLERY,
LONDON

Rococo. Towards the end of his life, in London, he painted a number of 'fancy pictures', in the manner of Murillo, largely of children in scenes of rustic simplicity.

Increasingly, around these great names of the second half of the eighteenth century appeared others, their strength and their weaknesses conditioned by the society they served. The English country house could be said to dominate English art in this century as the Industrial Revolution was to do a hundred years later. Outside, the tranquil, rolling parkland was informally devised on 'picturesque' lines. Inside, the lords, the squires and the gentry accumulated fine furniture and commissioned records of themselves, their wives and their children, their horses, their homes.

The young Gainsborough caught one aspect of this spirit with extraordinary felicity; another was given permanence by the portraitist and animal-painter George Stubbs (1724-1806). A whole school of 'sporting' artists, indeed, came into being to record the Englishman's love of horses and dogs, of hunting scenes and racing. Ben Marshall (1767-1835) was one; George Morland (1763-1804) a genre painter of rustic subjects, and James Ward (1769-1859) a Romantic landscapist and animal-painter, were others. Stubbs was distinguished from these by the precision of his frieze-like compositions and the delicacy of his tones and touch. His was an infinitely tactful, rational art, producing images of deliberate, yet curiously compelling, quietude. His lifelong study of human and animal anatomy was profound and it has even been suggested that the most wholly original contribution to European painting in the eighteenth century by an English artist is to be found in Stubbs' monumental study of *The Anatomy of the Horse,* published in 1776. Delacroix was among those influenced by his paintings of wild animals.

As the Royal Academy schools turned out succeeding generations of trained students, competition

EIGHTEENTH- AND NINETEENTH-CENTURY ENGLAND

grew among the portraitists following Reynolds. Allan Ramsay (1713-1784), George Romney (1734-1802), John Hoppner (1758-1810) and Sir Henry Raeburn (1756-1823) are among those who demand consideration. The first and last of these, it may be noted, were Scotsmen—an indication that Scottish portraiture was now to be reckoned with. Ramsay was the more graceful, Raeburn the more forceful interpreter of character. Ramsay's paintings—of women in particular—are notable for their delicate sensibility and their cool, muted tonalities. Raeburn, largely self-taught, but with the inevitable trip to Italy behind him, presented Edinburgh society and the Highland nobility to themselves with dramatic lighting and a broad treatment. The neurotic Romney, at his happiest with young and handsome sitters, achieved fashionable success by his compositional skill and easy flattery; his neo-classic drawings link him with Fuseli and Blake.

After Hoppner's death in 1880, the acknowledged successor to Reynolds was Sir Thomas Lawrence (1769-1830). He settled in London in 1786 as a Royal Academy student, exhibited there the following year, and succeeded Reynolds as 'Painter in Ordinary' to George III in 1792. His style, however, lacked Reynold's profundity. There is a flashing extravagance about his earlier work which turns a little thin and decorative in the great series of portraits of allied sovereigns and notables which he executed all over Europe between 1814 and 1820 for the Waterloo Chamber in Windsor Castle. Admired by Delacroix and Degas, Lawrence was nevertheless an important link between English and French Romanticism.

The Romantic movement not only began, but threw up some of its most eccentric manifestations, in Britain. The Gothic revival, marked most fancifully in architecture by Beckford's Fonthill Abbey, found expression also in the Gothic novel and in fantastication in the

RAEBURN. PORTRAIT OF MRS ELEANOR URQUHART, c. 1795. NATIONAL GALLERY, WASHINGTON

THOMAS LAWRENCE. 1769-1830. PORTRAIT OF PRINCESS LIEVEN, c. 1820. TATE GALLERY, LONDON

LAWRENCE. PORTRAITS OF JULIUS ANGERSTEIN AND HIS WIFE, 1792. LOUVRE, PARIS

EIGHTEENTH- AND NINETEENTH-CENTURY ENGLAND

HANS HEINRICH FÜSSLI, KNOWN AS HENRY FUSELI. 1741-1825.
THE LITTLE FAIRY, KUNSTMUSEUM, BASLE

FUSELI.
LADY MACBETH.
PRIVATE COLLECTION LONDON

WILLIAM BLAKE.
1757-1827.
DANTE AND VIRGIL AT THE ENTRANCE TO HELL,
1824-1827.
TATE GALLERY, LONDON

visual arts. The burning centre of all that was most visionary in English painting in the first quarter of the nineteenth century was William Blake (1757-1827). In retrospect, all others with comparable aims, whether older or younger, seem to spring from him.

Older than Blake was Henry Fuseli (1741-1825) born Hans Heinrich Füssli, in Zurich. First ordained as a clergyman, Fuseli came to England when he was twenty-two. Apart from eight years in Italy, he spent the rest of his life in England, where he came to have some influence as Professor of Painting at the Royal Academy (Lawrence owned no fewer than twenty-one paintings by him). Fuseli was capricious, mannered, morbid, extravagant. His nightmares of the weird, the illogical and the terrible could be said to preshadow Surrealism but seldom produce in the modern onlooker a suspension of disbelief. Considerably more strange than these theatrical set-pieces are his sinister and erotic drawings of women, which hold a genuine disquiet arising from a static sense of potential drama. These are closely related to very similar drawings by John Brown (1752-1787), though which artist influenced the other is not known. Much-quoted, however, has been Fuseli's admission that Blake was 'damned good to steal from'.

In actual fact, Fuseli was able to encourage the younger man in various ways. Blake is one of those English geniuses it is almost impossible to fit neatly into the history of painting. His reputation rests as much upon his very great poetry as his painting—poetry which became so subjective and mystical as to baffle the casual reader. Until he was sixty he lived in relative obscurity, considered mad by many and maintaining a simple existence by engraving other men's designs and his own illustrations to the Bible, Dante, Virgil and his own poems. Born in London, he lacked formal schooling, though he worked for

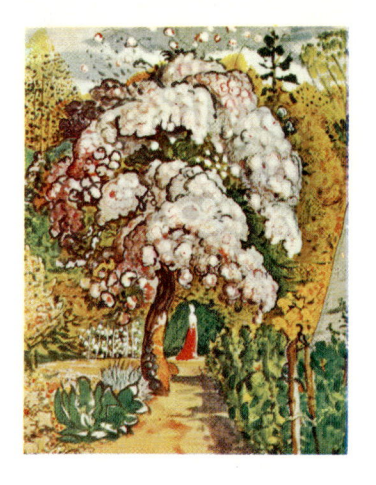

EIGHTEENTH- AND NINETEENTH-CENTURY ENGLAND

a time in the Royal Academy schools. His academically inadequate powers of draughtsmanship he sought, consciously and unconsciously, to supplement with borrowings from the past. What gives his works their potency is the sheer force of imaginative vision that sustains them. Blake believed himself to be under Heavenly guidance. He believed that the artist is sent into the world to make his visions real to other men. His passion for the hard, bounding contour line was part of his effort to express his religious symbols in as concrete a manner as possible. 'A spirit or a vision' he said 'are not a cloudy vapour or a nothing... Greatness of Ideas is Precision of Ideas.'

Towards the end of his life there gathered around him, for the most part through the person of John Linnell (1792-1882), a group of younger artists, almost disciples. They called themselves 'The Ancients' and among them, apart from Linnell himself, were John Varley (1778-1842), Edward Calvert (1799-1883) and Samuel Palmer (1805-1881). Their inspiration was to fade as Victorian values became established, but Palmer, in particular, shone for a brief decade with the brilliance of a falling star. Some of Blake's wood-engravings he described as 'visions of little dells, like unto Paradise... of the exquisitest pitch of poetry', and the words might equally be applied to his own pastoral landscapes of Shoreham in Kent. Seen with extraordinary intensity, often by moonlight, the foliage and corn full, ripe and abundant, these are ecstatic records of a mystical joy in nature.

An exact contemporary of Blake, and equally hard to place historically, was Thomas Rowlandson (1756-1827). Essentially, his world was Hogarth's, a world of comment and social satire, lapsing often into caricature and farce. Yet, at the same time, he was capable of investing his landscapes with a lyric poetry. Rowlandson, who studied at the Royal Academy

BLAKE.
THE SIMONIAC POPE,
1824-1827.
TATE GALLERY,
LONDON

BLAKE.
SATAN SMITING JOB WITH SORE BOILS,
c. 1825.
TATE GALLERY,
LONDON

SAMUEL PALMER.
1805-1881.
THE GARDEN AT SHOREHAM,
c. 1829.
VICTORIA AND ALBERT MUSEUM,
LONDON

217

EIGHTEENTH- AND NINETEENTH-CENTURY ENGLAND

JOHN CROME, KNOWN AS OLD CROME.
1768-1821.
THE PORINGLAND OAK,
c. 1818.
NATIONAL GALLERY, LONDON

JOHN CONSTABLE.
1776-1837.
VIEW AT EPSOM,
c. 1808.
TATE GALLERY, LONDON

CONSTABLE.
WILLY LOTT'S HOUSE,
c. 1814.
VICTORIA AND ALBERT MUSEUM, LONDON

schools, inherited wealth but squandered it and thereafter he threw off prints and drawings for a livelihood with boundless vitality. In sum these form a kind of boisterous roistering 'comic strip' that recalls the *Comédie Humaine* in its richness of character. Rowlandson never painted in oils, but the Rococo delicacy of his landscape sketches projects the 'picturesque' tradition of the eighteenth century forward into the nineteenth.

The topographical landscape had been popular in England for centuries. Its place was never stronger than in this hundred years, during which the Englishman became aware of the drama in the atmosphere, in the weather and the seasons. From the neo-classical game of separating the 'correct' views from the 'incorrect' he developed that Wordsworthian self-identification with the forces of nature which in turn led to the non-conceptual vision of landscape which was the nineteenth century's great contribution to the history of art. Ruisdael and Hobbema, Claude and Wilson were the starting points; by the middle of the nineteenth century a new tradition had been created and handed on to France.

Between these points is strung a necklet of names, adventurous in varying degree, often a little provincial, but never without a modest charm: Alexander Cozens (c. 1717-1786) and his son John Robert Cozens (1752-1797), in Constable's view the greatest genius that ever touched landscape; Paul Sandby (1725-1809); Thomas Girtin (1775-1802) the friend of Turner's youth, who broke away from the earlier tradition to register more Romantic effects; John Crome (1769-1821), founder of the Norwich Society of Artists — the only regional school in England of any consequence — who likewise represents the same transition; John Sell Cotman (1782-1842) also of the Norwich school, introspective, neurotic, remarkable for his austere sense of design; David Cox (1783-1859).

These were most of them water-

EIGHTEENTH- AND NINETEENTH-CENTURY ENGLAND

colourists. The true inheritor of Gainsborough's lyrical response to nature was John Constable (1776-1837), with Turner, the major English painter of the nineteenth century. In him culminated the tradition that had begun with Hobbema and Ruisdael. Constable sought to catch nature in motion and trembling with continual change; the sweep of clouds and all the exciting gleams of light playing over, and giving vitality to, the countryside. He wanted his pictures, he said, 'to have the dew and sparkle of trees and bushes and grass in the real, light-drenched world.' Fuseli said of his paintings that they make one want 'to call for one's great coat and umbrella.'

The son of a prosperous Suffolk miller, he divided his time between London and his beloved Suffolk. Though he never left England, his influence upon later nineteenth-century landscape was profound.

For many of his large scale compositions Constable painted both so-called sketches and more highly elaborated versions. To the modern eye it is the former—and such marvellously spontaneous impressions as the 'unfinished' sketch of *Weymouth Bay*—that have the greater freshness and vivacity; the creative nature of the latter was nevertheless grasped at once in France where *The Hay Wain* and *A View on the Stour* gained a Gold Medal at the Salon. There, Constable's free handling of paint was acclaimed by the Romantics and the precision of his observation was to affect the Barbizon school.

A further link in the chain by which this near-Impressionist vision was transmitted to France, was afforded by the talented but short-lived Richard Parks Bonington (1802-1828). Bonington was brought up in Calais and studied in Paris where he became friends with Delacroix. Both painters admired Constable, and Bonington's own landscapes express a somewhat formal vision with an equally spontaneous touch.

CONSTABLE.
WIVENHOE PARK,
ESSEX, 1816.
NATIONAL GALLERY,
WASHINGTON

CONSTABLE.
BRIGHTON BEACH,
1842.
VICTORIA AND
ALBERT MUSEUM,
LONDON

CONSTABLE.
SALISBURY
CATHEDRAL,
c. 1827.
NATIONAL GALLERY,
LONDON

RICHARD PARKES
BONINGTON.
1802-1828.
VIEW AT VERSAILLES,
1825.
LOUVRE, PARIS

EIGHTEENTH- AND NINETEENTH-CENTURY ENGLAND

JOSEPH MALLORD
WILLIAM TURNER.
1775-1851.
ROCKY BAY,
c. 1830.
TATE GALLERY,
LONDON

TURNER.
HASTINGS,
c. 1830.
TATE GALLERY,
LONDON

TURNER.
NORHAM CASTLE,
SUNRISE;
AFTER 1830.
TATE GALLERY,
LONDON

TURNER.
THE FIGHTING
TEMERAIRE TOWED
TO HER LAST BERTH,
1838.
NATIONAL GALLERY,
LONDON

The English Romantic movement culminated in Joseph Mallord William Turner (1775-1851). His contribution to the history of art was more varied and profound than that of any other English painter. If Constable sought light, Turner pushed the search even further, until, in the end, everything else was swallowed up in it. He raised his palette to the pitch where his pictures not only represented light but were themselves symbolic of it. Constable accused him of painting 'in tinted steam'; someone else said that his landscapes were 'pictures of nothing and very like'.

The truth is that Turner, born in the heart of London, son of a barber, looking like a slovenly coachman and generally a 'rum bird', was another English visionary. He could see all the universe in a cloud or in a sunbeam. The reckless, explosive mixture of scumbling and smearing, scratching and scraping, with which he ended his career was essentially an effort to reach and to grasp almost cosmic truths.

His youth was precocious. He was admitted to the Royal Academy schools in 1789 and first exhibited there two years later. By 1799 he was an Associate, by 1802 a full Academician. Until 1796 he remained a watercolourist; in the early 1800's he set himself to surpass Claude. He travelled incessantly in Western Europe, first making topographical records of the grandeur of the Alps, coming finally to the magic city of Venice.

Turner's work grew steadily more abstract and he took as his subjects snowstorms and deluges as expressive of the insignificance of man as those of Leonardo. Finally facts disappeared from his painting altogether.

From the last twenty years of his life date his most important works. His contemporary reputation was, however, a little dimmed when Ruskin came to his defence in the first volume of *Modern Painters* in 1843. It is odd that Ruskin,

EIGHTEENTH- AND NINETEENTH-CENTURY ENGLAND

who was to father the Pre-Raphaelite movement, could accept these late Turners as naturalism in any form. Or is it perhaps that his form is of another order, another scale, from that more normally encountered? The current modes of abstract expressionism provide a new gloss upon Turner's subjectivism.

Though Turner did not care a fig for the polite usages of life, he was utterly single-minded about his art. He early determined to win a place among the old masters of his choosing. He came to look upon his life-work as a single gesture and hoped that a public gallery might be founded where it could be seen as a whole. He began to hoard his paintings. He twice refused £100,000 for the work in his studio—a sum equivalent to perhaps five or six times as much today. He refused to sell *Dido Building Carthage* to the National Gallery, saying that it was a waste of public money since he had already left it to the nation in his will. Indeed the final bequest amounted to nearly 300 paintings and nearly 20,000 watercolours.

With Turner's death British painting now entered the long night of the Industrial Revolution. The chimneys belched smoke, a rural peasantry learned to live in the cities and a new middle class, of greater wealth than taste, came into being.

A bourgeoisie consisting of industrialists, traders, managers, technocrats and bureaucrats, seems always to have much the same taste in art, be it in seventeenth-century Holland, nineteenth-century Britain or twentieth-century Russia. It demands that a picture should tell a story with as great an illusion of reality as possible.

For a brief period, one group of artists contrived to combine realism with seriousness. In the Pre-Raphaelite Brotherhood, formed in 1848, the English Romantic movement found its final expression. The 'Brethren' included Dante Gabriel Rossetti (1828-1882), Wil-

TURNER.
THE PIAZZETTA,
1839-1840.
TATE GALLERY,
LONDON

TURNER.
THE LETTER,
c. 1830.
TATE GALLERY,
LONDON

TURNER.
PEACE. BURIAL AT
SEA
(OF SIR DAVID
WILKIE),
1842.
TATE GALLERY,
LONDON

221

THE PRE-RAPHAELITES

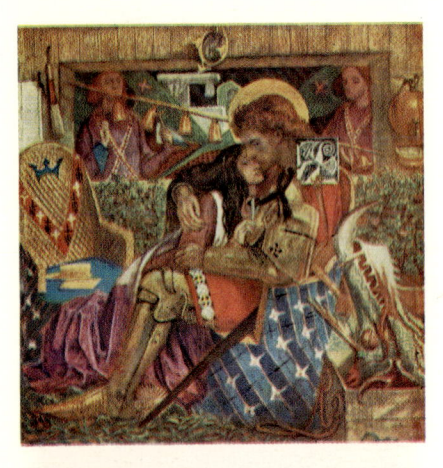

DANTE GABRIEL
ROSSETTI.
1828-1882.
THE WEDDING OF
ST GEORGE AND
PRINCESS SABRA,
1857.
TATE GALLERY,
LONDON

RICHARD WILSON.
1714-1782.
ON HOUNSLOW
HEATH.
TATE GALLERY,
LONDON

EDWARD
BURNE-JONES.
1833-1898.
PERSEUS RECIEVING
HIS ARMS,
1879-1888.
ART GALLERY,
SOUTHAMPTON

liam Holman Hunt (1827-1910) and John Everett Millais (1829-1896); Ford Madox Brown (1821-1893) was associated with them. The movement, which lasted less than five years, was a reaction against the pretentious rhetoric to which Sir Joshua's 'Grand Style' had led. It was compounded of mediaevalism, religious fervour and an intense observation of the objective world. In its love of meticulous detail and reliance upon bright local colour it may be compared with the German 'Nazarene' movement.

Rossetti's contribution was entirely personal, charged with emotion in his earlier years, increasingly hysterical in later life. Hunt's was the talent that accepted Ruskin's admonition (to students) to 'go to nature rejecting nothing, selecting nothing and scorning nothing.' With intense and unfaltering conscientiousness he accumulated the details of specific forms as painstakingly as the Surrealists were to do three quarters of a century later.

Lack of taste and pictorial intelligence marked all these painters, and none more so than Millais, whose ambition and technical brilliance (he was attending the Royal Academy schools at the age of twelve) led him to a knighthood and the presidency of the Royal Academy. Sir Edward Burne-Jones (1833-1898) broke away from his early admiration for Rossetti to a dream world of figures from a 'Golden Age' that was an escape from industrialism and from life. The sentiment that suffuses his near-monochrome figures, with their echoes of Botticelli and Mantegna, is exceptionally evocative of its period.

And thus, smothered by increasingly bourgeois standards, the creative impetus of the century evaporated. The energy of a true Romantic like James Ward was debased into the sentimentalities of a Landseer; Classicism turned into the insipid pageants of Alma Tadema and Lord Leighton. It was from this national abdication of taste that Whistler sought to turn Victorian England.

GERMAN ROMANTICISM

In Germany, Romanticism did not appear in literature at the same time as in the visual arts. When Gœthe was at Rome in 1787 his admiration for Gothic had long been supplanted by a renewed taste for Antiquity, whereas Romanticism was unknown to the numerous German artists in the Eternal City, who still obeyed the strict principles of Winckelmann and Mengs. Wilhelm Tischbein showed not the slightest urge for independence, when he painted the poet amid the ruins of the Campagna. A famous portrait if ever there was one, it gained its author the nickname 'Gœthe-Tischbein'.

German Romantic art really arose both at Rome, where Overbeck and the Nazarenes installed themselves in the disused monastery of Sant' Isidoro to share their religious fervour and admiration for painting prior to Raphael; and in northern Germany, where it took a very different form. Both its chief initiators there were born in Pomerania, and studied at Copenhagen. Philipp Otto Runge probably had the more many-sided character. Poetically inclined, he died young (1777-1810), leaving behind several masterly portraits, together with some rather tame symbolical pictures, which try to do too much at once. After being misunderstood for a long time, Caspar David Friedrich (1774-1840) has become one of the popular German artists. A far more gifted painter than his easel pictures suggest, he produced many spontaneous water-colours of skies and clouds. He was slow to turn to oils, which, in the studio, he used with the utmost diligence to produce the mirror-like surfaces of vast landscapes: seas reflecting the moon, crosses raised on mountains, ruined abbeys, the moors of his native region and of Rügen, whose wide horizons he specially loved. His friend Kersting depicted him at his easel in a cold, bare room. In reality, he had a little group of faithful admirers, and life was rather hard. Posterity has avenged him, however.

JOHAN HEINRICH
WILHELM TISCHBEIN.
1751-1829.
GŒTHE IN ITALY,
1787.
STÄDELSCHES
KUNSTINSTITUT,
FRANKFORT

CASPAR DAVID
FRIEDRICH.
1774-1840.
MOUNTAIN
LANDSCAPE
WITH RAINBOW.
FOLKWANG
MUSEUM,
ESSEN

CASPAR FRIEDRICH.
MORNING LIGHT,
1808.
FOLKWANG
MUSEUM,
ESSEN

CASPAR FRIEDRICH.
MAN AND WOMAN
GAZING AT THE
MOON,
1819.
BERLIN MUSEUM

FRENCH NEO-CLASSICISM

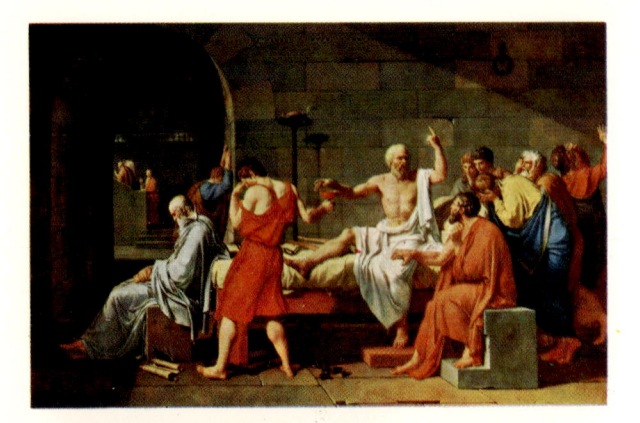

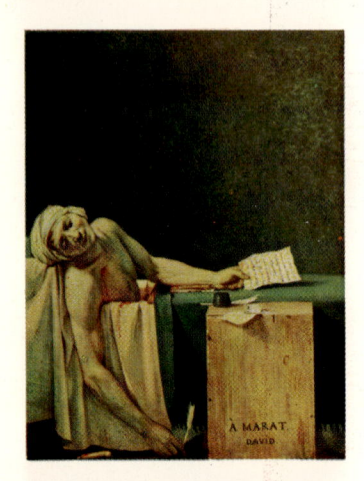

JACQUES-LOUIS
DAVID.
1748-1825.
THE DEATH OF
SOCRATES,
1787.
METROPOLITAN
MUSEUM,
NEW YORK

LOUIS DAVID.
THE DEAD MARAT
IN HIS BATH,
1793.
MUSÉE ROYAL DES
BEAUX-ARTS,
BRUSSELS

LOUIS DAVID.
BONAPARTE AT
MONT SAINT-
BERNARD,
1800.
PALACE OF
VERSAILLES

Jacques-Louis David, in Rome after winning the most covered prize in French art with his *Erisiratus identifying the Sickness of Antiochus* (1774), plunged with characteristic vehemence into the Antiquity that he had but dimly preconceived in Paris, and that incited him to react against the enervation and licentiousness of the age. Heeding the advice of his teacher Vien, he copied the masterpieces which detained him at every step in that museum of a city: monuments, detached sculpture, vases, sarcophagi, frescoes, and manuscripts. Like Poussin, of whom he was soon to be called the heir, he could have exclaimed: 'I never feel such an urge to work as when I've seen some beautiful object!'

On David's return to France in 1781, his *Belisarius begging for Alms* (Louvre)—after *The Obsequies of Patroclus* (Cherbourg)—met with a triumphant reception. Also in 1781, he opened a huge studio; in 1783 he painted *Andromache's Grief before the Body of Hector* (Montpellier); in 1784 *The Oath of the Horatii;* and in 1787 *The Death of Socrates,* which he exhibited at the Salon four years later with *The Lictors carry back to Brutus the Body of his Son* (Louvre). A deputy to the Convention in 1792 and an admirer of Robespierre, he protested against the lewd decorations in 'the apartments of the satraps and the boudoirs of the courtesans', and became director of the Republican festivals.

One could not be more violently wrong about oneself than was this violent man who, though an idealist on principle, had the temperament of a realist. When, in his declining years, he was alarmed at having caused French portraiture —by his example, but in spite of himself—to cultivate visual truth, he wrote to his favourite disciple Gros that it would serve to remind him that there was only one respectable form of art: history painting.

Yet it is not because of *The Oath of the Horatii* or *Leonidas at Thermopylae* (Louvre) that this precursor of Géricault, Delacroix, Ingres,

FRENCH NEO-CLASSICISM

and Courbet today compels our admiration. It is through the authority of his likenesses, his sincere response, and his uncompromising approach to his models, as in *The dead Marat in his Bath, The Coronation of Napoleon* (Louvre), or *The Distribution of the Eagles* (Versailles). Even if *Woman selling Vegetables, The three Ladies of Ghent,* and *The Gerard Family* are not, as formerly believed, by David, they follow his example. Like his admirable portraits of himself, Mme Récamier, the Sériziat family, or Pius VII (Louvre), they make us forget all the false Poussins and shoddy work mass-produced by so many uncultured prigs and sub-Davids, under the influence of a would-be heroic doctrine.

'Nothing is more deadly than the alleged rules and conventions, and the attraction that they exercise,' wrote Delacroix. Though he trained so many brilliant pupils, and had twice been a member of the Convention, David forgot that theories never create masterpieces, and that (again according to Delacroix) technique is expounded not through treatises or systems, but 'palette in hand'.

David was a prose-writer who thought himself a poet. The supernatural and unconscious never came to the aid of this compatriot of Poussin and Corneille, and, in the theatrical staging of his history pieces, not a single actor plays his part with conviction. A canvas like the famous *Sabine Women* in the Louvre, its dryness and crude colouring only emphasized by restoration, is made up of borrowings from Poussin. Delacroix was right in saying that David's inspiration came entirely from the head, and that, with all its vigour, his work lacked impulsive ardour, emotion, and expressive power. How cruelly his weaknesses are exposed by Rubens, whom he despised! *Paris and Helen,* painted at forty, leaves us just as cold as *Mars disarmed by Venus* (Brussels), a product of his old age. David was only really great when not aspiring after greatness.

LOUIS DAVID. PORTRAIT OF M. SÉRIZIAT, 1795. LOUVRE, PARIS

LOUIS DAVID. PORTRAIT OF MADAME RÉCAMIER, 1800. LOUVRE, PARIS

LOUIS DAVID. PORTRAIT OF MADAME HAMELIN, c. 1800. NATIONAL GALLERY OF ART, WASHINGTON

FRENCH NEO-CLASSICISM

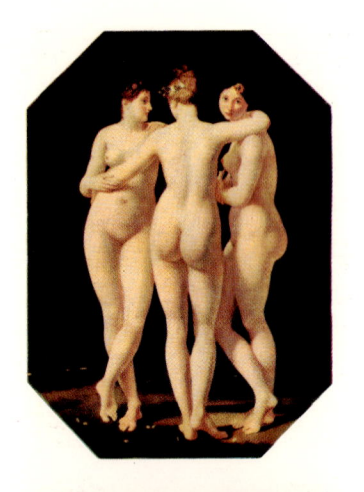

JEAN-BAPTISTE
REGNAULT.
1754-1829.
THE THREE GRACES,
1799.
LOUVRE, PARIS

FRANÇOIS-PASCAL,
BARON GÉRARD.
1770-1837.
PORTRAIT OF
MADAME RÉCAMIER.
LOUVRE, PARIS

ANNE-LOUIS
GIRODET-TRIOSON.
1767-1824.
THE BURIAL OF
ATALA,
1808.
LOUVRE, PARIS

Pierre Prud'hon, who formed a link between the eighteenth and nineteenth centuries, is sometimes called 'the French Correggio'. Sensual but not licentious and romantic without exaggeration, he may be described, with his 'languishing beauties', as the André Chénier of painting. No one has ever known how to play more tenderly with attributes and emblems. He is seen at his best in his caressingly soft drawings on blue paper and his many commissioned portraits, which he usually roughed out in greys. Yet he had nothing like the technical virtuosity of Greuze, whom at times he somewhat resembled.

Large compositions like *Crime pursued by Justice and Vengeance* (Louvre), which made his reputation, lack the charm of unfinished studies such as *Innocence, The Soul breaking its earthly Bonds* and, particularly, *The Rape of Psyche*. These have retained all their appeal, even though, through the use of bitumen, their colouring has rapidly turned olive or leaden.

The Louvre is rich in portraits that recall the fleeting fame of Baron Gérard, Jean-Baptiste Regnault, Girodet-Trioson, and Marie-Guilhelmine Benoist. All these were transitional artists in whom the qualities or conventions of the eighteenth century, into which they had been born, came to be more-or-less successfully combined with Davidesque and Romantic influences, or with memories of the English school.

Torn between a variety of temptations, Baron Gérard was brilliant, though a trifle cold, in full-length portraits like those of Isabey and Mme Visconti; insipid in his *Psyche*, which is just a lifeless Prud'hon; and charming in his *Comtesse Regnault*. A skilled technician but a superficial analyst, he was too much swayed by successive fashions to occupy a high place in French painting.

The same goes for Girodet-Trioson. Though a highly experienced teacher, whose studio Géricault attended, his figures in

FRENCH NEO-CLASSICISM

The Burial of Atala or *The Sleep of Endymion* were capable of causing his own master, David, to describe them as being made of crystal. Jean-Baptiste Regnault was another artist of this kind. He thought that he could match David's *Sabine Women* with his own *Hercules delivering Alcestis,* but he got no more out of his Pompeian or Raphaelesque borrowings than did his pupil Guérin in *Phaedra, Aurora and Cephalus,* or *Aeneas telling Dido of the Misfortunes of Troy* (Louvre). How many even less inspired future winners of the Prix de Rome took these sham Antiquities and gimcrack furnishings as their models!

The name of Marie-Guilhelmine Benoist, a pupil of Vigée-Lebrun and David, certainly would not be remembered but for her beautiful and most unexpected portrait of a negress. Painted in 1800, it gives a foretaste of Géricault. Under the First Empire, many good qualities were smothered by the theories of David, the aesthetics of Quatremere de Quincy, and the complete misunderstanding of both Poussin's greatness and the coming greatness of Ingres, as revealed not in *The Apotheosis of Homer,* but in his nudes and portraits. Guérin summed up better than anyone the aberrations of which he himself was guilty, when he said of Girodet-Trioson that he carried the School's vice—that of painting statues—even further than the others.

Gros's career was founded on a nine year's stay in Italy, the discovery in turn of Michelangelo, Rubens, and Raphael, and his providential meeting with Napoleon. These events brought him official status, but he always guarded his independence. He recreated history, and invented a truth more credible than that of merely keeping to the facts, which, in *The Plague-stricken of Jaffa, The Battle of Aboukir,* and *Napoleon at Eylau* (Louvre 1804, 1806, 1808), he recomposed as Rubens would have done.

Delacroix has shown how, abandoning the Academic form-

PIERRE-PAUL PRUD'HON. 1758-1823. THE RAPE OF PSYCHE, 1808. LOUVRE, PARIS

PRUD'HON. PORTRAIT OF THE EMPRESS JOSEPHINE, 1805. LOUVRE, PARIS

MARIE-GUILHELMINE BENOIST. 1768-1826. PORTRAIT OF A NEGRESS, 1800. LOUVRE, PARIS

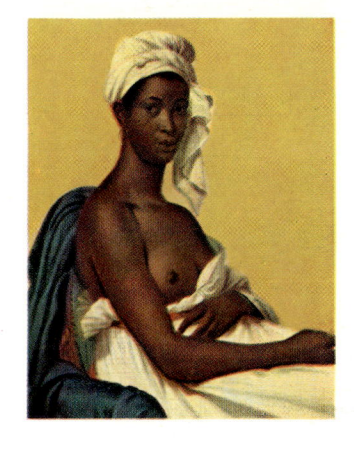

NINETEENTH-CENTURY FRANCE

JEAN-ANTOINE GROS.
1771-1835.
BONAPARTE AT THE
BRIDGE
AT ARCOLA, 1796.
LOUVRE, PARIS

JEAN-ANTOINE GROS.
THE BATTLE OF
ABOUKIR (DETAIL).
PALACE OF
VERSAILLES

THÉODORE
GÉRICAULT.
1791-1824.
OFFICER OF THE
CHASSEURS OF
THE GUARD, 1812.
LOUVRE, PARIS

ulae, Gros dared to paint real dead, real fever victims, the sweat streaming down the horses' croups, the fiery breath issuing from their nostrils, and the flash of the sword as it it thrust into the enemy's throat. He showed how Gros dared to lavish on his battle-pieces the 'poetry of detail' that makes each of them a picture composed out of a hundred pictures.

Never before in French art had any one had the courage to evoke reality with so much feverish excitement and imagination on such vast surfaces. Gros applied the scrupulousness that he acquired from David to depicting heroic events, and he succeeded in doing something that. was beyond his master: organize, without freezing it, disorder itself.

David demanded of his greatest pupil that, late in life, he too should go against his own nature. This poet of history in the making was obliged to return to musty tales of the distant past. Forsaken by inspiration and no longer knowing wherein lay the truth, he died of this uncertainty, to be reborn in those who without his example, would have painted neither *The Raft of the 'Medusa'* nor *The Massacre on Chios*.

Géricault's artistic activity extended over less than twelve years (1811-1823), and during his lifetime he only exhibited three canvases, including *The Raft of the 'Medusa'* (Louvre, 1819). Had he not died when still under thirty-three as the result of a riding accident (horses were one of his passions), he might indeed have become the Rembrandt of French painting.

His fire and the variety of his gifts amazed Guérin, his first teacher. As Delacroix wrote of Bonington, he was one of those men who are born fully armed. Inspired to begin with by the Napoleonic epic, on which he drew for his first pictures (*Light-cavalry Officer of the Imperial Guard, Wounded Cuirassier withdrawing from Action,* Louvre), he was the most brilliant heir of David and Gros.

228

NINETEENTH-CENTURY FRANCE

To an even greater extent, however, he was self-taught, deriving his basic principles from the most varied old masters, whose works he copied freely.

The term 'Romantic' only fits this clear-headed man in so far as it designates a dynamic temperament with a leaning towards the sublime.

Although he was born at Rouen —like Corneille—not far from Poussin's birth-place, he could have been called a Roman even before he had set foot in Rome (1816) and visited the Sistine Chapel. For he already possessed all that David lacked—'that vigour, that boldness which is to painting what the *vis comica* is to the art of the theatre, those beauties which incorrectness does not mar' (Delacroix).

A universal genius who opened up infinite horizons for painting, he was as great in the evocation of individual character as in landscape or still-life; and with equal passion he practised every technique simultaneously, including drawing, lithography, and sculpture.

For convenience, his work has been divided into three periods: an early one up to 1816; his Roman period dominated by Michelangelo; and his late years, marked by a two-year stay in London, on returning from which he painted his *Derby at Epsom* (Louvre) and studies of lunatics, and planned huge compositions like *The Slave-trade* and *The Freeing of the Victims of the Inquisition*.

His untimely death caused the tremendous contribution of his work to be swiftly forgotten or passed over, and it has taken more than a century to reconstruct it in all its richness. Pen drawings, often heightened with gouache and sepia, heralded not only Delacroix, but Raffet, Daumier, Guys, and Rodin. With Gros, he was one of the first to give lithography an epic quality, and the least of his sketches commands our attention by reason of its monumental proportions.

GÉRICAULT. THE MAD ASSASSIN, 1822-1823. MUSÉE ROYAL DES BEAUX-ARTS, GHENT

GÉRICAULT. SIGN-BOARD FOR A BLACKSMITH, 1818-1819. PRIVATE COLLECTION, PARIS

GÉRICAULT. MADMAN WITH DELUSIONS OF MILITARY GRANDEUR, 1822-1823. OSKAR REINHART COLLECTION, WINTERTHUR

NINETEENTH-CENTURY FRANCE

JEAN-DOMINIQUE
INGRES.
1780-1867.
PORTRAIT OF
MADEMOISELLE
RIVIÈRE,
1805.
LOUVRE, PARIS

INGRES.
PORTRAIT OF
MADAME AYMON;
'LA BELLE ZÉLIE',
1806.
ROUEN MUSEUM

INGRES
LA GRANDE
ODALISQUE, 1814.
LOUVRE, PARIS

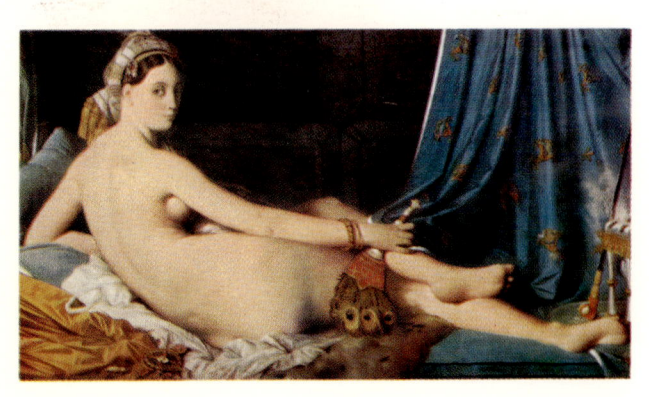

Really to admire Ingres, one almost has to disregard what mattered most of all to him—his large compositions. Skilful pastiches of Raphael, Titian, Poussin and David, they form an unbroken succession from *The Envoys of Agamemnon,* which gained him the Prix de Rome at twenty-one, to *Christ among the Doctors* (Montauban), by way of *Oedipus and the Sphinx* or *The Virgin with the Host* (Louvre). One must also forget his 'historical miniatures', in which what little vitality the contours possess comes nowhere near to bringing the story to life. Some kind of inadequacy or obtuseness only allowed Ingres to be truly himself in a limited space. The inspiration and nobility that he lacked when representing characters from history returned to him in front of some middle-class woman 'dressed up like a monkey' (to use one of his own expressions) or before a good-looking model. He was small when he throught he was great, and great the moment he stopped aiming high.

It was in his portraits and nudes that Ingres rose to the level of the best painters of all times. In them he was truly creative, while remaining intensely traditional. His powers of imagination were confined to visually possessing a face or a body. Thousands of drawings tell of his delight in evoking the rhythms of the only kind of landscape to move him—that of a woman's body; and in seeing the silent development of the only play of light that seemed to him worth recording—that on the back or stomach of a woman bather, whether seated or lying, and whether he called her Odalisque, Andromeda, Venus Anadyomene, or the Source.

His smooth handling, which when employed by Academic painters so quickly became soapy, suggests a caress: it inflames the flesh, which seems to swell and coo like a dove. *The Turkish Bath,* from his virile old age, recalls the odalisques he painted when he was twenty-five. They weigh deli-

NINETEENTH-CENTURY FRANCE

ciously down on carpets and cushions, mingling curves with curves. The miracle thus took place within a harem, where Ingres was at last fired by the imagination so cruelly denied to him when reconstructing a scene from Antiquity or composing a history picture. It was there that he won his surest victories—there and in his portraits.

One will not begrudge these portraits the fullness evenly applied to their sausage arms, fat hands, or necks like columns. Indeed, one is glad that this Realist—a term applied to him before Courbet—betrayed his own principles, correcting nature, ruining (as he said) 'the health of the form', and reconstructing in his own way all these comfortable, well-fed women, who are just right for showing off satins, feathers, Cashmere shawls, lace, or embroidery. In each portrait he has compelled lines and colours to join in a wonderfully orchestrated symphony.

Here, there is no conflict between the drawing and the colour. Ingres was embroiled with colour (as he was with Delacroix), but, far from appearing a superfluous addition, it asserts its indispensability, weight, and brightness, contributing to the singular charm of admirable portraits such as *Mlle Rivière, Mme Aymon (la belle Zélie), Mme de Senonnes,* or *Mme Panckoucke* (Louvre). One may deliberately mix up types, ages and conditions, because, in the soul of Ingres, all these sitters were reduced to a common denominator. With equal ardour and indifference, he passed from one or other of his wives to Princess de Broglie, Mme Leblanc, or Baroness James de Rothschild. He was the least inquisitive and sentimental of men, yet every remarkable physical quality moved and astonished him. His male portraits, such as those of Pastoret (New York), Cordier, or the elder Bertin (both Louvre), have no less authority; and, so unflagging was his vitality, that one is amazed to find them spread out over more than half a century.

INGRES. PORTRAIT OF MADAME DE SENONNES, 1816. NANTES MUSEUM

INGRES. THE TURKISH BATH, 1859-1863. LOUVRE, PARIS

INGRES. PORTRAIT OF MADAME LEBLANC, 1823. METROPOLITAN MUSEUM, NEW YORK

231

NINETEENTH-CENTURY FRANCE

EUGÈNE DELACROIX.
1798-1863.
THE MASSACRE
ON CHIOS
(FRAGMENT),
1824.
LOUVRE, PARIS

DELACROIX.
LIBERTY LEADING
THE PEOPLE:
JULY 28, 1830.
LOUVRE, PARIS

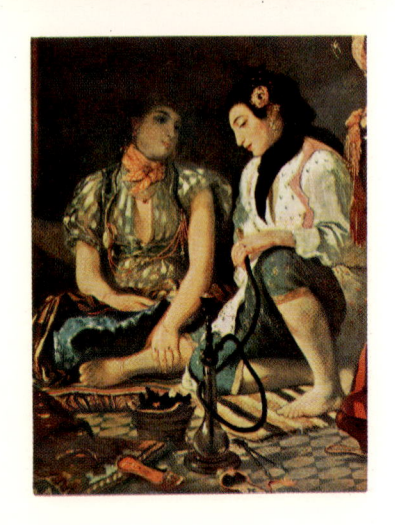

DELACROIX.
WOMEN OF
ALGIERS IN
THEIR APARTMENT
(DETAIL), 1834.
LOUVRE, PARIS

How is one to separate Delacroix from his first friends and the earliest objects of his admiration? It was in the Louvre that, as a very young man, he first met Bonington, who was making water-colour copies there after the masters. Bonington appears to have taught him how to use the copal varnish that imparts such brilliance to his early canvases. Even before he left for London in 1825, Delacroix had experienced the revelation of Constable, under whose influence he repainted *The Massacre on Chios* in four days, discovering the separation of brush-strokes and the law of optical mixtures. One must also remember his youthful admiration for Lawrence and Reynolds, whose influence is as apparent in his portrait of Baron Schwiter as in his *Agony in the Garden;* for Rowlandson, whose prints he copied; and, finally, for the British writers—Shakespeare, Sir Walter Scott, and Byron—who served to kindle his imagination. It could be said that the greater part of Delacroix's training was English; for the rest, his formation was due to Watteau, Prud'hon, and Goya.

His second great friend, twelve years his senior, was Géricault, whose very universality encouraged Delacroix to avoid becoming confined to any one branch of painting, and to be bold enough to cover vast surfaces, while working from memory. Like Géricault, it was by copying in turn the great Venetians, Rubens (who remained his god), Rembrandt, and Watteau that Delacroix perfected his technique, without becoming the slave of any one method or imitating any single school. He also helped to do so by making endless drawings, wherever he was and at every period, looking on nature as an inexhaustible store of signs and images—a kind of dictionary. Hidden influences provided this reputed son of Talleyrand with official commissions, in spite of the incomprehension—he was accused of 'painting with a drunken broom' —that he struggled against for more than thirty years. His trip

NINETEENTH-CENTURY FRANCE

to Morocco in 1832 was one of the great events of his settled life. He discovered that Rome—which he never visited, any more than Venice—was 'no longer in Rome', for it was in Morocco that he found the beauty of Antiquity, together with a light and colours that would continue to haunt his eyes. Fortified with the contents of his notebooks, he tirelessly added to the number of his scenes representing lion hunts, fantasias, horses fighting, and Arab cavalry charging, without lapsing into the technical exhibitionism and repetitiveness of a Decamps. 'I only began doing something possible', he wrote, 'the moment I had forgotten about the petty details, and remembered only the striking and poetic aspects. Up to then, I had been possessed by a love of the exactitude that the majority take for truth.'

Touchy, solitary, and regarding painting as his 'one and only mistress', Delacroix worked ceaselessly by night and by day, even though he looked so frail. All the work of anybody not abundantly creative was bound, he thought, to show signs of fatigue. Passionately fond of music, he found in painting 'a very special kind of emotion that one could call the picture's music'. He also said that the chief merit of a canvas lay in its being 'a feast for the eye'.

After *The Massacre on Chios*, *The Death of Sardanapalus*, and *Liberty leading the People*, came *Algerian Women*, *The Jewish Wedding*, and *The Entry of the Crusaders into Constantinople* (Louvre). Though engrossed in his vast decorative schemes for the Chamber of Deputies (1837-1838), the Luxembourg (1845), the Louvre (1849), the Hôtel de Ville, Paris (1853), and St Sulpice, Paris (1857), Delacroix found time to write up his *Journal*, which ought to be every artist's Bible. As clear-headed as he was passionate, he was an austere genius, the last great all-rounder of French art. To have realized everything that seethed inside him, he would, as he said, have needed several lives.

DELACROIX.
THE BRIDE OF
ABYDOS, 1843.
LOUVRE, PARIS

DELACROIX.
WOMAN WITH A
PARROT,
1827.
LYON MUSEUM

DELACROIX.
THE ABDUCTION
OF REBECCA,
1846.
METROPOLITAN
MUSEUM, NEW YORK

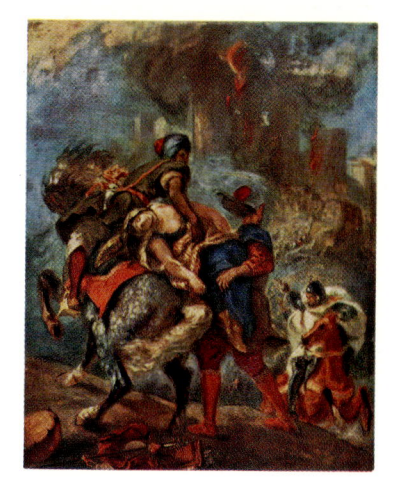

NINETEENTH-CENTURY FRANCE

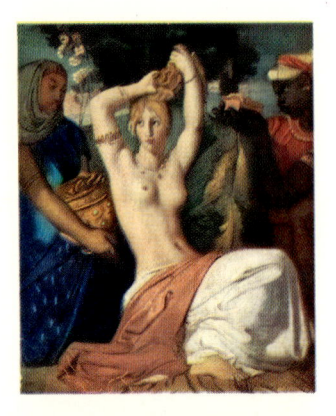

THÉODORE CHASSÉRIAU. 1819-1856. ESTHER ADORNING HERSELF TO APPEAR BEFORE AHAZUERUS. LOUVRE, PARIS

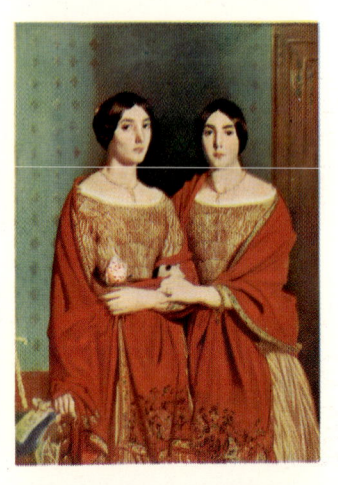

CHASSÉRIAU. TWO SISTERS, 1843. LOUVRE, PARIS

CHASSÉRIAU. PORTRAIT OF FATHER LACORDAIRE, 1840. LOUVRE, PARIS

One cannot read without amazement the rapturous eulogies that Decamp's canvases evoked from all the critics of his day. 'Decamps, the most original of painters', exclaimed Théophile Gautier. At the Salon of 1831, his *Turkish Patrol* was more admired than *Liberty leading the People*. The Universal Exhibition of 1855 brought together thirty-five of his works. His performing monkeys disguised as painters, story pictures, and hunting scenes alternated with countless imaginative reconstructions of Turkish life: *A Street in Smyrna, The Guard-house, The Turkish Butcher* (the wonder of wonders, according to the Goncourts). Posterity is content to give this deft craftsman credit for having been one of the first 'Orientalists', admiring his virtuosity and the undeniable earthy richness of his style.

Chassériau's works, on the other hand, are now enjoying a renewal of favour. Born in 1819 on San Domingo, at twelve he entered the studio of Ingres, who regarded him as 'the future Napoleon of painting'. From his seventeenth year, he exhibited admirable portraits of his close relations, which foreshadowed Degas—who was to declare Chassériau's *Two Sisters* the finest portrait of the century. *Daphne, Venus Anadyomene,* and *Esther adorning herself to appear before Ahazuerus* exhale a creole charm, a sensual delight that distinguishes the artist from Ingres, and recalls Correggio and Prud'hon.

On returning from Africa in 1846, did Chassériau, who was made for expressing the firm and lasting, really increase his stature by depicting under the obvious influence of Delacroix quantities of market scenes, tepidaria, and Arab horsemen, which suffer from excessive ornament and detail? An oustsanding decorative scheme for the Cour des Comptes (1844-1848) seems to prefigure Puvis de Chavannes. To what heights this restless genius, whose black-lead drawings reconcile Ingres and Delacroix, promised to rise, had he not died at thirty-seven!

NINETEENTH-CENTURY FRANCE

One cannot help associating Jean-François Millet with the twelve-years-older Théodore Rousseau: they worked side by side for so many years, and with Diaz and Dupré formed the Barbizon school. Millet may almost be regarded as self-taught. An admirer of Poussin, he began by painting trifling subjects in the eighteenth-century tradition and some admirable portraits, but then devoted himself entirely to evoking country life and putting 'the commonplace at the service of the sublime', as he expressed it. Contrary to what has too often been said, though raised on the Bible, he was not making humanitarian speeches when he depicted his reapers, woodcutters, and diggers in the same style. His sketches, almost all from memory, show how vigorously he weighed the form, concentrated the light, and summarized the action. The beauty of his peasant women is of a rugged kind, though he regarded them with love. He was an even better draughtsman than painter, for his colouring is at times heavy and dull.

Rousseau, who emulated the great Dutch landscapists and admired Bruegel and Rembrandt, was debated as fiercely as Delacroix. Through the different versions that he liked to produce of the same view, and the richness and multiplicity of the intermingled touches by which he evoked the play of light, he appears with Daubigny as the herald of the Impressionists. Consequently, he saw his *Avenue of Chestnut Trees* (Louvre) rejected without mercy at the Salon of 1837—like his *Descent of the Herds* before it. Unfortunately, though he took care to give his works a firm, enduring substructure, many have been impaired by an over-elaborate analysis of effects and the abuse of bitumen. Landscapes that once shocked people through the violence of their hues are now obscured by darkness. Today, only the drawings and preparatory sketches of this great contemplator of the sky and the forces of the cosmos allow us to judge him truly.

THÉODORE ROUSSEAU. 1812-1867. EVENING. MUSEUM OF ART, TOLEDO (OHIO)

JEAN-FRANÇOIS MILLET. 1814-1875. THE GLEANERS, 1857. LOUVRE, PARIS

MILLET. THE WOOD CUTTERS. VICTORIA AND ALBERT MUSEUM, LONDON

MILLET. SPRING, 1873. LOUVRE, PARIS

235

NINETEENTH-CENTURY FRANCE

JEAN-BAPTISTE
COROT.
1796-1875.
PORTRAIT OF
MLLE OCTAVIE
SENNEGON, 1833.
RENAND
COLLECTION,
PARIS

COROT.
THE CHURCH OF
MARISSEL,
1866.
LOUVRE, PARIS

COROT.
MARIETTA,
'THE ROMAN
ODALISQUE',
1843.
MUSÉE DES
BEAUX-ARTS,
PARIS

Although they lived at the same period, Corot, Jongkind, and Courbet—who, with Théodore Rousseau, were at the root of all the conquests and emancipations of modern landscape painting—seem hardly to have known each other, and exerted no mutual influence.

The vain Courbet called himself the pupil of Nature; Corot thought the same applied to him—but in all modesty. Did not his first teacher Michallon, who in his turn had received the advice from Valenciennes, tell him to represent with the greatest precision what he had before his eyes? The secret of his art seems to be contained in the following: 'Let us yield to the first impression. If we have been really moved, our emotion will be conveyed to others.'

Eliminating all notion of slavish imitation and all systematic construction, Corot knew that though pictures are made with lines and colours, above all they are made, as Chardin said, with feeling; and he knew, too, that the greatest skill is compatible with the greatest humility. That is why he so often recalls the 'primitives'.

In the studio of his second teacher, Bertin, he met young men divided between over attention to style and over attention to finish. Unlike them, Corot effortlessly achieved a wonderful balance between the gift that is only obtained by grace and the craftsmanship only acquired through will-power. His visual memory allowed him to reconcile working directly from nature and fidelity to his model with working from memory in the studio. 'It is not so much the site as the interpretation that makes the work.'

Well after his return from each of his three journeys to Italy (1826, 1834, 1843), he was to be seen starting out from black-lead drawings or little studies made on the spot to compose rather more comprehensive canvases. Even if he did make the sally: 'I don't give a damn about Poussin, broad outlines, or the Classical, I'm in the woods', and though his historical

NINETEENTH-CENTURY FRANCE

landscapes *(Homer and the Shepherds, Rebecca)* do not come up to the others, he went on painting 'animated compositions' in the seventeenth- or eighteenth-century manner.

For him, studying the tone values was the essential basis of every picture; the arrangement of the colours and actual execution followed afterwards. 'Colour is only a supplementary charm to be used with discretion . . . Above all, I love unity, harmony in the tones.' He made continual use of those greys that are free from all opacity and establish the transitions. They were already apparent in the work of Chardin, Vernet, Louis Moreau, Valenciennes, and Bidault, and became the olive or almond greens, ochres, or delicate blues that provide the connecting links in each picture.

Just as happy at Arras, Mantes, Honfleur, or St Lô as at Avignon or La Rochelle, Corot found everywhere a sort of compound of Roman or Venetian light and that of the Ile-de-France. At the Louvre one can see—whether in *Chartres Cathedral, Douai Belfry,* or the views recorded during his first visit to Italy *(The Bridge at Narni, The Forum,* etc.)—how an inborn sense of when to leave things out secured the foundations of a landscape, while allowing some passages the look of a sketch in order the better to eliminate inessentials. Corot did not sell a canvas until he was fifty-one. Overshadowed by showy painters, he only experienced success the moment that, subordinating colour still more to nuances of tone, he began to delight in the twilight hours form fades, night descends, and the first stars appear *(Recollection of Mortefontaine,* Louvre). It was not until well after the death of this great but modest man, that he was seen to be a master of universal scope, whose portraits (like *Young Woman with a Pearl Ring* or *Woman with a Mandolin*), and nudes, are in no way inferior to his best landscapes, and set him among the greatest painters of all the schools.

COROT. THE BELFREY OF DOUAI, 1871. LOUVRE, PARIS

COROT. YOUNG WOMAN WITH A PEARL RING, 1868-1870. LOUVRE, PARIS

COROT. THE BRIDGE OF NANTES, 1868-1870. LOUVRE, PARIS.

NINETEENTH-CENTURY FRANCE

HONORÉ DAUMIER.
1808-1879.
CRISPIN AND SCAPIN,
c. 1860.
LOUVRE, PARIS

DAUMIER.
THE BATH,
1855-1860.
PRIVATE
COLLECTION,
PARIS

DAUMIER.
ADVICE TO A
YOUNG ARTIST,
1855-1860.
NATIONAL GALLERY
OF ART,
WASHINGTON

Baudelaire, Jean Gigoux, Champfleury, and Banville all described Daumier as a sound middle-class citizen, not very different from the ones that he drew or painted, and they all agreed in speaking highly of his good nature, straightforwardness, freedom from vanity, and unselfishness. He said little, and wrote even less. A few landmarks from his life tell us nothing about his formation as an artist: born at Marseilles in 1808; spent his apprentice years in Paris working for a process-server, a bookseller, and a lithographer; began his career with Ricourt, then moved to Aubert; joined the staff of *la Caricature* (1831); imprisoned at Ste Pélagie (1832); married in 1846; died aged seventy-one in the little house at Valmondois that he owed to Corot's generosity.

From 1830, when his first lithograph appeared, to 1872, when his eyes, worn out by the four thousand plates that he contributed to *la Caricature* and then to *le Charivari*, refused any longer to guide his hand, he unwittingly built a huge edifice that helped to reanimate France under three regimes. He very soon shook off the influence of Pigalle, Grandville, Charlet, Monnier, and the English caricaturists, to march abreast of Rembrandt, Goya, Géricault, and all the great artists to whom he was related.

It must be acknowledged that he was first and foremost a draughtsman, a master of black and white, and that he transposed to his canvases the very methods of his drawings. The closer he got to monochrome, the more powerful he became. Even if working in the dense medium of paint was too slow to suit him, his light effects are always resplendent. Using the brush like a pen or charcoal, his hand emphasized the contours, and the life and interconnexion of the planes.

We know of a few landmarks in the evolution of his technique, and it certainly seems as though it was from 1848, and particularly from 1860, that the caricaturist, sacked (for three years) by *le Charivari*,

NINETEENTH-CENTURY FRANCE

turned to painting. Thenceforward his association with—and, no doubt, the advice of—Corot taught him to produce the fluid brushwork, modulations, and delicate impasto to which we owe masterpieces like *The Print Collector* or *The Washerwoman* (1861) in the Louvre. More static than their predecessors, these compositions enabled Daumier to master the impatience and frenzy that, when he had to catch a fleeting pose or expression, and convey strife and tumult, sometimes drove him to hurry his execution and distort the values. All the same, how successful *The Thieves and the Donkey* is, painted with little, close-packed touches in a range of warm, russet hues; and also *The Fugitives* (Montreal) or *Don Quixote galloping across the Plain,* beside which Delacroix's action seems like slow-motion !

Many compositions miraculously succeed in reconciling the rhythm of a figure caught in an attitude with that of one or more moving figures, as in *Crispin and Scapin, The Melodrama* (Munich, Neue Pinakothek), *The Chess-players* (Paris, Petit Palais), or the numerous scenes showing Don Quixote and Sancho Panza, barristers, and third-class railway carriages.

Elsewhere, whether because the artist had the misfortune to use bitumen, or because he overdid the tonal contrasts in his impasto, one meets with pictures that, though their expressive force is admirable, appear summary, and have often not progressed beyond sketches. All the beauty of the golds, crimsons, and earth colours does not cover up the feverish, and sometimes hasty execution, which omits the transitions and destroys the charm. Canvases such as these are related to the fantastic, visionary images with which Goya in his old age covered the walls of the Quinta del Sordo. Let us admire them for all that they held in promise, while regretting that an artist of such exceptional quality could only devote himself to painting in his spare time between two lithographs.

DAUMIER.
THE THIRD-CLASS
CARRIAGE,
c. 1862.
METROPOLITAN
MUSEUM, NEW YORK

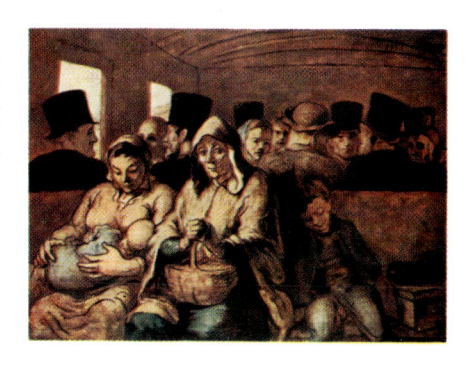

DAUMIER.
DON QUIXOTE,
c. 1868.
NEUE PINAKOTHEK,
MUNICH

DAUMIER.
THE PRINT
COLLECTOR,
1857-1860.
MUSÉE DES
BEAUX-ARTS,
PARIS

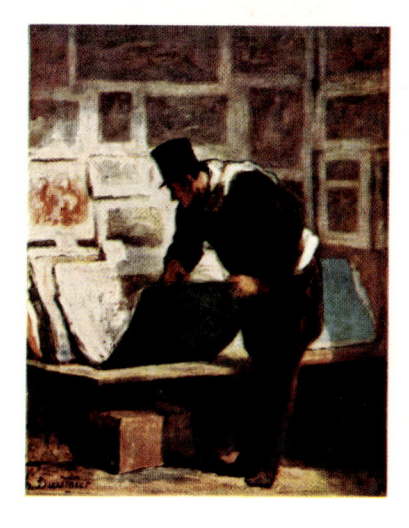

FRENCH REALISM

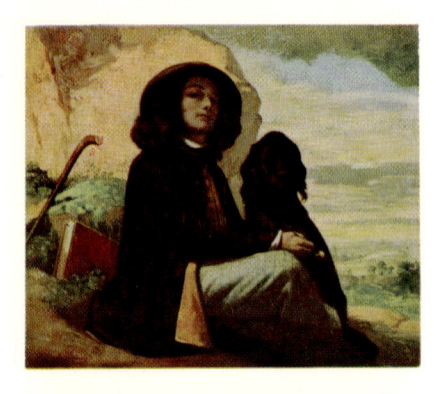

GUSTAVE COURBET.
1819-1877.
SELF-PORTRAIT
WITH A BLACK
DOG,
1842.
MUSÉE DES
BEAUX-ARTS,
PARIS

COURBET.
PORTRAIT OF
JULIETTE COURBET,
1844.
MUSÉE DES
BEAUX-ARTS,
PARIS

COURBET.
WOMAN COMBING
HER HAIR,
c. 1847.
A. MORHANGE
COLLECTION,
LONDON

He called himself 'the Master-painter', and inscribed below his own likeness: 'Courbet, without ideal and without religion'. The most arrogant words of our contemporaries pale beside his. 'In everybody's opinion, I am the foremost man of France', he wrote to a friend at Ornans, the village where he was born; and to Bruyas: 'I triumph not only over the moderns, but over the ancients.' He believed it; for without having passed through any school, had he not as a very young man equalled the Venetians in his portraits of himself and his sisters? Like Corot or Daumier, he was almost self-taught.

Uninvolved in the conflict that set Ingres against Delacroix, he trod firmly on solid ground, consulting only his instinct and that superior common sense which deserted him as soon as he wanted to play the thinker or the wit. His theories were prompted to him by philosophers and poets, and luckily they seldom influenced his art. There were moments when he himself recognized the emptiness of the term Realism, which designates the movement of which he was the standard-bearer, and when he felt that a painter only justifies himself by painting.

The freedom with which he laid bare a landscape or a human being, restoring to his model its animal splendour, caused a scandal at the Salon of 1853. In 1856, he dared to commit the sacrilege of representing life-size two street women of his day sprawling under the open sky in the drowsiness of summer, as though on a bed *(The Young Women on the Banks of the Seine)*. Like the biggest, the smallest of his canvases gain their weight and durability from their force and unity. Unaware of the enormous work of transfiguration going on inside him, this 'Realist', who only believed his eyes and refused to paint angels, encountered the supernatural in the forests and meadows that he rough-cast with a trowel in areas of impasto that give his canvas the glitter of enamels. He

240

FRENCH REALISM

makes us aware of the secret rising of the sap and the irresistible thrust towards the light of the forces in the plants. Never before had the vehemence of torrents and seas been so powerfully expressed.

With him there are none of the tender qualities of Corot or Boudin. Whatever he painted, it was always himself that he asserted. Landscapes sprinkled with snow or shimmering with summer, still-lifes, nudes, or portraits — he treated them all alike, and it was his own vitality that he found in *The Wave* (Lyons) or *The Trout* (Zurich, Kunsthaus). If he remained earthy and sometimes even vulgar, this was due less to theory than to temperament. He lacked a sense of the infinite, but not of breadth. Though his costumes and types came from the present — as in *The Burial at Ornans* (Louvre), which caused a scandal in 1850, *Bonjour, Monsieur Courbet* (Montpellier), *The Village Maidens* (New York), or *The Painter's Studio* (Louvre) — the individual hardly interested him. In short, his best portraits are those that he did of himself at every period of his life, and the ones of his sisters. This vine-grower's son, gay dog, and scoffer derived his merit less from his humanitarian aims, which he thought he had expressed in his *Stone-breakers* (Dresden), than from his vitality and all that relates him to the Venetian, Rubens, and Frans Hals — or to Manet and Renoir, whom he heralded in *After Dinner at Ornans* (Lille).

We will not recount the deplorable events that led up to his death in exile in 1877, the victim of his own bragging and morally crushed by the Vendôme Column in revenge for its destruction. The collaboration of mediocre pupils like Pata and, later, the thousands of forgeries explain how it has been possible to talk of his decline. Nevertheless, when almost sixty, he was still painting masterpieces in Switzerland, and from start to finish his genius, which no external force could curb, went on asserting its magnificent health and invigorating unity.

COURBET.
THE YOUNG
WOMEN ON THE
BANKS OF THE
SEINE, 1856.
MUSÉE DES
BEAUX-ARTS, PARIS

COURBET.
THE PAINTER'S
STUDIO,
1855.
LOUVRE, PARIS

COURBET.
THE RÉVEIL,
1866.
KUNSTMUSEUM,
BERNE

241

SYMBOLISM

PUVIS DE CHAVANNES. 1824-1898. THE POOR FISHERMAN. 1881. LOUVRE, PARIS

GUSTAVE MOREAU. 1826-1898. SKETCH FOR 'LEDA' (?). MUSÉE GUSTAVE MOREAU, PARIS

HENRI FANTIN-LATOUR. 1836-1904. STILL-LIFE. 1866. NATIONAL GALLERY OF ART, WASHINGTON

There were several painters active during the second half of the nineteenth century whose talent and independence gain them universal respect, but who only evoke rather luke-warm admiration. Puvis de Chavannes was over thirty-five when, in 1861, he began his murals at Amiens, one of the great decorative schemes that were to win him fame. Decorations in Marseilles, Poitiers, Paris, Lyon, Rouen, and Boston followed; all form balanced and harmonious wholes, strongly drawn and deliberately painted in rather pale colours so as not to stand out from the wall. Puvis enjoyed a success that he had only sought by the most noble means. At the Salon of 1881, he exhibited *The poor Fisherman,* which was much discussed.

His contemporary Gustave Moreau, another independent, belonged even more than he to the heirs of Chassériau. His cold manner and involved subjects have dispelled an admiration that was always cliquish, though some of his watercolours shine with the brilliance of book illuminations. He was unprejudiced and the studio of this member of the *Institut* was a nursery for innovators, including Matisse, Marquet, Manguin, Rouault, and Camoin, while Desvallières was his friend. They all revered their liberal teacher, who, perhaps without always understanding them, encouraged them to follow their own courses.

Manet's friend Fantin-Latour was closer to the Impressionists. His copies after the masters and Delacroix are the most beautiful that exist, and he revived the taste for the group portraits once beloved by Netherlandish artists. The Louvre possesses his *Homage to Delacroix, The Studio at les Batignolles,* showing most of the Impressionists, another for poets, and a fourth for musicians. Not only are they invaluable documents, but, low in key with a predominance of browns, they are extremely harmonious, too. Fantin also painted still-lifes and wonderfully fresh bouquets.

WHISTLER

James Abbot McNeill Whistler, equally at home in Paris and London yet wholly of neither, was born in Lowell, Massachusetts. After failure at the West Point Military Academy and a year as a naval cartographer, be came to Paris in 1855 to learn painting. There he became friendly with Fantin-Latour, Manet and Degas among others. In 1859 he moved to London, but still visited Paris frequently, and thus became the first channel of importance by which the ideas of French painting began to filter back to England.

Whistler's admiration for Velasquez was coloured by Courbet's realism, the Impressionists' handling of tone, and a prolonged flirtation with Japanese art, from which he learnt to restrict his palette, flatten his forms and dispose them with great economy of means. He emphasised the purely pictorial qualities of his subdued and delicate compositions by calling them 'Symphonies' or 'Nocturnes' or merely 'Arrangements', though his purpose was always consciously and deliberately aesthetic; it lacked, that is to say, the element of genuine visual research which gave French Impressionism its vigour.

Dandy, wit, self-conscious bohemian and ready litigant, Whistler relished public polemics. In 1877 Ruskin accused him of 'flinging a pot of paint in the public's face'. In the libel case which followed, Whistler scored a brilliant tactical victory which was, however, rewarded by a farthing damages.

Bankrupted by his costs, he went to Venice, hoping to recoup himself by his etchings — a medium in which he excelled. An important retrospective exhibition in 1892, however, was a complete success and the last decade of his life was spent in the full glow of public recognition regained.

Whistler, Sickert, William Morris and a handful of architects — with these began the long-drawn-out process of bringing Britain back into the main stream of European art, not to be completed until after the second world war.

JAMES MCNEILL WHISTLER. 1834-1903. BATTERSEA BRIDGE: NOCTURNE IN BLUE AND GOLD, 1865. TATE GALLERY, LONDON

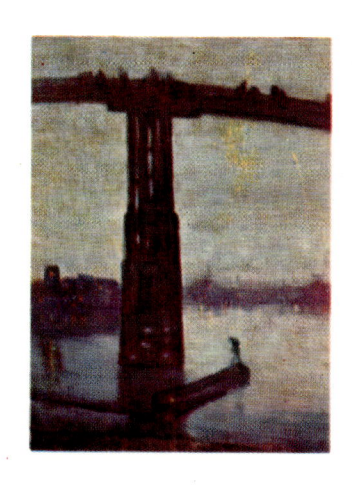

WHISTLER. PORTRAIT OF WHISTLER'S MOTHER, 1871-1872. LOUVRE, PARIS

WHISTLER. PORTRAIT OF MISS CECILY ALEXANDER, 1872-1874. TATE GALLERY, LONDON

ÉDOUARD MANET.
1832-1883.
LE DÉJEUNER
SUR L'HERBE,
1863,
LOUVRE, PARIS

MANET.
MADEMOISELLE
VICTORINE
IN THE COSTUME OF
AN ESPADA,
1862.
METROPOLITAN
MUSEUM, NEW YORK

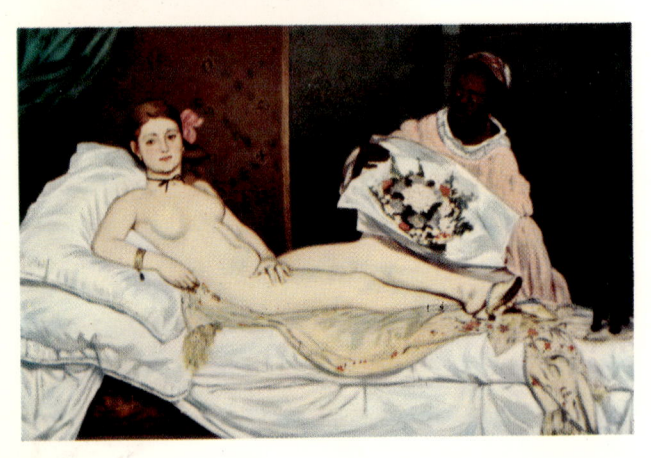

MANET.
OLYMPIA,
1863.
LOUVRE, PARIS

IMPRESSIONISM

The tremendous scandal caused by Manet's *Olympia* in 1865 shows that he stood at the beginning of an entirely new phase in art. It was, of course, established practice that the nineteenth-century public should cry shame at any innovation in painting and, therefore, that any true creator should be called shocking. But no others had caused such an outcry of resentment and irritation as Manet. No others had made such a breach with existing tradition while still maintaining a certain contact with it.

Manet was not ignorant of the old masters: he borrowed the idea and the composition of his *Déjeuner sur l'Herbe* from Raphael and Giorgione and his *Olympia* was obviously inspired by Titian's *Venus of Urbino*. But if he drew inspiration from the painting of the past it was always to show with all the more force that his aims were quite different. Far from being a goddess, his *Olympia* is a young Parisienne of the period, with a puny-looking body and individualized face. The black cat and the negress in a pink dress bringing flowers suggest that, not content with cocking a snook at the nobility of the subject, Manet came very close to cocking a snook at the subject itself. They are there mainly to justify the choice of colours, and indeed the colour-relationships are more important than the relationships between the figures. In other words the picture is not, as of old, an illustration of a theme or idea but essentially a fine piece of painting. The aspect of art which for centuries the public had considered only as a means to an end becomes an end in itself.

As regards manner, too, Manet departed from the traditional practices. He reduced the depth, flattened volumes, replaced modelling with variations of outline, spread colours over large areas and made light areas join on to dark ones without any transition. There can be no doubt as to the inspiration for these daring liberties: Manet had been studying the Japanese

IMPRESSIONISM

prints which were just filtering into Europe at that period. He was one of the first to realize how much Western painting could learn from them; after him they contributed much to its regeneration.

However, Manet was not out only to innovate, shock. And he admired the old masters, particularly Velasquez, Titian and Frans Hals, too much to spend all his time contradicting them. And so among his works are many which, while clearly marked with his own individual imprint, reveal a less original vision and more conventional manner.

In 1874 he fell under the spell of the Impressionists. Setting up his easel in the open air near the Seine at Gennevilliers or at Argenteuil, he focussed his attention on effects of light and atmosphere and painted what he saw in prism-colours. It is significant that he rarely painted a landscape as such and was always preoccupied by composition: in this, too, he followed the old masters. Finally he managed to reconcile the still potent qualities of traditional painting with the results of modern re-thinking; in pictures such as *A Bar at the Folies-Bergère*, the instantaneous quality is blended, perfectly naturally, with a solid, well thought-out plan.

Manet made a point of having human figures in his works not only because he remained preoccupied with tactile values but because he took pleasure in observing the society around him. 'You will never be anything more than the Daumier of our age,' his teacher, Thomas Couture, had told him. But in fact he did not see the world with the eyes of a Daumier. He was an interested spectator, but he never moralized or sat in judgment. Only his retina was moved by what he saw. In this too he belongs to his period—that of the growth of photography with its 'objective' pictures. Nevertheless there is nothing cold about his art. His eye is penetrating, his touch spontaneous, his line confident. And his colour, both direct and distinguished, has an acid tang.

MANET.
A BAR AT THE
FOLIES-BERGÈRE,
1881-1882.
COURTAULD
INSTITUTE
OF ART,
LONDON

MANET.
NANA,
1877.
KUNSTHALLE,
HAMBURG

MANET.
PORTRAIT OF
MADAME
MICHEL LÉVY
(PASTEL),
1882.
NATIONAL GALLERY
OF ART,
WASHINGTON

245

IMPRESSIONISM

When *Olympia* was moving the crowds to ribald laughter, the painters who were given the name of 'Impressionists' in 1874 were still searching for their own solutions. They were encouraged by Manet's disdain of official painting, but although the attacks launched at him moved them to rally round him, few of them modelled their style on his. In that respect they were more inclined to look towards Courbet or Corot or the Barbizon painters, to seek the advice of Boudin and Jongkind.

Boudin had a decisive influence on Monet, in particular, the painter who from the first stood out as the moving force behind the group. Boudin had said that 'everything which is painted directly and on the spot has a force, power and liveliness of touch which one never recaptures in the studio.' And Monet, working with him in about 1860 by the sea-shore in Normandy, watched him creating works full of a delicate light which caressed every object, and an atmosphere of freshness that surrounded and softened them.

His meetings with Jongkind were no less crucial. For although the Dutch painter still bowed down to the gods of Romanticism in his oil-paintings, his limpid water-colours glowed with a freshness of vision and alertness of style which showed even more authoritatively than Boudin's work the worth of an image which retained only instantaneous appearance.

Monet put all this to good use, and as early as 1866 he was painting not only open-air studies but finished pictures such as *Women in the Garden* (Louvre). By 1869, three years later, he had given up enclosing forms in hard-and-fast outlines, and his interest in the iridescence of the reflections in the Seine had led him to use small brush-strokes and divide up his colours. His friends Renoir, Bazille, Pissarro and Sisley explored similar avenues, with varying degrees of urgency, so that by 1870 there were already a certain number of pictures in existence which might

EUGÈNE BOUDIN. 1824-1898. CRINOLINES ON THE BEACH, 1869. PRIVATE COLLECTION, PARIS

JONGKIND. 1819-1891 VIEW OF ROUEN (WATERCOLOUR), 1864. LOUVRE, PARIS

JONGKIND. SUNSET ON THE MEUSE (WATERCOLOUR), c. 1866. MME G. SIGNAC COLLECTION, PARIS

CLAUDE MONET. 1840-1926. IMPRESSION, SOLEIL LEVANT, 1872. MUSÉE MARMOTTAN, PARIS

IMPRESSIONISM

be said to herald a new kind of painting. The Franco-German War cut short Bazille's career, but it hastened Monet's and Pissarro's development: seeking refuge in London, they discovered the work of Turner and Constable which reinforced their own convictions.

Shortly after his return Monet painted his famous picture of the port of Le Havre in the morning mist; it was shown in 1874 in the first exhibition of the group at Nadar's gallery in Paris. The title of the picture *Impression, Soleil Levant (Impression, Sunrise)* caused a reporter on the Paris *Charivari* to christen the painter and his associates 'Impressionists'.

Once again the public was scandalised. The same reporter called the show an attack on 'artistic morals, on the cult of form and respect for the great masters.' If by masters he meant those of the academic school, it must be admitted that there was a good deal in what he said. The exponents of the 'new painting' differed in many of their preoccupations, but there was one thing which united them all—those already mentioned and Degas, Cézanne, Guillaumin, Berthe Morisot (and Mary Cassatt, who joined the group later): they were all sworn enemies of 'official' painting, all rejected historical, mythological and sentimental subjects, dark colouring and 'overpolished' form. All of them strove to make painting a part of contemporary life by taking their themes from the everyday reality of the age. To a certain extent they all agreed that a picture should present only the image which struck the painter's eye at the moment of painting—in other words, only surface appearance, only what one saw, not what one knew to be there. And in addition, since every image was only a product of light, they agreed in showing it only in those pure colours which are obtained when light is broken up. Thus even shadows became colours (blues, greens, mauves) and painting became pale before later becoming bright.

FRÉDÉRIC BAZILLE. 1841-1870. PORTRAIT OF RENOIR, 1867. MUSÉE DES BEAUX-ARTS, ALGIERS

BERTHE MORISOT. 1841-1895. ON THE TERRACE AT MEUDON (WATERCOLOUR), 1884. ART INSTITUTE, CHICAGO

MARY CASSATT. 1845-1927. THE LITTLE SISTERS, c. 1885. ART GALLERY, GLASGOW

IMPRESSIONISM

CLAUDE MONET.
1840-1926.
LA GRENOUILLÈRE
(MARSH),
1869.
METROPOLITAN
MUSEUM, NEW YORK

MONET.
HOUSES OF
PARLIAMENT,
LONDON,
1871.
J. J. ASTOR
COLLECTION,
LONDON

MONET.
SAILING-BOAT
AT ARGENTEUIL,
c. 1894.
F. W. BRAVINGTON
COLLECTION,
HENLEY-ON-THAMES

MONET.
GARE
SAINT-LAZARE,
1877.
LOUVRE, PARIS

Until 1874 Monet was the leading spirit of the Impressionist movement; he would always be its most convinced and daring exponent. Shortly after 1880 the group broke up and the painters of the generations following his own resolutely opposed many of the ideas he stood for, but he himself continued in the same path to the end of his life.

Not that Monet remained static: quite the contrary. After starting out as a Realist he ended by lending his art a strangely unreal quality. But this was only because he was not afraid to take the principles of his early years to their logical conclusion. In reality, however much the Impressionists quested after realism, they could not reduce everything to a visual phenomenon without exercising a certain principle of abstraction. They could not translate feelings into pure colours without using a certain freedom in choosing those colours, without realising that to a certain extent the imagination is bound to interpret what the eye sees. The part played by imagination became more and more prominent in Monet's work, although it was always based on an analysis of reality.

If there was any period in his life when he painted as naturally, in his own phrase, 'as birds sing', it was in about 1874. He was then living at Argenteuil and his favourite subjects were the Seine and its banks. With exquisite perfection he captured the trembling of the reflections on the river and the fine, fresh dampness of the air which heightens the pleasure to be derived from a summer's day.

But Monet did not confine himself to singing the praises of the idyllic life. His eye was also open to the metal railway bridge that crosses some of his pictures diagonally and elsewhere is 'framed' in an unexpected way, showing that he too had made a profitable study of Japanese prints. In 1876 he went so far as to set up his easel in the Saint-Lazare railway station

248

IMPRESSIONISM

at Paris and paint a series of pictures showing engines, rails and metal structures. No doubt he was attracted by the modernity, the novelty of the subject. But it also had something even more attractive to a lover of the evanescent than water: the smoke of the engines with its enchanted iridescence and capricious metamorphoses.

Other series followed the Saint-Lazare: the *Ice-Drifts,* the *Poplars,* the *Haystacks,* the *Rouen Cathedrals.* Although Monet went on painting 'single' pictures, it is his series which show most clearly what he was getting at and how much his art was, basically, speculative. The fact that he was able to produce more than twenty different versions of the same façade of a cathedral seen from more or less the same angle proves beyond any shadow of doubt that for him it was not the object that counted but the effect it produced at a given time, in sunlight or under a cloudy sky, in clear air or mist. The cathedral itself lost its substance and its structure practically disappeared. What was left was a sort of subtly coloured veil.

This 'dissolving' of objects, already visible in *The Houses of Parliament* and *The Doge's Palace,* reaches its height in the *Water-Lilies* and *Gardens* which occupied the last twenty-five years of his life. At the beginning the vegetation is still easily identifiable but later one can only distinguish blobs and streams of colour which very nearly become completely self-sufficient.

Monet's works seem to express a sort of pantheistic lyricism, couched in terms of a broad, sweeping style, full of freedom and dash. It might be said to lack backbone but its author must nevertheless be recognised as a real painter, one who never slides into facility. Moreover his qualities have been haloed with a new prestige since some of the 'free style' painters of the present day have been seen to derive from him and, indeed, take him for a model.

MONET. HOUSES OF PARLIAMENT, LONDON: SUNLIGHT THROUGH FOG, 1904. LOUVRE, PARIS

MONET. ROUEN CATHEDRAL: THE DOOR AND THE 'TOUR D'ALBANE' IN FULL SUNLIGHT, 1894. LOUVRE, PARIS

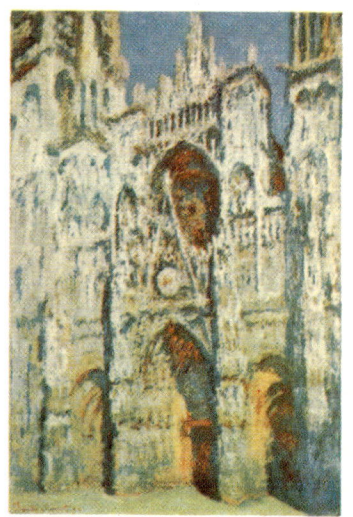

MONET. WATER-LILIES, c. 1916. KUNSTHAUS, ZURICH

249

IMPRESSIONISM

CAMILLE PISSARRO,
1830-1903.
ENTRANCE TO THE
VILLAGE
OF VOISINS,
1872.
LOUVRE, PARIS

PISSARRO.
RED ROOFS,
1877.
LOUVRE, PARIS

PISSARRO.
RUE DE L'ÉPICERIE,
ROUEN; MORNING,
DULL WEATHER,
1898
PRIVATE
COLLECTION,
PARIS.

Pissarro and Sisley both began as disciples of Corot and when, afterwards, they opted for Impressionism they still continued to have strong affinities with each other. Both were less bold than Monet, more humble in their attitude towards the external world and consequently much less given to speculation; they were too sensitive and discerning to attempt to sacrifice reality to lyricism.

If both are essentially landscapists, Pissarro's choice of subjects is frequently reminiscent of Millet. A peasant-woman pushing a wheelbarrow, a ploughman on horseback returning from the fields, washerwomen near the Oise—these are a few of his themes. Obviously he is not as sentimental about country life as Millet—the man who painted *The Angelus* (Louvre) —but he is not entirely preoccupied by the action of the light and the variations in atmosphere: the human element interests him not a little. And he contemplates objects with an affection which effectually prevents him from reducing them to mere light-vibrations: in his pictures they always preserve a certain solidity and embody a realistic conception.

Though by nature eminently unsuited to theoretical argument, he allowed himself to be converted to Neo-Impressionism in about 1886. Nevertheless it did not take him long to realize that this had been a mistake, that in attempting to make his art more scientific, he had merely made it drier and colder, not truer. In about 1890 he abandoned Pointillism and returned to more direct painting.

The most original works of his later years were inspired by urban landscapes. One after another, Rouen, Dieppe and Paris claimed his affections and he proved equally good at evoking the calm of a quiet provincial side-street and the bustle of a Paris square or boulevard. By looking at his subject from a high window he was able to extend his view over wide areas, plunge the spectator into deep perspectives and reveal the road, passers-by,

IMPRESSIONISM

etc. from unusual aspects which anticipate Marquet.

But Pissarro's work had less influence on the future than the advice and encouragement that he lavished on artists younger than himself. He guided the early attempts of Cézanne and Gauguin, encouraged Seurat and Van Gogh. Towards the end of the century even Matisse consulted him and profited from his advice.

Sisley approached nature with even more reserve than Pissarro. The image of it that he presents is even more delicate and peaceful. But despite the tenderness with which he contemplates the external world, he is still an acute observer, a subtle analyst, a man capable of distinguishing between the most delicate shades of difference.

He travelled about the Ile-de-France, stopping casually to paint a river or a canal, a sleepy little market-square, a cluster of houses looking like the purest virginity under their robe of snow. And each choice proves a success, each moves and charms the spectator.

With Pissarro one sometimes senses a certain disquiet, the world sometimes takes on a slightly gloomy air. With Sisley, on the other hand, not even a flood looks like a catastrophe. The clouds rising in the skies are not tossed by the storm; winter adds a touch of melancholy but no severity; the summer sun is not unbearably hot.

Sisley is one of those painters who exert very little influence on the evolution of painting but whose best works are distinguished by a harmony and aptness that more pioneering artists often miss, because of their very boldness. In fact, between 1872 and 1876 Sisley produced some of the most 'true' and accomplished paintings of the whole period. Later, modelling himself on Monet, he too attempted to use brighter, more sustained colour. But this was, as it were, a contradiction of his own nature and from then onwards he sometimes fell into the trap of crudity and artificiality.

PISSARRO. L'ISLE LACROIX, ROUEN: FOG EFFECTS, 1888. MUSEUM OF ART, PHILADELPHIA.

ALFRED SISLEY, 1839-1899. BOAT DURING A FLOOD, 1876. LOUVRE, PARIS

SISLEY. SNOW AT LOUVECIENNES, 1878. LOUVRE, PARIS

IMPESSIONISM

PIERRE AUGUSTE
RENOIR,
1841-1919.
MOULIN DE LA
GALETTE (DETAIL),
1876.
LOUVRE, PARIS

RENOIR.
PORTRAIT OF
MADEMOISELLE
GRIMPEL WITH
A BLUE RIBBON,
1880.
PRIVATE
COLLECTION,
PARIS

RENOIR.
AFTER
THE BATH,
1888.
OSKAR REINHART
COLLECTION,
WINTERTHUR

In his early formative years Renoir often showed close affinities with Monet, but his individual temperament was always evident. Even *Les Grenouillères,* (Stockholm Museum and Oskar Reinhardt collection, Winterthur) which he painted in his friend's company, show quite clearly that he was less attracted by the fleeting qualities of optical phenomena than by the enchantment of light and the pleasantness of the atmosphere. He was sensual, more interested in a close-up of the transfiguration of a nude or a face than the distant metamorphoses of water, sky or trees. And the light whose effects he carefully observed not only caresses the surface of the skin: it penetrates deep into the flesh, heightens its glow and charm. In addition, he is not satisfied by vision alone; he has to have, and convey, the sensation of touching. In other words he never makes any attempt to dissolve form; his objects never lose their substance.

Basically, he started from much the same position as Manet. Like him he believed that 'one learns to paint in a museum' and he admired Titian, Rubens, Boucher and Delacroix above all other painters. Like him, he was fond of portraying certain aspects of the Parisian life of his day—particularly before 1880. Perhaps he even got the idea for his *Moulin de la Galette* from Manet's *Musique aux Tuileries,* of some fifteen years earlier. But even so his originality stands out in a brilliant and unmistakable fashion. First of all he makes no attempt to play the detached, distant observer; on the contrary he stresses that he has been part of this group of *grisettes* and art-students —a group certainly less elegant and fashionable but much more cheerfully gay than Manet's. There is much more ease in Renoir's composition and he is, of course, much more of an Impressionist. There is a supreme delicacy in the way he notes the caprice of the sun filtering through the leaves, lighting up a mouth or a cheek here, gilding an arm or a brow or a head

IMPRESSIONISM

there. Renoir deliberately applied the principles of Impressionism to the human figure; none of the other Impressionists did so as naturally or with such success.

He applied these principles even to portraiture, a branch of painting which occupied him a good deal, although he was not especially interested in the psychological aspect of it. It is no use looking for character-penetration or psychological insight in his work, for he deliberately ignores all complications, all confusion, all impenetrability. His sitters are usually women, girls or children whose straightforward personalities shine out through their transparent faces, full of sweetness and grace.

In about 1883 he went through a crucial phase. After creating so many pleasing, harmonious works he began to introduce more strictness into his art. Following the example of Raphael, whom he had learned to admire during a visit to Italy, he laid more stress on line, gave more precision to form and a more polished appearance to his surfaces. But on the whole he lost more than he gained from this change—at least for the time being. When he returned to his old freedom it was clear that his period of asceticism had not been in vain.

From then on his form was ampler, stronger, but no less sensitive. His colour took on a more intense lyricism and a more glowing warmth. By now he lived principally in the south of France and as he approached old age he was more successful than ever before in fulfilling his ambition to paint 'human beings like beautiful fruit'. Though he continued to paint portraits, notably of his children, his favourite subject was now the nude, particularly women with ample curves. He was especially fond of linking it with landscape; the nude figure does not melt into the landscape but shares intimately in the dionysian life of nature which, knowing nothing of good or evil, gives way to the intoxication of a bountiful existence in a glorious light.

RENOIR. GIRL COMBING HER HAIR, 1894, LEHMAN COLLECTION, NEW YORK

RENOIR. GABRIELLE WITH A ROSE, 1911. LOUVRE, PARIS

RENOIR. NUDE GIRL RECLINING, 1917. HARRY BAKWIN COLLECTION, NEW YORK

IMPRESSIONISM

EDGAR DE GAS,
KNOWN AS DEGAS.
1834-1917.
ABSINTHE,
1876.
LOUVRE, PARIS

DEGAS.
JOCKEYS,
1881-1885.
YALE UNIVERSITY
ART GALLERY,
NEW HAVEN

DEGAS.
DANCER
IN A
PINK DRESS,
c. 1880.
CHAUNCEY
MCCORMICK
COLLECTION,
CHICAGO

It may seem strange to rank Degas with the Impressionists. In his early years he painted many remarkable portraits and he was always attracted by the human figure; on the other hand, he rarely painted landscapes and was never fond of open-air painting. Moreover, in comparison with the other Impressionists he did a great deal of drawing and his basic ambition was to 'be a colourist through line'.

Nevertheless it was no accident that he exhibited under the same banner as Monet, Pissarro and Renoir, even though that banner never particularly attracted him. First of all, he too believed that re-thinking was necessary. Though in his early years, when he was influenced by Ingres, he painted works like *Spartan Girls and Boys Exercising* (London, Nat. Gall.) or *Misfortunes of the Town of Orleans* (Louvre), after 1865 he gave up historical themes and turned a steady gaze on the reality of his own age. In fact even a few years before he had jotted down ideas in his notebooks for a series of pictures on contemporary subjects and his first *Race-Horses* (Louvre) date from 1862. Like the more characteristic Impressionists, Degas was interested in certain fleeting aspects of things and certain light-effects. But neither were those which interested Renoir or Monet.

It was in the movements of an agile, alert body, the skilled gestures of ballet-dancers, or race-horses that Degas wanted to trap down the fleeting moment. And the light which he was most interested in observing was the light in interiors. He analysed both daylight and artificial light, revealed their softness or liveliness, the way in which they heightened or distorted volumes, brightened or dulled colours, divided up space and gave an unusual appearance to even the most familiar objects.

The unusual was the main goal of his researches, but in fact he was to find it not on the fringe of every-day life but at the very heart of it. Everyone who has been to Paris can vouch for the reality of his

IMPRESSIONISM

cafés—the slightly dreary *bistro* of *Absinthe* or the fashionable *Café-Concert at the Ambassadeurs* (Lyons). And yet, like the workroom of *The Laundresses* or the shop of *At the Modiste's,* there is nothing outstanding about them in themselves. Nevertheless, they seem like revelations. The shock comes not only from the light but also, and often especially, from the design. Perhaps because of the influence of Japanese prints, perhaps because of the photographs which had come into such vogue and which he himself used, Degas gave composition great importance in his work—an importance which cannot be over-stressed, and it is from the unusual design that his art derives some of its most original qualities. He never tired of inventing new viewpoints and ways of 'framing' the scene. He knew exactly how much expressive power lies in lay-out, knew all its resources and brought them into play with all the more energy since what he was interested in was not (conventional) beauty but true novelty.

Look at his ballet-dancers and nudes. He rarely shows the former on the stage or executing their more graceful movements but nearly always in the practice-room and in the most peculiar, strained and tiring of their poses. In fact he heightens their ugly side. His nudes are usually women scrubbing themselves crouched in a bathtub or drying themselves after getting out of it: he surprises them in the very positions which they would least like to be seen. There is nothing sympathetic about his vision; it is very far away from Renoir's generous presentation. For Degas the female body is merely a subject of study; it may excite the curiosity but it moves neither the heart nor the senses.

Though in about 1875 Degas made his colour subservient to form, by the end of his life it became more and more free. And finally Ingres' erstwhile disciple came to advocate an art made up of allusive forms, invented tones and brilliant harmonies.

DEGAS.
THE LAUNDRESSES,
c. 1884.
LOUVRE, PARIS

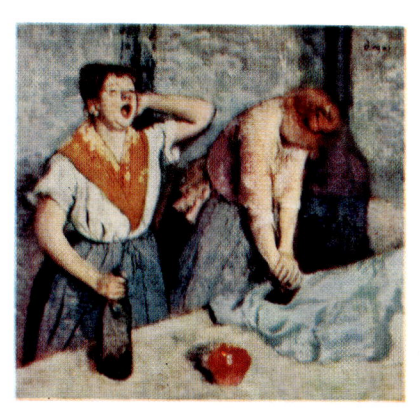

DEGAS.
THE TUB (PASTEL),
c. 1890.
ART INSTITUTE,
CHICAGO

DEGAS.
DANCERS (PASTEL),
1899.
MUSEUM OF ART,
TOLEDO (OHIO)

CÉZANNE

PAUL CÉZANNE.
1839-1906.
THE BLUE VASE,
1885-1887.
LOUVRE, PARIS

CÉZANNE.
PORTRAIT OF
MADAME CÉZANNE,
1883-1887.
PRIVATE
COLLECTION,
USA

CÉZANNE.
CARD-PLAYERS,
1885-1890.
LOUVRE, PARIS

For Cézanne Impressionism was only a transient phase, but a phase which left its mark on him and, most important of all, enabled him to find his true path. When, in 1872, he settled in Auvers-sur-Oise so as to be able to work near Pissarro, he had behind him some ten years of painting, and yet few of his works were anything more than tentative efforts. Moreover, though he had long been a member of the group that had grown up round Monet, his works had remained 'Romantic' in inspiration and style. They reveal a certain violence of feeling and only rarely are the forms not distorted. Although in places there are brilliant tones, in general the drama of the colour is derived from tension between light and dark. From 1872 his palette grew lighter, his spirit calmer and his hand more disciplined. In his landscapes, which had now begun to breathe a spirit of serenity, straight lines became more important than curves, and the precise shapes of houses, with their firm solidity, contrast more sharply with the vaguer forms of the leaves.

Returning to his birthplace, Aix-en-Provence, where he lived almost continuously from 1878, Cézanne increased the clarity of his composition still further. Although he still probed deep into the subject (whether the Gulf of Marseilles, Gardanne or the Mont Sainte-Victoire) and strove to convey the sharpness and intensity of his feelings, he now concentrated on sorting them out, filtering them, making them subservient to the plastic needs of the picture. He succeeded in this aim only at the cost of a hesitancy and slowness in painting which troubled him but which in the end produced dense, vibrant and strongly constructed works.

His landscapes are not, of course, iridescent in the same sense as Monet's. The light is not brilliant or scintillating, the water does not sparkle with millions of reflections which appear and disappear with every passing second. In his desire to 'make Impressionism into something solid and last-

CÉZANNE

ing like the art of the old masters' Cézanne tended to give a certain substance even to liquids and impose an order reminiscent of geometry on the natural confusion of the landscape. In the final analysis, his pictures are autonomous organisms in which, basically, each object moves the spectator by reason of its pictorial qualities.

His portraits have even less psychological interest than Renoir's and, far from radiating charm, convey the idea of a taciturn, defiant, almost fierce human species. His nudes are even less sensual than Degas'. His still-lifes are composed of stiff cloths, fruits which, to him, seem to have neither flesh nor juice.

Yet the serious, monumental quality of his portraits is enough to make them imposing. There is an extraordinary eloquence about the forms of his bodies inscribing curves, triangles and pyramids on the landscape—figures which fit the movements of the trees and serrations of the clouds like answering rhymes. The volumes of the fruits are exquisite in their purity and sensitivity, while their colours are rich and vibrant. What does it matter if such objects have lost some of the qualities of real life? They have acquired others of a rarer zest.

'When colour is at its richest,' Cézanne declared, 'form is at its fullest. The secret of drawing and modelling lies in the contrasts and harmonies of the colour.' In his last pictures—as in his inspired water-colours—he demonstrates the truth of this dictum with peculiar clarity. On occasion objects are only suggested by blobs of colour, but one can still feel their solidity, and the picture as a whole lacks neither structure nor space. Sometimes, too, a broad, sweeping rhythm takes over, as though Cézanne had recaptured the Baroque lyricism of his early years. But even in this he never forgets another of his maxims: 'The most valuable adjunct to sensitivity in creating a work of art is a mind which can organize powerfully.'

CÉZANNE. L'ESTAQUE, c. 1885. R. A. BUTLER COLLECTION, LONDON

CÉZANNE. BOY IN A RED WAISTCOAT, 1890-1895. E. BÜHRLE COLLECTION, ZURICH

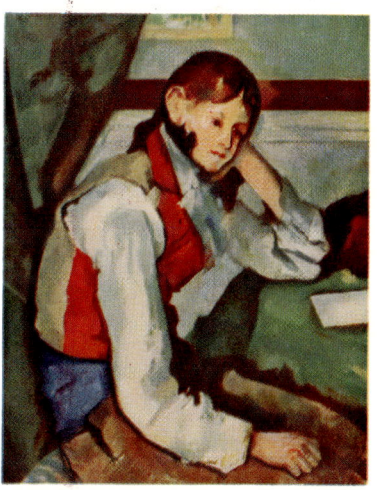

CÉZANNE. MONT SAINTE-VICTOIRE, SEEN FROM LAUVES, 1904-1906. KUNSTHAUS, ZURICH

NEO-IMPRESSIONISM

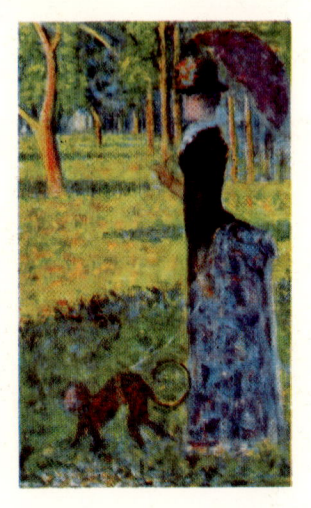

GEORGES SEURAT.
1859-1891.
LA BAIGNADE,
1883-1884.
TATE GALLERY,
LONDON

SEURAT.
STUDY FOR
SUNDAY
AFTERNOON AT
THE GRANDE JATTE,
1885.
SMITH COLLEGE
MUSEUM OF ART,
NORTHAMPTON, USA

SEURAT.
HONFLEUR: END
OF THE JETTY,
1886.
RIJKSMUSEUM
KRÖLLER-MÜLLER,
OTTERLO

The last exhibition by the Impressionist group was held in 1886. Monet, Renoir and Sisley no longer took part. But in place of them there was a young artist called Seurat, whose picture *Sunday Afternoon at the Grande Jatte* (Chicago, Art Institute) seemed to be the manifesto of a new trend which was soon to acquire a name of its own: Neo-Impressionism. However, there can be no doubt that in essentials it differed from Monet's manner much more often than it resembled it. Perhaps it should be called a new school rather than a new trend. One hesitates to apply the term 'school' to the Impressionists, who never had a programme worth the name, but one can hardly avoid using it in connection with Seurat and his friends; they loudly proclaimed their clearly defined creed and all believed in the same method.

Signac, their spokesman, called it 'a precise and scientific method' in his essay 'From Eugène Delacroix to Neo-Impressionism'. And it is true that, whereas their predecessors had relied mainly on instinct in analysing and conveying their feelings, the Neo-Impressionists consulted Chevreul's *Simultaneous Contrast of Colours,* studied the most recent works of scientists such as Helmholtz, Maxwell and N. O. Rood and, in general, insisted on making use of science.

They began by making a precise distinction between an object's 'local' colour and the colour it acquired from the light, and then noted the reactions of these on each other. Then, following the principles of Pointillism, they laid on these colours in little spots or strokes instead of the usual pigmentary mixture which ran the risk of dulling them. By their method, on the other hand, they maintained that the luminosity was preserved and the effect of the complementary colours heightened.

The Neo-Impressionists also attached importance to 'the moral effect of lines and colours' and to the 'decorative' composition of a picture. In other words, they saw

NEO-IMPRESSIONISM

the painter as more than a mere recording eye: he was also to select, calculate and organize. Unfortunately the Neo-Impressionist usually calculated only too much and, in trying to apply the method with complete scrupulousness, often stifled his own sensitivity and deprived his painting of some of its most valuable qualities. One cannot help saying that neither Signac, Cross, Camille Pissaro, his son Lucien, nor Maximilien Luce (to name only these) derived as much benefit from their scientific principles as they had hoped. It is true that when Signac and Cross had confidence in their own spontaneous impulses they were able to create remarkable watercolours; they also did much to liberate colour. But when all is said and done, only Seurat really managed to avoid dryness and produce works which are among the most important of his period.

The fact is that Seurat was one of those artists for whom methodical work and rigid rules are not a hindrance but a true stimulus. Moreover his sensitivity was so acute that it could bring even the most calculated compositions to life. Like Cézanne he liked solidity, stability and the strictness of geometry. However, movement is of little importance in his work. Except in *The Circus,* he lacks ease; he found difficulty in starting and grew stiff before finishing a convincing figure. Even the many walking figures in *Sunday at the Grande Jatte* do not give an impression of real animation. For instead of belonging to real life, Seurat's figures, despite the fact that they wear the fashions of the day, usually have the regularity and measured gestures of archaic statues. His painting is attractive not for its realism but for its stylistic qualities—the delicacy of the colours, the purity of form, the poetry of the design. These are even more marked in his landscapes than in his large compositions. In them the light is particularly delicate and strictness is miraculously blended with subtlety.

SEURAT. THE CIRCUS, 1891. LOUVRE, PARIS

PAUL SIGNAC, 1863-1935. WOMAN COMBING HER HAIR, 1892. MME G. SIGNAC COLLECTION, PARIS

HENRY-EDMOND DELACROIX, KNOWN AS CROSS, 1856-1910. THE WAVE, c. 1907. MME G. SIGNAC COLLECTION, PARIS

THE REACTION AGAINST IMPRESSIONISM

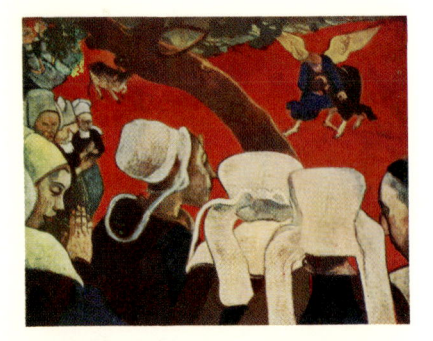

PAUL GAUGUIN.
1848-1903.
VISION AFTER
THE SERMON,
1888.
NATIONAL GALLERY
OF SCOTLAND,
EDINBURGH

GAUGUIN.
TAHITIAN WOMEN,
1891.
LOUVRE, PARIS

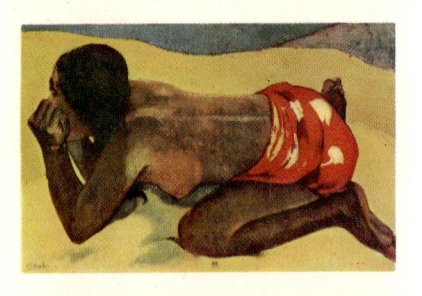

GAUGUIN.
OTAHI (ALONE),
1893.
PRIVATE
COLLECTION,
PARIS

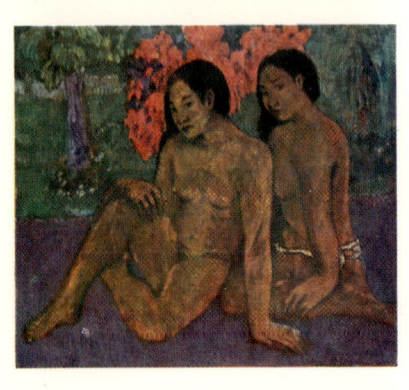

GAUGUIN.
ET L'OR DE LEUR
CORPS...
1901.
LOUVRE, PARIS

At the very time when the Neo-Impressionists were seeking to provide a new future for painting by adopting a 'scientific' approach to its problems, another artist was looking for his answer in a different direction: Primitivism—in life as well as in art. This was Paul Gauguin, whose extraordinary life has fascinated biographers and public more perhaps than that of any other artist. He was born in 1848 and as a young man went into business (stock-broking and banking). He prospered, married, and his life seemed settled and conventional.

His painting began as a hobby. In 1876 a picture of his was accepted by the Salon. Soon afterwards he met Pissarro, who developed his genius to such a degree that by 1883 he gave up his job and devoted himself entirely to painting, living in unaccustomed poverty and cutting himself off almost completely from his wife and children.

At first he went to Brittany, the 'wildest' part of France, then to Martinique and Panama. In 1888 he stayed for two months with Van Gogh at Arles, but the two artists soon quarrelled. Finally in 1891 he left for the South Sea Islands, remaining there (with a break in 1893-1895) until his death. He said that for him 'barbarism' was 'a rejuvenation'; as applied to his art this was true, although his life undoubtedly wore itself out more rapidly in the Tropics than if he had stayed in Europe. Yet this intensity never brought him peace, and wherever he went he was filled only with bitterness and despair.

At first Gauguin took his inspiration from Pissarro, then from Cézanne, Puvis de Chavannes and Japanese prints. It was not until 1888, when he was working at Pont-Aven with Emile Bernard, a young painter of much originality but little strength, that he found his true style. It was then that he painted *Vision after the Sermon,* a statement of his own personality and a brilliant exposition of a new aesthetic attitude. He retained only the palette of Im-

260

THE REACTION AGAINST IMPRESSIONISM

pressionism, and even so he did not use it to copy light effects but to express his thoughts and feelings. Instead of being a subject for close analysis, the external world was only a starting-point, a springboard, a means to an end. Thus a field becomes a bright red colour, so that Jacob's stuggle with the angel (in *Vision after the Sermon*) takes place on an entirely unreal plane.

From this time onwards Gauguin's painting went beyond realism in every respect: the colour was not only pure but laid on in flat areas; forms were defined less by modelling than by outline and space was suggested by 'sign-posts' rather than linear perspective. Aerial perspective is banished altogether. And the same is true, in the majority of cases, of cast shadows. To find anything comparable in European art, one has to go back to the painting of the Middle Ages or to folk art. Gauguin was probably the first modern artist to see that it had something to offer 'high art'. By the twentieth century, of course, there were to be hundreds of artists who admired the freshness of primitive art, often in a very different way from Gauguin. But it was he who started the trend. 'Greek art' he declared, 'was the biggest mistake of all, however beautiful it was' and 'I have gone back much further than the horses of the Parthenon to the hobby-horse of my childhood, a nice, solid wooden horse.'

The forms he discovered in Brittany blossomed in Tahiti. His drawing became ever more vigorous and the colour more opulent — no doubt partly inspired by the exotic scenery: he sought to capture its luxuriance, light, smell and mystery. But he avoided exoticism: he was always more interested in pictorial qualities and their specific poetry than in mere picturesqueness. He also managed to avoid literary painting. Although he valued ideas, he thought of himself only as a painter, his primary obligation to produce harmonies of a sensuous originality and expressive simplifications of form.

GAUGUIN. TAHITIAN WOMEN ON THE BEACH, 1891-1892. LEHMAN COLLECTION, NEW YORK

GAUGUIN. RIDERS ON THE SHORE, 1902. FOLKWANG MUSEUM, ESSEN

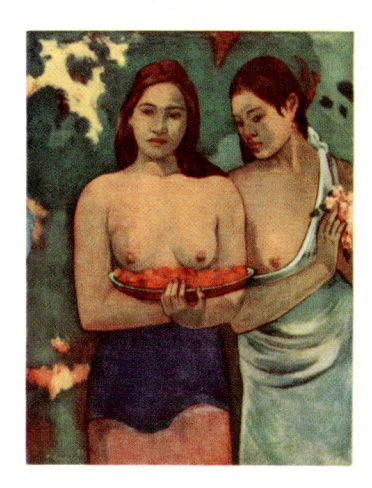

GAUGUIN. TAHITI WOMEN BY THE MANGO TREE, 1899. METROPOLITAN MUSEUM, NEW YORK

THE REACTION AGAINST IMPRESSIONISM

VINCENT VAN GOGH.
1853-1890.
SUNFLOWERS,
1888.
TATE GALLERY,
LONDON

VAN GOGH.
LE PONT DE
L'ANGLOIS,
1888.
WILDENSTEIN
COLLECTION,
NEW YORK

VAN GOGH.
SELF-PORTRAIT
WITH BANDAGED
EAR, 1889.
LEIGH B. BLOCK
COLLECTION,
CHICAGO.

'I should not be surprised if in a short while the Impressionists begin to take exception to my manner, which owes more to Delacroix' ideas than theirs. For, instead of trying to give an exact translation of what I see, I use colour more arbitrarily to express myself with force.' Vincent van Gogh, who in these words so accurately sums up his artistic method, was the son of a Dutch pastor. He began life by studying for the church and became a missionary in the Belgian mining-district of Borinage, sharing the hardships of the miners. Throughout his life he remained concerned with these problems, but his career as a missionary ended in failure.

Although he had odd lessons in Antwerp and the Hague, he largely taught himself to paint and draw. In Holland where he had made a point of stressing his identity with the peasants, their life, their work and their land, his forms had been rough and unpolished, his colours dark.

After he arrived in Paris in 1886 both his mood and his manner changed: his outlook became less gloomy, his palette brighter, and his touch lighter. But no aesthetic programme which gave primary importance to the mere appearance of things could wholly satisfy Van Gogh.

Even in Paris he was never an orthodox Impressionist. He approached subjects not only with interest but with tenderness. Although after coming in contact with Signac and Seurat he attempted to show them by means of small dots and dashes, this method was never an end in itself but a means of making them vibrate more dramatically in a pure, burning colour.

His colour became even more lively and dazzling after he had moved to the south of France, driven there by a sort of nostalgia for the sun. Whether his subject was a landscape or an interior, flowers (as in *Sunflowers*) or a portrait, he heightened and enriched his colours, putting them on to the canvas in writhing, flame-like shapes (even

262

THE REACTION AGAINST IMPRESSIONISM

solid masonry is represented in these terms). At the same time he strengthened his drawing, which still played a vitally important part in his work and was as strong and authoritative as his colour. The *Pont de l'Anglois* is a particularly good example of this with its subtle interplay of verticals, diagonals, horizontals and curved shapes.

But, although Van Gogh was mainly interested in expressive power he was too great an admirer of Japanese prints to undervalue the virtues of delicacy and refinement. Later he would be considered as a precursor of Expressionism, and there can be no doubt that his work shows Expressionist tendencies. But there can be no doubt, either, that these tendencies never made him slap-dash or led him to despise pictorial beauty.

Nevertheless his spirit was constantly haunted, torn, wrenched by the most horrible torments. His first fit of insanity, when he cut off his ear, struck him down in 1888. (His *Self-portrait with bandaged Ear* was painted immediately afterwards.) Gauguin, with whose artistic aims he felt a strong affinity, had joined him at Arles and the two men had quarrelled. From then onwards the insanity was always in the background, a continual threat, and periodically it came to the surface. Van Gogh was admitted as a voluntary patient to the mental hospital at Saint-Rémy before going in May 1890 to Auvers-sur-Oise where he committed suicide two months later. But even at the height of his sickness the fits of frenzy and despair were interspersed with phases of lucidity when his hand regained its creative dynamism (*The Church at Auvers* is of this period).

The Wheatfield was painted shortly before his suicide. The colours are no longer joyous, but like all his works it is far more than an unconsidered outpouring. The œuvre of Van Gogh is not only one of the most moving in art history, but also one of the most harmonious and strong.

VAN GOGH.
SELF-PORTRAIT,
1889.
LOUVRE, PARIS

VAN GOGH.
THE CHURCH
AT AUVERS,
1890.
LOUVRE, PARIS

VAN GOGH.
CROWS OVER
THE WHEATFIELD,
1890.
V. W. VAN GOGH
COLLECTION,
LAREN

THE REACTION AGAINST IMPRESSIONISM

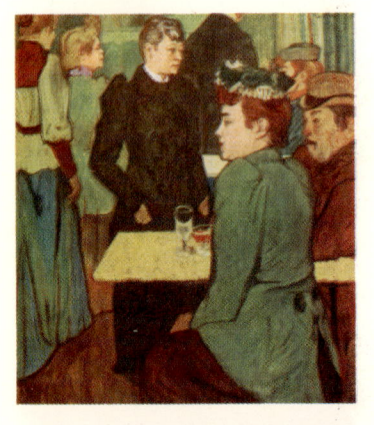

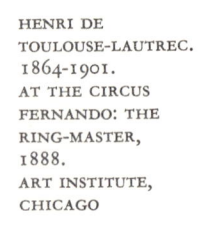

HENRI DE
TOULOUSE-LAUTREC.
1864-1901.
AT THE CIRCUS
FERNANDO: THE
RING-MASTER,
1888.
ART INSTITUTE,
CHICAGO

TOULOUSE-LAUTREC.
MOULIN DE LA
GALETTE, 1892.
NATIONAL GALLERY
OF ART,
WASHINGTON

TOULOUSE-LAUTREC.
LA GOULUE
ENTERING
THE MOULIN ROUGE,
1892.
DAVID M. LEVY
COLLECTION,
NEW YORK

Van Gogh hoped to find a refuge and a richer fund of inspiration in Arles. Gauguin sought the same benefits in the Tropics. Toulouse-Lautrec could find them only in Paris. And not even Paris as a whole, but the city within a city which is made up of bars, music-halls, circuses—the city of nocturnal pleasures and debauchery.

Gauguin was fleeing from civilization but Toulouse-Lautrec was fleeing from himself. Or rather he was trying to escape from the tortured cripple he had become after two accidents in his childhood which had left him a dwarf incapable of easy movement. If he had remained amongst the society of his own class—he was a descendent of the Counts of Toulouse—he would have been condemned to live as an outsider, condemned to resignation or completely impotent resentment. But Montmartre provided an environment where his deformity did not prevent him from taking part in the frenzied life all around. And yet although he appreciated the fact that Montmartre society gave way to its desires without any inhibitions and made fun of the barriers set up by respectable morality, he cherished no illusions. His eye was too penetrating, his mind too lucid and his heart too full of bitterness for him to present an idealised or sentimental image of the world in which he lived. Toulouse-Lautrec had no pity for the human creatures he observed. On the contrary, he used a sharp, cutting, implacable style which sometimes made his works become not merely expressive but caricaturish.

One cannot help thinking that his vision is moulded by a certain envy and frustrated desire, particularly when he shows movement—that of horses, of male or female dancers, or acrobats. He never tired of watching them, of painting them in every posture, usually choosing the moment when they had taken on a grotesque, not merely unusual, appearance. This is one of the points in which he differs from Degas, whose influence

THE REACTION AGAINST IMPRESSIONISM

he felt and with whom he had many affinities. Like Degas he was a master of line, even in his painting. Like him, too, he liked unexpected design and lighting, and even more than him, his interest was directed entirely towards the behaviour of human beings. But the human beings he observed were of a different type from those who had attracted his predecessor.

The women whom Toulouse-Lautrec shows in various intimate situations were prostitutes in a brothel. His dancers were the stars of places like the Moulin Rouge or Jardin de Paris. And instead of leaving them anonymous, he stressed the most characteristic features of each face or dancer. He even helped to impress their outlines on Paris—and on posterity—by making them appear in striking posters. La Goulue, Jane Avril, the singer Aristide Bruant and others owed a large portion of their fame to him.

In 1891 he did his first poster, and it emerged as a masterpiece. In general, Toulouse-Lautrec was particularly at ease in lithography; few of his paintings show such supreme mastery as his posters and prints. In them the composition is extraordinarily bold, the colour more full of brilliance and refinement than anywhere else. Nowhere else is the modelling so radically banished, and each figure reduced to an area of colour energetically outlined with an incisive, terse line. It is true that this style owes something to the Japanese prints which had such a wide influence at this period, but Lautrec did not merely follow an example; he turned it into something very personal. The freedom of his drawing, the boldness and acidity of his harmonies, the touch of insolence one often senses in the way he arranges his picture, all his biting wit, irreverence and cynicism mark him out as a thoroughly Western artist who, with a vigour peculiar to himself, portrayed a certain milieu and at the same time laid bare a soul tortured by a horrible stroke of fate.

TOULOUSE-LAUTREC. WOMAN AT HER TOILET, 1896. LOUVRE, PARIS

TOULOUSE-LAUTREC. THE ENGLISHWOMAN AT THE 'STAR', LE HAVRE, 1899. MUSÉE D'ALBI

TOULOUSE-LAUTREC. THE MODISTE, 1900. MUSÉE D'ALBI

THE SYMBOLISTS AND THE NABIS

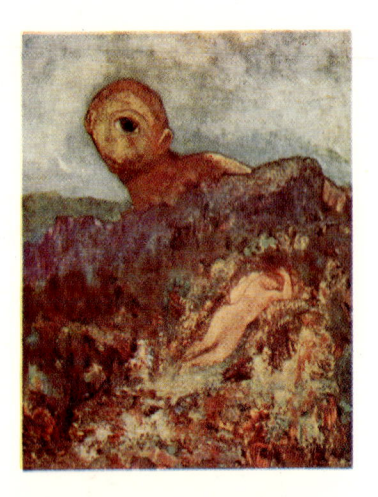

ODILON REDON.
1840-1916.
THE CYCLOPS,
1895-1900.
RIJKSMUSEUM
KRÖLLER-MÜLLER,
OTTERLO

ODILON REDON.
SAILING BOATS
AT VENICE, 1906.
PRIVATE
COLLECTION,
PARIS

ÉDOUARD VUILLARD.
1868-1940.
PORTRAIT OF
TOULOUSE-LAUTREC.
MUSÉE D'ALBI

In about 1890, the reaction against Impressionism became apparent in almost all the studios producing art that was going to affect the future. Everyone, from Cézanne to Seurat, Van Gogh to Gauguin, or Degas to Lautrec, was coming to regard painting far more as something created by the mind, than as just a record of sense-impressions. During the same period, an anti-naturalistic movement known as Symbolism was developing in literature, and it is not surprising that the two currents tended to converge, particularly as the idea of giving symbolic value to forms had occurred to Gauguin, Van Gogh and Seurat. In 1891 and 1892 the critic Albert Aurier defined Symbolist painting as 'ideist, synthetic, subjective, decorative'. Admittedly, the movement's most characteristic representative was Gauguin, but Aurier also mentioned as being among the Symbolists Van Gogh, Redon and a number of young artists. In 1888, most of these, including Sérusier, Denis, Ranson, Roussel, Bonnard and Vuillard, had formed a group, calling themselves the Nabis—a Hebrew word meaning 'prophets'. As a matter of fact, the differences between these artists were in some cases very great, and the one thing that they all had in common was their opposition to Impressionist naturalism, as well as to official painting.

According to Odilon Redon, everything that transcended, transfigured or magnified an object, and that caused the mind to ascend into the realm of mystery had been a closed book to the Impressionists. In so saying, Redon also indicated what mattered to him and the general direction of his own investigations. Until about 1890 he expressed himself chiefly in black and white, but later he tended to use pastel to translate his observations and conceptions into iridescent effects of colour. For though he was a visionary, he did not neglect to study nature. He would examine with a botanist's or zoologist's eye the plants, flowers and

266

THE SYMBOLISTS AND THE NABIS

butterflies that he liked to depict, before transferring them to the fabulous clime peculiar to his art, where they grew lighter, and became fragile, mannered, unreal.

The importance that Redon attached to the subjective element in art made him popular with the Nabis, who, in other respects, were influenced by Cézanne, Degas and Puvis de Chavannes, as well as by Gauguin. When he met Gauguin at Pont-Aven in 1888, Sérusier listened to his advice and passed it on to his friends. 'Thus,' wrote Maurice Denis, 'we recognized that every work of art was the transposition, caricature and emotionally heightened equivalent of a perception.' No less strong than Gauguin's influence was that of the Japanese. They it was who gave the Nabis their taste for long and supple arabesques, which form the link between their art and the plant- and flower-based style that became famous in Europe about 1900. It is variously known as Art Nouveau, *Jugendstil* and 'the Modern style'. It was also to the Japanese that the most fertile artists of the group, Pierre Bonnard and Edouard Vuillard, owed their subdued colouring, which differed so radically from that of the Impressionists. They used it just as much for their indoor scenes as when they were representing the streets or public parks of Paris. At that period, both painters were Intimists even in their landscapes, and their light was always soft and dreamy. In very ordinary subjects, like a family sitting round a table, a woman serving, or women and children in the park, they found a most charming poetic quality. If anything, Vuillard's work shows even greater refinement than that of Bonnard, and, in any case, nothing outshines the success with which he harmonized his ranges of browns, beiges, rosy whites and subdued blues. His evocations of form are always unobtrusive, and he achieved them with the slightly timid tenderness characteristic of him; how effortless it all seems!

VUILLARD. PORTRAIT OF THE ARTIST'S MOTHER AND SISTER, c. 1893. MUSEUM OF MODERN ART, NEW YORK

VUILLARD. PORTRAIT OF MADAME SERT. PRIVATE COLLECTION, WINTERTHUR.

MAURICE DENIS. 1870-1943. THE MUSES, 1893. MUSÉE D'ART MODERNE, PARIS

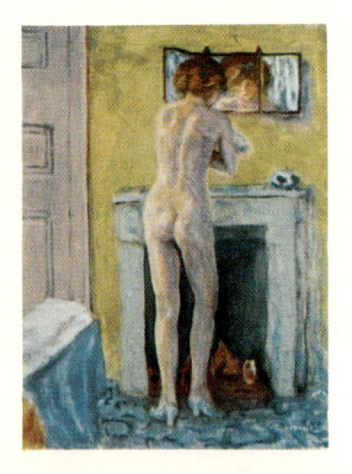

THE SYMBOLISTS AND THE NABIS

PIERRE BONNARD.
1867-1947.
NUDE IN FRONT
OF THE FIREPLACE,
1917.
MUSÉE DE
L'ANNONCIADE,
SAINT-TROPEZ

BONNARD.
THE RED BODICE,
1925.
MUSÉE D'ART
MODERNE, PARIS

BONNARD.
AT THE CASINO,
1924.
PRIVATE
COLLECTION,
PARIS

Though he excelled in suggesting the secret life of inconspicuous things—all that was not too weighty and too clearly defined in its features—Vuillard was rather at a loss when he wanted to be precise and 'literal', or when he found himself confronted with a model from a world that was not his. After 1900 his success led him to become the portraitist of a middle-class society that he never really managed to get used to. From then onwards, the unobtrusiveness and diffidence that formed the charm of his work when he steered his own course became a disadvantage to him. For he hesitated to assert himself and, instead of imposing his own vision, adopted the tastes of his clientèle. His art thus ceased to be delicately allusive and became based, instead, on an often emphatic realism. In some pictures only incidentals, such as a table-cloth or a bowl of fruit, recall the exquisite qualities of his earlier work. Bonnard's evolution was entirely different; without haste and without ever taking on the air of an aggressive revolutionary, he developed a style that became increasingly bold. So that, by the end of his life, he appeared as one of the most original and inventive painters of his times.

Moreover, even at the period when he was fairly close to Vuillard, he differed from his friend in being less respectful. He could never contemplate the world without a trace of humour and mischief. Moreover, he retained the unsophisticated eye of a child right up to his death. Everything dazzled and amazed him: his wife washing; a café in the evening at Montmartre; part of a table, with a camembert and a few grapes on it; the harbours at Cannes and Trouville; houses in the green countryside around Le Cannet; the Mediterranean, ecstatic in a fiery sunset. His astonishment was never feigned or forced, nor was his expression of it. Undoubtedly he wanted the spectator to share his amazement, and exercised his ingenuity to prepare surprises for him; but,

THE SYMBOLISTS AND THE NABIS

though mischievous, he never became unreasonable. However novel his 'frame' and view-point, he always seems to present us with a slice of life, cut at random. One is often conscious that he has run the most serious risks with the balance and unity of his compositions; but he always evades the hazard, like a clever acrobat.

Whereas some of the subjects that Bonnard chose and the way that he presented them may recall Degas, his feeling for life brings him closer to Renoir. Like Renoir's, his work is an expression of the enjoyment of living and of the sense of wonder that invades us when the world is transfigured by a friendly sun, but he expressed himself with even greater freedom than did his predecessor.

While Bonnard, too, most certainly took nature as his starting-point, his imagination interpreted his impressions with such creative license, and he made his colouring such a law unto itself, that, in the end, his works took on a completely unrealistic appearance. Moreover, after 1910, his palette became increasingly brilliant, while, at the same time, his colour harmonies grew progressively bolder and more delightful.

What, in fact, he did with his brush was to transform reality into a fairyland. Changing the world into a state of perpetual florescence, he coupled sonorous hues with the most subtly iridescent effects: vivid reds and oranges that radiate the light of the midday sun with the delicate vibrations of morning light reflected in the dew. And he certainly knew how to make the best of lilac and violet, which painters so seldom use without lapsing into prettification and insipidity. Absolutely everything, including his brush-work, adds to the magic of his pictures. His touch was light, and the paint seems to have settled in flakes on the canvas, like snow upon a meadow. The colour is never flat, never opaque; on the contrary, it consists everywhere in delicate gradations, and emits a kind of soft shimmer.

BONNARD. THE FARM AT LE CANNET, 1923. PRIVATE COLLECTION, PARIS

BONNARD. PANORAMA, LE CANNET, 1924. MUSÉE D'ART MODERNE, PARIS

BONNARD. CORNER OF THE DINING ROOM AT LE CANNET, c. 1932. MUSÉE D'ART MODERNE, PARIS

FAUVISM

HENRI MATISSE.
1869-1954.
PORTRAIT OF
MADAME MATISSE.
'PORTRAIT WITH
THE GREEN STRIPE',
1905.
J. RUMP
COLLECTION,
STATENS MUSEUM,
COPENHAGEN

MATISSE.
COLLIOURE
LANDSCAPE,
STUDY FOR
'LA JOIE DE VIVRE',
1905.
J. RUMP
COLLECTION,
STATENS MUSEUM,
COPENHAGEN

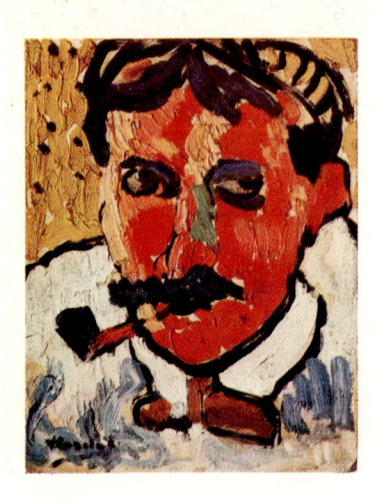

MAURICE DE
VLAMINCK.
1876-1958.
PORTRAIT OF
ANDRÉ DERAIN,
1905.
PRIVATE
COLLECTION,
PARIS

Has there ever been such a fertile period in the history of art as the beginning of the twentieth century? At any rate, from 1905 to 1914 innovations followed one another at what it is hardly an exaggeration to call a giddy speed. Moreover, they were important, radical innovations, which laid the foundations of every subsequent creative development.

1905 saw the birth of Fauvism and Expressionism, 1908, that of Cubism, 1910, that of Futurism and of metaphysical and abstract painting. Naturally enough, these different movements did not all appear in a single country: while Fauvism and Cubism arose in France, Expressionism was chiefly a German development, and the promoters of Futurism and metaphysical painting were all Italians. With regard to abstract art, for which Fauvism, Expressionism, and Cubism jointly prepared the way, it is generally agreed that it originated at Munich, though it soon also emerged elsewhere.

Seen in relation to the second half of the nineteenth century, this sharing of the lime-light by several different countries is a new development that deserves emphasis. Nevertheless, it was still in France that most of the decisive research took place, just as it was there that the works most outstanding for their purely pictorial qualities were created.

If one had to sum up Fauvism in a few words, one could say that it represents the triumph of colour —but with the rider that this triumph does not just consist in the purity and brilliance of the colour. What provoked the critic Louis Vauxcelles to refer to 'Fauves' was undoubtedly the brightness—even the crudeness—of the hues that confronted him at the Salon d'Automne of 1905 in the room where the works of Matisse, Vlaminck, Derain, Friesz, Manguin, Jean Puy, and Valtat were. This was also the significance the word had for Vlaminck, who announced that he wanted to burn down the Ecole des Beaux-Arts

FAUVISM

with his cobalts and vermilions. However, for Henri Matisse, the group's leader, the problem was more involved; to him, the thing that mattered was to increase the power not only of bright but also of delicate colouring.

By and large, Vlaminck was impulsive, declaring that it took more courage to obey one's instincts than to die a hero's death on the battle-field; Matisse objected that it was necessary to restrain instinct, as one prunes a tree to improve its growth. On both artists Van Gogh left his mark; but whereas Vlaminck saw him as a painter who had abandoned lucidity in his work, contented simply to lay bare his soul and keep nothing in reserve, Matisse understood more clearly what he had to teach. Moreover, to Van Gogh's lesson he added those of Gauguin and Cézanne; and there was, besides, a brief period when he was attracted by the Neo-Impressionists. Working alongside Signac and Cross at St Tropez in 1904, he divided up his colours; but, at the same time, he paid heed to the decorative organization of his pictures. In 1905 he painted a few at Collioure in which he was a trifle negligent about form—but this was only a passing phase.

By comparing Vlaminck's portrait of Derain with Matisse's *Portrait with a green Stripe,* one can judge the distance between the two artists, and get a clear idea of the opposing extremes of Fauvism. In the first picture, the colouring is harsh and violent to the point of brutality, while the drawing is heavy, summary and imprecise; briefly, it is an art that compels recognition through its verve, punch, and earthy poetry far more than through its sensibility and 'correctness'. In the second, one finds a richer palette, colour harmonies that are not only sonorous, but of rare beauty, drawing that is more precise, and above all, a more conscious approach to volume. What the Fauves actually wanted to do, when they deliberately gave up modelling in light and shade,

VLAMINCK. LES BATEAUX-LAVOIRS, 1906. PRIVATE COLLECTION, PARIS

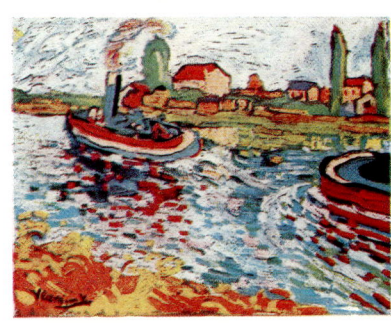

VLAMINCK. TUG-BOATS ON THE SEINE, 1906. JOHN HAY WHITNEY COLLECTION, NEW YORK

ANDRÉ DERAIN. 1880-1954. HOUSES OF PARLIAMENT, LONDON, 1905. PIERRE LÉVY COLLECTION, TROYES

DERAIN. LONDON, BLACKFRIARS, 1907. ART GALLERY, GLASGOW

FAUVISM

OTHON FRIESZ.
1879-1949.
LANDSCAPE,
LA CIOTAT,
1907.
PIERRE LÉVY
COLLECTION, TROYES

ALBERT MARQUET.
1875-1947.
JULY 14TH
AT LE HAVRE,
1906.
PRIVATE
COLLECTION,
PARIS

MARQUET.
SERGEANT
OF THE COLONIALE,
1907.
LEHMAN
COLLECTION,
NEW YORK

was to express form purely in terms of colour and line. Hence, Matisse devised his green stripe, which, by descending from the subject's forehead towards the chin, so to speak pushes back the temples and cheeks without any loss of intensity in their colouring. Neither in Van Gogh's *œuvre* nor that of Gauguin does one find similar solutions or such freedom in the use of colour; and this, rather than the violent impact of the colouring, is Fauvism's really novel contribution to art.

Obviously, a work like Matisse's portrait is not produced without long and careful thought. It is not surprising, therefore, that its author believed that 'one could judge an artist's vitality and power by his ability, on being directly moved by the spectacle of nature, to organize his feelings, and even to come back several times on different days in the same state of mind, so that he could continue to experience them; such a faculty implied that a man had sufficient self-mastery to discipline himself'.

There were other Fauves who also recognized the need for discipline. Notwithstanding his friendship with Vlaminck, André Derain tended to follow the course set by Matisse. Emotionally, he differed from his friend, for whereas Vlaminck was rough and hot-headed, Derain was urbane and prepossessing. Even his daring work has an engaging quality about it, as well as a certain sweetness, grace, and at times, indeed, prettiness.

If one were to judge only by the pictures that Matisse, Derain, Friesz, or Braque painted in the Midi, one might well conclude that the Fauve palette owed its brilliance solely to the intensity of the southern light. However, Vlaminck employed fiery hues to depict the roads of the northern department of Seine-et-Oise, and Derain's colouring was perhaps never more resonant than when, on a visit to London in 1905-1906, he painted some of the most wonderful landscapes that Fauvism produced. Though he at first

FAUVISM

applied his paint in small, oblong touches, later he laid it on in fairly broad, flat areas, of which the boundaries are sometimes emphasized by an encircling line. He also showed increasing freedom in his choice of colours, but this did not stop him paying attention to form and disposition.

Émile-Othon Friesz, too, learned how to control his impulses; on the other hand, violence and excess are foreign to the nature of Georges Braque, whom Friesz helped to find his bearings, and there is consequently something almost wary about the way he distributed his colours. Friesz's handling could be impetuous, whereas Braque's was slow and measured. As for Albert Marquet and Raoul Dufy, who were inclined to work together between 1904 and 1906, they too saw Fauvism as something more than just another form of Expressionism. Nevertheless, while Dufy, particularly in his *July 14th* paintings, already revealed his fondness for vivid, cheerful hues, Marquet found it more natural to express himself in ranges of greyish tones, even though he was a friend of Matisse.

Of all the Fauves, it is the Dutch artist Kees van Dongen who came closest to Vlaminck in the importance that he attached to direct expression. He differed from his French colleague, however, in having a more sensitive eye, more exacting taste, and a sounder technique. During the Fauve period, indeed, Van Dongen, who after 1918 became the best-known society portraitist in Paris, was a colourist full of exuberance, bite, and even delicacy.

It must be added that, whereas he remained a supporter of Fauvism until about 1912, Vlaminck, Derain, Friesz, Dufy, and Braque all changed course as early as 1908 (see p. 279). Denying the gods that up till then they had adored, they set about creating a sober, austere, and more-or-less systematically developed form of art, which claimed Cézanne as its starting point, and emerged as Cubism.

RAOUL DUFY.
1877-1953.
JULY 14TH
AT LE HAVRE,
1907.
PRIVATE
COLLECTION,
PARIS

GEORGES BRAQUE.
BORN 1882.
LANDSCAPE,
COLLIOURE,
1906-1907.
PIERRE LÉVY
COLLECTION,
TROYES

KEES
VAN DONGEN.
BORN 1877.
'LA BELLE FATMA'
AND HER TROUPE,
1906.
B. J. FISZ
COLLECTION,
PARIS

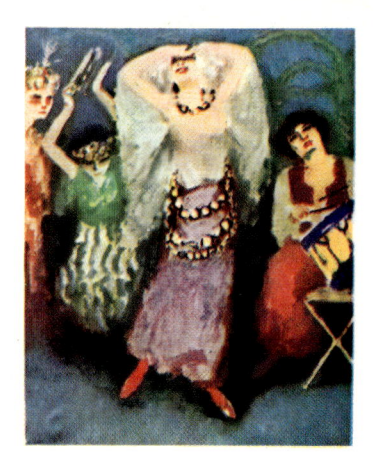

FAUVISM

HENRI MATISSE.
1869-1954.
STILL LIFE
WITH ORANGES,
1912.
PABLO PICASSO
COLLECTION,
PARIS

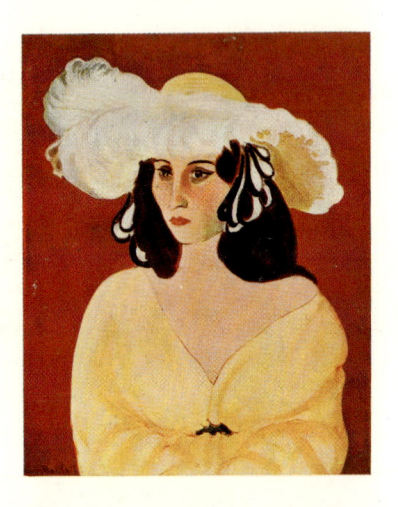

MATISSE.
WHITE PLUMES,
1919.
ART INSTITUTE,
MINNEAPOLIS

MATISSE.
THE GREEN
SIDEBOARD,
1928.
MUSÉE D'ART
MODERNE, PARIS

The reason why Matisse remained faithful to Fauvism at a time when almost all his former associates were moving away from it is that, in his opinion, he had by no means exhausted its possibilities. How pure colour was to be reconciled with a suggestion of space and volume seemed to him a problem of fundamental importance that artists had hardly begun to tackle. So, for years he devoted himself to finding solutions, and the methods that he used were varied and subtle. Light, too, he expressed in terms of colour; instead of being thought of as the luminous opposite of shadows, it emanated from the very brilliance of his colour harmonies.

No doubt there came a time when the example of Cubism led Matisse in his turn to make his colouring less hot, and give his forms and compositions as a whole more severity. However, even if his style took on a more severe appearance, far from becoming anaemic, it remained profoundly personal and bold. In about 1916, as a result, the artist produced some canvases, such as *Moroccans at Prayer* and *The Piano Lesson,* that are among the least ornate, most vibrant, freest, and most solidly constructed of all his works.

The pictures that he executed after the first world war, on the other hand, did tend to be less adventurous. He was working at this period on the Côte d'Azur, and his chief desire seems to have been to pass on the enjoyment of life that he experienced there. In the '20s his space and form became less novel, while his colour grew very attractive. Odalisques now formed his favourite subject-matter, not only because he liked recalling the visits he made to Morocco in about 1912, during his travels, but because they provided a theme that tempted him to draw even closer to the Persian miniaturists he had long admired.

At all events, 'When one's means (of communication) become so refined and so subtle that they are drained of their expressive power,'

274

FAUVISM

he declared in 1936, 'one has to go back to the principles that have created human language. It is the principles that then revive, return to life, and give life to us.' When he made this pronouncement, he had, in fact, already been back for some time pursuing his daring investigations. From then onwards, a new Fauvism became apparent in his work, differing from the old in its maturity. In transcribing nature, Matisse thenceforward displayed as much boldness as before, but even more authority and fluency. Numerous drawings and patient study enabled him to get to know objects so well that he could enclose them in a single line without making them seem schematic. As for his colouring, it was no less vivid than before, but even more exceptional, more luminous and more opulent. He varied his harmonies inexhaustibly, and gave unflagging thought to what they could be made to express; for it was not the subject itself that mattered, but the composition of the picture, which transformed the subject.

For all its boldness, the art of Matisse never ceased to be harmonious, felicitous, balanced. He was as unaware of violently agitated forms as he was of violent mental agitation. No line or wrinkle puckering the features of his women reveals to the spectator that they have known anguish, suffering or merely worry. In general, these figures express not passiveness but emotional peace and a sublime spiritual tranquillity that borders on serenity and defies definition. Consequently, their role in the pictures is hardly different from that of flowers and fruit, as Matisse never aimed to disturb or to upset. He wanted to charm his spectators (and 'charm' is here used with the full force of its original meaning), ravish them, carry them away to a world of his own creation; its felicity is his triumph, and in it one's soul gains new strength, as in the most richly flowered and headily scented garden.

MATISSE. ASIA, 1946. TOM MAY COLLECTION, BEVERLY HILLS

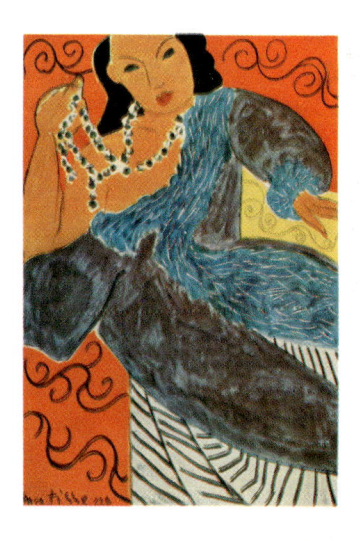

MATISSE. PINK NUDE, 1935. MUSEUM OF ART, BALTIMORE

MATISSE. PLUM-TREE BRANCH ON GREEN BACKGROUND, 1948. A. D. LASKER COLLECTION, NEW YORK

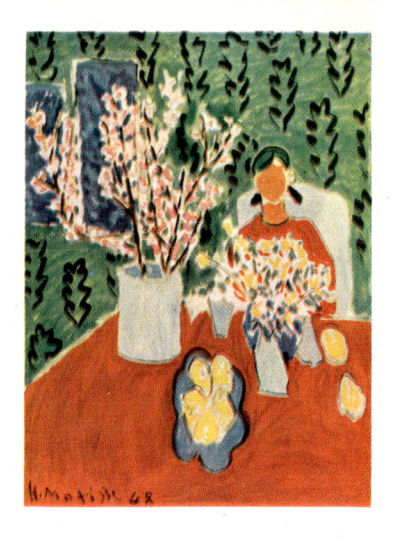

FAUVISM

RAOUL DUFY.
1877-1953.
SAIL-BOAT
AT SAINTE-
ADRESSE,
1912.
MUSEUM OF MODERN
ART, NEW YORK

DUFY.
HOMAGE TO MOZART
(WATERCOLOUR),
1915.
ALBRIGHT ART
GALLERY, BUFFALO

DUFY.
PORTRAIT OF
MICHEL BIGNOU,
1934.
MICHEL BIGNOU
COLLECTION, PARIS

Raoul Dufy was steered towards Fauvism by a Matisse composition, *Luxe, Calme et Volupté*, which he had seen at the Salon des Indépendants of 1905. 'In front of this picture,' he later disclosed, 'I understood all the new reasons for painting; Impressionist realism lost its charm for me as I gazed at this miraculous introduction of imagination into drawing and colour.' Nevertheless, in 1908 he was among the artists who deserted the Fauve movement, and, working in the company of Braque at l'Estaque, he developed a style that was characterized by stony, geometrical forms and a palette limited almost entirely to ochres, greens and blues. Such severity and asceticism were little suited to his vivacious character, however, and so he gradually reverted to brighter colouring, while his drawing became lighter and more supple. The result was that, round about 1920, he began to develop the witty style by means of which he asserted, and from then on maintained, his artistic originality. As he loved all sights and spectacles that make one feel how good it is to be alive, Dufy painted Nice, with the dazzling sea beside her and sky above her; he captured the feverish excitement and vitality of racecourses and regattas, the solemn atmosphere of concert halls, and the stretching of the soul which is produced by music. Sometimes he gained his inspiration from man's labours, too, as when he depicted his own studio, harvest-time, and threshing; in other words, he took as his subject-matter the moments when life is exalted by the joy of creation or by the happiness that summer brings. 'Yet do what I may,' he once said, 'I only give you a fraction of my inward joy.' No one has ever infused more jubilation into the blue of the sky, more pleasure into the blue of the sea, or more dewy and fragrant freshness into the green of a meadow. To the hues that he derived from nature, Dufy imparted an intonation that he alone could produce.

FAUVISM

Fantasy was never absent from his art; it led him, without any appearance of affectation, to make the greenish blue of the sea overflow into the sky, and to paint a horse with a blue body and a brown neck and withers. It is as though he was too fond of things not to add the charms that man's poetic imagination could bestow.

A picture by Dufy is first and foremost a juxtaposition of areas of colour. Objects make their appearance in it through the mediation of his extremely agile drawing, which seems to seize objects on the wing, and which, instead of describing things, evokes them. Moreover, the lines are superimposed on the patches of colour without regard for the edges of these patches, so that line and colour remain independent of each other. Objects appear to have been caught, quivering, at a moment when they are still seeking their final form. Their size does not necessarily correspond to reality, for Dufy did not construct space in the light of what he saw, but of what he felt. When representing things, he gave them the dimensions and the weight that they had in his mind.

Towards the end of his life, he began to simplify his painting style by giving up contrasts and spreading a single bright colour over almost the entire canvas, which he brought to life by inscribing it with objects or ornaments briskly expressed in line. Far from impoverishing his works, this economy of means is as effective as the purest brilliance. On the other hand, it was then that Dufy became interested in black, which he used to fill broad areas in the middle of some of his canvases. He may have endowed it with symbolic value, flooding a bull-ring with it in order to suggest the presence of death. A more probable explanation, however, is that he used black to indicate the blinding glare of intense light; for he also introduced it into completely undramatic views of ports and harbours, in which it is surrounded by joyous colours.

DUFY. REGATTA AT DEAUVILLE. PIERRE LÉVY COLLECTION, TROYES

DUFY. ASCOT (WATERCOLOUR), 1931. DR ROUDINESCO COLLECTION, PARIS

DUFY. MOZART CONCERTO, 1948. PRIVATE COLLECTION, SWITZERLAND

DUFY. THE BLACK CARGO, 1952. PRIVATE COLLECTION, PARIS

THE REACTION AGAINST FAUVISM

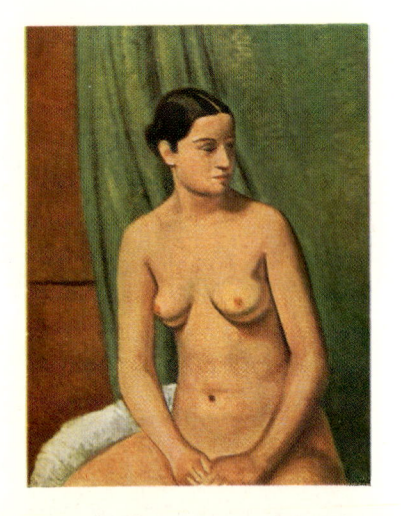

ANDRÉ DERAIN.
1880-1954.
NUDE WITH
GREEN CURTAIN,
1923.
MUSÉE D'ART
MODERNE, PARIS

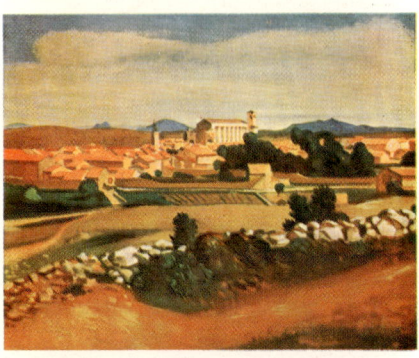

DERAIN.
VIEW OF
SAINT-MAXIMIN,
1930.
MUSÉE D'ART
MODERNE, PARIS

DERAIN.
THE CUP OF TEA,
1935.
MUSÉE D'ART
MODERNE, PARIS

In 1902, André Derain wrote: 'Doctrines appear to counsel us to belong to our times; but that's not simple, and, in my uncertainty, I intend to belong instead to all times.' Though, later on, there were occasions when he forgot these words, the idea behind them never entirely lost its hold on him. After the Fauve experiment he continued for several years to advance with the *avant-garde*. In 1908, he painted nudes and landscapes with hard, massive volumes, not far removed from those of Braque and Picasso at the same period; and shortly afterwards he, too, turned to still-life. However, despite his friendship with Picasso, he was wary of following him, because at heart he wanted only to take Cézanne's advice to express nature in terms of the cylinder, sphere, and cone.

Besides, he did not continue in this style for long. Increasingly, he seemed to believe that the only way 'to belong to all times' was by relating his own work to the 'timeless' art of the museums. Not without affectation, he began to elongate his bodies and faces in a way that gave them a Gothic look. The fact that he turned to the Middle Ages no doubt shows that he was still aware of the preoccupations of his period, since other artists were trying — or would try — to regenerate painting by relating it to non-classical art. Had he advanced further in this direction, he would at least have shown an urge to produce something new.

After 1918, however, all his work was done in reaction against the bold experiments of his contemporaries, and he took as his models only artists in the realist tradition: Raphael, Poussin, the Bolognese school, seventeenth-century Dutch painters, Corot, Renoir, and the artists of Pompeii. He translated what he learned from them into a style that differed from theirs in possessing a certain offhandedness and some deliberately clumsy features, owing to his desire not to seem adroit. His is the art of a virtuoso, and underlying

278

THE REACTION AGAINST FAUVISM

it one is aware of lofty ambitions, a restlessness, and a dissatisfaction that compel respect; but also of a lack of faith and the absence of the passion that, in art, can never be replaced by culture.

Until about 1914, Vlaminck, too, kept in step with the other disciples of Cézanne. The artist who had declared that Van Gogh meant more to him than his own father, now consented to discipline himself, accentuate depth, make his forms geometrical, and emphasize the structure of his compositions by means of outlines. He also softened and darkened his palette, so that, instead of incandescent colouring, one finds him using cooler greens, greys, and blues.

After the first world war, he again gave way to his feelings. Once more he hurled shrill whites, muddy browns, and greyish or blackish blues on to his canvases, contrasting them in one passage with a few slashes of red, in another with a confused medley of sulphurous yellows. As for his drawing, it became choleric, while his brushwork grew more impetuous than ever. The emphatic contrast between light and shade produced effects in his landscapes intended to be moving but now and again merely theatrical. Nevertheless, when he has not given too free reign to his violent instincts, he can affect us through his rugged atmosphere and dramatic feeling for life.

As already mentioned, Marquet's palette was never very bright (see pages 272, 273), and, after 1908, he remained by and large what he had been before. He was basically a landscape artist, but with the difference that, instead of setting up his easel before a view of nature from which man was absent, he preferred to do so in towns and, above all, on the waterfront. With his delicate perception of tone values and liking for outdoor subjects, he never really lost contact with Impressionism. Yet the way he emphasized the structure of his works with long but succinct lines is a distinctly post-Impressionist feature.

DERAIN. STILL-LIFE. PIERRE LÉVY COLLECTION, TROYES

MAURICE DE VLAMINCK. 1876-1958. SNOWY LANDSCAPE. DR ROUDINESCO COLLECTION, PARIS

VLAMINCK. WINTER LANDSCAPE. DR ROUDINESCO COLLECTION, PARIS

KEES VAN DONGEN. BORN 1877. VERSAILLES. MME WAUTERS COLLECTION, BRUSSELS

279

CUBISM

GEORGES BRAQUE.
BORN 1882.
HOUSES IN
L'ESTAQUE,
1908.
H. RUPF
COLLECTION,
BERNE

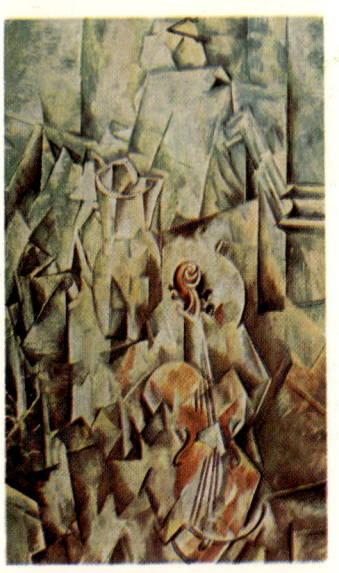

BRAQUE.
VIOLIN
AND JUG,
1909-1910.
LA ROCHE
COLLECTION,
KUNSTMUSEUM,
BASLE

BRAQUE.
THE MUSICIAN'S
TABLE,
1913.
KUNSTMUSEUM,
BASLE

One always runs the risk of mistaking the significance of an art movement, if one lays too much stress on its name. After Louis Vauxcelles had written in 1908: 'M. Braque . . . reduced everything—scenery, houses, and figures—to geometric diagrams, to cubes,' it was no doubt natural to talk of 'Cubism'. All the same, the Cubists—which means, first and foremost, Braque and Picasso —were not content just to make form geometrical; prompted by Cézanne and primitive art, they also analysed it, took it to pieces and then recreated it. In short, they brought about a real revolution. All the conventions of visual realism, such as modelling, the perspective introduced by the Renaissance, and naturalistic distribution of light, were repudiated by them in the most uncompromising manner. This they did because, far from meaning to turn their back on objects, they wanted to study them from close to, and aimed at a more complete representation of them than traditional realism made possible. The conventional method of adopting a single view-point had, in effect, condemned artists to depicting things only as a motionless spectator sees them. Now, the Cubists were fully aware of the fact that modern man tends increasingly to move about at speed, so that he gets a complex idea of things. To express this complexity they came to juxtapose different facets of the same object, combining in a single image what the eye only sees successively.

But the Cubists were not merely concerned with presenting a new realism. They had just as much pleasures in varying natural appearances—even ignoring them and replacing them with forms of their own invention. So it is not surprising that, from then on, their favourite subject was a still-life composed of a group of more or less insignificant objects, like a bottle, a glass, a pipe, a newspaper, a violin, and a guitar. However, the Cubists did also represent the human form, although they remain-

280

CUBISM

ed completely indifferent to all psychological considerations. Having taken it to pieces, joint by joint, and put it together again to look a bit like Negro sculpture (which had just been 'discovered' in Europe), they began, in 1909, to turn the human body into an assemblage of polyhedrals, concave and convex volumes, facets, and angles of intersection. A little later, they broke it up into still smaller pieces, and flattened it out so much that, merging here and there into the background, it became hardly recognisable.

During the same period, it was the turn of objects to break, crumble, and finally to disintegrate. In other words, Braque and Picasso had arrived at the frontier of abstract art; but instead of crossing it, they set about 'reviving' objects by breaking them up less and defining them more clearly.

In about 1912, they introduced printed lettering into their works to form words like *Bal, le Torero,* and *Ma Jolie;* their general effect was decorative but, in a way, evocative of reality, too. Besides this, they invented the *papier collé*, which consisted of bits of newspaper, wallpaper, and wrapping paper stuck, just as they were, on to a support; to characterize an object, the artists would add a few lines or passages of colour. Transmuted reality thus became contiguous with crude, commonplace reality, and now at last the latter, too, was transformed; not only did it acquire pictorial value, but it also took on a poetic quality. Moreover, *papiers collés* helped Braque and Picasso to pass from the analytical to the synthetic phase of Cubism, leading them to produce an impression of space with the aid of only the most elementary means. Finally, it enabled them to rediscover colour. Since the two artists were principally concerned with the problem of form, they in fact developed an extremely ascetic palette, usually limiting themselves to delicately gradated ranges of greys, ochres, and browns shown in a non-naturalistic light.

PABLO RUIZ PICASSO. BORN 1881. THE RESERVOIR OF HORTA DE EBRO, 1909. PRIVATE COLLECTION, PARIS

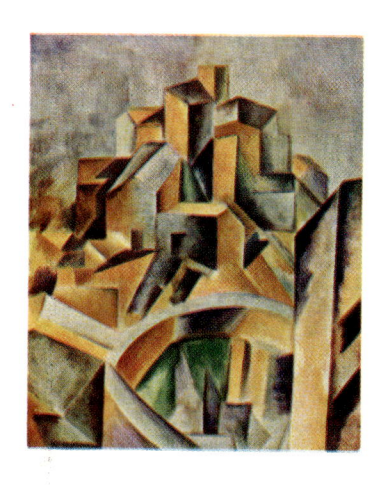

PICASSO. PORTRAIT OF AMBROISE VOLLARD, 1910. MUSEUM OF MODERN ART, MOSCOW

PICASSO. STILL LIFE WITH CANE CHAIR, 1911-1912. ARTIST'S COLLECTION, PARIS

281

CUBISM

JUAN GRIS.
1887-1927.
STILL-LIFE,
1912.
RIJKSMUSEUM
KRÖLLER-MÜLLER,
OTTERLO

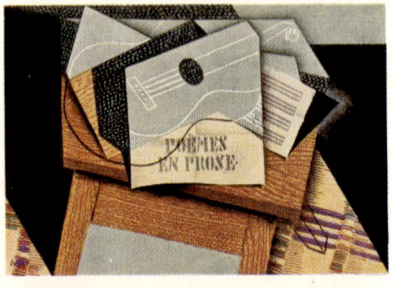

JUAN GRIS,
POEMS
IN PROSE,
1915.
PRIVATE
COLLECTION,
PARIS

JUAN GRIS.
STILL-LIFE,
1921.
HOFFMANN-
STIFTUNG,
KUNSTMUSEUM,
BASLE

Even though Braque and Picasso were the creators of Cubism and illustrate its different phases most logically and with the greatest authority, they were not its only champions. Cubism was a vast movement, which attracted sculptors as well as painters, and affected the development of architecture, the poster, typography, scenic design, and the cinema; its influence was felt in every sphere.

A point of interest is that whereas the fire of Fauvism burned itself out in three years, Cubism had lost none of its vitality when, in 1914, the first world war put an end to it as a movement. And it left a deep impression on its adherents. Naturally enough, they evolved; but whatever the ultimate development of their art may have been, they never renounced the new, 'modern' outlook, which Cubism had done so much to establish.

Among the artists whose advance entailed following in the footsteps of Braque and Picasso, Juan Gris and Louis Marcoussis left behind them the most notable works. Despite the fact that he was a Spaniard, like Picasso, and that the two painters came to be on friendly terms, Gris was fundamentally very different from his compatriot. He was as deliberate, as devoted to method and its strict application, as Picasso was adventurous. Having made Paris his home since 1906, Gris witnessed the birth of Cubism in close-up, but he did not join the movement until 1911, and always refused to analyse objects to the point of abolishing them altogether. Although, in the pictures that he executed between 1915 and 1920, he geometrized his form so resolutely that it became almost diagramatical, it is not to be mistaken for the product of chilly stylization. Moreover, his colouring, which was both sonorous and sensitive, counteracted any danger of his construction growing too severe. 'I try to make concrete what is abstract,' he said. 'Cézanne made a cylinder out of a bottle; I . . . make a bottle out of a cylinder.'

CUBISM

Or: 'I begin by organizing my picture, then I characterize the objects.' He defined objects more precisely after 1920. From then onwards, his line exactly enclosed the different patches of colour, whereas previously it had been inclined to proceed rather independently. Besides this, his general approach became less lordly, and, through the effect of the disease that was undermining his health, it seemed in places to betray, if not irresolution, at least a little weariness. By way of compensation, the artist's colour grew more velvety, and increased the warmth of its muted harmonies.

Delicate sensibility, a subtle and captivating poetic quality, and a tendency to divest Cubism of everything brusque and haughty — these are the characteristics of the Polish-born artist Louis Marcoussis, who began to be attracted by Braque's work in 1910. It could be said of him that he brought a smile to the stern face of Cubism; but, in any case, nobody spoke the new language more pleasantly than he or gave it a more direct power of attraction. Whether straight or undulating, his lines are generally light and supple; while his colouring, which was sober at first, grew more rich and vivid after 1918, but never ceased to be delicately concordant. It became particularly vibrant in his glass-painting, where its soft radiance is enhanced by the medium, and its harmonies are at times so refined that they border on preciosity.

Though, in 1912, Albert Gleizes and Jean Metzinger produced the first book devoted to the new aesthetic doctrine, *Du Cubisme,* they were not really among the leaders. If they geometricised objects, if here and there they put a hollow instead of a bulge, it visibly cost them something to drive away the memory of the real form from their minds. Even Gleizes, who pushed his researches farthest, only escaped stylization with difficulty. By and large, they did not go beyond the point reached by Picasso and Braque in 1908.

JUAN GRIS.
WOMAN,
1926.
GALERIE
LOUISE LEIRIS,
PARIS

LOUIS MARCOUSSIS.
1883-1941.
TWO POETS,
1929.
REDFERN GALLERY,
LONDON

ALBERT GLEIZES.
1881-1953.
WOMAN AT
THE PIANO.
ARENSBERG
COLLECTION,
MUSEUM OF ART,
PHILADELPHIA

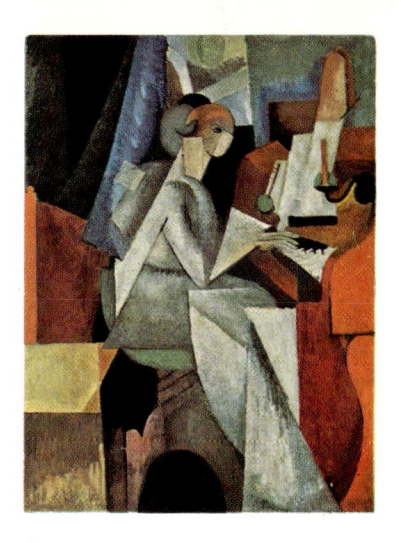

CUBISM

ROBERT DELAUNAY.
1885-1941.
THE WINDOWS,
1911.
JEAN CASSOU
COLLECTION,
PARIS

FERNAND LÉGER.
1881-1955.
CONTRAST IN
FORMS,
1913.
H. RUPF
COLLECTION,
BERNE

JACQUES VILLON,
BORN 1875.
SOLDIERS
MARCHING,
1913.
PRIVATE
COLLECTION,
PARIS

Robert Delaunay and Fernand Léger represent a completely different aspect of Cubism. Not only did they deviate from Braque and Picasso, but, on fundamental issues, they were categorically opposed to them; yet their originality and creative powers are just as unmistakable as their rivals'.

Like Braque and Picasso, they most certainly acknowledged a debt to Cézanne. Like them, too, they put everything they had into producing a new transcription of form; but even though they broke it up and reconstructed it, they refrained from smashing it to smithereens. On the other hand —and this is even more important —they were unwilling to make use only of subdued colours. Delaunay, who sought his natural style with the help of Neo-Impressionism and, no doubt, Fauvism too, always displayed his love for the colours of the spectrum. From 1912 onwards, Léger, too, showed himself to be extremely fond of pure, bright hues. However, each of them was a colourist in his own special way. Whereas for Delaunay, the different hues formed the elements of a melodiously developing song, in Léger's art each one of them asserts its own individual quality, while the combinations are harsher.

Another feature distinguishing both these painters from the other Cubists is the fact that their favourite art-form was not still-life. Over and over again Delaunay depicted the interior of the church of St Séverin. More often still, he was inspired by the Eiffel Tower (page 292), which, according to Blaise Cendrars, 'he took to pieces in order to get it into his frame; he also truncated and tilted it so as to give it its 300 metres of dizziness'. Léger's subjects, on the other hand, include *The Roofs of Paris, July 14th, Woman in Blue,* and *The Wedding* (Paris, Musée d'Art Moderne), and his vision was still more revolutionary than Delaunay's; or, at any rate, it was even more anti-Impressionist. Most of the forms that he invented are really based

CUBISM

less on things observed than on geometry. Hence, in 1913, his *Contrast in Forms,* which consists mainly of truncated cones, pyramids, and cylinders. For, at this period, it was chiefly volume that interested him, and, without recourse to orthodox modelling, he suggested it by means only of line and two bands of colour separated by a strip of white.

A little earlier, Delaunay had already made some excursions into abstract painting, towards which, moreover, he had been advancing since 1911. In his *Simultaneous Windows* pictures, which are to be counted among the most vibrant works of his times, he subordinated everything to colour, which, he said, became 'form and subject'. The different hues are subtly gradated, and flare up energetically to evoke the fervent exaltation of light that seems to shift and change its form before our very eyes.

Movement, which played a part in other works by Delaunay, also absorbed Jacques Villon and his brother Marcel Duchamp. By means of a play of straight lines and acute angles, Villon translated the swift, staccato pace of a group of soldiers on the march; while his brother made use of a combination of gently oscillating straight and curved lines in order to juxtapose the successive phases of the movement of a *Nude Figure descending a staircase* (Philadelphia Museum).

Roger de la Fresnaye and André Lhote saw Cubism chiefly as a recall to order and as a means of giving a picture solidity and stability. While they, like their associates, appealed to Cézanne's authority, they also consulted Seurat (who, it must be added, influenced other Cubists as well); it follows that they liked clear forms lucidly interrelated. They enclosed objects in simplified contours, which, while defining them, bring out their strictly pictorial qualities. In the last analysis, both these artists remained fairly close to the appearances of the external world; and they aimed not so much to subvert tradition, as to rejuvenate it.

ROGER DE LA FRESNAYE. 1885-1925. STILL LIFE, 1913. A. L. COLLECTION, PARIS

LA FRESNAYE. CONQUEST OF THE AIR, 1913. MUSEUM OF MODERN ART, NEW YORK

ANDRÉ LHOTE, BORN 1885. RUGBY, 1917. MUSÉE D'ART MODERNE, PARIS

CUBISM

PABLO PICASSO.
BORN 1881.
WOMAN WITH
A FAN,
1905.
MRS AVERELL
HARRIMAN
COLLECTION,
NEW YORK

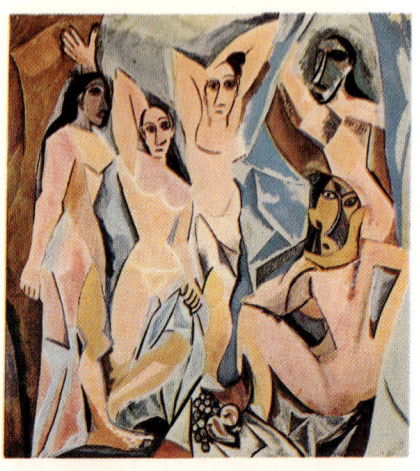

PICASSO.
LES DEMOISELLES
D'AVIGNON,
1907.
MUSEUM OF
MODERN ART,
NEW YORK

PICASSO.
THE THREE
MUSICIANS,
1921.
MUSEUM OF
MODERN ART,
NEW YORK

When, in 1900, Pablo Picasso left Spain to pay his first visit to Paris, his mind was far from Cubism; for, at that period, he had only just begun to free himself, under the guidance of Lautrec, from the Academic style. A year later, his personality was more firmly established, and, with the aid of a palette dominated by a cool blue, he painted anaemic young women, puny children, and thin, tremulous old men. This Blue Period was followed in 1906 by a Pink Period; but though the colouring is a little warmer, and though the harlequins, strolling entertainers, and acrobats who people the new pictures appear to suffer less than the earlier figures, they still have a serious, anxious look.

In 1906, Picasso gave up the softness and sentimentality that had been characteristic of his art up to then; his line grew taut, and his form underwent a somewhat crude simplification. In short, he was moving towards Cubism. Before long, he painted *Les Demoiselles d'Avignon*—and the die was cast. For ten years he remained a reckless and uncompromising Cubist; then, in 1917, he appears to have returned to the realist tradition, for he began producing portraits that recall those of Ingres. But he still did work in the Cubist spirit, with the result that the summer of 1921 saw him depicting his *Three Women at a Spring* in a Greco-Roman style, and creating *The Three Musicians* in a manner entirely of his own invention.

Later on, when he had again given up borrowing from the realist tradition, his art began to appear in a variety of most contradictory and unexpected styles. But far from being evidence of a lack of individuality, these sudden changes simply demonstrate the inexhaustible fertility and endless youthful vigour of his genius. They also reveal his need always to express himself with complete freedom. Picasso demands the right to play, even at the cost of irritating us, just as he demands the right to shake us to the depths of our soul.

CUBISM

In 1937, the Spanish civil war produced a new atmosphere in his art. Thenceforward, no longer content to attend only to problems that affected him as an artist and an individual, he became equally concerned about the fate of a people and their country. Thus, to proclaim his horror at the bombing of the little Basque town of Guernica by the German air-force on behalf of Franco, he painted one of the most poignant compositions ever inspired by war. Other works, too, owe their origin to the same event, particularly the *Weeping Woman,* with its mournful colouring and bitter, harrowing design. Picasso also took sides actively in the second world war; for it was not just due to chance or a taste for aggressive exaggeration that, at this period, he produced his series of seated women with monstrously but pitifully deformed faces. These figures give a shattering account of the anguish and torment of those years.

Thus, Picasso's painting does not belong to an ivory tower or a laboratory; on the contrary, it is a 'committed' art, intimately bound up with the life of the artist, and expressing his joys, affections, disappointments, rages, and revolts. Since about 1928, Picasso has shown himself to be at heart an Expressionist, but one who, from Cubism onwards, has succeeded in devising a far more revolutionary language, and one with far greater impact, than that of Expressionism properly so called. It is a harsh and authoritarian, often a rough and abrupt language, in which form has even more importance than colour. It shows a great urge to dominate. In fact, whatever arouses Picasso's interest—whether it is a human being, an object, or the work of another artist—he has to transform. And it is not enough for him to stamp it with the seal of his own sensibility; he has to make it into something that belongs to him alone, and that bears witness to his power, his disrespect, and unquenchable thirst for the unknown.

PICASSO.
WEEPING
WOMAN,
1937.
ROLAND PENROSE
COLLECTION,
LONDON

PICASSO.
COCK AND
KNIFE,
1947.
V. W. GANZ
COLLECTION,
NEW YORK

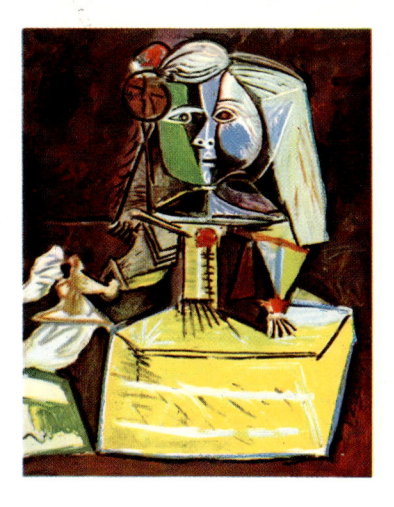

PICASSO.
LAS MENINAS,
1957.
ARTIST'S
COLLECTION,
PARIS

CUBISM

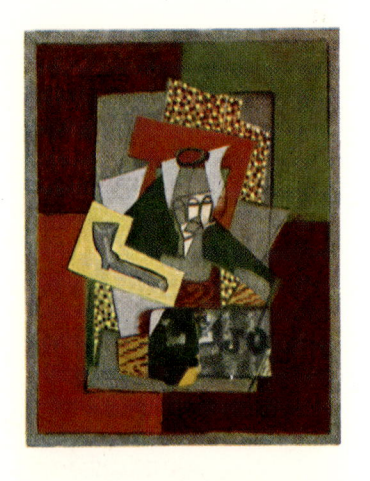

GEORGES BRAQUE.
BORN 1882.
GLASS AND PIPE,
1917.
ERIC ESTORICK
COLLECTION,
LONDON

BRAQUE.
THE TABLE,
1928.
PHILLIPS
COLLECTION,
WASHINGTON

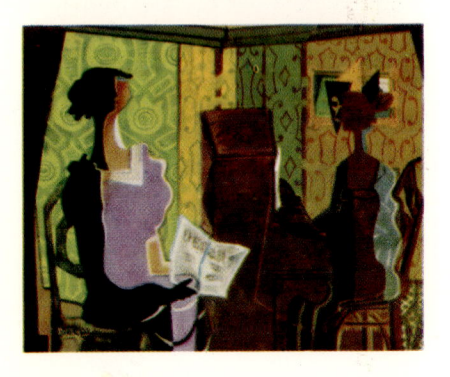

BRAQUE.
THE DUET,
1937.
MUSÉE D'ART
MODERNE, PARIS

During the whole of the Cubist period, Braque and Picasso were very close to each other; they advanced side by side, posed the same problems, and provided identical solutions. Then the first world war separated them; and thereafter they each followed their own distinct line of evolution, revealing more clearly than before what distinguished them at the core of their being. While Picasso tended continually to extend the limits of freedom, Georges Braque declared his love for 'the rule that corrects the emotion'. There was nothing anarchic in his spirit, and nothing hurried in his step. Yet, although he advanced slowly and cautiously, he was far from being irresolute, and from the moment that he chose the road of Cubism, he never retraced his steps. Thus, throughout his whole career, he has been applying one of the most revolutionary principles of the new aesthetics: 'inverted perspective'. This means that, in the artist's works, objects are disposed vertically rather than into depth, and that, instead of receding from the eye, they glise towards it.

However, after 1918, Braque's style changed, becoming less austere, and more sensual and fleshy. Not only did objects cease to be broken up into small pieces, but they also lost some of their geometric regularity. At the same time, they became thicker, and seemed to bear a closer relation to certain features of their prototypes in the material world. All the same, as —according to Braque himself— the artist does not try to reconstitute an incident, but to constitute a (new) pictorial fact, objects continued to be wholly incorporated into the scheme and atmosphere of the picture. If the scheme and atmosphere required it, they became distorted and changed their colour, as though they were obligingly submitting to the artist's will. Actually, there is nothing tyrannical about the line that defines them; on the contrary, it embraces them rather gently and dreamily. If the curves of a guitar

288

CUBISM

become less exact, if they stretch out and change into triangles, it appears to be the object itself that is urging them to free themselves, so that they may find a more striking form than the one they possess in the real world.

Likewise, the non-naturalistic colouring seems to enable things to reveal hidden virtues and secret yearnings; or, at any rate, with its beiges, browns, greens, blues, and blacks, it brings out everything that is calm, meditative, and poetic in the life of simple objects. Besides, it is not only the colour harmonies that act in this way. The paint itself also emphasizes the contemplative character of this art.

Braque, whose sensitivity relates him to Chardin and Corot, is essentially an Intimist. It is true that he has also produced some landscapes; but, as a rule, he paints still-lifes and figure compositions. Among the latter, those that he executed round about 1937 are marked out by charms of a special order. For each figure embodies two different beings: from the front, it tenders the prettily plump face of a modern young woman; while, in profile, it presents the delicate features, standing out in black like a shadow, of a head with a general look of gracefulness and intelligence. These aristocratic silhouettes are reminiscent of the figures on Greek vases of the Archaic period. Yet one would never dream of describing them as pastiches; for Braque never ceases to be himself and belong to this age.

About ten years ago, the painter began to flatten out objects again, to choose his colours with even greater freedom, and, above all, to present more complex impressions of space. Particularly in his *Studio* paintings, flat, horizontal surfaces and a sense of depth continually assert themselves and contradict each other. He repeatedly inscribed these canvases with the figure of a great bird in flight. This bird reappears in other, more recent works by the artist, filling them with its light, supple, majestic movement.

BRAQUE.
FLOWERS AND
PALETTE,
1941.
PRIVATE
COLLECTION,
ITALY

BRAQUE.
WASHSTAND
BY A
WINDOW,
1943.
PRIVATE
COLLECTION

BRAQUE.
L'ÉCHO,
1956.
AIMÉ MAEGHT
COLLECTION,
PARIS

CUBISM

FERNAND LÉGER.
1881-1955.
COMPOSITION,
1918.
PRIVATE
COLLECTION,
PARIS

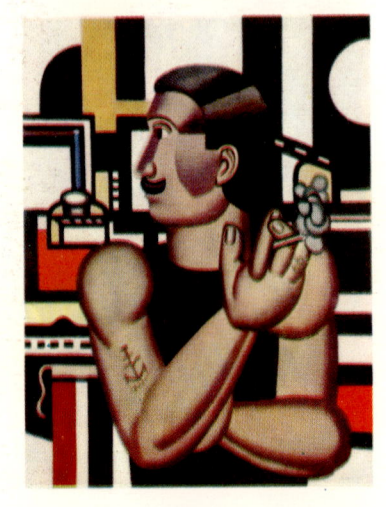

LÉGER.
THE MECHANIC,
1920.
GALERIE LOUIS
CARRÉ, PARIS

LÉGER.
LA DANSEUSE
AUX CLÉS,
1930.
MUSÉE D'ART
MODERNE, PARIS

Generally speaking, the first world war is not reflected at all in the work of the Cubists, whether they were called up or not. For example, when Braque was able to return to painting, he took up his researches where he had left off on becoming a soldier, despite his wound and consequent trepanning operation.

Fernand Léger, however, admitted that, for him, the war had been a tremendous event, which had brought him down from the clouds. For, firstly, he had made contact with a new section of humanity: 'miners, navvies, iron- and wood-workers.' Secondly, he had been constantly in the presence of guns, which he saw less as instruments of destruction than as formidable machines with precise and powerful mechanisms. To be sure, even before the war, modern engineering had impressed him, and he had painted human figures like robots with limbs that appear to be slightly out of joint. From 1917 onwards, however, he stressed the 'mechanical' character of his art. The 'plasticity' of the machine and its products filled him with such wonder that for years he turned every figure and object into something metallic, apparently mass-produced in a factory. At this period, his drawing and colour became completely clear; all signs of his brush-strokes, which up to then had been visible, were erased; his handling became impersonal; his paint grew thin and meagre.

Thus, while most artists of his generation ignored or inveighed against our industrial civilization, Léger felt completely at home in it. He admired its vitality, its inexhaustible power of invention, and its continual urge to construct. To give an account of all that aroused his enthusiasm, he did not hesitate to make himself hard and 'inhuman', banishing from his art every trace of sentimentality and romanticism, as well as all psychological interest. Nothing could be more lacking in 'expression' than Léger's figures; and yet somehow they seem more than just sturdy

CUBISM

aluminium dummies. With their strictly spherical heads, impassive faces, and massive bodies, some of his female figures from the 'twenties remind one of goddesses.

The forms of the divers, cyclists, and circus folk whom he depicted later on are less regular and more supple, but just as vigorous. This applies equally to objects, among which forms that had come out of a factory gave way more and more to those borrowed from nature. It is also true that Léger was inclined to juxtapose both types, just as he liked to present side by side a bunch of keys and a girl dancer, pincers and a cigar-box, or a vase of flowers and logs, thus giving each amazing eloquence.

To his contrasted objects, Léger added contrasts of form and colour. Since he loathed the least suspicion of prettification, and liked to make nothing but the frankest artistic statements, he only allowed relationships that were strained to the utmost limits to appear on his canvases. His expressive power derives not just from the firmness of his drawing and the brilliance of his colour, but also from the fact that, in his work, all opposing elements are reconciled and united by the way they emphasize and enhance one another. In 1942, Léger began superimposing abstract colour schemes on representational drawings, with the result that, by being developed on two levels, such works move the spectator in two different ways. However, these colours were neither picked out at random or arbitrarily arranged. It is surely clear that in *The Grand Parade,* for example, they express the brassy music of the circus, while at the same time, through their disposition, suggesting feats of horsemanship and swinging on the trapeze.

But Léger's art is not just a demonstration of his principles; and however deliberate his approach may have been, there was absolutely nothing highbrow about him. In his work intellect never predominates over temperament and instinct.

LÉGER.
WOMAN BATHING,
1931.
GALERIE LOUIS
CARRÉ, PARIS

LÉGER.
BUTTERFLIES AND
FLOWERS,
1937.
GALERIE LOUIS
CARRÉ, PARIS

LÉGER.
FOUR CYCLISTS,
1943-1948.
MME LÉGER
COLLECTION,
PARIS

LÉGER.
THE GRAND PARADE,
1954.
GALERIE MAEGHT,
PARIS

CUBISM

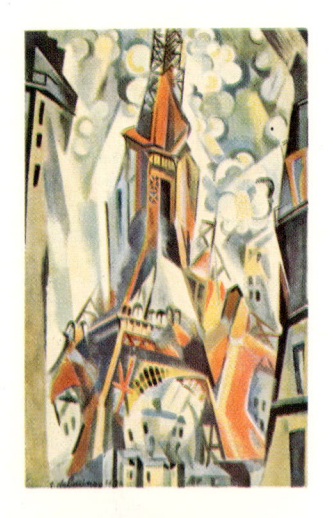

ROBERT DELAUNAY,
1885-1941.
EIFFEL TOWER,
1910-1911.
KUNSTMUSEUM,
BASLE

DELAUNAY.
SIMULTANEOUS DISC,
1912.
MRS BURTON
TREMAINE
COLLECTION, USA

DELAUNAY.
RUNNERS,
1926.
MME DELAUNAY
COLLECTION,
PARIS

Like Léger's art, that of Robert Delaunay radiates health and optimism. In it, the reds, yellows and oranges seem to pass on their glee even to the greens and blues. Delaunay's pictures are usually animated by a gyrating, upward movement, strongly apparent not only in his abstract *Circular Forms* series, dating from 1912-1913, or in his *Homage to Blériot* of 1914 (Grenoble, Museum), but even in the nudes and still-lifes that he executed in Spain and Portugal during the first world war. Nevertheless, however vigorous his impulse, it never got out of control.

As we have seen, the Cubists were all looking for a new pictorial language. For Delaunay, nothing was more expressive or constructive than colour. Through the distribution of the various hues and the play of what, following Michel-Eugène Chevreul, he described as 'simultaneous contrasts', he aimed to make it possible for colour alone to be the constructive element in a picture, to create the forms, suggest space and movement, and, in a word, express the dynamic aspect of the modern world.

However, as he was anxious to discover and apply what he called 'the laws governing colour', Delaunay did not always avoid giving his pictures the appearance of a practical demonstration, particularly after 1930. Broadly speaking, one has to admit that he created his most poetic works during the Cubist period. It is quite true that, later still, he was able to communicate his masculine high spirits in a striking way, especially in the large pictures inspired by football matches and running races. Likewise, the *Rhythms* series that he painted during the thirties are not without their merits, for, in them, this vigorous movement has been richly developed. They also possess the decorative and architectural qualities that the artist was then bent on introducing into his work. However, these pictures have a systematic quality that is not without coldness, and reduces their emotive power.

CUBISM

Jacques Villon excludes neither grey nor black from his palette, but, like Delaunay, he prefers to use the pure colours of the spectrum. No doubt this is a legacy from the Impressionists, because the artist also pays careful attention to the effects of light, and, particularly from 1939 onwards, he has shown himself to be responsive to open-air subjects. Nevertheless, he replaces the wonder of the fleeting moment with more enduring wonders, enriching what he perceives with what he invents. His participation in the Cubist movement was not in vain, since he has retained from it not only a habit of freely interpreting his observations of the external world, but also a liking for geometrical form, and a careful attention for precise grouping. However, even in the sometimes very inornate non-representational compositions that he produced in about 1920 and 1930-1932 *(Allégresse)*, there is nothing severe, dry or cold about his 'geometry'. Whether the lines are thin or broad, they are never heavy, and the general effect of his colour is thoroughly refined and pleasing.

The more Villon has advanced, the more subtle his palette has become, and the more unusual and flowery he has made his colour-combinations. Pinks, lilacs, yellows, purples and pale or intense violets are set beside ethereal blues and a whole range of vernal greens. Here and there he has added softly luminous whites and velvety blacks to produce harmonies whose novelty, faint but somewhat piquant acidity, and occasional subtle dissonance may seem surprising, but which never shock or betray the slightest crudity. The artist's painting style is one of the most exquisite that exist. In it, there is no noticeable disorder, division, or want of balance. Villon is a sorcerer who makes even the most daring invention look natural, because it takes its place as part of a whole in which everything is measured, weighed, and arranged with unerring precision.

JACQUES VILLON, BORN 1875. ALLÉGRESSE, 1932. LOUIS CARRÉ COLLECTION, PARIS

VILLON. VERS LA CHIMÈRE, 1947. PRIVATE COLLECTION, PARIS

VILLON. ICARUS, 1956. PRIVATE COLLECTION, PARIS

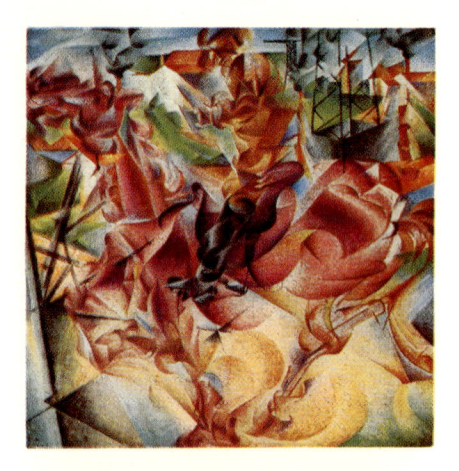

FUTURISM

UMBERTO BOCCIONI.
1882-1916.
ELASTICITY,
1912.
PRIVATE
COLLECTION,
MILAN

GINO SEVERINI.
BORN 1883.
DANCER,
1913.
ERIC ESTORICK
COLLECTION,
LONDON

GIACOMO BALLA.
BORN 1871.
DYNAMISM OF A
DOG ON A LEASH,
1912.
A. CONGER
GOODYEAR
COLLECTION,
NEW YORK

Although Futurism was a strictly Italian movement, its first manifesto was launched in 1909 at Paris. Composed by the poet Marinetti, it urged the destruction of 'the museums, those graveyards', proclaiming that 'a work of art must be aggressive' and that 'at all cost one must be original.' Further, it declared that 'a racing car is more beautiful than the *Victory of Samothrace*.' A year later, at Milan, appeared the 'Manifesto of the Futurist Painters', signed by Boccioni, Carrà, Russolo, Balla, and Severini. This, too, protested violently against the cult of the past, and asked: 'Can we remain indifferent to the frenzied activity of the cities, to the new mentality of the night-birds, the feverish figures of the playboy, the good-time girl, the tough and the drunk?' It is hardly surprising that Italian artists should have claimed so violently the right to belong to their own times. Indeed, their excesses and their challenging tone can readily be explained by the fact that their object was to rouse a society still completely hypnotized by a tradition that was certainly great, but whose principles could now produce only paralysis. To have sounded the reveille of a living art in Italy is probably the Futurists' one great merit, since—as artists themselves—they made fewer innovations than their manifestos might lead one to suppose. In their desire to express the 'frenzied activity of the cities', they naturally came to pay special attention to movement. Thus, Giacomo Balla, in his famous *Dynamism of a Dog on a Leash,* multiplied the creature's paws and indicated the different positions of its tail; while Umberto Boccioni, in his *Elasticity,* reconstructed the bodies of a horse and rider almost entirely out of curved planes and jerky lines. Both artists did, however, respect the essential form of nature, unlike Duchamp in his *Nude descending a Staircase,* or Villon in his *Soldiers on the March.* Gino Severini worked at Paris; his dancers manifest greater freedom, but their bodies

294

METAPHYSICAL PAINTING

are so broken up and the fragments so scattered that the eye often has difficulty in assembling them and in discerning their movement.

The zest of the Futurist pioneers did not survive the first world war, and their influence fell far short of that of the Cubists. All the same, it affected a few painters in France, as well as in Germany. That the Futurists were themselves influenced by Cubism is clearly shown by the fragmentation of their forms. Moreover, the colour and handling of some of their works reveal that they owed a debt to the Neo-Impressionists, too. Be this as it may, they still produced an atmosphere of their own; their works make one feel the opposing forces that struggle and clash noisily in a tumultuous world. In 1913, however, Balla turned to abstract painting, in which he suggested movement in a highly convincing way.

It is an odd fact that, during the very period when the Futurists were in revolt against the art of the past, another Italian painter, Giorgio de Chirico, was haunted by the presence of Antique statues in the world of today. In 1911 he settled in Paris, and, at a time when all other modern painters were disclaiming Renaissance perspective, saw a 'disturbing connexion between perspective and metaphysics.' But although Chirico used traditional means, his aim was not to present the spectator with reassuring images, but to bewilder him. The cardboard architecture, the squares, which make an impression of emptiness, even though they are peopled with stray statues and solemn dummies, the sharply outlined shadows—all have an enigmatic, obsessive quality, like certain dream landscapes. For a time, this style—known as 'metaphysical painting'—was also adopted by the former Futurist Carlo Carrà and the Bolognese artist Giorgio Morandi. Later it attracted the Surrealists, who considered Chirico one of their masters, whereas he himself was evolving an ever more literary, even Academic, style.

GIORGIO DE CHIRICO. BORN 1888. THE ENIGMA OF THE HOUR, 1911. GIANNI MATTIOLI COLLECTION, MILAN

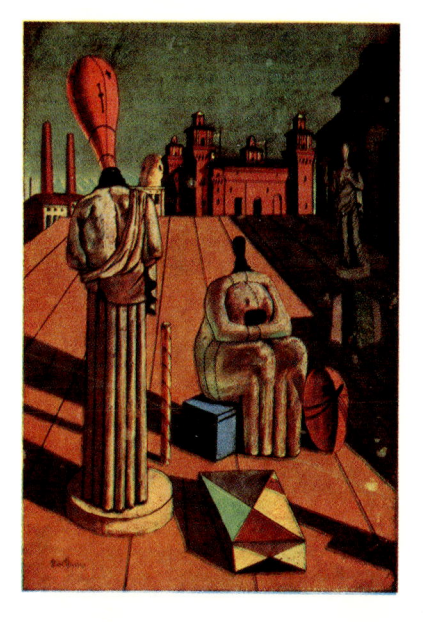

CHIRICO. THE DISQUIETING MUSES, 1917. GIANNI MATTIOLI COLLECTION, MILAN

GIORGIO MORANDI. BORN 1890. METAPHYSICAL STILL-LIFE, 1915. JUCKER COLLECTION, MILAN

EXPRESSIONISM

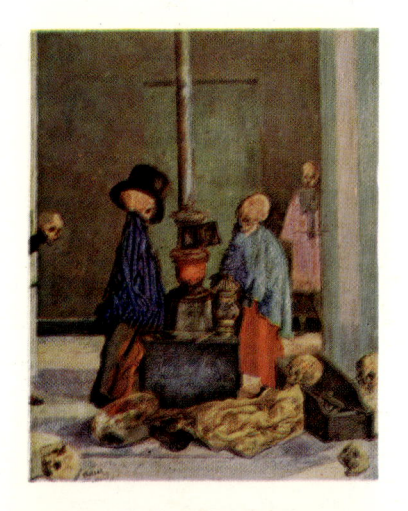

JAMES ENSOR,
1860-1947.
SKELETONS WARMING
THEMSELVES ROUND
A STOVE,
1889.
WINDFHOR
COLLECTION,
DALLAS

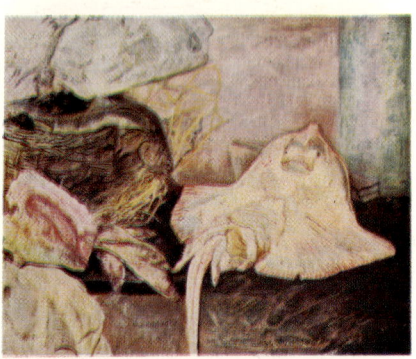

ENSOR.
THE SKATE,
1892.
MUSÉE D'ART
MODERNE,
BRUSSELS

ENSOR.
THE INTRIGUE
(MASKS),
DETAIL,
1890.
MUSÉE DES BEAUX-
ARTS, ANTWERP

The term 'Expressionism' comes from Germany, where it originally covered everything in modern art opposed to Realism and Impressionism. However, it is expedient to limit its meaning, although it is not an easy word to define precisely. One might, perhaps, say that, to the Expressionists, strictly formal problems counted for less than the urge to externalize their innermost feelings in a direct and striking manner. Broadly speaking, this is true; but one could name artists who, though they are certainly to be classed as Expressionists, were still concerned with the beauty of their vehicle of expression. Can it be said that they remained faithful to chiaroscuro, to modelling, and to the traditional way of treating space? In fact, they did make fewer innovations than the Fauves and Cubists, although they were not unaware of the contributions of these movements, and in many cases learned something from then. But however their styles may have differed in other respects, one thing that they all had in common was their maladjustment to life as it existed for them. At times it disappointed them, at others it scared, tormented and sickened them; and, to express their dissatisfaction or anguish, some of them resorted to sarcasm and invective, while others created an atmosphere that was harsh, dramatic, and often even intensely distressing. The movement had many adherents, and not only in Germany. No doubt it was there that Expressionism took its most violent form, but, sooner or later, it also appeared in Holland, Belgium and Luxembourg. Even France experienced it, and not only through Vlaminck; in Spain it was represented by Solana; and it also had exponents in Mexico, Brazil, and the United States, as well as in other countries. As for its origins, the truth is that there exists a permanent current of expressionism in art, though its first representatives in modern times were the Netherlander Van Gogh, the Belgian James Ensor, and the

EXPRESSIONISM

Norwegian Edvard Munch. Furthermore, all the painters who, in France, reacted against Impressionism prepared the way for it.

The nineteenth century had not yet ended when Ensor and Munch created the works that were to mark the way for those who followed them. From 1883 onwards, the Belgian artist abandoned the sombre style he had employed up to then; but though he adopted an Impressionist palette, he had too much imagination and too caustic a wit to be content simply to transcribe what he saw. As an ironical observer of the human comedy, he wanted to show up everything in human behaviour that was silly, pretentious, ridiculous, absurd; and his favourite subjects were masks and skeletons dressed in rags. But though his art reveals his taste for violent satire and low comedy, it does not contain any real spite. The moral climate of Ensor's work may remind one of Bosch and Bruegel, but his clear, bright colouring and the freedom of his form make him a painter who belonged to his own times, and who was also an innovator and a harbinger. In some of his still-lifes and iridescent landscapes he even appears to herald Bonnard.

Munch, whose colouring was both less decorative and less dense, produced a different atmosphere. Pessimistic, morbid, never at ease, he had an agonizing sense of man's loneliness, both amid the city crowds and before the terrifying immensity of nature. Women attracted him, but at the same time they frightened him. In his view, the rapture that they brought only led to conflict, regret and bitterness; and he expressed these feelings by means of lines that stretch and bend mournfully and colours that remain nostalgic even when they are bright. Whereas his palette shows that he regarded Van Gogh and Gauguin with admiration, his handling of line provides a slight link with the Nabis. Munch owed his fame to Germany; he exerted a decisive influence on German art.

EDVARD MUNCH,
1863-1944.
THE MORNING
AFTER,
1894-1895.
NATIONAL GALLERY,
OSLO

MUNCH.
ANXIETY,
1894.
MUNICIPAL
COLLECTION, OSLO

MUNCH.
ON THE BRIDGE,
1901
NATIONAL GALLERY,
OSLO

EXPRESSIONISM

GEORGES ROUAULT.
1871-1958.
LE CHAHUT,
1905.
PRIVATE
COLLECTION,
PARIS

ROUAULT.
THREE JUDGES,
1913.
MUSEUM OF
MODERN ART,
NEW YORK

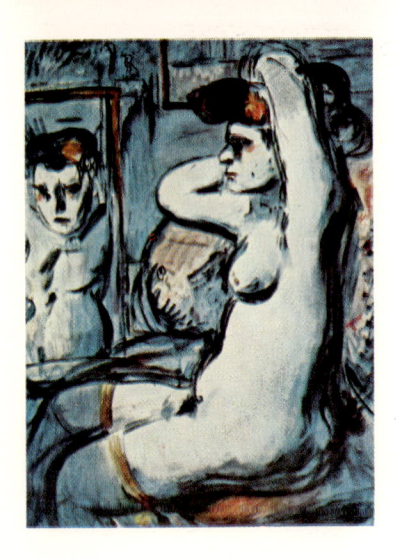

ROUAULT.
IN THE MIRROR,
1906.
MUSÉE D'ART
MODERNE, PARIS

Georges Rouault belonged to the same generation as the Fauves, and — like them — exhibited at the Salon d'Automne of 1905 works that shocked the public by their violence and lack of restraint. All the same, he cannot be regarded as a champion of Fauvism, because he certainly did not proclaim the pleasures of the senses or seek the exhilaration of pure colours. He aimed not so much to delight the eye as to move the heart. In a word, he was an Expressionist — and he bore the title with unsurpassed authority.

Although he showed no less impetuosity than Vlaminck or certain German painters, there was nothing hasty or slack about his technique. Even the works dating from 1903 to 1910, in which the form seems to be lashed into existence, are very far from being mere rapid outpourings; yet one can tell that he was impatient to let the spectator know what moved or shocked him. With all his soul and with all his body, Rouault was a Christian. The sin that he saw around him wounded him; the injustice made him indignant; and as for the poverty and affliction, he felt the need to express his compassion for them. One is tempted to say that he had something in him of the Old Testament prophets who suffered in the presence of the world's wickedness, and who denounced it with fierce ardour. On the other hand, he revealed both an earthy, accusatorial zest that related him to Daumier; and a sense, not of the ridiculousness of the grotesque, but of its poignancy and dreadfulness, which brought him close to Goya. Look at his prostitutes. He stripped them of every attraction they might once have possessed; their bodies are weary and ashen, their faces hideous and stupid. Then there are his judges. No human feeling is capable of disturbing the cruel indifference expressed by these pig-like heads, which sit heavily on top of red-draped mounds of flesh. On the other hand, he observed his clowns with a brotherly eye,

EXPRESSIONISM

and made them into beings whom life had ill-treated, filling their hearts with sorrow, resignation, and sometimes bitterness. In addition, Rouault depicted religious subjects; no one since El Greco and Rembrandt has done so more naturally. One feels the religious atmosphere of this works even before one has identified their theme. It is, moreover, a fiery, mystical atmosphere, far removed from the affected grace of nineteenth-century sacred art but very close to the fervour embodied in Byzantine churches, or Romanesque and Gothic cathedrals. Rouault recovered in its entirety the religious spirit of the great periods of Christianity.

He imbued his landscapes with the same pathos and spirituality as his figures. Moreover, whether these views evoke depressing industrial suburbs, or whether they are inspired by the Palestine of the Gospels, they always owe less to the external world than to the artist's private visions. They are bathed in an ecstatic light, as exalted as the setting sun or the uneasy tremor of a lurid moon.

Though Rouault's line was tempestuous at first, after 1910 it became heavier, broadened out, and began to move rather slowly. From then onwards, it was suggestive of the lead that surrounds the forms in stained-glass windows. Rouault's palette, too, grew more and more closely related to the colouring of leaded glass. The gradations of blue and pink that dominated his early works gave way to fiery reds, sulphureous yellows, and greens and blues, sometimes bright, sometimes dark. Often these hues seemed to vibrate with light from a source behind the picture. This translucent quality of the colours is made even more remarkable by the rich impasto; because, for all his spirituality, Rouault did not neglect the physical substance of his paintings. Moreover, he is distinguished by the richness, relish and, indeed, refinement of his palette, even in works that embody ugliness.

ROUAULT. HEAD OF CHRIST, 1933. MUSÉE D'ART MODERNE, PARIS

ROUAULT. CHRIST ON THE SEA OF GALILEE. PRIVATE COLLECTION, PARIS

ROUAULT. PIERROT. PRIVATE COLLECTION, PARIS

DIE BRÜCKE

ERNST LUDWIG KIRCHNER. 1880-1938. WOMAN ON A BLUE DIVAN, FRAENZI, 1907-1908. INSTITUTE OF ARTS, MINNEAPOLIS

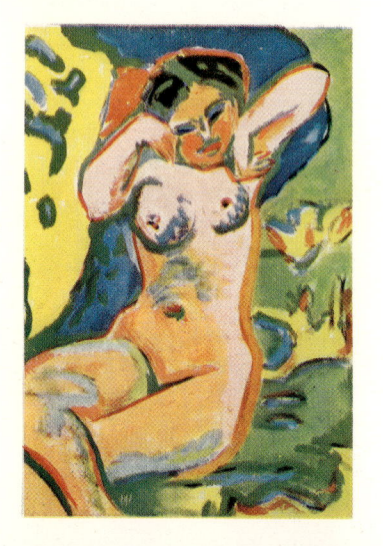

KIRCHNER. GIRL IN A FLOWER MEADOW, 1908. BUCHHEIM COLLECTION, FELDAFING

KARL SCHMIDT-ROTTLUFF. BORN 1884. NORWEGIAN LANDSCAPE, 1911. BUCHHEIM COLLECTION, FELDAFING

The first artists to represent German Expressionism formed themselves into a group at Dresden in 1905. They chose as their motto the words *die Brücke* (the bridge), because they wanted to muster 'the entire younger generation' and 'everyone ... who expresses his creative impulses honestly and directly.' The four founders of the movement—Fritz Bleyl, Erich Heckel, Ernst Ludwig Kirchner, and Karl Schmidt-Rottluff—were joined by a number of other painters, notably Max Pechstein, Otto Mueller and, for a while, Nolde.

The work of these German artists reveals a combination of Munch's influence with that of Van Gogh, Gauguin, Lautrec and Ensor. They also came under the spell of Negro and Oceanian art and late mediaeval wood-cuts. No doubt it was to the latter that they owed the angular, crude and summary drawing of so many of their works. However, their colouring is not without crudeness, too. Though it comes close to the Fauve palette (of which the Brücke group was not unaware), it differs from it in that the harmonies are usually shrill, strident and aggressive—even more aggressive than those of Vlaminck. Indeed, it was not only in the sphere of art that these German painters aimed to be non-conformists; they were also in revolt against the moral values of bourgeois society. When painting a nude, they did not, following the example of Matisse, conceive it as a beautiful structure or as a pretext for creating arabesques. On the contrary, they liked to present it—with a hint of defiance—in an atmosphere of eroticism. Moreover, as they wanted to express their opposition to the prettiness of Academic nudes, they distorted their own sometimes going so far as to make them ugly and repulsive.

The strongest personality of the group was Kirchner, who, in 1911, went to Berlin, where he spent several years. There his art became somewhat calmer; the colour grew less crude, and the drawing

300

firmer and more constructive. Yet although he liked to represent all that was not genuine in those who promenaded the city, he remained ill at ease. This shows even in the landscapes that, from 1917 onwards, he produced in Switzerland, where he had hoped to find a refuge amidst the unspoiled scenery of the high mountains.

However violent Kirchner's art, it is less so than that of Nolde, whose style shows the least restraint of all the German Expressionists. Convinced that the most brutal expression was also the strongest, there was no excess or crudity at which he drew the line; his colours are glaring, his impasto coarse, and his form seems to have been hacked into shape. All the same, there can be no denying that he was a visionary; that fact is proclaimed in his figures, his religious scenes, and also his landscapes. One could nevertheless wish that the visionary was matched by a painter who, instead of just seeking to shock, had aimed to communicate more lasting emotions. However, the vulgarity that so often mars his easel pictures does not appear in his water-colours, which are the most satisfactory and convincing of all his works.

The Austrian painter Oskar Kokoschka developed a form of Expressionism that, at bottom, is more tormented than Nolde's, but nevertheless possesses more solid pictorial qualities. At the start of his career Kokoschka executed portraits—both at Vienna and Berlin—that usually represent hypersensitive beings with stormy emotions and souls quivering with anxiety; in each of these works he laid bare the innermost self of his model. Although, at that period, he expressed himself by means of incisive lines that twist and cockle, he soon began to make colour play a more important role in his compositions. Nevertheless, his handling has never lost its nervous quality; it is particularly impulsive in the spacious, yet strongly agitated townscapes that he produced during his extensive travels.

EMIL NOLDE. 1867-1956. VAGABONDS, 1910-1915. WALLRAF-RICHARTZ MUSEUM, COLOGNE

KOKOSCHKA. MARSEILLE, 1925. CITY ART MUSEUM, SAINT-LOUIS

OSKAR KOKOSCHKA. FATHER HIRSCH, c. 1907. NEUE GALERIE, LINZ

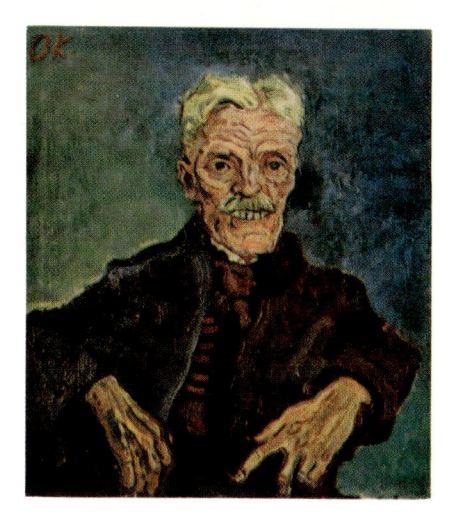

DER BLAUE REITER

WASSILY KANDINSKY.
1866-1944.
CHURCH AT
MURNAU,
1910.
STEDELIJK VAN
ABBE MUSEUM,
EINDHOVEN

ALEXEI
VON JAWLENSKY.
1864-1942.
MEDUSA.
LYONS MUSEUM

FRANZ MARC.
1880-1916.
BLUE HORSE,
1911.
BERNHARD KÖHLER
COLLECTION,
BERLIN

It is customary to include among the Expressionists the painters who, in 1909, founded the Neue Künstlervereinigung at Munich, out of which emerged, two years later, the Blaue Reiter group. However, at Munich the spirit was not the same as at Dresden, Berlin or Vienna. It is true that the Russian-born artists Alexei von Jawlensky and Wassily Kandinsky used vivid, even violent, hues; but in general the colour-combinations of the Munich painters are more harmonious than those of the Brücke group. Both Jawlensky and Kandinsky visited Paris, where they came under the influence of Matisse. On the other hand, the Germans Franz Marc and August Macke, and Paul Klee, who had a German father but a Swiss mother, were in touch with Delaunay; and none of them showed any tendency to unburden themselves without bothering about stylistic problems. So it is not surprising that it was among this group that two personalities destined to play a leading part on an international level, first asserted themselves—namely Kandinsky and Klee.

Although at first Wassily Kandinsky used his sparkling palette to paint views of the Bavarian countryside and compositions embodying memories of a voyage to Tunisia, as early as 1910 he decided in favour of a completely new mode of expression: abstract painting. On the other hand, Klee, who moved cautiously, did not become convinced that he was a colourist until 1914, though it is true that he had previously produced some water-colours announcing the direction that he subsequently took.

Alexei von Jawlensky showed less inclination to explore unknown territory. On the whole, his style in about 1910 was Fauve; but his sumptuous and stately colour-combinations recall Russian choirs, in which the high voices blend so remarkably with the deep, warm resonance of the basses. A broad blue line surrounds the forms, rather like wire that has gained thickness at the expense of its

DER BLAUE REITER

flexibility. Later on, Jawlensky's drawing became entirely geometrical, and, despite the spiritual significance with which he intended to endow his faces and masks, they sometimes look schematic.

Marc and Macke did not have time to produce an extensive *œuvre*, for both were killed during the first world war. Nevertheless, they are among the most interesting artists to have worked in Germany during this century. Convinced that man was ugly, and that animals were both more beautiful and more pure, Franz Marc became *the* animal painter. He was not content to depict them tenderly in an atmosphere of legend, but strove, as it were, to get inside them, to see the world with their eyes. In the long run, however, he discovered even in animals things that offended his sensibility, with the result that his art became increasingly abstract. In a work such as *Tyrol*, completed in 1914, objects have almost disappeared, to be replaced by a conflict between opposing forces, and between contrasting forms and colours.

Less speculative than Marc, but more of a painter by nature, August Macke seems to have consulted Seurat as well as Delaunay. He liked to depict figures with the slender, rounded appearance of columns, walking beneath the trees or pausing before shop-windows. His is an art full of calm and balance, instinct with well-being, simultaneously grave and pleasing.

Lyonel Feininger did not live in Munich, and only exhibited with the Blaue Reiter painters in Berlin in 1913; but even before this, he could have appeared in their company. He, too, got to know Delaunay, and throughout his life retained from his contact with Cubism a liking for strictness and clear disposition. On the other hand, he was so sensitive to effects of light that, with the aid of his delicate and mysterious colouring, he imparted an ethereal, and sometimes transparent, quality even to the geometric solidity of ships and houses.

FRANZ MARC.
GAZELLES,
1913.
MARIE LANGE
COLLECTION,
KREFELD

AUGUST MACKE.
1887-1914.
GIRLS IN A WOOD,
1914.
PRIVATE
COLLECTION,
AUSTRIA

PAUL KLEE.
1879-1940.
IN THE QUARRY
(WATERCOLOUR),
1913.
KLEE FOUNDATION,
BERNE

LYONEL FEININGER,
1871-1956.
TOWERS AT HALLE,
1931.
WALLRAF-RICHARTZ
MUSEUM, COLOGNE

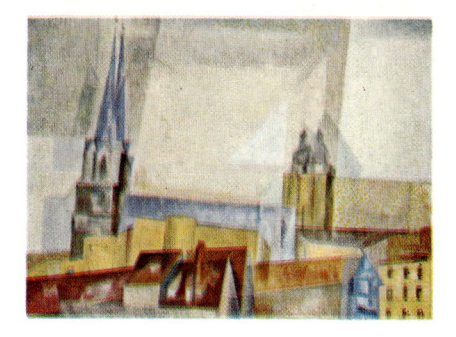

KLEE

PAUL KLEE.
1879-1940.
THE NIESEN,
1915.
HERMANN RUPF
COLLECTION,
BERNE

KLEE.
WITH THE EAGLE,
1918.
KLEE FOUNDATION,
BERNE

KLEE.
LANDSCAPE WITH
YELLOW BIRDS,
1923.
R. DOETSCH-
BENZIGER
COLLECTION,
BASLE

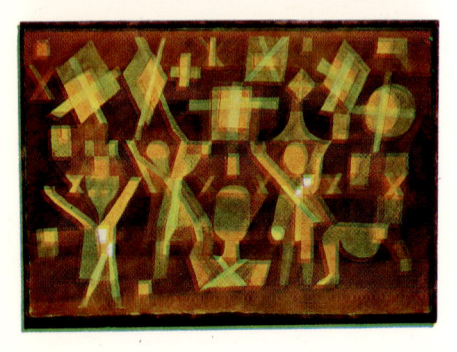

KLEE.
TOWARDS THE STARS,
1923.
ROLF BÜRGI
COLLECTION,
BERNE

When, in 1914, Paul Klee wrote in his diary: 'I am possessed by colour ... I am a painter,' he was on a visit to Tunisia with Macke. Even if it was the enchantment of the journey that caused this certainty to blossom in his mind, the fact, of course, remains that he had already glimpsed it through the fog of his doubts; for he had long been seeking his true self. But before openly coming to grips with colour, of which Van Gogh and Cézanne had revealed to him the properties, he had wanted to explore the possibilities of line and tone values. This artist, who at first glance seems to have followed only his fantasy, only what was most spontaneous and least controllable in his inspiration, actually felt the need to use his intellect to guide his means. Furthermore, he wanted each of these means to keep its elemental purity. To him the artist was a kind of constructor bent on 'grouping the formal elements in such a pure and logical way that each occupies the place that belongs to it and none of them does harm to another.' True enough, he also said that nothing could replace intuition; and he mentioned the phases of the creative process, which mainly take place in the subconscious. But when working, his basic concern was with pictorial problems. It therefore became the rule, after 1914, that the title of a work and the idea it expressed did not exist prior to the composition of the picture. Far from determining the latter, they were themselves generated by it. The urge to use his means with a lucid mind went on growing until, in 1921, he became a teacher at the Bauhaus, newly founded at Weimar by the architect Gropius. Here, where the aim was to knock down the 'high wall between the artisan and the artist', and the most advanced artistic conceptions were propounded, Klee taught alongside Feininger and Kandinsky, among others. In everything, he went back to first principles, and his course was extremely systematic.

KLEE

On the other hand, he also considered it absolutely essential to find his bearings in the realm of nature. He advised teachers to induce children 'to see how a bud takes form, how a tree grows, how a butterfly develops, so that they may become as rich, as changing, as original as great nature.' He practised what he preached, studying not only the appearance of nature, but its functions and laws—so much so that he could evoke it through works that appear completely abstract.

Taken all round, his art is distinguished by its high poetic content and the diversity of its pictorial qualities. In fact, no other modern artist has produced a more varied and richly inventive *œuvre* than he. Here a thin, sharp line nimbly makes its way; there it seems to tremble with timidity; elsewhere a broad stroke advances slowly and heavily. Though the general effect of the colour is usually gently toned down, it can also assert itself without restraint, to become bright and emphatic. It is chiefly in the last works that its sonority increases, just as it is there that the drawing appears at its firmest, freest and most elliptical. Then again, Klee would sometimes spread his compositions out vertically or horizontally, and sometimes produce an impression of depth, distance and relief. Nevertheless, whatever his style, he could never be mistaken for any one else. He was at once grave and mischievous, full of naïvety and supremely reflective. His humour was free from spite, his tenderness from prettification. He evoked tragedy without becoming grandiloquent, and told stories without his works ever growing anecdotal. He loved caprices, but only as liberties to be taken with rules. He knew how to combine firmness with grace, and spontaneity with calculation. Thus he established an extremely subtle understanding between his poetic leanings, his taste for symbols, his constant urge to meet the demands of the picture.

KLEE. INDIVIDUALISED MEASUREMENT OF THE BEDS, 1930. KLEE FOUNDATION, BERNE

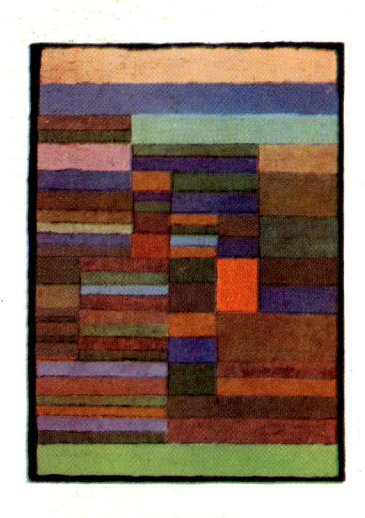

KLEE. INTOXICATION, 1939. HANS MEYER COLLECTION, BERNE

KLEE. SAILOR, 1940. VICTOR BABIN COLLECTION, SANTA FE

FLEMISH EXPRESSIONISM

RIK WOUTERS.
1882-1916.
ANNIVERSARY
FLOWERS,
1912.
C. JUSSIAUT
COLLECTION,
ANVERS

CONSTANT PERMEKE.
1886-1952.
PEASANT FAMILY
WITH CAT, 1928.
MUSÉE DES
BEAUX-ARTS,
BRUSSELS.

JOSEPH KUTTER.
1894-1941.
CLOWN,
1937.
STEDELIJK MUSEUM,
AMSTEEDAM

James Ensor certainly influenced not only the German Expressionists but also painting in his own country, though he did not have any true disciples there. Even if Rik Wouters owed to him his taste for hues that are vivid and pearly by turns, the two men had nothing else in common. Besides, Wouters also admired Cézanne and Renoir, so that sensuality and severity are intimately blended in his works. Just as he combined delicacy and brightness in his colouring, he applied his paint spiritedly, but without neglecting the organisation of his composition. His early death during the first world war occurred just when the true pioneers of Expressionism in Belgium, Permeke, Gustave de Smet, and Frits van den Berghe, were beginning to discover the new movement. Though spurred on by Ensor's example, they, too, moved in a different direction from him.

In Constant Permeke's work, for instance, one finds the colours of damp clods, creamy milk, and old oak timber—all the hues seen by peasants as they plough and harvest. His subjects could not be more humdrum: people eating potatoes or black bread; a sow and her piglets; a cow being milked in a cowshed; a village fair. Yet he viewed all this with a sort of religious solemnity, translating it into a style that gives it pathos and poetry, without causing it to lose its rugged, fiercely uncompromising reality. Above all, he knew how to lay on his thick paint so that it became vibrant, rich, sometimes luminous.

If, in his pessimism, dramatic chiaroscuro, and at times distressing solemnity, the Luxembourg artist Joseph Kutter offers points of comparison with the Flemish Expressionists, his fundamental originality is nevertheless clearly apparent. He is more controlled, his colouring is richer and more radiant than theirs. Even in his *Clowns,* in which his crushing sorrows are most movingly revealed, his art is distinguished by its pungency, solidity, and stability.

306

TWENTIETH-CENTURY ENGLAND

With Walter Richard Sickert English painting entered a new phase. The son and grandson of artists, he was, with Wilson Steer, the most important of the British painters influenced by Impressionism—most profoundly in his own case by Whistler, whose assistant he was for some years, and Degas, whose friendship he valued. He came to mistrust, however, the surface brilliance of the former and what he regarded as the facile charm of the lesser Impressionists. His own earlier work is low in tone, his realism at once sensitive and robust. The shabby vistas of Camden Town, Dieppe and Venice; the interiors — these most greatly appealed to him. Sickert etched much, wrote forcefully, founded the Camden Town Group and was elected a Member of the Royal Academy.

No less great than Sickert's personal dynamism was the self-effacing reticence of Matthew Smith, the sources of whose art are nonetheless equally to be found in France. From 1910 he divided his life between France and England. The impact upon him of Matisse and the Fauves was decisive. Flowers, still-life, the female nude and, less often, landscape he depicted in the most sumptuous manner: his colour was rich, his forms were opulent, his handling florid. A late starter, his first proper exhibition was not until 1926.

Markedly more English in feeling was the work of Paul Nash, whose firm sense of design and gently disturbing romanticism allied him first with the aftermath of Wyndham Lewis' Vorticism and later with the Surrealists. Between his angular records of the first world war and his more poetic memories of the Battle of Britain, he evolved a landscape vision based on animistic correspondences and encounters which were to influence Henry Moore and Graham Sutherland. It is perhaps in his watercolours, firmly rooted in the English tradition, that Nash's art found its most delicate and lyric expression.

WALTER RICHARD SICKERT. 1860-1942. INTERIOR OF ST MARKS, VENICE. TATE GALLERY, LONDON

MATTHEW SMITH. 1879-1959. APPLES ON DISH, 1919. TATE GALLERY, LONDON

PAUL NASH. 1889-1946. PILLAR AND MOON, 1932-1942. TATE GALLERY, LONDON

307

SOUTINE

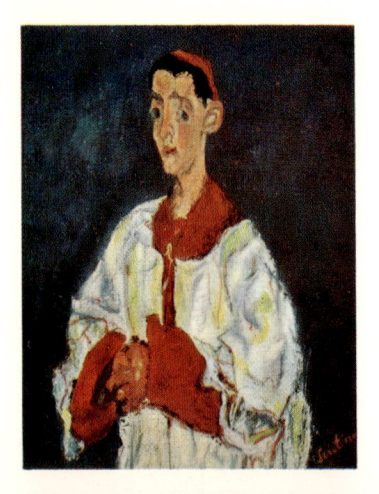

CHAIM SOUTINE.
1894-1943.
CHOIRBOY,
1928.
MME JEAN WALTER
COLLECTION, PARIS.

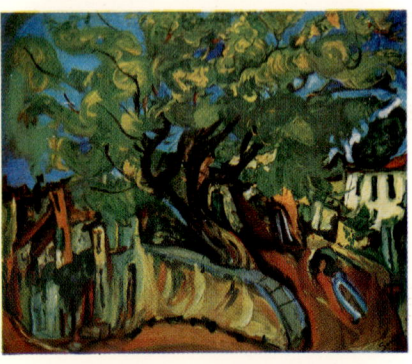

SOUTINE.
LANDSCAPE,
1926.
PRIVATE
COLLECTION,
LONDON

SOUTINE.
WOMAN IN RED.
HARRY BAKWIN
COLLECTION,
NEW YORK

Generally speaking, there is nothing chaotic about the Expressionism that took root in the studios of various French artists after the first world war. It does not even seem to be threatened with disorder, and the barriers show no sign at all of being shaken by those violent waves that come surging up from the painfully agitated depths. When all is said and done, an artist like Marcel Gromaire is closer to the Cubists than to Permeke. Nevertheless, the painter who, of all the Expressionists, produced the most tormented, tormenting and frenzied pictures — namely, Chaim Soutine — worked in France. Of Jewish parentage, he spent his childhood in a Lithuanian ghetto. Pogroms were a constant menace. Soutine lived in fear and in dire poverty; and fear, like hunger, dogged him to the art school at Vilna as well as, later on, to Paris, where he arrived in 1913. His anguish did not even leave him when he ceased to be poverty-stricken, and whatever he painted became a projection of his anxiety, his despair, and his incurable loneliness. His figures are degenerate creatures with misshapen bodies and demented, sottish, or crafty faces. Moreover, he felt that they were so irreparably damned that he looked on them without the slightest compassion or shocked indignation. Far from finding consolation among the animals, he only painted them when they were dead; the flayed carcass of an ox or a skinned rabbit; a plucked pheasant hanging above some tomatoes that look like clots of blood. Nor did his attitude change before a landscape. Those that he recorded appear to be in the grip of an earthquake; the tottering houses seem about to collapse, while the trees struggle against the hurricanes that shake and twist them. Steep roads thrust aggressively upwards towards the sky, where they are engulfed in the void. Even the sunny landscapes of southern France appear to be groaning in a sadist's clutches. All this nihilism

MODIGLIANI

is, however, redeemed by the life Soutine imparted not so much to his form (which is simply that of realism—after being slashed to ribbons) as to his colour and impasto. To be sure, it is an impure and sometimes a muddy kind of life; but how vibrant and how rich in visual delights it can be! Next to violent reds, nocturnal and leaden blues, one actually finds tender pinks (and what if they *are* the pinks of putrefaction!) and bluish or yellowy whites. In short, the delicate and delectable are here placed side by side with the shocking and corrosive.

The so-called 'Jewish pathos' also appears in Amedeo Modigliani's art, but in a different way. Modigliani was an Italian. He studied at Florence, and never lost his admiration for the Tuscan masters of the fourteenth and fifteenth centuries. In 1906, or just before, he arrived in Paris, where he associated with the Cubists. The result was that, however fond he may have been of riotous living, in art he favoured a disciplined approach. Moreover, contrary to Soutine's, the dominant factor in Modigliani's handling is line—geometrical at first, then more and more supple. Sinuously, it stretches out in long curves, advancing languidly with an elegance that is soft and delicate, and sometimes even with a hint of mannerism. The forms that it traces contain patches of colour that are carefully confined within their boundaries.

As he was really only interested in human beings, Modigliani painted hardly anything but nudes and portraits. Although his nude figures are far from being unaware of the pleasures of the flesh, they always exhale a sense of melancholy. As for the portraits, however varied his models may have been in reality (and they included artists, poets, children and women he had loved or simply met), in his pictures they almost all belong to the same race. They confront the spectator in formal poses, inviting him to measure their sadness and the difficulty they find in living.

AMEDEO MODIGLIANI. 1884-1920. PORTRAIT OF THE POET LEOPOLD ZBOROWSKI, 1917. MUSEU D'ARTE, SAO PAULO

MODIGLIANI. NUDE, 1917-1918. GIANNI MATTIOLI COLLECTION, MILAN

MODIGLIANI. ELVIRA, 1919. W. HADORN COLLECTION, BERNE

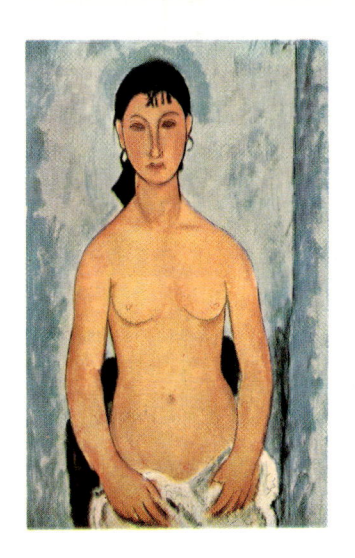

309

CHAGALL

MARC CHAGALL.
BORN 1887.
LE MARCHAND
DE BESTIAUX,
1912.
KUNSTMUSEUM,
BASLE

CHAGALL.
GREEN VIOLINIST,
1918.
SOLOMON
R. GUGGENHEIM
MUSEUM,
NEW YORK

CHAGALL,
LES MARIÉS
DE LA TOUR EIFFEL,
1938-1939.
PRIVATE
COLLECTION

Although shortly after he came to Paris, in 1910, Marc Chagall painted a few canvases that can be described as Expressionist, his *œuvre* on the whole differs from that of any of the Expressionists who have just been mentioned. He has affinities only with the Flemish painter Edgar Tytgat. For Chagall is a story-teller, too, although in a different language and recounting different tales. Like Soutine, he was born in Russia, and he has never ceased recalling what he saw there during his childhood as a member of a large, poor Jewish family at Vitebsk. Other events, such as his happy home life and the persecutions suffered by others of his race, have also left their mark on him; but nothing has effaced the image charged with nostalgic tenderness that he bore away from his homeland. Likewise, though his style may have altered—Cubism, having imposed geometrical severity on the tortuous forms of his early days, gave way in its turn during the 'twenties to supple drawing—the spirit of his art does not change at all. Imagination is always stronger than probability; or, rather, what prevails is the truth that he knows and feels—that of the spirit and the heart, not that of the eye. In the universe he has created, the laws of the physical world are suppressed. There are no barriers between the various realms of nature or different periods of time. The distant past may be mixed with, and is often no less important than, the present. Things that in the external world have nothing to do with each other are here related, and combine together in a natural way. What is normally inanimate comes to life like everything else: a clock or a candelabrum flies just as well as a pair of lovers. Marc Chagall distributes his colours with complete freedom, too. One would be tempted to believe that he was only interested in their poetic value, were it not for his own words: 'I admit nothing that does not first justify itself plastically.'

NAIVE PAINTING

Side by side with modern painting properly so called, there has developed a type of art that in itself is nothing new, but to which circumstances have given a new significance: the art of the painters sometimes known as 'twentieth-century primitives' and sometimes as 'folk masters of reality'. Put very briefly, it is the continuation of an old craft tradition, which the principles of the Renaissance have certainly influenced, but which they have never succeeded in dominating completely. Consequently, it shows signs of awkwardness and clumsiness, some of which are due to ignorance and an inexperienced hand, others to naïvety of vision and mind. The result is that this art, too, deviates from 'visual realism' in order to present a more complete image of objects, and one that is 'truer' and more arresting, than that offered by academic painting. This explains why it is not more surprising that its most significant representative, Henri Rousseau, was specially appreciated by the advocates of Cubism; for they found in him, if not their speculative turn of mind, at least certain solutions that were related to their own.

Was Henri, called 'le Douanier', Rousseau—the erstwhile customs officer and 'Sunday painter', who retired at the age of forty to devote himself entirely to painting—really as naïve as this or that episode from his life suggests? Whatever the answer may be, he produced solidly constructed and magnificently painted pictures that hold their own beside the most powerful works of his time. As Rousseau's fame was established chiefly by the Cubists, it is easy to forget that he was born only four years after Monet. All the same, no one was less amenable to Impressionism than he. Never dwelling on the accidental or transitory, he painted what is, what lasts, and what can be measured, felt and weighed. Indeed, the story goes that, before setting to work on his portrait of Apollinaire. *The Muse and the Poet,* he took the

HENRI ROUSSEAU, CALLED LE DOUANIER. 1844-1910. PORTRAIT OF PIERRE LOTI, *c.* 1890. KUNSTHAUS, ZURICH

HENRI ROUSSEAU. THE SNAKE CHARMER, 1907. LOUVRE, PARIS

HENRI ROUSSEAU. THE MUSE AND THE POET: APOLLINAIRE AND MARIE LAURENCIN, 1909. KUNSTMUSEUM, BASLE

311

NAIVE PAINTING

LOUIS VIVIN.
1861-1936.
NOTRE-DAME
DE PARIS,
c. 1933.
MUSÉE D'ART
MODERNE, PARIS

ANDRÉ BAUCHANT.
1873-1958.
FÊTE DE LA
LIBÉRATION
(DÉTAIL),
1945.
MUSÉE D'ART
MODERNE, PARIS

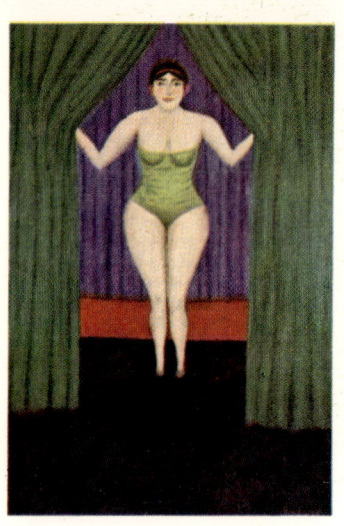

CAMILLE BOMBOIS.
BORN 1883.
THE DANCER,
1926.
PRIVATE
COLLECTION,
PARIS

measurements of his sitter's nose, forehead, mouth and ears. Nevertheless, he did not confine himself to painting what he could observe —portraits, landscapes, flowers, and still-lifes; he also treated subjects that came out of his imagination, such as his *War or the Ride of Discord, The Snake Charmer,* and *The Dream of Yadwigha.* Since the two latter works represent scenes in luxuriant virgin forests, it was formerly believed that they were to be explained by a journey that the artist made to Mexico. It seems more probable, however, that Rousseau based his creations on what he found in the Jardin des Plantes at Paris. After all, might it not be precisely because he had never set foot in a virgin forest that he could endow it with such intense poetry. He always affirmed, moreover, that he was a visionary. At all events, in his art dwells a solemn mystery; and instead of dispelling it, the clearness of the drawing, the monumentality of the form and the crystalline transparency of the atmosphere only add to its fascination.

Though none of the other modern primitives have achieved Rousseau's authority, some of them do nevertheless confront the spectator with a reality to which their artlessness has conveyed its mysterious fullness of substance and its total clarity. Besides, each of them leads one into a different world. Louis Vivin painted mainly buildings, which he constructed stone by stone like a mason, whereas André Bauchant liked to represent biblical or historical scenes, setting them in enchanting landscapes. While Camille Bombois, with working-class vigour, displays fair- and circus-performers as well as buxom female figures, Séraphine Louis—sometimes called Séraphine de Senlis—presented luxuriant bouquets of flowers and rich bunches of fruit gathered in some fabulous garden. The painting of this simple charwoman goes far beyond all realism. In fact, there are few works that so fully deserve the name 'Surrealist'.

UTRILLO

Maurice Utrillo has not the same claim to be called a naïve painter as Henri Rousseau or André Bauchant. He possessed neither their attitude of wonder, not their simplifying and scrupulously careful style. When, in 1903, his mother Suzanne Valadon, herself an accomplished painter, put a brush into his hand in order to try to cure him of his alcoholism, he began by producing landscapes that were influenced by Pissarro. Later on, as well, he continued to uphold a kind of primitive Impressionism — an Impressionism, that is to say, which did not dissolve form or analyse colour. In short, there is nothing new about Utrillo's pictorial language; yet he occupies a unique place in twentieth-century painting.

No one before him had looked at the streets of Montmartre with such penetrating melancholy; no one had provided such a sorrowful image of its old walls. Utrillo restored their cracking and crumbling coat of rough-cast, which was growing leprous and mildewy. He even seems to imitate it in the white or greyish impasto that gives his best works an air of simultaneous decay and distinction. On the other hand, he displayed a passion for solid composition; and, particularly in the numerous churches that he painted either directly from nature or else after picture-postcards, he distributed the architectural masses with a superlative sense of balance. A master of whites and greys, to which he added subdued greens, blues and browns, Utrillo virtually never managed to create a substantial work from the moment that he began to use clear, gay colours. Moreover, as the man succeeded in escaping from his sorrow, his painting languished. From about 1920, Utrillo, who during his years of debauchery and disorder had given evidence of the most unerring pictorial qualities, was reduced to copying himself; and thenceforward it was generally in vain that he strove to regain the genius that had abandoned him.

MAURICE UTRILLO. 1883-1955. L'ÉGLISE SAINT-PIERRE ET LE SACRÉ-CŒUR, 1910. GALERIE PÉTRIDÈS, PARIS

UTRILLO. SNOW IN MONTMARTRE. PRIVATE COLLECTION, NEW YORK

UTRILLO. L'ÉGLISE DE DEUIL, 'LA PETITE COMMUNIANTE', 1912. GALERIE PÉTRIDÈS, PARIS

UTRILLO. CABARET DU LAPIN AGILE (GOUACHE). GALERIE PÉTRIDÈS, PARIS

DADAISM

MARCEL DUCHAMP.
BORN 1887.
LE PASSAGE DE LA
VIERGE À LA MARIÉE,
1912.
MUSEUM OF MODERN
ART, NEW YORK

FRANCIS PICABIA.
1879-1953.
OPTOPHONE.
H. P. ROCHÉ
COLLECTION, PARIS

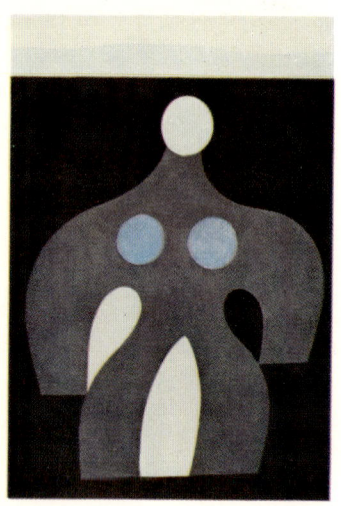

HANS ARP.
BORN 1887.
THREE-NAVEL-MAN,
1920.
PRIVATE
COLLECTION,
MERIDEN, CONN.

If the irrational already played a considerable role in the art of most of the Expressionists, it became even more important with the promoters of Dadaism and Surrealism. The Dada supporters began to appear on the scene during the first world war, and it was the war itself that accounted for their state of mind and their activities. Sickened by a world in which absurdity and death triumphed, and disgusted at the uses they saw being made of reason, logic and science, they jeered at these activities, proclaiming them to be noxious and baneful. The very name that they gave themselves in 1916 is significant, in that it was meant to signify nothing; they found it by opening a dictionary at random.

This took place in Zurich among a group that included, among others, the Rumanian poet Tristan Tzara, the German writers Hugo Ball and Richard Hülsenbeck, and the Alsatian painter and sculptor Hans Arp. At the same moment, however, the Dada spirit asserted itself in New York, too, where the leading lights were two painters from France: Marcel Duchamp and Francis Picabia. A little later, other centres appeared in Paris, Berlin, Cologne and Hanover. While the Dadaists in Berlin were concerned about politics, elsewhere their revolutionary action was limited to the sphere of art and culture. Moreover, whereas some of them only attacked conceptions that seemed false or sterile, for others it was a matter of destroying the idea of art itself.

Thus, in his desire to show that absolutely any 'ready-made' object could be promoted to the rank of a work of art, Marcel Duchamp bought a urinal, signed it with the name of a manufacturer of sanitary installations, R. Mutt, entitled it *Fontaine,* and sent it to the New York Independents' exhibition of 1917. Similarly, he took a reproduction of the *Mona Lisa,* gave it a moustache, and in 1920 exhibited it at Paris with the title LHOOQ. Picabia, for his part, proceeded to paint 'ironic machines' with

SURREALISM

precise but absurd mechanisms. In short, having produced some remarkable pictures (about 1913 Picabia was one of the promoters of abstract art), these two painters ceased to set any store by real artistic creation. Henceforward, their aim was to cast ridicule on the idols of society, like machinery and the art that people admire with their eyes shut, knowing that it is enshrined in a venerable museum. They only wanted to upset: the main thing for them was not the work itself but the confusion that they could arouse in people's minds. On the other hand, Arp, who later became one of the great sculptors of the twentieth century, did not aim at the mere negation of all values. 'We were looking for an elemental art,' he has since said, 'that would, we thought, save mankind from the raging madness of those times. We were aspiring after a new order that would re-establish the balance between Heaven and Hell.' So, relying on the fruitfulness of chance he created abstract paintings and reliefs whose strictly artistic interest its indisputable. The same applies to the works that the Hanover Dadaist Kurt Schwitters began to produce after the first world war, by assembling fragments of objects that others had dropped in the street or thrown on rubbish dumps. In his hands, bits of envelope, stamps, tram-tickets, came to form little pictures that sometimes recall Cubist *papiers collés*, sometimes water-colours by Paul Klee; now and then, one finds the refinement of a Persian miniature.

Surrealism arose in 1932 at Paris, in the very midst of the Dada movement. It, too, extolled the virtues of the irrational, but, in so doing, its aim was not destructive. Directed by poets who had read Freud, its intention was to explore the subconscious and cast new light on the hidden depths of the soul. André Breton, in the first manifesto of Surrealism (1924), sang the praises of 'pure psychic automatism', 'the dictates of thought, in the absence of any

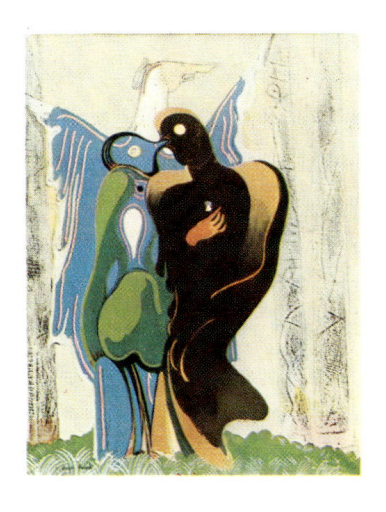

MAX ERNST.
BORN 1891.
THE CHASTE JOSEPH,
1928.
A. D. MOURADIAN
COLLECTION,
PARIS

MAX ERNST.
MOTHER AND
CHILDREN ON
THE TERRESTRIAL
GLOBE,
1953.
KUNSTHALLE,
MANNHEIM

YVES TANGUY.
1900-1957.
MAMAN,
PAPA EST BLESSÉ !
1927.
MUSEUM OF MODERN
ART, NEW YORK

315

SURREALISM

SALVADOR DALI.
BORN 1904.
THE PERSISTENCE
OF MEMORY,
1931.
MUSEUM OF
MODERN ART,
NEW YORK

DALI.
BACCHANAL,
1939.
PRIVATE
COLLECTION

RENÉ MAGRITTE.
BORN 1898.
THE STEPS OF
SUMMER,
1937.
PRIVATE
COLLECTION,
PARIS

JOAN MIRÓ.
BORN 1893.
CATALAN
LANDSCAPE,
THE HUNTER,
1923-1924.
MUSEUM OF
MODERN ART,
NEW YORK

control exercised by reason, and exterior to any aesthetic or moral prejudices'. Thus a strictly Surrealist painting was important not for its pictorial research but as a psychological document; and since it was held that images and anecdotes were more revealing than form, orthodox Surrealists, like the German Max Ernst, the Belgian René Magritte and the Spaniard Salvador Dali, deliberately expressed themselves by means of 'photographic' realism. But, as with Chirico, their guiding star, however realistic the details may be, the total effect is strange—full of caprice and abnormalities. Unquestionably, it is Ernst who has created the richest and most complex body of Surrealist works. Though less aggressive than Dali's, it plainly responds to more deep-rooted needs, and its mystery is more genuine. Then again, while Dali delights in the chromatic vulgarity of a bad colour-print, Ernst has recently chosen a style that takes into account some of the contributions of Cubism and abstract art. This enabled him to endow Surrealist painting with the pictorial qualities that it had rather too nonchalantly sacrificed.

It is true that André Masson and the Spaniard Joan Miró, who had also become members of the group, never lost interest in formal problems. Nevertheless, like Klee, who took part in the first Surrealist exhibition at Paris in 1925, both these painters went beyond orthodox Surrealism. All things considered, the movement's importance stems more from the ideas that it spread than from the pictures that faithfully illustrate its conceptions. Its great merit is to have directed people's attention to the hidden recesses of the soul, of which artists like Bosch, Blake, Redon and Chagall had, indeed, already revealed aspects, but which in periods of too narrow rationalism had tended to be denied or ignored. Thus, even Picasso has been influenced by it; one can still see its effects in the work of certain abstract painters of today.

316

SURREALISM

Joan Miró's meeting with the Surrealists in 1925 constituted his second and final liberation (the first was his contact with Picasso in 1919). However, some importance must no doubt be attached to the fact that Cubism had left its mark on him before he began to associate with André Breton and his friends. Besides, in 1925 he was already in possession of a style that belonged exclusively to him; for by then he had invented those mischievous signs by means of which he commented on objects at the same time as evoking them. Surrealism merely induced him to express himself with an even freer fantasy, in a style still more impulsive and capricious.

It is clear that Miró and Klee are kindred spirits, since both introduce the spectator into a primitive world. Nevertheless, while there is a certain restraint in Klee's primitivism, Miró's reveals itself impetuously and without reserve —though not without humour. Then again, it cannot be denied that an element of cruelty enters into Miró's art. His smile is not altogether pleasant when he constructs his odd, rudimentary figures, and gives them their bewildered, dazed, and sometimes voracious and wicked look. He likes to place them near strange, multiform birds, with which, moreover, they tend to merge—unless it is the birds that merge with them. Miró is fond of ambiguous figures, and enjoys suggesting unusual relationships between dissimilar creatures. Though his men and women sometimes recall prehistoric cult images, they never have anything majestic or terrifying about them, since they always show signs of being dominated by the humour that helped to produce them. For all its air of casualness, Miró's drawing is not without character, and the highly capricious manner in which his lines can roam about is not incompatible with firmness. As for his colour, it is sometimes governed by an effect of muted richness, sometimes by one of sprightly and comical brilliance.

MIRÓ.
NOCTURNAL BIRD,
1939.
MME GIEDION-
WELCKER
COLLECTION,
ZURICH

MIRÓ.
THE WHITE
LADY,
1950.
PRIVATE
COLLECTION,
PARIS

MIRÓ.
THE MAUVE
OF THE MOON,
1951.
PRIVATE
COLLECTION,
PARIS

ABSTRACT PAINTING

WASSILY KANDINSKY. 1866-1944. ABSTRACT COMPOSITION NUMBER 2, 1913. JOSEPH SLIFKA COLLECTION, NEW YORK

KANDINSKY. ON WHITE, 1923. PRIVATE COLLECTION, PARIS

KANDINSKY. PINK COMPOSITION. WALLRAF-RICHARTZ MUSEUM, COLOGNE

Wassily Kandinsky's first abstract work, painted in 1910, is a water-colour. It looks a little like a stylistic exercise or a daring experiment, and it probably appeared as such even to the artist, who for years had been convinced that objects were detrimental to his painting. He hesitated to give them up, however, because of the danger of getting bogged down in merely decorative art. In fact, memories of the external world continue to play a part in his work right down to 1913. True enough, they are distorted, and often they can barely be identified; for even if Kandinsky was obsessed by them, on his canvases he wanted them to be reduced to simple lines and patches of colour. The lines he created spring up impetuously, snake, swirl, bristle or buckle, while his bright, glowing colours seethe, explode and collide. For Kandinsky, painting was now 'a thunderous clash of different worlds, whose struggle results in the creation of a new world termed the [finished] work.' 'Every picture,' he added, 'is born, in the same way as the cosmos, of catastrophes, which, from the chaotic dinning of the instruments, create in the end a symphony that is called the music of the spheres.' There really is something cosmic about a good many of his works; they carry one off up above the earth into the realm of the planets.

After the first world war, and particularly from 1922, when he joined the teaching staff of the Bauhaus, Kandinsky imparted a less 'romantic' character to his art; but though the tumult disappeared from his works, though he geometrized his drawing and clarified his composition, the dynamic vitality remained. Almost all the forms express movement, impetuosity or impatience. The colours can be frivolous and gay, but in general they are stately and sumptuous. Among them, one finds all the timbres of a great orchestra, from the riotous brilliance of the trumpets to the graceful melodies of the violins.

318

ABSTRACT PAINTING

Shortly after it appeared in Munich, abstract painting also found supporters in Paris, Italy and Russia. For many of them, however, it was not a question of complete and final conversion. Truth to tell, there are not many artists who through the weight and compass of their work deserve to be included among the pioneers of non-figurative art. However, along with Kandinsky and Delaunay, we must mention the Czech Kupka, the Russian Malevitch, and the Dutchman Mondrian.

Frank Kupka's researches are manifold. Sometimes his compositions appear to have been painted in emulation of music, as with his series of *Fugues in two Colours* and the *Solo of a brown Line*. At others, he erects works of architecture, as when he constructed a kind of building in which the action of the different colours creates a mystical space evoking a *Cathedral*. Then there are occasions when he directs towards the spectator successive waves of curved or ogival forms, which seem to well up from the depths of the universe. Or else his pictures may be filled with a swelling, floral mass, of which the expansion is so strong that it runs the risk of overflowing. The artist restrains it, however. Often he even represses his lyricism; sometimes his work becomes cold, through being too strictly controlled.

Wishing to establish 'the supremacy of pure sensibility', Casimir Malevitch, the founder of Suprematism, used only flat, elementary geometrical forms. Though on one occasion—so as to be able to start again at the very beginning—he confined himself to drawing a black square against a white background, his geometrical forms are usually filled in with various colours. These help to give each of them a personality of its own, so that they all appear charged with a different message. Malevitch does indeed seem to have been the first to show that strict geometry can be given real emotive power.

CASIMIR MALEVITCH, 1878-1935. SUPREMATIST COMPOSITION, 1915-1916. LENINGRAD MUSEUM.

FRANK KUPKA. 1871-1957. BLUE AND RED VERTICAL PLANES, 1913. GALERIE LOUIS CARRÉ, PARIS

KUPKA. PHILOSOPHICAL ARCHITECTURE, 1913. GALERIE LOUIS CARRÉ, PARIS

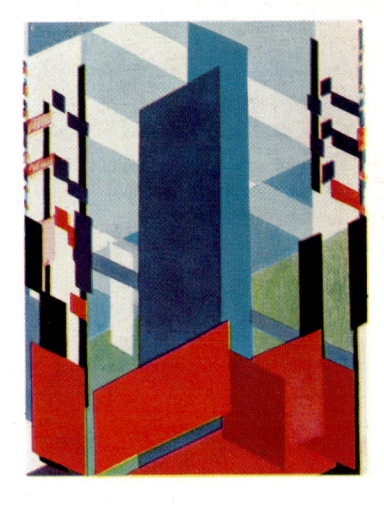

ABSTRACT PAINTING

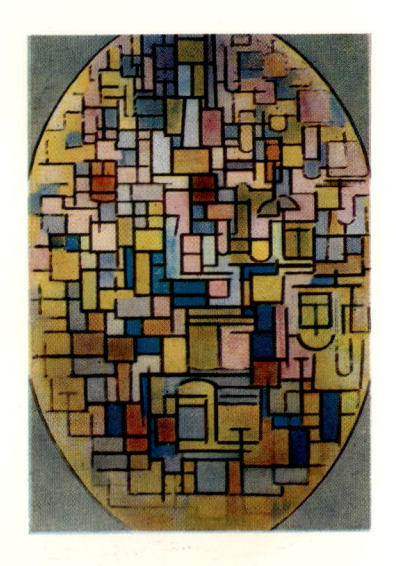

PIET MONDRIAN.
1872-1944.
OVAL COMPOSITION
(TABLEAU III),
1914.
STEDELIJK MUSEUM,
AMSTERDAM

MONDRIAN.
COMPOSITION IN
RED, YELLOW AND
BLUE, 1926.
H. M. ROTHSCHILD
COLLECTION, USA

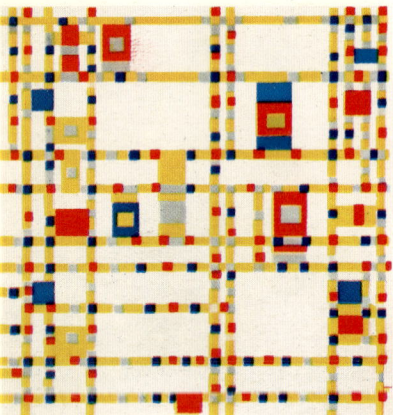

MONDRIAN.
BROADWAY
BOOGIE-WOOGIE,
1942-1943.
MUSEUM OF MODERN
ART, NEW YORK

Piet Mondrian also made use of geometry, but in a more austere and puritanical spirit than Casimir Malevitch. As soon as he had found his own style—from 1921 onwards, that is to say—he no longer allowed anything to appear on his canvases except compartments bounded by vertical and horizontal lines. At the same time, he limited his palette to red, yellow, and blue, in combination with black, white and grey. Moreover, he never mixed his colours, and none of the three necessarily appears, so that some of his pictures present only white surfaces divided up by two or three black lines. Such a reduction to essentials does not mean a lack of sensibility; the works done at Paris between 1911 and 1914 under the influence of Cubism are extremely vibrant. It was just that he became convinced that what mattered was the expression not of 'subjective states of soul' but of 'pure reality'. This he located behind the changing appearances of nature, and he considered that only pure plastic relationships were capable of giving an account of it. Yet, however exact the relationships that he taxed his ingenuity to establish, one is bound to admit that, by and large, he confined himself for twenty years to varying the same formula. Only in his very last works did something new become apparent, when, having settled in New York, he abandoned essentially static compositions, in order to express the hectic vitality of the great city. All the same, he did not repudiate his principles.

Thus, thanks to Mondrian and to Kandinsky as he was between 1910 and 1914, abstract painting indicated right from its heroic age the extremes between which it would never cease to oscillate and developed.

On the one hand, there are manifest an almost frenzied lyricism, volcanic outpourings, and handling that is full of dash and brilliance; on the other, the rejection of all romanticism, and a concern for the most lucid balance.

320

AMERICAN PAINTING

From the early years of settlement in the North American colonies there is evidence of art in some form, but the story of picture making in America begins with the eighteenth century, when the colonies had achieved coherence and a native society which made demands far beyond the immediate necessities of life. The Protestant affiliations of the American settlers almost excluded religious themes, and the Puritans' aversion to anything less than the serious narrowed the subject matter for painting to portraiture. Robert Feke, Charles Willson Peale, Thomas Sully, Benjamin West, John Singleton Copley and Gilbert Stuart carried the crest of the tide, leaving to posterity a pictorial record of the respected and great of the era.

Of these, the work of Copley and Stuart is of genius, both men bringing to it a full knowledge of human nature; the former through a sharp and brilliant delineation of character, the latter through a penetration to the inner man. One fond of informal poses and harmonious color, the other often dispensing with all but a powerful statement of the inner life of his subject.

Limited opportunities for instruction and the urge to see the works of the immortal masters of Europe drew West, Copley, Stuart and others to England, where West and Copley settled. Stuart, however, returned to America "to paint Washington" and remained there. In England, West, Copley and others became absorbed in the European art movements, and the historical and classical subjects they painted reflect the Rococo and Neoclassical mode.

In strong contrast to these sophisticated pictures executed under European influences stands the homegrown work of the remarkable sign painter from Pennsylvania, Edward Hicks. For him as ardent Quaker and itinerant preacher of his faith, art and style served only the purpose of translating the burning message of his pictures, love for his country and for his religion. His principal theme, of

JOHN SINGLETON COPLEY, 1738-1815. NATHANIEL HURD, AFTER 1765. THE CLEVELAND MUSEUM

GILBERT STUART, 1755-1828. MRS. RICHARD YATES, c. 1793. NATIONAL GALLERY OF ART, WASHINGTON

EDWARD HICKS, 1780-1849. THE PEACEABLE KINGDOM, c. 1835. COLLECTION MRS. HOLGER CAHILL, NEW YORK

321

AMERICAN PAINTING

GEORGE INNESS,
1825-1894.
JUNE,
1882.
THE BROOKLYN
MUSEUM

WINSLOW HOMER,
1836-1910.
THE GULF STREAM,
1899.
METROPOLITAN
MUSEUM, NEW YORK

THOMAS EAKINS,
1844-1916.
THE AGNEW CLINIC,
1889.
UNIVERSITY OF
PENNSYLVANIA,
PHILADELPHIA

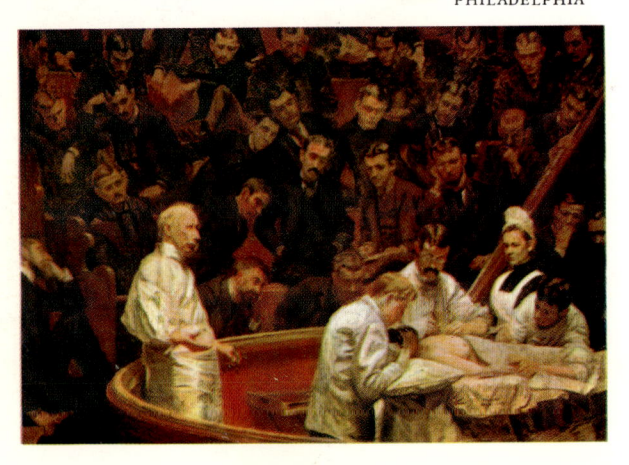

which more than a hundred versions exist, was the Peaceable Kingdom, here incorporating a view of William Penn signing a peace treaty with the Indians and a vista of the Delaware Water Gap.

Throughout the nineteenth century landscape painting developed into an important trend culminating in the art of George Inness, who started as a member of the Hudson River School, and reached a universality in his subject matter unknown in America. He understood and interpreted the spaces and aerial distance of his native land, the languid peace of nature uninhabited, the drowsy heat and hot shimmer of its summers and the atmospheric moods created by masses of storm-laden clouds gathering over the wide expanse of American skies.

If the cosmopolitan character of art drew men like James McNeil Whistler (see p. 243) to Europe to work and live because he considered the confines of the art world in America too narrow by contrast, Winslow Homer, Yankee born and bred and almost entirely self-taught, found strength and greatness on his native soil. He brought to maturity a pictorial expression which had grown out of the pioneer spirit and the nature of a new continent. Homer's range of subject matter and style was wider than that of any of his predecessors. He began as a successful illustrator and in this capacity covered the Civil War for *Harper's Weekly*. But already in this commissioned work his deep interest in the common stands out, for the scenes he chose for the campaign are the unheroic activities of soldiers at camp. Though Homer portrayed contemporary life in the United States, his art is also devoted to the stirring aspects of nature, chiefly of the sea and man's relation to it.

Like Homer, Thomas Eakins pictured the America of his day. However, a scientific aptitude combined in him with artistic talents and determined his creative goals. He was a student of anatomy and received art training at the Penn-

AMERICAN PAINTING

sylvania Academy of Fine Arts in Philadelphia and at the École des Beaux-Arts of Paris. In his early years Eakins painted varied subjects, domestic genre, sporting scenes and compositions of the clinic where he studied. When his work was ignored or received with indifference the artist turned to portraiture exclusively. His subjects were his friends and his family. Through his insight, mastery and sensitive selection he exposed the inner personality, unflattered but alive, of his sitters.

The most unworldly of the painters who hold a distinguished position in American art is Albert Pinkham Ryder. He described his own life when he said, "The artist needs but a roof, a crust of bread and his easel and all the rest God gives him in abundance." Ryder lived in poverty and squalor, completely absorbed in giving form to his visions. His pictures, though small in scale, are monumental in effect. The themes are based on nature or drawn from the Bible, Shakespeare or Wagner. His wind-blown trees, clouds, oceans and vessels exist in a world as fundamental as the days of Genesis. To achieve such results Ryder reworked his paintings again and again sometimes for years. Wrestling with envisioned effects made him a careless technician, mixing his media indiscriminately. His output is limited to about 150 paintings, many of them in deplorable condition.

In the 1870's painting rose to one of its peaks in Europe, especially in France, inducing the new generation of American students to study abroad under prominent artists. The largest contingent of these sought instruction in Paris. Two major figures of the Paris-trained artists were John Singer Sargent and Mary Cassett (see p. 247). Sargent's phenomenal talent and thorough training soon made him an international figure in the art world. Born in Florence, the son of expatriate Americans, he travelled widely, ultimately settling in London. His brilliant technique,

ALBERT P. RYDER, 1847-1917. THE FLYING DUTCHMAN, BEFORE 1890. NATIONAL COLLECTION OF FINE ARTS, WASHINGTON

JOHN SINGER SARGENT, 1856-1925. MR. & MRS. I. N. PHELPS STOKES, 1897. METROPOLITAN MUSEUM, NEW YORK

JOHN MARIN, 1870-1953. MAINE ISLANDS (WATERCOLOR), 1922. PHILLIPS COLLECTION, WASHINGTON

AMERICAN PAINTING

GEORGE BELLOWS,
1882-1925.
ELINOR,
JEAN AND ANNA.
1920.
ALBRIGHT
ART GALLERY,
BUFFALO

EDWARD HOPPER,
BORN 1882.
EARLY SUNDAY
MORNING,
1930.
WHITNEY MUSEUM,
NEW YORK

JACK LEVINE,
BORN 1915.
THE SYNDICATE,
1939.
COLLECTION OF
JOSEPH
H. HIRSHHORN,
NEW YORK

vivid sense of color and unproblematic and ingratiating subjects, which told little about the people portrayed and much about the elegance of the elite, made him a much-sought-after society painter in Boston and Europe.

In 1899 John Marin relinquished a career in architecture to study art, first in Philadelphia and New York, then for six years in France. Annual exhibits at Alfred Stieglitz' "291" gallery in New York laid the basis for the important retrospectives of his work at the New York Museum of Modern Art in 1936 and at the Venice Biennale in 1950, the first American to be thus honored. From his student years, the craft of etching, which he learned largely by consulting the prints of Rembrandt and Whistler, and a play of color not unlike that of the Fauves, remained to influence his mature work. Working largely in watercolor, but with a sweep and vigor not usually associated with this medium, he sought in the skyscrapers and bridges of New York and the mountains and seacoasts of New England form and outline and color for his highly expressive paintings, which are often executed in a highly personal shorthand that borders on abstraction.

Soon after the beginning of the twentieth century, a group of young artists known as "The Eight," portrayed in rather somber, but solid colors the boisterous raw life of a crowded city. George Bellows, pupil of one of them, Robert Henri, not only carried on the tradition of "The Eight," but developed it to its fullest. The style suited Bellows' extrovert nature. Through the free and dashing brush work of his pictures shines the artists's robust vitality and quick mind. These gave sparkle to his Hudson River scenes, power to his paintings of sport, and tactile warmth and tenderness to his portraits.

Bellows and most of "The Eight" were instrumental in organizing the Armory Show of 1913 which acquainted the American public with the radical movements existing abroad and prepared the way

324

AMERICAN PAINTING

for a slow acceptance of such directions as Expressionism. However, the greatest impetus to Expressionism was the depression of the 1930's. Jack Levine's art was one of satirical and vitriolic comment on the brutal and hypocritical aspects of society, although his lyrical colors and highly sensitive and soft modeling of form stand in strange contrast to the subjects he painted.

An older painter, Edward Hopper, did not focus on man but brought him into his pictures as the silent partner of his surroundings. If man is not in sight, his spirit is behind the deserted look of Main Street in *Early Sunday Morning*. Hopper's art symbolizes the principal characteristic of American painting, the devotion to the actual. Except for the interlude and special moment for the depression, American painting up to the late nineteen thirties, the period covered in this book, is mainly an art of careful observation, an observation which is tempered and qualified by the era and by the individual practitioner. American painting in its many aspects, therefore, is truly a mirror of the growth of the nation.

MEXICAN PAINTING

The great period of modern Mexican painting found its inception in the revolution of 1910. Under government patronage, it was employed to decorate schools, hospitals and other types of public edifices and serves a didactic function. It speaks of and for the people of Mexico, their heritage, hardships, oppression and victories. Two of its leading muralists, Diego Rivera and José Clemente Orozco, found welcome in certain circles in the United States. The latter's murals are at Pomona College, California, Dartmouth College, and the New School for Social Research and the Museum of Modern Art, New York. Orozco's vision transcends nationalism, fascism and war and forecasts a universal holocaust unless a Promethean humanism prevails.

JOSÉ CLEMENTE OROZCO, 1883-1949. COMBAT, 1920. COLLECTION DR. ALVAR CARRILLO GIL, MEXICO

OROZCO. SELF-PORTRAIT, 1940. MUSEUM OF MODERN ART, NEW YORK

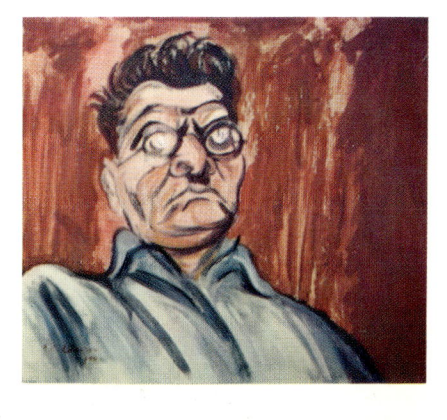

OROZCO. ZAPATISTAS, 1931. MUSEUM OF MODERN ART, NEW YORK

325

Index of Artists

Artists who are discussed in
some detail or whose works are illustrated,
and the main references of series, are shown
by roman lettering or numbers.
Passing mentions are denoted by italics.

INDEX OF ARTISTS

Aertsen, Pieter   176
Albertinelli, Mariotto   112
Allegri, Antonio, see Correggio
Altdorfer, Albrecht   132, 135, 136, 138
Andrea del Castagno   52-53
Angelico, Fra   27, 44-5, 50, 51, 106
Antonello da Messina   61, 62, 63
Apelles   11, 69
Arp, Hans   314, 315
Arpino, Chevalier d'   154
Audran, Claude   194
Aved   199

Bakhuysen, Ludolf   183
Baldovinetti, Alesso   51, 67
Baldung Grien, Hans   132, 136-7
Balla, Giacomo   294, 295
Bandol, Jean de   73
Barbarelli, Giorgio, see Giorgione
Barbari, Jacopo de'   132
Bartolomeo, Fra   112
Baschenis, Evaristo   157
Bassano, Jacopo   125
Bastiani, Lazzaro   64
Bauchant, André   312, 313
Baugin   157, 177
Bazille, Frédéric   246, 247
Beaumetz, Jean de   73
Beauneveu, André   73, 74
Bellechose, Henri   72, 73
Bellegambe, Jean   80
Bellinis, the   59, 117
Bellini, Gentile   62, 64, 65
Bellini, Giovanni   61, 62-3, 65, 118, 124
Bellini, Jacopo   40, 62, 116
Bellotto, Bernardo   203
Bellows, George   324
Bencovitch, Federico   206
Benoit, Marie-Guilhelmine   226, 227

Benvenuto di Giovanni   43
Berchem, Nicolaes   182
Berghe, Frits van den   306
Bernard, Émile   260
Bertin, Victor   236
Bertram, Master   38, 39, 99
Beuckelaer, Joachim   176
Blake, William   215, 216-7, 316
Blanchard, Jacques   188
Bleyl, Fritz   300
Boccioni, Umberto   294
Boilly, Louis-Léopold   201
Bombois, Camille   312
Bonington, Richard-Parkes   219, 228, 232
Bonnard, Pierre   181, 266, 267, 268-9, 297
Bordone, Paris   120, 121
Borrassa, Luis   96
Bosch, Hieronymus   93, 94-5, 143, 144, 147, 148, 149, 170, 297, 316
Botticelli, Sandro   68-9, 70, 222
Boucher, François   196-7, 200, 252
Boudin, Eugène   241, 246
Bouts, Dieric   87, 88-9, 90, 92, 101, 142
Bramante, Donato   56, 108
Braque, Georges   272, 273, 276, 278, 280, 281, 282, 283, 284, 288-9, 290
Broederlam, Melchior   73
Bronzino, Angelo   113
Brouwer, Adriaen   170-1
Brown, Ford Madox   222
Brown, John   216
Bruegel the Elder, Pieter   74, 93, 147-9, 170, 181, 235, 297
Bruegel the Younger, Pieter   149
Bruegel, Velvet, Jan   166, 171
Brunel the Younger, Jean   128
Brunelleschi, Filippo   46, 47, 48

Buonarroti, See Michelangelo
Burne-Jones, Edward   222

Caliari, Paolo, see Veronese
Callot, Jacques   174
Calvert, Edward   217
Camoin, Charles   242
Campin, Robert   81, 84
Canaletto, Antonio   203, 204
Cappelle, Johannes van de   184
Caravaggio, Michelangelo Merisi   154-5, 156, 157, 167, 173, 185, 189, 193, 198
Caron, Antoine   130, 131
Carpaccio, Vittore   64-5
Carrá, Carlo   294, 295
Carracci, Annibale   189, 193, 205
Carrucci, Jacopo, see Pontormo
Cassatt, Mary   247, 323
Castagno, see Andrea del
Cavallini, Pietro   28-9, 30
Cellini, Benvenuto   127
Cézanne, Paul   247, 251, 256-7, 259, 260, 266, 267, 271, 273, 278, 279, 280, 282, 284, 285, 304, 406
Chagall, Marc   310, 316
Champaigne, Philippe de   178, 184, 187, 188
Chardin, Jean-Baptiste   179, 181, 198-9, 200, 205, 236, 237, 289
Charlet, Nicolas   238
Charton, Enguerrand   77, 78, 79
Chassériau, Théodore   234, 242
Chirico, Giorgio de   295, 316
Christus, Petrus   86-7, 88
Cimabue   28, 29, 30, 32
Claesz, Pieter   176, 177
Cleve, Joos van   145
Clouet, François   128, 139, 130
Clouet, Jean   128, 129, 130
Codde, Pieter   181
Coecke van Aelst, Pieter   147

INDEX OF ARTISTS

Coelho, see *Sanchez Coelho*
Colantonio *61*
Constable, John 213, 218-9, 220, 232, 247
Copley, John Singleton 321
Corneille de Lyon 130, *131*
Corot, Jean-Baptiste *177*, *197*, 202, 236-7, 238, 239, 240, 241, 246, 250, 278, 289
Correggio Antonio Allegri 89, 114-5, *124*, *179*, 226, 234
Cosimo, see *Piero di Cosimo*
Cossa, Francesco del 60
Costa, Lorenzo 114
Cotán, Sanchez 157, 177
Cotman, John Sell 218
Courbet, Gustave *259*, 225, 231, 236, 240-1, 243, 246
Cousin, Jean *126*, 127
Couture, Thomas 245
Cox, David 218
Cozens, Alexander 218
Cozens, John-Robert 218
Cranach the Younger, Lucas 139
Cranach the Elder, Lucas *132*, 138-9
Credi, see *Lorenzo di Credi*
Crivelli, Carlo 59
Crome, John 218
Cross, Henry-Edmond *259*, 271
Cuyp, Albert 182, *183*

Dali, Salvador 316
Dalmau, Luis 96
Daubigny, Charles 235
Daumier, Honoré 229, 238-9 240, 245, 298
David, Gerard 142-3
David, Louis 224-5, 226, 227, 228, 229, 230
Decamps, Alexandre 233, 234
Decourt, Jean 130
Degas, Edgar 215, 234, 243, 247, 254-5, 257, 264, 265, 266, 267, 269, 307
Delacroix, Eugène *200*, 214, 215, 219, 224, 225, 227, 228, 229, 231, 232-3, 234, 235, 239, 240, 242, 252, 262
Delaunay, Robert 284, 285, 292, 293, 302, 303, 319
Denis, Maurice 266, 267
Derain, André 270, 271, 272, 273, 278-9
Desportes, François 196, 197
Desvallières, Georges 242
De Troy, see *Troy, François de*
Deutsch, Niklaus Manuel 137, *139*
Devis, Arthur 210
Diaz, Narcisse-Virgile 235
Dombet, Guillaume 76, 78
Domenico Venziano 44, 50, 51, 52, 54, 106
Donatello 46, 47, 53, 58, 60, 110
Dongen, Kees van 273, 279
Doni, see *Uccello, Paolo Doni*
Dossi, Dosso 115
Dou, Gérard *177*, *180*, *181*
Doyen, Gabriel 200
Dubois, Ambroise 131
Dubreuil, Toussaint 131
Duccio di Buoninsegna 32-3, 34
Duchamp, Marcel 285, 294, 314
Dufy, Raoul 273, 276-7
Dujardin, Karel 183
Dumoutier, Daniel 130
Duplessis, Joseph 200
Dupré, Jules 235
Dürer, Albrecht, *100*, *103*, 113, 129, 132-3, *134*, *135*, *136*, *138*, *140*, *145*, *147*, *174*
Duval, Marc 130, 131
Duyster, Willem-Cornelisz *181*
Dyck, Anthony van *166*, 168-9, 172, *193*, 210

Eakins, Thomas 322-3
Elsheimer, Adam 156, *174*
Engelbrechtsz, Cornelis 147
Ensor, James 296-7, 300, 306
Ernst, Max 315, 316

Eyck, Hubert van 81, 82, 83, 85, 86, 87, 88, 90
Eyck, Jan van 27, 61, 73, 80, 81-3, 84, 85, 86, 87, 88, 90, 96, 97, 143, 164

Fabius Pictor 12
Fabritius, Carel 176, 177, *178*
Fantin-Latour, Henri 242, 243
Feininger, Lyonel 303, 304
Fetti, Domenico 204
Floris, Frans 145
Fouquet, Jean 74-5, 76-7
Fouquières, Jacques 187
Fragonard, Jean-Honoré 200-1
Francesco di Giorgio Martini 43
Francke, Master 98, 99
Fréminet, Martin 131
Friedrich, Gaspard-David 223
Friesz, Othon 270, 272, 273
Froment, Nicolas 77, 78-9
Frueauf the Elder 102, 103
Fuseli, Henry 215, 216, 219
Fyt, Jan 176

Gainsborough, Thomas 213, 214, 219
Gauguin, Paul 251, 260-1, *263*, 264, 266, 267, 272, 279, 300
Geertgen tot Sint Jans 88, 89
Gellée, see *Lorrain, Claude*
Gentile da Fabriano 40, *41*, 43, 45, 51, 62
Gentileschi, Orazio 156
Gérard François, Baron 226
Géricault, Théodore 224, 226, 227, 228-9, 232, 238
Ghiberti, Lorenzo 48, 51
Ghirlandaio, David 67
Ghirlandaio, Domenico 67, *110*
Giorgione Giorgio Barbarelli 63, 116-7, *118*, *120*, *125*, *179*, *195*, 244
Giotto di Bondone 30-1, 33, 34, 35, 40, 46
Girard of Orleans 38, 39

INDEX OF ARTISTS

Girodet-Trioson, Anne-Louis 226, 227
Girtin, Thomas 218
Gleizes, Albert 283
Goblen, Van 187
Goes, Hugo van der 67, 89, 90-1
Gogh, Vincent van 251, 260, 262-3, 264, 266, 271, 272, 279, 296, 297, 300, 304
Gonçalves, Nuño 97
Gossaert, Jan 143, 144, 145, 146
Goya, Francisco de 94, 208-9, 232, 238, 239, 298
Goyen, Jan van 182, 183
Gozzoli, Benozzo 51, 106
Graf, Urs 137
Grandville 238
Greco, El 125, 152-3, 160, 299
Greuze, Jean-Baptiste 199, 200, 226
Grien, see Baldung Grien
Gris, Juan 282-3
Gromaire, Marcel 308
Gropius, Walter 304
Gros, Jean-Antoine 224, 227, 228, 229
Grünewald, Mathias 132, 133, 134-5
Guardi, Francesco 204-5
Guardi, Gianantonio 204
Guérin Pierre, Baron 227, 228
Guido da Sienna 28, 29
Guillaumin, Armand 247
Guys, Constantin 229

Hals, Frans 170, 172-3, 180, 241, 245
Heckel, Erich 300
Heda, Willem Claesz 176, 177
Heem, Davidsz de 176, 177
Heemskerck, Martin van 146
Helst, Bartholomeus van der 173
Hemessen, Jan van 144
Herlin, Friedrich 102, 103

Hesdin, Jacquemart de 74
Heyden, Jan van der 203
Hicks, Edward 321-2
Highmore, Joseph 210
Hillyarde, Nicholas 210
Hobbema, Meindert 182, 183, 218, 219
Hogarth, William 205, 210-1, 212, 217
Holbein the Elder, Hans 140
Holbein the Younger, Hans 129, 132, 139-140-1, 150
Homer, Winslow 322
Honthorst, Gerard van 156
Hooch, Pieter de 181
Hopper, Edward 324, 325
Hoppner, John 215
Huguet, Jaume 96
Hunt, William Holman 222

Ingres, Dominique 209, 224, 227, 230-1, 234, 240, 254, 255, 286
Inness, George 322
Isenbrant, Adriaenen 143

Jawlensky, Alexei von 302, 303
Jones, Inigo 210
Jongkind, Johan-Barthold 236, 246
Jordaens, Jacob 167, 170
Juanes, Juan de 151
Justus of Ghent 90

Kalf, Willem 277
Kandinsky, Wassily 302, 304, 318, 319, 320
Kirchner, Ernst-Ludwig 300, 301
Klee, Paul 302, 303, 304-5, 315, 316, 317
Kneller, Godfrey 210
Kokoschka, Oskar 301
Koninck, Philips 182, 183
Kupka, Frank 319
Kutter, Joseph 306

La Fresnaye, Roger de 285
Lagneau, Pierre 130
Lancret, Nicolas 196
Landseer, Edwin 222
Largillière, Nicolas de 193, 197
Lasterman, Pieter Pietersz 174
La Tour, Georges de 157, 184-5, 186, 190
La Tour, Maurice-Quentin de 197, 198
Laurana, Francesco da 61
Lawrence, Thomas 215, 216, 232
Le Brun, Charles 188, 192, 193
Léger, Fernand 284, 285, 290-1, 292
Leighton, lord Frederick 222
Lely, Peter 210
Lemoine, François 193
Le Nain, Antoine 186
Le Nain, Louis, 178, 184, 186-7
La Nain, Mathieu 186
Leonardo da Vinci 46, 66, 70, 71, 95, 104-5, 108, 110, 111, 112, 114, 116, 126, 140, 143, 220
Le Sueur, Eustache 184, 188
Levine, Jack 324, 325
Lewis, Wyndham 307
Leyden, Lucas van 146, 147, 174
Leyster, Judith 181
Lhote, André 285
Limbourg, Pol de 73
Limbourg brothers, Pol, Hennequin and Herman de 74, 83
Linard 176
Linnell, John 217
Lippi, Filippino 47, 70
Lippi, Filippo 50, 51, 68, 70
Lochner, Stephan 39, 100-1
Longhi, Pietro 205
Lorenzetti, Ambrogio 36-7
Lorenzetti, Pietro 35, 36
Lorenzo di Credi 66, 71
Lorenzo Monaco 40, 44, 50

INDEX OF ARTISTS

Lorrain, Claude *184, 188, 189, 218, 220*
Lotto, Lorenzo *121*
Luce, Maximilien *259*
Luciani, see Sebastiano del Piombo
Luini, Bernardino *114*
Lys, Jan *204*

Mabuse, see Gossaert
Mack, August *302, 303, 304*
Magnasco, Alessandro *204*
Magritte, René *316*
Maler, Hans *103*
Malevitch, Casimir *319, 320*
Malouel, Jean *72, 73*
Mander, Karel van *172*
Manet, Édouard *159, 209, 241, 242, 243, 244-5, 246, 252*
Manfredi, Bartolomeo *156*
Manguin, Henri-Charles *242, 270*
Mantegna, Andrea *56, 58-9, 60, 62, 63, 64, 102, 114, 124, 132, 174, 222*
Marc, Franz *302-3*
Marcoussis, Louis *282, 283*
Marieschi *204*
Marin, John *323, 324*
Marmion, Simon *80*
Marquet, Albert *242, 251, 272, 273, 279*
Marshall, Ben *214*
Martini, Simone *33, 34, 35, 42*
Masaccio, Tomaso di Giovanni di Simone *40, 42, 44, 46-7, 48, 49, 50, 52, 53, 54, 55, 70, 154*
Masolino, Tomaso di Cristoforo Fini *42, 46, 47*
Masson, André *316*
Massys, Quentin *142, 143, 144*
Master of the Bicker Portraits *147*
Master of the Death of the Virgin, see Cleve, Joos van
Master E. S. *94*
Master of Flémalle *81, 84-5*
Master of the Heures de Boucicaut *83*

Master of the Life of the Virgin *100, 101*
Master of the Moulins *78-9, 90*
Master of the Osservanza *43*
Master of the Registrum Gregorii *20*
Master of St Bartholomew *101, 102*
Master of St George *96*
Master of St Giles *80*
Master of St-Jean-de-Luz *80*
Master of the St Peter's Altarpiece *29*
Master of St. Sebastien *80*
Master of the St Ursula Legen *101*
Master of St Veronica *98*
Master of the Trébon Altarpiece *38, 39*
Master of the Upper Rhine or Middle Rhine *98*
Master of the Virgin of Benediktbeuren *98, 99*
Master of the Virgo inter Virgines *86, 87*
Master of Werden, see Master of the Life of the Virgin
Master of 1456 *76, 80*
Matisse, Henri *242, 251, 270, 271, 272, 273, 274-5, 276, 300, 302, 307*
Mazzola, Francesco, see Parmigianino
Meer, van der *183*
Melozzo da Forli *56*
Memlinc, Hans *64, 91, 92-3, 142*
Merisi, Michelangelo, see Caravaggio
Metsu, Gabriel *176, 181*
Metzinger, Jean *283*
Michallon *236*
Michelangelo Buonarroti *56, 67, 103, 108, 109, 110-1, 113, 120, 122, 126, 227, 229*
Michelozzo *45*
Mignard, Pierre *184, 188, 192*

Millais, John Everett *222*
Millet, Jean-François *235, 250*
Miró, Joan *316, 317*
Modigliani, Amedeo *309*
Mondrian, Piet *319, 320*
Monet, Claude *246, 247, 248-9, 250, 251, 252, 254, 256, 258, 311*
Monnier, Henry *238*
Moor, Anthonis, see Moro
Moore, Henry *307*
Morales, Luis de *151*
Morandi, Giorgio *295*
Moreau, Gustave *242*
Moreau, Louis *237*
Morisot, Berthe *247*
Morland, George *214*
Moro, Antonio *150, 151*
Morris, William *222, 243*
Moser, Lucas *99, 100*
Mueller, Otto *300*
Multscher *100*
Munch, Edvard *297, 300*
Murillo, Bartolome Esteban *151, 159, 162, 214*

Nash, Paul *307*
Nattier, Jean-Marc *196, 197*
Negretti, Jacopo, see Palma Vecchio
Neithart, Mathis, see Grünewald
Neroccio de' Landi *43*
Nicolas of Hagenau *134*
Nolde, Emil *300, 301*
Noort, Adam van *167*

Old Crome, see Crome, John
Orley, Bernard van *145, 146, 147*
Orozco, José Clemente *325*
Ostade, Adriaen van *181*
Oudry, Jean-Baptiste *197*

Pacher, Michael *101, 102*
Palamedesz, Anthonie *181*
Palladio, Andrea *124*

INDEX OF ARTISTS

Palma Giovane, Jacopo Negretti 119
Palma Vecchio, Jacopo Negretti 120
Palmer, Samuel 217
Palmezzano, Marco 56
Pannini, Giov. Antonio 202
Pantoja de la Cruz, Juan 150
Parmigianino, *Francesco Mazzola* 115, *122*, *127*
Pata 241
Patenier, Joachim 143-44
Pater, Jean-Baptiste 196
Patinir, Joachim, see *Patenier*
Pechstein, Max 300
Permeke, Constant 306, *308*
Perréal, Jean 79
Perugino, *Pietro Vannucci* 66, 106-7, *108*, *112*, 114
Piazzetta, Giovanni-Battista 206
Picabia, Francis 314, 315
Picasso, Pablo Ruiz 208, *278*, *280*, 281, *282*, 283, 284, *286-7*, *288*, *316*, 317
Piero della Francesca 50, *51*, 54-5, 56, *60*, *61*, *63*, 106
Piero di Cosimo 71
Pinturicchio, Bernardino 107
Piranesi 202
Pisanello, Antonio 40-1, 60, 72
Pisano, Nicola 32
Pissarro, Camille 246, 247, 250-1, 254, 256, 259, 260, *313*
Pissarro, Lucien 259
Pizzolo, Niccolo 58
Pleydenwurff, Hans 102-3
Pollaiulo, Antonio 53, 56, 66, 68
Polygnotos 11, 13
Pontormo, *Jacopo Carrucci* 112, *113*
Porcellis, Jan 183
Potter, Paulus 183
Pourbus the Younger, Frans 131, 187
Poussin, Nicholas *131*, *157*, *184*, *188*, *189*, 190-1, *192*, *196*, 224,

225, 227, 229, 230, 235, 236, 278
Primaticcio, Francesco 126, 127
Prud'hon, Pierre-Paul 226, 227, *232*, 234
Pucelle, Jean 74
Puvis de Chavannes, Pierre 234, 242, 260, 267
Puy, Jean 270

Quarton, Enguerrand, see *Charton*
Quesnel, François *130*, *131*

Raeburn, Henry 214-5
Raffet 229
Ramsay, Allan 215
Ranson, Paul 266
Raphael Sanzio 75, *106*, *107*, 108-9, *110*, *112*, 121, 122, 124, 125, *126*, *189*, 223, 227, 230, 244, *253*, 278
Redon, Odilon 266, *316*
Regnault, Jean-Baptiste 226 227
Rembrandt, Harmensz van Rijn 156, *173*, 174-5, *177*, *178*, *179*, 182, *183*, *185*, *190*, 228, *232*, *235*, *238*, *299*, *324*
Renoir, Auguste *179*, *181*, *213*, 241, 246, 252-3, 254, *255*, 257, 258, 269, *278*, 306
Reymerswael, Marinus van 144, 145
Reynolds, Sir Joshua *179*, 212, *213*, 215, 222, 232
Ribalta, Francisco 158
Ribera, José de *156*, 158
Ricci, Sebastiano 206
Rigaud, Hyacinthe *193*
Robert, Hubert 200, *201*, 202
Roberti, Ercole de' 60
Robusti, Jacopo, see *Tintoretto*
Rodin, Auguste 229
Romano, Guilo 122, 124, *125*, *126*
Romney, George 214, 215
Rossetti, Dante-Daniel, 221, 222

Rosso, Giovanbattista 126
Rouault, Georges 242, 298-9
Rousseau, Théodore *183*, 235, 236
Rousseau le Douanier, Henri 311, *312*, *313*
Roussel, Ker-Xavier 266
Rowlandson, Thomas 217, 218, *232*
Rubens, Peter-Paul *131*, 148, 149, 164-5, *166*, *167*, *168*, *169*, *170*, *171*, *172*, *183*, *187*, *188*, *190*, *193*, *194*, *195*, *200*, *209*, 225, 227, 232, 241, 252
Rublev, Andrei 27
Ruisdael, Jacob Isaacksz 182, 183, *213*, 218, 219
Ruisdael, Salomon van 182
Runge, Philipp Otto 223
Russolo, Luigi 294
Ryder, Albert P. 323

Saenredam, Pieter Jansz 176-7
Sanchez Coelho, Alonso *150*, 151
Sandby, Paul 218
Sano di Pietro 42, 43
Saraceni, Carlo 156
Sargent, John Singer 323-4
Sarto, Andrea del 112, *113*
Sasetta, *Stefano di Giovanni* 42, 43
Schiavone, Andrea 122
Schmodt-Rottluff, Karl 300
Schongauer, Martin *102*, *103*, 132
Schwitters, Kurt 315
Scorel, Jan 146, *147*
Sebastiano del Piombo, *Sebastiano Luciani* 120
Seghers, Hercules 182, *183*
Séraphine, Louis 312
Serodine, Giovanni 156
Sérusier, Paul 266, 267
Seurat, Georges 251, 258-9, 262, 266, *285*, 303

INDEX OF ARTISTS

Severini, Gino   294, 295
Sickert, Walter-Richard   243, 307
Signac, Paul   258, 259, 262, 271
Signorelli, Luca   45, 56-7, 107
Simone Martini, see Martini
Sisley, Alfred   246, 250, 251, 258
Smet, Gustave de   306
Smith, Matthew   307
Snyders, Frans   166, 176
Sodoma, Giovanni Bazzi   107
Solana, José Gutierrez   296
Solario, Andrea   114
Soutine, Chaïm   308, 309 310
Spranger, Bartholomeus   145
Squarcione   58, 60
Steen, Jan   180, 181
Steer, Wilson   307
Stoskopff, Sebastian   176
Stroganov   27
Strozzi, Zanobi   45
Stuart, Gilbert   321
Stubbs, George   214
Sutherland, Graham   307
Suttermans, Justus   166
Swanenburgh, Isaac Claesz van   174

Tadema, Alma   222
Tanguy, Yves   315
Teniers the Younger, David   171
Ter Borch, Gerard   180, 181
Terbrugghen, Hendrick   156, 178
Theodoric of Prague   39
Theophanes the Greek   27
Thornhill, James   210, 211
Tiepolo, Giambattista   200, 206-7
Tiepolo, Giandomenico   207
Tintoretto Jacopo Robusti   118, 122-3, 124, 125
Tischbein, Wilhelm   223
Titian, Tiziano Vecellio   63, 75, 116, 117, 118-9, 120, 121, 122, 124, 164, 168, 174, 179, 188, 207, 209, 230, 244, 245, 252
Tocqué, Louis   197

Torriti, Jacopo   29
Toulouse-Lautrec, Henri de   264-5, 266, 286, 300
Troost, Cornelis   181
Troy, François de   196, 197
Tura, Cosimo   60
Turner, William   189, 218, 219, 220-1, 247
Tytgat, Edgar   310

Uccello Paolo Doni   48-9, 52, 53, 54, 58
Ushakov, Simon   27
Utrillo, Maurice   313

Valadon, Suzanne   313
Valenciennes, Pierre-Henri   236, 237
Valentin de Boullongne   156, 157
Valtat, Louis   270
Van de Cappelle, van Cleve; van Dongen, van Dycke; van Eyck; van Goblen, van der Goes, van Gogh, van Goyen; van Heemskerck, van der Helst, van Hemessen, van der Heyden, van Honthorst; van Leyden, van Mander, van Noort; van Orley, van Ostade; van de Velde; van der Weyden : see under Capelle, Weyden, etc.
Vannucci, Pietro, see Perugino
Varley, John   217
Vasari, Giorgio   48, 52, 81, 113, 115, 116
Vecchietta, Lorenzo di Pietro   43
Vecellio, Tiziano, see Titian
Velasquez, Diego   156, 162-3, 169, 190, 208, 243, 245
Velde, Esaias van de   182
Velde the Younger, Willem van de   183
Veneziano, see Domenico Veneziano
Vermeer, Jan   87, 156, 177, 178-9, 181, 182, 183

Vernet, Joseph   202, 237
Veronese, Paolo Caliari   123, 124-5, 188, 207
Verrocchio, Andrea   66, 67, 68, 71, 104, 106
Vien, Joseph-Marie   244
Vigée-Lebrun, Élisabeth   220-1, 227
Villatte, Pierre   78
Villon, Jacques   284, 285, 293, 294
Vivarini, Bartolomeo   59
Vivien, Joseph   193
Vivin, Louis   312
Vlaminck, Maurice de   270-1, 272, 273, 279, 296, 298, 300
Vlieger, Simon de   183
Vos, Cornelis de   166
Vos, Paul de   166, 167
Vouet, Simon   131, 157, 184, 188, 190
Vuillard, Édouard   179, 181, 266-7, 268

Ward, James   214, 222
Wassenhove, Joos van, see Justus of Ghent
Watteau, Antoine   179, 194-5, 196, 201, 232
Weyden, Rogier van der   61, 73, 80, 84-5, 86, 87, 91, 92, 101, 102, 103
Whistler, James McNeill   222, 243, 307, 322, 324
Wilson, Richard   212, 213, 218, 222
Witte, Emanuel de   177, 181
Witz, Conrad   99, 100, 101, 102
Wohlgemut, Michael   103, 132
Wouters, Rik   306
Wouwerman, Philips   183

Zeuxis   11
Zurbarán, Francisco de   157, 160-1, 177